The Collegiate Churches
of England and Wales

Paul Jeffery grew up in Bournemouth, where the proximity of Christchurch, with its castle and priory, stimulated an early love for things medieval and has led to a long-standing enthusiasm for exploring old churches. Music, too, is important to him, and he plays the violin. A graduate of Cambridge University, he works in the computer industry. He is married, with two children, and lives in Winchester.

Paul Jeffery

Cobham Church, 9th. May '09

In memory of my mother, Lilian Jeffery, with whom as a child I first cycled 10 miles each way to see Wimborne Minster.

THE
COLLEGIATE CHURCHES
OF
ENGLAND AND WALES

PAUL JEFFERY

Robert Hale · London

ISBN 978-0-7090-8368-9

Robert Hale Limited
Clerkenwell House
Clerkenwell Green
London EC1R 0HT

A catalogue record for this book is available from the British Library

2 4 6 8 10 9 7 5 3 1

Printed in Singapore

Contents

Foreword

Secular colleges were a conspicuous feature of the ecclesiastical landscape of medieval England and have long merited the comprehensive study which this admirable book provides. They bear witness in a special way to the vitality of our Christian past and, insofar as many were founded by laymen and women – up to the eve of the Reformation – they are further evidence of the ability of the medieval Church in England to respond to the changing needs and aspirations of the laity.

Some were pre-Conquest foundations: 'minsters' which did not become cathedrals or former cathedrals demoted to collegiate status. Others were royal or noble private chapels and their chaplains. Most of the colleges founded in the later Middle Ages were essentially super-chantries, often with schools and almshouses attached; or they were communities of secular priests employed by the larger religious guilds; or they were colleges in the modern sense, i.e. places of education like Winchester and Eton and the Oxbridge colleges (but often with a strong chantry motive as well).

Their variety, often intricate evolution and elaborate organization are unravelled here with the greatest skill. Then follows a gazetteer giving details of every known medieval collegiate foundation in England and Wales, most of which suffered grievously during the Reformation. Armed with this guide, however, the reader will be able to spend many happy hours discovering some of the most magnificent buildings we have inherited from the Middle Ages.

J.J. Scarisbrick
Emeritus Professor of History, University of Warwick
August 2002

Preface

Many books have been written about the English parish churches. The abbeys and priories, too, have an extensive literature. However, very little attention has been given to the collegiate churches. My own interest in them stemmed from early encounters, and was stimulated by those occasions when I visited a church, usually fine, and found that it was collegiate. I learned much about what this means from the one book that has been devoted to them (by G.H. Cook, published in 1959), but it left me wanting to know more and to see a treatment of all the examples. So I long hoped for a new book to appear. As this did not happen, that hope gradually became an idea, an ambition and finally a task – one I have found absorbingly interesting.

Why do I think the subject of collegiate churches deserves more attention?

First, perhaps, because they represent a superb body of ecclesiastical architecture. Beverley Minster (Yorkshire, ER), St. George's Chapel, Windsor, and King's College Chapel, Cambridge, are unsurpassed of their types. Four former collegiate churches have in the nineteenth and twentieth centuries become cathedrals: Derby, Manchester, Ripon (Yorkshire, WR) and Southwell (Nottinghamshire). Many more are outstandingly fine: Fotheringhay (Northamptonshire), Howden (Yorkshire, ER), Merton College Chapel at Oxford, Ottery St Mary (Devon), Warwick, and Wimborne Minster (Dorset) are major churches by any reckoning. Others, though relatively small, are of especially fine quality: for example Battlefield (Shropshire), Denston (Suffolk) and Shottesbrooke (Berkshire). There is a great range, and many are less distinguished than these, but few are insignificant.

My second reason is that medieval colleges, though a very important class of medieval institution, are little known and often misunderstood. In this, they contrast with the monasteries. Yet colleges, like monasteries, were religious houses, and the two types have many parallels. Perhaps colleges lack romance: they have given us no great and evocative ruins, no collegiate equivalent to Fountains, Tintern or Rievaulx. A comparison of numbers is of interest: England and Wales had well over 700 monasteries, but the melancholy outcome of their dissolution under Henry VIII is that only a small fraction of their churches now survives wholly or partly in use or as a substantial ruin. The number of churches here accounted collegiate is over 170, and most still exist: almost as many collegiate churches may be visited today as monastic.

Thirdly, their histories are so often interesting. Many were founded by or closely connected with important ecclesiastical, secular or royal figures. Some of the secular founders belonged to the aristocracy; some were self-made men. A few colleges were founded not by individuals but by associations of ordinary people. Colleges also have certain connections with worldly matters: they illuminate for us more than just the religious side of medieval life. Moreover, unlike monasteries, colleges were not totally extinguished in the sixteenth century. Two classes, the academic colleges and the colleges of vicars, were largely untouched, one to thrive, the other gradually to wither. Also existing are a very few living representatives of the 'classic' colleges of the Middle Ages, most notably St George at Windsor and Westminster Abbey, uniquely protected by their royal connections. The latter was not collegiate in medieval times but, having ceased in 1540 to be an abbey in the true sense, it has survived in collegiate form.

I intend this book as both a general survey for the interested reader and a handbook for prospective visitors to the churches. I have myself visited all the standing churches that appear in the gazetteer, as well as many churches and other sites listed in the appendices. All the photographs were taken by me between July 1999 and May 2002.

Many people and organizations have been consulted for assistance, and it has been a pleasure to find how willingly help has been given. I appreciate the generous provision of material by the National Monuments Record (now part of English Heritage), and by its Welsh equivalent CADW. I am most grateful to Professor J.J. Scarisbrick for his foreword and for suggestions. I thank John Bowles and Dr John Leonard for reading and commenting on portions of the draft typescript. Christopher Dalton gave me valuable advice concerning photography. My thanks are due to Guildhall Library, Corporation of London, for the reproductions of early illustrations. I much appreciate the assistance of Anthea Jones, especially concerning portionary churches. Others I would like to thank include: Revd Paul Abram; Colin Arnold; Mrs Liz Bartlett; Dr J. Blatchly; Prof. Christopher Brooke; Revd Alasdair Coles; Dr Chrystal Davies; Mrs Enid Davies; Mrs Angela Doughty; Nick Evans; Christine Faunch; Philip R. French; Revd Mark Griffin; Mrs Marjorie Harrison; The Hon. Arthur Hazlerigg; Chris Henderson; Penny Icke; Estelle Jakeman; Richard Knox; Mrs Sue Ladipo; Richard Langley; Edward Martin; Prof. Nicholas Orme; Richard Parker; David Phillips; Prof. Colin Platt; Revd Leigh Richardson; Marten Rogers; Edwin J. Rose; Marie-Hélène Rousseau; Mike Sanders; P.R. Saunders; Prof. D.M. Smith; Ms Linda Smith; Mike Stokes; Tim Tatton-Brown; Revd Nigel Whitehouse; Jo Wisdom. To those I cannot mention by name, I apologize, but I am grateful to them all. Most of all I thank my wife Margy and my daughters Philippa and Harriet for encouraging me to undertake this project, the achievement of which has amazed me!

1

The Nature of a Collegiate Church

A collegiate church was the church of a medieval college. But what was a medieval college? The word is derived from Latin *collegium*, meaning a partnership or association: its original meaning was a community of people (colleagues) performing a shared function. In a religious context, it was a college of priests. It had in general no connection with education or learning. A college was a religious house containing a body of priests, and sometimes other clergy, who had not taken monastic vows. Their life was governed by the canons or rules of the Church, and so the priests came to be called canons. Unlike monks, the priests lived in contact with the world, and so could be called secular priests or secular canons.

The ideal of medieval religious life was the maintenance of the highest possible standard of liturgical observance. This meant the celebration in a church building of the canonical hours, also known as the divine office, a cycle of services at set times through every twenty-four hours. These comprised Matins, Lauds, Prime, Terce, Sext, None, Vespers and Compline. Established by the ninth century, this cycle remained unaltered throughout the Middle Ages, and indeed continued unchanged in the Roman Catholic Church until the mid-twentieth century. In addition, one or more masses should take place every day. The principal or solemn high mass was to be celebrated with as much magnificence as possible, including rich decoration of the altar, the use of incense and the employment of many candles. If possible, the celebrant should be assisted by two or more other priests and by others in the lower ranks of the holy or minor orders. There should be music, with choral singing of plainchant; in later periods, polyphonic music might be sung, with boy choristers singing a treble part, and perhaps instrumental support from an organ. The liturgy varied in a cycle through the week, and through the year. Additional masses and even richer ceremonial would be employed on Sundays and feast days. The larger and more important the church, the finer should be its liturgy. It was finest in the cathedrals, the major monasteries and the most important collegiate churches, but even humble parish churches strove for the best they could achieve. This was the *opus Dei* or work of God, the central purpose of the life of a religious house.

In this context, a college differed from a monastery only in that its community was of secular priests rather than monks or nuns. The centre of both was a church building, often large and splendid. Both had domestic buildings for the common life of its members, who slept in its dormitory or rooms and ate together in its common hall. The difference between them lay in the fact that monks and nuns were bound by the central vows of obedience, poverty and chastity, and so had no property and normally lived their lives entirely within the monastic confines. Secular priests could and did own property, and received a stipend or monetary reward for the positions they held. They were not enclosed: when not engaged in their tasks in the college, they could move in the world and have contact with laymen. They were not members of a religious order. If they wished, they could leave their position in a college, and move elsewhere. An incidental difference is that since they were in holy orders, they had to be men: there was no collegiate equivalent of a nunnery!

Normally a college had a head, for whom there were many possible titles: most often dean or master, but also warden, provost, precentor, prior, custos, archpriest, sacrist, rector or vicar. The head and the other members formed a body known as the chapter, as they did too in monasteries and cathedrals. A college was a corporation; it had statutes defining its function, and its identity would usually be expressed in the possession of a common seal for use on letters and documents. Like monasteries, colleges ranged in size from small houses with only two or three clergy up to major institutions with thirty or more. In addition to their priests and other members of the holy orders (deacons and sub-deacons), the larger colleges almost always had some clerks in minor orders; these were not members of the chapter. They also often had boy choristers (as did some monasteries). Both monasteries and colleges, particularly in later periods, often supported secular functions for the general good, such as a school.

The histories of monasteries, cathedrals and colleges were sometimes related. Several early cathedrals, including those of Crediton (Devon) and St John at Chester, lost their cathedral status but remained as collegiate churches. There were many examples of a college subsequently being reestablished as a monastery; the opposite change also sometimes took place.

By the twelfth century, the cathedrals of England had become almost equally divided into those that were served by canons, the secular or collegiate cathedrals, and those served by monks, the monastic cathedrals, which were rare outside England and had first appeared in the tenth century. A major collegiate church essentially differed from a secular cathedral only in that it was not the seat of a bishop. These cathedrals and colleges developed similarly as the Middle Ages progressed.

Colleges were constitutionally very variable; one could almost say that no two were alike. This absence of standardization applied also to the physical character of their buildings. In this they contrast with the monasteries which, within their particular orders, were in many respects largely uniform. The type of college that first reached maturity in the eleventh and twelfth centuries may be called the 'college of canons'. Many had pre-Conquest origins. Colleges of canons continued throughout the Middle Ages, but their character changed considerably in later years. They also came to be joined by other classes of college. One of these was the chantry college, which became numerous in the later Middle Ages. Another was the academic college, smaller in number and mostly located in Oxford or Cambridge. Although these new types differed from the colleges of canons in having particular new objectives and also usually in their organization, they had much in common with their earlier counterparts. The newer types continued to be founded into the sixteenth century, a period when the foundation of other types of religious house had almost ceased.[1]

2

Historical Development

Before the Norman Conquest

Christianity, through the centuries from its first appearance in this country until the Norman Conquest, had a chequered development. In the Roman Empire, it first became widespread after its recognition under the Emperor Constantine I in 313, and from this early date there was certainly some Christianity in England. However, these were the years of the decline of Roman power, with the final withdrawal of Roman forces from Britain in 410. There followed successive invasions, first from Scotland and then of Angles, Saxons and Jutes from what are now Holland and northern Germany: these were pagans, and by the middle of the fifth century Christianity was almost extinguished except in the western 'Celtic fringe' of Wales, Cornwall and west of the Pennines.

In this Celtic fringe, Christianity was nurtured mainly from Ireland, where it had spread from Gaul and was established on firm foundations largely by St Patrick. Irish missionaries came to Wales and Cornwall, and to Iona in Scotland and thence to Holy Island off Northumbria. In these regions there developed a distinctive Celtic style of Christianity. Meanwhile, in Italy and much of western Europe, different Christian practices had been developing, and these came to the south-east of the country when Pope Gregory I in 597 sent St Augustine with forty monks on his famous mission, which established Canterbury as a great Christian centre. Through the seventh century, most of Britain was brought to Christianity. The reconciliation of the Celtic forms with Roman practice was largely achieved at the Synod of Whitby in 663, although Christianity in Wales and Cornwall long remained recognizably different from elsewhere. In this flowering of Christianity, monasticism was prominent, but it was not organized in the way that became familiar later. Religious houses were centres of Christianity where some lived who had taken vows that we would recognize as monastic, while others had not taken vows and were what would later be known as secular priests. Both lived a communal life, and both were involved in evangelization and preaching. Similar arrangements probably applied in the cathedrals established in these years. Some centres had nuns as well as monks; this was a period notable for some famous holy women, such as St Hilda of Whitby.

For these religious houses, the term 'minster' was employed, from the Old English *mynster*, itself derived from the ecclesiastical Latin *monasterium*, a monastery. It soon came to be used for any important church, especially those established in the seventh and eighth centuries at the beginnings of what became the parochial system: these 'mother-churches' served a large district, and in time other dependent churches were established beneath them. It is hard to distinguish between these two types of minster, those of monastic character and the mother-churches; indeed, it is doubtful whether, at least at this period, any distinction was meaningful[2]. In the eighth century, moves began to bring a stricter organization to the religious houses, breaking up the mixed communities of monks and nuns, and separating from monks the priests who chose not to take monastic vows. However, this reform was soon overtaken by waves of attack by pagan Vikings and Danes, beginning in the late eighth century and continuing into the tenth century. By 900, religious life was at a low ebb.

Much of the country was conquered by the Danes in this period, but Wessex remained undefeated. It was from here that the revival came, both political and religious, beginning under Alfred, who ruled from 871 to 899 and is the only English king to have been awarded the epithet 'Great'. The unification of England followed under Athelstan (ruled 924–39). In the religious revival, the heirs of Alfred re-established and augmented old religious houses and founded new ones: some were of monks, others of secular priests. Monasticism was now on a stricter basis under the rule of St Benedict. Alongside this, houses of secular priests were also given a stricter communal life, often based on a rule devised by St Chrodegang, Bishop of Metz (in what is now Lorraine in France) from 742 to 766, for the secular clergy of his cathedral. After 975, there was a distinct movement against monasteries, and in many of them monks were replaced by secular priests[3]. By the end of the Anglo-Saxon era, colleges of secular priests were well established and often highly important, as exemplified by Earl Harold's great and prestigious foundation of the 1050s at Waltham (Essex). By this period, such houses may properly be called collegiate churches, having the life that this implies.

Meanwhile, the smaller minsters or mother-churches of pastoral function were in decline. The creation of local churches in their districts had deprived them of much of their purpose. Some retained multiple clergy, whose life was probably usually more pastoral than collegiate.

Many English place names contain the element 'minster', for example Exminster (Devon), Lytchett Minster (Dorset), Southminster (Essex) or Warminster (Wiltshire). Most of these, whatever their early origin, had a church that was later no more than parochial. Other places to which the term has adhered had churches that became or remained monastic, as at Westminster (London) or Leominster (Herefordshire). It has also remained in use for a few cathedrals, especially York Minster, or collegiate churches, as at Beverley Minster (Yorkshire, ER) or Wimborne Minster (Dorset). In general, however, the word carries no collegiate implication.[4]

Colleges of Canons after the Norman Conquest

After the Conquest, Normans soon took over most of the important positions in the Church, and began to impose changes, taking their leadership from Lanfranc, enthroned in 1070 as Archbishop of Canterbury. A policy was introduced that cathedrals should be in important and populous towns, as a result of which several sees were moved from their previous locations. Normans were responsible for many new foundations of religious houses. They also built; perhaps the most astonishing evidence of their vigour is the immense campaign of new construction that began to transform church buildings throughout the country. The architectural style they brought with them from Normandy; and the scale was greater than anything the country had seen before. Most of the labour for these achievements was of course provided by their new subjects.

The decline of the old small minsters of pastoral function continued, but many are recorded or implied in the Domesday Survey of 1086. In the larger minsters or collegiate churches and the secular cathedrals, the most far-reaching change was the widespread adoption of the prebendal system, a process that had begun just before the Conquest. The word 'prebend' derives from the Latin *praebere*, to grant or supply, hence *praebenda*, things to be supplied. From early times, the support for a church or religious house had been arranged by an endowment of property, usually land; the tithe on that property, one tenth of its produce, provided the income. This income had been managed as a common whole, from which in a church of multiple clergy a stipend would be provided for each, probably mostly in the form of food, clothing and other necessaries. The prebendal system was quite different: the endowments, in the form of manors, estates or churches, were divided into separate properties, each known as a prebend. This was treated as the endowment of a place in the chapter and stall in the church, and was allocated to a canon as a freehold; he thereby became both a prebendary (holder of a prebend) and a canon (member of the collegiate or cathedral church).[5]

Each prebend had a name, often that of the manor or the place in which the property lay. Sometimes the names derived from other sources, such as the different masses said in the church, or the different altars of the church. A prebend often derived from a parish church, with its property, in which case it carried responsibility for providing its cure of souls: this would be discharged by the appointment of a vicar (Latin *vicarius*, a substitute) or curate, paid by the prebendary out of the income of the prebend. The entitlement of the owner was known as the rectorial or great tithes, while that allotted to the vicar derived from the vicarial or small tithes. Because of their nature, appointments to prebends were normally made by the patron of the college. The adoption of this system had far-reaching consequences, about which more is said below.

The establishment of the prebendal system marked a move away from the old ideal of life in common. Already in the late eleventh or early twelfth century, at such churches as Chester St Werburgh and Christchurch (Hampshire), there is evidence that the canons were living in separate houses. This became the norm in both colleges of canons and secular cathedrals. Interestingly in the light of later developments, it seems that these canons already included a few who were non-resident.[6]

The canons of a collegiate church were in holy orders, but not necessarily all priests; a number might be deacons or sub-deacons (that is, clerks in holy orders, but of orders lower than priest). Some, of course, had to be priests: only priests could celebrate mass, the role of deacons and sub-deacons being as assistants. At Heytesbury (Wiltshire), the dean and two canons were priests, and the other two canons were deacons.

Although some new colleges of canons were established in Norman times, this was a period in which the trend of the late Anglo-Saxon years was reversed, and the climate of thought swung away from colleges towards monasteries. Monasteries were founded in large numbers, and many existing collegiate churches as well as small minsters were lost. We have seen that the small minsters were in decline. They did not usually adopt the prebendal system. Many that appear in Domesday Book simply ended over the next century or more, perhaps as a result of rationalization by bishops or patrons. There were probably some that have left no record. Other establishments, both large and small, ceased when they were given, with their property, as endowments to newly founded monasteries, as with St Alkmund at Shrewsbury, granted about 1145 to the newly founded Lilleshall Abbey.

But some of the most important colleges were brought to an end in another way. There was a growing awareness that life in many of the Benedictine monasteries was too slack, and in reaction to this there appeared a series of new orders, each aspiring to a more perfect monastic life; such were, for example, the Cistercians and the Cluniacs. A comparable movement affected the secular canons. Critics made unfavourable comparisons between the lives of secular clergy, living in individual houses, sometimes married, and those of monks. The response was to reform the canonical life by the adoption of a rule, which included celibacy and the renunciation of property; this rule appeared in the writings of St Augustine and was attributed to him. Canons who embraced it were known as Augustinian canons, Austin canons, regular canons or canons regular. During the twelfth century, many colleges of canons adopted the Augustinian rule. The life of canons regular was very similar to that of monks. Their houses were monasteries; what had been a college became an Augustinian priory or abbey. Henry I favoured the Augustinians, and was associated with some of these transformations. The pre-Conquest colleges of St Werburgh at Chester, Dover (Kent), Launceston (Cornwall), St Frideswide at Oxford and Plympton (Devon) are a few among the many that made this change. Most have no further part in the story of the collegiate churches. It is interesting to realize that the great Norman naves of Christchurch (Hampshire) and Waltham (Essex) were collegiate when built, or at least begun, although they soon became Augustinian. Details of collegiate churches that subsequently became monastic appear in Appendix III.

Waltham Abbey (Essex): the twelfth-century nave, collegiate when built

The Development of Colleges of Canons from about 1200

When the prebendal system became established, it was usual (if not universal) for a prebendary to reside at the college or cathedral and in person fulfil his liturgical duties. But by the thirteenth century, this was rapidly changing. Since a prebend constituted a freehold, the holder could receive the income without necessarily himself taking part in the duties in the church; instead he could employ a deputy, i.e. a vicar, to undertake them on his behalf. There were normally additional payments made by the college to those in residence, taken from the 'communia' or common fund; so a non-resident canon would not receive these. However, the income from a prebend was usually such that it could allow the holder to pay a relatively small part to a vicar and retain a substantial income for himself. It is in this context that money and personal advantage become a significant aspect of the story. This is not to say that the religious purpose of these houses was perverted to something different; indeed, many devout men were canons, whether resident or not, and they often used the money they obtained from the system for good purposes. Moreover, as will be seen later, the use of vicars itself had important positive effects. But the financial rewards of the prebendaries, and the fact that many were absentees, became a significant dimension to the life of the colleges and secular cathedrals. What drove the system was that the ability to give prebends was highly useful to patrons. It was an age in which most literate and educated people were in holy orders, and so for patrons, be they bishops, the crown or powerful laymen, the giving of a prebend was a way of providing an income to a servant whose principal work often lay outside the college.

By their nature, the incomes provided by different prebends attached to a church were not identical; moreover, as conditions changed with time, an individual prebend might become poorer or richer. At Hastings (Sussex) in 1275, of ten prebends, the prebend of Peasmarsh was worth 30 marks (£20) a year, while that of Wartling was worth 50 marks (£33 13s 4d).[7] Others were worth varying values down to 9 marks (£6), except for Stone and Marlrepast, which were worth less; indeed the latter was worth only 1 mark (13s 4d). In this college, a vicar was paid 2d a day (£3 1s 0d a year): so most prebendaries could readily afford to provide one. Clearly, however, this was not the case for the unfortunate prebendary for Marlrepast, since the cost of a vicar would exceed the income from his prebend: so he could not afford to be an absentee. Nevertheless, we should perhaps limit our sympathy, since as a resident he would receive substantial support from the common fund, and was probably better off than a vicar. Of the high values, the prebend of Wartling was soon divided into three, but it was not unusual for a college or cathedral to have a large or 'golden' prebend. Also normally larger than the others was the prebend held by the head of a college: for example, at Tamworth (Staffordshire) in 1535, the value of the dean's prebend was listed as £21 a year, whereas the other prebends were worth £10, £8, £8, £7 and £3 6s 8d.[8]

Many of the absentee prebendaries of the thirteenth century and later were pluralists, holding posts in several different places from which they drew income but which they might seldom or never visit. It has been suggested that, from the fourteenth century onwards, only about a quarter of all canons were actually in residence at any one time.[9] They provided vicars, who took their places in the stalls for the services; but the vicars were not members of the college, so there was no collegiate life. However fine its liturgy, it may be felt that the religious life of such a college fell short of the highest ideals. This view is probably supported by the fact that, by the fourteenth century, hardly any new foundations used prebends. As will be seen later, chantry colleges normally employed a different system.

This state of affairs was not necessarily seen as an abuse. Concerning benefices with cure of souls (the pastoral care of a parish), the medieval

Church regarded pluralism and non-residence as an evil and tried to eliminate them, with some success. But prebends did not have cure of souls, and the practice was accepted. Prebends were in the gift of the patrons of the houses concerned, and it was not easy for any central authority to prevent those patrons from giving them to whomever they chose. Some absentees did make an active contribution; they might be present for a limited period each year, or they might play a significant role in chapter, attending on occasions when there was an important meeting or an episcopal visitation. Others, however, probably never had any intention of using their prebends as other than a source of income. There are many records of men who held five or more prebends, rectorships, masterships of hospitals and other such positions, often in locations far apart. A spectacular pluralist was John of Droxford, later Bishop of Bath and Wells, who is recorded in 1307–8 as holding fifteen prebends and five rectories of parish churches.[10] In the later Middle Ages, many figures prominent in both Church and State held multiple prebends and other preferments, and it was this that gave them the means to pursue their wide interests. It is no surprise to encounter familiar names in the lists of prebendaries and deans of a collegiate church.

In some collegiate churches, usually small, there might be no canons at all in residence. Occasionally in later years, it was worse: at Darlington (Co. Durham) in 1439, none of the four canons was resident, nor had they provided vicars, so the entire maintenance of religious life fell upon the vicar, who had the cure of souls. This certainly was seen as an abuse by Bishop Neville, who stepped in and changed the constitution to prevent it.[11]

Whether or not they were of the same order as their canons, vicars were regarded as of lower status; and as we have seen, their financial rewards were usually lower. The statutes of later colleges, or those of earlier colleges as revised later, often addressed the vicars. For example, the statutes of 1292 at Auckland (Co. Durham) specified that residence was not required of the canons, and that they should appoint vicars.[12] There were five priest canons, whose vicars should be priests, to be paid £3 6s 8d annually; the vicars of the four deacon canons should be deacons and receive 40s (£2); and the sub-deacon vicars, with the clerks, were to receive 30s. In important colleges and in the secular cathedrals, the liturgy required a high standard of music, so it was desirable that it be sung by men who were musical specialists. This need for professional musicians increased as the music became more complex and its techniques developed, especially with the introduction of polyphony, so it became established that these vicars were chosen for their skill as singers, and were known as 'vicars choral'. The use of vicars choral was important in the development of the musical aspect of the liturgy in succeeding centuries.

In the secular cathedrals and the larger colleges, the canons included four dignitaries (*personae* or *dignitates* – the *quattuor majores personae* or four principal persons).[13] These were the positions of highest precedence, and the holders of some or all of them were often required to be resident. These canons had stalls in the choir in positions corresponding to their status: that of first precedence was usually the first stall on the south side at the entrance to the choir, the second was the first stall on the north side, the third the second stall on the south, and so on. These positions still apply in cathedrals and elsewhere today. The first dignitary was the head of the college. The second was the precentor or cantor, who as his title implies was the chief singer, responsible for the music. Third in precedence was the chancellor, who was responsible for the instruction of the choristers and vicars, for keeping the books and documents, and for reading the lessons in the services. Fourth was the treasurer, responsible for finance, including the vestments and other valuables. There might be further posts: for example, as the music grew more complicated in later years, the precentor was often assisted by another canon known as the succentor or sub-chanter. In a church that was also parochial, the head had responsibility for the cure of souls. This might be discharged by the appointment of a curate or vicar (not a vicar choral).

The patronage of a college of canons represented a very desirable possession, not only for the opportunities it gave the patron to provide support for servants. Equally important was its religious life, with its almost continuous liturgy and rich ceremonial, satisfying the real and sincere motivation to use individual wealth for the glory of God, and for the corresponding merit and benefit which the patron and his family could expect in the afterlife. Some founders were anxious to locate their college close to their principal residence, perhaps particularly because of the use that could be made of its literate clerks in the administration of the patron's affairs. This led to what might seem a surprising occurrence: some colleges were established inside castles. This conjunction of the religious and the military must sometimes have been uncomfortable, but was accepted. A few later colleges were established in a manor house or palace, notably the College of St Stephen in the Palace of Westminster. The outstanding example of a college in a castle is that unique survival, the College of St George at Windsor. Collegiate churches in castles are listed in Appendix V.

Collegiate churches were founded by ecclesiastical patrons mainly for similar reasons to those that motivated lay founders, but an element of ecclesiastical politics could also be a factor.[14] One group in ecclesiastical patronage stands alone: the great collegiate churches of Beverley, Ripon and Southwell in the diocese of York. These large and splendid establishments were little short of subordinate cathedrals in this large diocese (two of them actually became cathedrals in the nineteenth century). York was a secular cathedral, and in addition to his cathedral, in which the chapter of secular canons was led by the dean, the archbishop had these three important chapters in his patronage. Most archbishops spent some of their time near these colleges, which seem to have given them a power base to balance that of the dean in the cathedral. Another diocese with a secular cathedral containing important collegiate churches under the patronage of the bishop was Exeter: it had major colleges at Crediton, Ottery St Mary and Penryn. Bishops sometimes had the patronage of a college outside their diocese: for example, the bishop of Exeter was patron also of that of Bosham (Sussex).

A similar need for a collegiate chapter was felt by some bishops of monastic cathedrals, as a counterweight to their monastic chapters. It was this that led to the phenomenon of the diocese with two cathedrals: Bath and Wells, and Coventry and Lichfield. In each case one cathedral was monastic, one secular. A long and contentious period passed before the acceptance in these dioceses of the compromise whereby the bishop had two cathedrals. This need also led to the extraordinary attempts of Archbishop Baldwin of Canterbury in the late twelfth century to establish a major chapter of secular canons, which he pursued in the face of the strongest opposition from the monastic chapter in his cathedral. First he founded a college at Hackington on the edge of the cathedral city; then he founded one at Lambeth, later continued by his successor. Both were brought down as a result of appeals to the pope by the monastic community of the cathedral (*see* Appendix IV). Later, the archbishops of Canterbury did successfully establish a smaller college at Wingham, and they had another at South Malling (Sussex), outside the diocese. The bishops of Durham had the patronage of five collegiate churches within their diocese. In the diocese of Worcester, there were interesting episodes concerning the collegiate church of Westbury-on-Trym (Gloucestershire), which two bishops had ambitions of raising in status to give another diocese with two cathedrals.

Other bishops, however, of both secular and monastic cathedrals, had no college in their patronage.

Churches of Portioners

As we have seen, not all churches with multiple clergy in the eleventh and twelfth centuries adopted the prebendal system; those that did not were mostly the surviving small minsters that had originated as mother-churches. Typically, the income of such a church was simply divided amongst its clergy. These clergy were known as portioners (or sometimes portionists), and the establishment was a church of portioners, or portionary church. In its basic form, it was small, lacked a charter of incorporation, did not form a chapter and had no dean or head. Its function was probably pastoral rather than collegiate. Arguably, such an establishment was not a college. An often-quoted illustration is the inquiry ordered in 1384 by Bishop Gilbert of Hereford into the status of the churches of Ledbury and Bromyard in his diocese, which concluded that they were churches of portioners, and as such were parochial and not collegiate.[15] At Bromyard the three portions were reported to run 'in equal shares': so the incomes provided by each portion were equal, unlike those from prebends.

This, however, is an incomplete view of a complicated and difficult subject.[16] It is often not easy to decide whether a church should be categorized as portionary. Portions were also known as bursal prebends, and scribes often simply used the word *praebenda* for them. Moreover, the financial arrangements in a portionary system were very variable, and not all gave equal portions. Some, for example Pontesbury and Burford (both in Shropshire), might be described as part-way between portionary and prebendal. Further, not all portionary churches were former minsters: some, for example Holdgate (Shropshire) or Tiverton (Devon), were founded or became portionary in Norman or even later times. Nor were they always small: the canons of several important colleges, and even of Exeter Cathedral, were supported by portions rather than prebends. Several churches of portioners were later reconstituted as regular colleges with prebends, as at Wingham (Kent) and Auckland (Co. Durham).

Equally vexed is the question of the function of portionary churches: they cover a wide range, and not all are to be dismissed as parochial. Some were functionally indistinguishable from colleges of canons, and their clergy had nothing to do with pastoral duties. Examples are Norton (Co. Durham), where there were eight portioners, or Gnosall (Staffordshire), with four. The latter had royal free status (see below), its portioners were usually absentees, and the church was served by vicars. In others, it is difficult to know whether the function was collegiate or parochial.

Thus it is not easy to draw a clear distinction between churches of portioners and colleges of canons. Uncertainties are often compounded by the limitations of the historical record. A thorough treatment of the subject is not attempted here; some portionary churches are regarded as collegiate, but others appear only in Appendix IV.

Colleges of Vicars Choral

In the secular cathedrals, and also in some collegiate churches, it became by about the thirteenth century a requirement that all canons, whether resident or not, should have a vicar. As explained above, these were musical specialists, known as vicars choral. Such a vicar would at first either live in the house of the canon to whom he was deputy or would lodge in the town. But later, in all the English cathedrals and in some of the collegiate churches, separate accommodation was provided for them. Eventually, in most of these cathedrals, the common residence of the vicars was legally incorporated. The college of vicars was a full college: it could hold property in common and manage its affairs independently of the cathedral chapter. One of the vicars was chosen by the members as the head, usually known as the succentor of the vicars, sub-chanter, custos or principal. Even where there was a college of vicars, however, responsibility for the music remained in the hands of the precentor, one of the canons normally resident.

At St Paul's Cathedral in London, alone among the English secular cathedrals, the vicars choral were never incorporated, but in a role connected with them were twelve 'minor canons', who were incorporated in a college of this name. Of the four Welsh cathedrals, a college of vicars was incorporated only at St Davids; the others had insufficient vicars to warrant a college. Collegiate churches where a common residence was constructed for the vicars were both large and small; they included Beverley (Yorkshire, ER), Gnosall (Staffordshire), Heytesbury (Wiltshire) and Howden (Yorkshire, ER). Only at Ripon (Yorkshire, WR) among the collegiate churches were the vicars separately incorporated.

Colleges of vicars choral appear as Appendix I.

Chantry Colleges

A matter of real concern to many people in the Middle Ages was the doctrine of Purgatory. Purgatory is 'a place or state in which the souls of those who have died in a state of grace undergo a period of suffering or punishment to become purified from their sins'. Thus, while most hoped that their final destination would be Heaven rather than Hell, it was recognized that only a saint could hope to go there directly. So the sufferings of Purgatory loomed large and were a preoccupation for many. Inherent in this was the belief that not only could people ease their future passage through Purgatory by good works in their lifetimes, but that after their deaths this could be assisted by the prayers of the living, by the intercession of the saints, by gifts of alms in their names, and above all by the mass as a propitiatory sacrifice on their behalf.

To meet this need, chantries were founded. In the basic form, a person left by will money or goods to pay for a priest to sing mass daily for some period at a particular altar in a church. The period might be up to a few years, depending on the value of what was given. These 'soul-masses' would be offered for the founder or founders and for others specified by them, equally when living or dead. Most chantries were of this temporary nature, but those who had sufficient means might leave an endowment for what was called a perpetual chantry, providing for the maintenance of a priest for this purpose in perpetuity.

Chantries first appeared in the twelfth century. Their popularity increased, and during the last two centuries of the medieval era numerous perpetual chantries were established in parish churches everywhere. They came to support altogether a large population of priests. The establishment of a perpetual chantry required the construction of a chantry chapel, usually a small area within the church surrounded by timber screens, containing the chantry altar. Towards the end of the Middle Ages the aisles of many churches came to be filled with such chapels. Often an important church with many chantries was enlarged for their accommodation by the addition of further aisles or chapels. In cathedrals or other major churches, chantry chapels might be gloriously elaborate stone-built structures. Churches in which individual chantries were established naturally included some belonging to colleges of canons; usually the chantries were served by separate priests, but sometimes clergy of the college would supplement their incomes by also serving as chantry priests. In cathedrals, this was frequently done by vicars choral.

It should not be thought that the only function of the chantries was the maintenance of daily soul-masses for the benefit of those specified. The chantry priests usually assisted in the regular parish services; moreover the chantry masses contributed to 'the increase of divine service', which was regarded as of benefit to the whole community. Chantry priests might make a valuable contribution to pastoral work, especially in a large and scattered parish. Furthermore, chantry foundations usually included some provision of good works for the living. These could include regular gifts to the poor, often on the anniversary of the death of the founder; they might provide funds for the maintenance of roads and bridges; and frequently they included a provision for education, a chantry priest being required to spend some time teaching grammar and other subjects.

The extent of the provisions associated with a perpetual chantry depended on the resources committed to it by the founder. Some very wealthy founders might endow a chantry served by more than one priest. The wealthiest might endow not just a chantry but a chantry college, in which multiple chantry priests would live together as a community.[17] In addition to the construction of buildings for communal living, the establishment of a chantry college frequently involved the appropriation of a parish church in which it was to function. In many chantry colleges, each priest spent much of his time serving at a particular altar; but there were also services in which all celebrated together in the chancel, perhaps with the assistance of choristers and other clerks. The provision for good works might be on a very substantial scale, and the educational function sometimes included accommodation for a number of boys.

Surviving statutes give details of those who are to benefit from the chantry function. For example, at Cotterstock (Northamptonshire) in 1340, it is specified that each chaplain celebrating mass should remember John Gifford, the founder, with his father, mother and other relations; other benefactors; the kings and queens of England with their progenitors and children; Henry, bishop of Lincoln, and the canons of Lincoln cathedral; William de Kyrkeby and his wife Christina; John de Honby; John Knyvet and his wife Joan; Richard Knyvet and his wife Joan; Walter de Honby; and the heirs and children of all these.[18] They may also give extremely detailed instructions for the life of the college, including such matters as the vestments to be worn, the lights to be maintained in the church, and special observances for feast days. Other provisions such as for education may also be described in detail.

Most chantry colleges did not employ the prebendal system. Instead, the income of the college was used to provide its priests with a fixed stipend.[19] In this, a chantry college might be thought to resemble a church of portioners, but the system was quite different. The nomination of the head of the college would be the responsibility of the patron, but (unlike the position with prebendaries or portioners) the filling of vacancies within the college was normally the responsibility of the college, the head and the chaplains acting together. The stipend of the chantry priests was a payment for the specified tasks they were to perform, and the statutes normally stated that they could not appoint deputies to undertake these tasks. Thus there were no absentee holders of positions in chantry colleges, and no vicars. Appointments to these colleges could not be used by patrons as rewards for clerks in their service. As with individual chantries, the remuneration of the clergy was usually fixed by the founder and defined in the statutes. At Guildhall College in London, for example, the master received a stipend of 13 marks (£8 13s 4d) per year, and the remaining chaplains 10 marks (£6 13s 4d).[20] At Clifton (Nottinghamshire) in 1535, the warden received £6 13s 4d, and the two fellows £6 exactly.[21] At Tong (Shropshire), the statutes of 1411 specified an annual stipend of 10 marks (£6 13s 4d) for the warden, and of 4 marks (£2 13s 4d) for the chaplains, with an additional 6s 8d for those who undertook the functions of subwarden, parochial chaplain, steward and schoolmaster.[22]

The system described here is often referred to as the chantry system, but it was a matter of organization and did not automatically mean that the principal purpose of the college was the chantry function, although it was usually so. The prebendal system had perhaps been seen as open to abuse, so the new system gained favour, and since most later colleges had a chantry purpose, the two went hand in hand. It was also perhaps favoured for colleges of chantry purpose because the founders wished them to function exactly as they specified. However, the College of St Edmund at Salisbury, for example, founded in 1269, had this organization but was not a chantry college, and maintained a religious life similar to that of a college of canons. Conversely, the great College of St Mary at Warwick, founded in 1123, had a dean and canons holding prebends, but from the first the chantry purpose was a major part of its function. In fact, the founder or founders were remembered in the services of most colleges of canons, and this was sometimes specified in their statutes. Whatever the differences in purpose and organization, chantry colleges and colleges of canons had a great deal in common.

A few later colleges with a chantry function did have prebends, notably Edward III's great foundations of 1348 at Windsor and Westminster. However, these were bursal prebends, worth at these colleges just 3 marks (£2) a year, to which much greater sums were added for those who were in residence: residence was expected.[23] Other late colleges which adopted a system involving prebends were Hemingbrough (Yorkshire, ER), Irthlingborough (Northamptonshire), Newarke College at Leicester and Stoke by Clare (Suffolk).

In the last two centuries of the medieval era, when very few further monasteries were being founded, something of the zeal that had earlier been devoted to them was now applied to founding chantry colleges. They were popular equally amongst great churchmen, the nobility and the newly rich. A few chantry colleges, such as that of Fotheringhay (Northamptonshire), specified a quasi-monastic rigour of life, with obedience to a rule, usually that of St

Augustine. New foundations continued to the eve of the Reformation; the last was Kirkoswald (Cumberland), of about 1523.

There were some chantry colleges in which a parish church was used by the college and contained the college's chantry altar or altars, but was not appropriated, i.e. transferred to the ownership of the college. In the strictest sense, such a church was not collegiate. However, it met the same functional requirements as an appropriated church, and could still in consequence of the foundation of the college benefit by enlargement or the installation of new furnishings. Some were notable establishments: at Cobham (Kent), the college founded about 1362 was large, the spacious church was partly reconstructed for it, and the still surviving quadrangle of collegiate buildings stands right alongside and was connected to the church, almost like that of a monastery. Some such colleges used a church that was already of particular size and splendour, as at Higham Ferrers (Northamptonshire), or Rotherham (Yorkshire, WR). In some instances an unappropriated church used by a college was appropriated later. For example, at Stratford-on-Avon (Warwickshire), the college was founded in 1331, but the church was not appropriated until 1415. At Greystoke (Cumberland) in 1548, there was uncertainty as to whether the church had been appropriated, and the matter had to be decided by a court.

There was another type of college of chantry priests. By the fifteenth century, many important parish churches, especially in towns, had a considerable number of associated chantry priests, responsible for individual chantries. For example, in 1417, Salle (Norfolk) was served by seven chantry priests. Such a church was not collegiate: the priests were independent, and lived in whatever accommodation they could obtain, usually in lodgings. This was not always ideal; the temptations of so living in the world were perhaps not conducive to the demeanour expected of a priest. For this and other reasons, a common residence was sometimes built for these priests. Occasionally a college was founded for them, or an earlier common residence was incorporated. The establishment of such a college involved the provision of statutes specifying rules for its communal life; but there would be no necessity for the church in which they served to be involved, or for it to be appropriated. Again, such a church was strictly not collegiate, but may be regarded as effectively so. An example is the College of Jesus at Bury St Edmunds (Suffolk).

Other chantry colleges were not associated with a parish church at all: they were 'non-parochial' (or, less correctly, 'extra-parochial'). They had a church building solely for their own use: strictly, this was a collegiate chapel and not a collegiate church. Examples include Battlefield (Shropshire), founded for the souls of those killed in the Battle of Shrewsbury in 1403; Carnary College at Norwich, founded in 1316; Marwell (Hampshire), the earliest of the type, founded in the later twelfth century; and Stoke-sub-Hamdon (Somerset), licensed in 1303.

There were other variants. A chantry college was sometimes founded, with the appropriation of the parish church, which would also absorb one or more chantries already existing in the church. The college had a chantry purpose specified by its founder, but would also continue the function of the pre-existing chantries. In just one or two chantry colleges, as at Ruddington (Nottinghamshire), the priests formed a single incorporated body, but served and even resided in more than one place.

In the later Middle Ages, all cathedrals contained chantries, and at several a college was founded for the priests who served them: the best example is St William's College at York. Monastic churches, too, often contained chantries, and a college could be founded for the priests who served in them. Such colleges appear in Appendix II.

Royal Free Chapels

This term appeared only in the thirteenth century, but many royal free chapels originated before the Norman Conquest. They were collegiate churches that had been founded or made collegiate by the sovereign, or in a few cases had later come under the control of the sovereign. As a result, originally by custom, they were not under normal ecclesiastical jurisdiction. Such a college was a 'peculiar': it was exempt from the jurisdiction of the 'ordinary', the bishop of the diocese in which it was located. Other than by possession of this privilege, the royal free chapels were like other colleges, and only a few were especially large or important. Several were associated with castles which had been royal, at least at the time of the establishment of the college. By convention, the head of a royal free chapel had the title of dean, and its estates were known as a deanery; the dependent churches in the deanery were sometimes called prebendal chapels, with incumbents referred to as chaplains rather than vicars.[24]

The royal origin of some royal free chapels was lost in pre-Conquest history, but the status had become established by usage. There was a particular concentration of eight early examples in the diocese of Coventry and Lichfield, five of them in Staffordshire.

In the eleventh and twelfth centuries, the special status of these colleges was generally accepted, though not necessarily clearly defined. Royal chapels were sometimes used in this period as gifts from the sovereign to political supporters. In the thirteenth century, and especially after the accession of Edward I in 1272, the crown became more determined to make its jurisdiction over them as complete as possible. The motivation was no doubt their value as a means of providing secure and well-paid appointments for royal retainers who were in effect senior civil servants. Being under royal jurisdiction, bishops could not raise objections to appointments or to other aspects of their life; they were not subject to episcopal visitation. There was also an economic aspect: their freedoms included freedom from ecclesiastical exactions. The significance should not be exaggerated, however; they functioned much as other colleges, but they were useful to their royal masters.

At the same time, however, some bishops became increasingly intolerant of peculiars within their dioceses. As a result, particularly in the later thirteenth

century, there were many disputes over the royal free chapels, which sometimes exemplified the more arcane aspects of medieval affairs. Physical force
was occasionally involved, appeals to the pope were frequent, and an episcopal weapon was excommunication or interdict of individuals and
communities. An example is at Stafford, where the church was certainly royal
in the twelfth century, though not necessarily claiming exemption from the
authority of the bishop. A dispute arose in 1244, under Henry III. Papal
declarations in their favour were obtained first by the king and then by the
bishop of Coventry and Lichfield, Roger Weseham. The dispute continued,
and in 1258 the next bishop, Roger Meuland, came to the church with a band
of armed men, who forced entry and were alleged to have ill-treated the
clergy. Meuland also suspended the chapter and excommunicated the dean
and two of the canons. Lengthy litigation followed. This failed to resolve
matters, and the case was again referred to Rome, which eventually, after
further complications, in 1267 supported the bishop, and the chapter
remained suspended. This verdict was not accepted in Stafford or by the king.
In 1280, the energetic new Archbishop Pecham of Canterbury came to the
town determined to make a visitation. With the encouragement of the king,
now Edward I, the Sheriff of Staffordshire and the townspeople physically
prevented the archbishop from entering the church. Following this, in 1281,
Bishop Meuland finally capitulated, and recognized the exemption from his
jurisdiction of Stafford and six other royal free chapels in his diocese.[25]

By the end of the reign of Edward I in 1307, the exemption of most royal
free chapels from normal episcopal jurisdiction was fully established, though
their status still varied in detail. Where the patronage of royal free chapels
had been given away, aspects of their royal freedoms remained, and could still
be of value to the sovereign. Some later returned to full royal control.

Several of the early royal free chapels later lost their collegiate status; and
in the twelfth century, four became monasteries. No new royal free chapels
were established between the mid-twelfth and the mid-thirteenth century, but
after that time several more were founded, or existing colleges were raised to
royal free status. Some were of chantry function, including the great colleges
of Fotheringhay (Northamptonshire), St Stephen at Westminster and St
George at Windsor. With the exception of the last, the royal free chapels were
dissolved in the 1540s. Their churches, however, usually retained their status
as royal peculiars until the nineteenth century, when most ecclesiastical peculiars were abolished.

A list of royal free chapels is given as Appendix VI.

Academic Colleges

The inception and development of the academic college took place almost
entirely in or associated with the towns of Oxford and Cambridge.[26] In both
places, the university appeared before there were any colleges. Oxford first

became established as a centre of learning in the late twelfth century; by the end of the century there were perhaps 200 students in the town, and a century later that number may have risen to as many as 2,000. The university became a corporate entity in the early thirteenth century, the first chancellor being appointed in 1214. Cambridge followed soon after, partly as a result of disturbances in Oxford in 1209 that caused many teachers and students to leave; some went to Cambridge, and though many subsequently returned to Oxford, some remained. Cambridge University had a chancellor by 1226. In both universities, students normally lived either in lodgings or inns, or in academic halls, which were houses licensed by the university for the purpose. In time the number of academic halls in Oxford exceeded 100.

The first mover in the entry of the college to this scene was Walter de Merton, Chancellor of England and later Bishop of Rochester. Concerned to improve the education of the clergy, he began his activities to this end in 1262 in Surrey (*see* Malden, Appendix IV), but his work soon led to the beginning of what became Merton College at Oxford. Like most colleges of the day, this was attached to and appropriated an existing parish church. It was a lavish foundation, which established a pattern for the subsequent growth of academic colleges. Two more institutions appeared at Oxford in the same period, which in time became Balliol and University Colleges; but they were initially small and were not constituted as colleges until after Merton. Exeter College (originally Stapledon Hall), Oriel College and Queen's College followed in the early fourteenth century. A similar process took place at Cambridge, the first college being Peterhouse, founded in 1284. It was followed in the fourteenth century by Clare Hall, Gonville Hall, Trinity Hall and others. Some of these early colleges, though constituted as such, used the title 'hall'; they were usually later renamed. They are not to be confused with the academic halls, most of which eventually disappeared, though just a few later developed into colleges.

Further colleges were founded in both universities through the following centuries, but it was not until the sixteenth century that the majority of students were members of a college. These further foundations include three which stand out from the rest both because of their size and because of an important new aspect. William of Wykeham, Bishop of Winchester from 1369 to 1404 and a great man of affairs, founded New College, Oxford, in 1379, at the time easily the largest college in either university town. Its particular innovation was that it was conceived as part of a dual foundation: Wykeham also founded a college at Winchester to educate boys and act as a feeder to the Oxford college. This concept was followed from 1440 by Henry VI in his magnificent foundations of King's College, Cambridge, and Eton College (Buckinghamshire). A third great dual foundation was planned in the sixteenth century by Cardinal Wolsey, and has given us Christ Church, Oxford; but its associated foundation at Ipswich (Suffolk) was lost on Wolsey's fall from royal favour.

In their constitution and function, academic colleges developed from the chantry colleges, which were also growing in number through these years. The difference was mainly one of degree. Most chantry colleges included in their function an element of education, and some provided accommodation for boys who were being educated. In the academic colleges, education and the accommodation of scholars were major and essential objectives; but all pre-Reformation academic colleges retained the chantry element as an important factor. Their fellows were priests and were required to maintain religious observances in the collegiate church or chapel, and to say daily masses for the souls of the founder or founders and others. Several included an important provision for music, with an establishment of singing men and boy choristers: this is a function they usually retain today, most famously at King's College, Cambridge. Only a few had a parochial responsibility. The great royal foundations of King's Hall and King's College at Cambridge were exempt from episcopal authority in much the same way as the royal free chapels.

In these colleges, the fellows were expected to be pursuing higher studies, as well as giving instruction. The scholars might study such subjects as law and medicine, and in the feeder colleges grammar, but the most important subject was theology; the prime function of higher education was seen as the better education of the clergy. In the Oxford and Cambridge colleges, students as well as fellows were always at least in minor orders. Although the chantry element disappeared with the Reformation, the clerical element remained strong; it was not until the nineteenth century that the fellows of the Oxford and Cambridge colleges were permitted to marry[27].

Colleges of Fraternity Priests

Fraternities were also known as religious guilds, confraternities or brotherhoods: these are synonymous terms. A fraternity was an association mainly of lay people, women as well as men, that provided its members with religious benefits on their deaths: a good funeral, and after this prayers and soul-masses. It could thus be regarded as a poor man's chantry. (Fraternities should not be confused with the trade or craft guilds which, although they sometimes had a prominent religious aspect, were primarily concerned with economic matters). Fraternities were popular; some existed before the Conquest, and they became very numerous in later medieval times. Many were small organizations operating in villages, with no endowments and little property, but some town fraternities became large and important, and included worldly as well as religious benefits. For example, they might help members who got into trouble with the law. Large fraternities also often ran almshouses and schools, and were responsible for other good works.[28]

The larger fraternities employed their own priests, in just a few cases a significant number who formed an incorporated body, as part of the fraternity or otherwise. The church they served could be non-parochial, as with the Guild of St John the Baptist at Coventry. In others, the priests might serve in a parish church, as at All Saints, Northampton, which was not appropriated. Colleges of fraternity priests were closely analogous to colleges of chantry priests, and are often referred to as such, but there was a distinction. Some, however, also had priests serving chantries, and so were mixed in their function. At Corpus Christi, Cambridge, fraternities were responsible for the foundation of an academic college.

Colleges Associated with Hospitals

As we have already seen, many colleges, especially chantry colleges, in addition to their religious observances included functions for the benefit of the living, which could include the accommodation and maintenance of a few poor, aged or infirm people. Such colleges also functioned as hospitals. This function could be substantial: the chantry college of Tattershall (Lincolnshire), in addition to its master, six chaplains and others, supported thirteen poor people. It could apply even with an academic college: the early constitution of Eton College included the support of twenty-five poor men. Conversely, some major hospitals had a staff of several priests, and might maintain a high standard of religious life, so that they had a collegiate aspect. The great hospital of St Cross at Winchester, which in the sixteenth century had an annual income of £184 and accommodated twenty-seven poor brethren, had a staff of six priests, six clerks and six choristers. In several cases, an establishment that began as a hospital was later enlarged or refounded as a college, as at St Mary in the Fields at Norwich. Sometimes, a hospital and a college would be found in association, though with separate buildings for the two functions, as at the great Newarke College at Leicester.

The status of most colleges and hospitals is not in doubt. A very few houses are sometimes referred to either as a hospital or as a chantry college. Examples are Herringby (Norfolk) and Knolles Almshouses at Pontefract (Yorkshire, WR).

The Foundation of a College

The process of establishing a new college was complicated and could be lengthy. For example, at Wye (Kent), royal licence for the foundation was obtained in 1432, but staff were not appointed until 1448. It is no surprise that there are cases (some of which appear in Appendix IV) where the process is known to have been begun but never reached completion. The foundation of a college was usually due to a wealthy or powerful patron, who had to make a very large commitment of resources for the purchase or allocation of land, for construction, for furnishing, and especially for the provision of an endowment. The college could not begin to function until necessary permissions had been obtained, legal arrangements completed, an income secured, and church and domestic accommodation made ready. Foundation dates quoted in published sources may refer to different elements of the process, which can explain why they sometimes differ.

The greatest part of the income of a college normally came from its endowments, though this would be supplemented by the oblations and contributions of the faithful. Only when sufficient endowments had been secured would the college be able to maintain its intended establishment. Endowments would often be added, by the founder and others, over many years following the foundation.

In most cases the process of foundation involved the appropriation of an existing parish church ('appropriation of the rectory' means the same). Often it was appropriated to become the collegiate church. A church or churches might also be appropriated to become a part of the endowment: this was a common process, also used by monasteries. As already mentioned, if appropriated to a college of canons, it was usually allocated as a prebend. Appropriation meant the ownership of the church building and of the tithes and endowments belonging to it, but also carried its responsibilities in terms of pastoral care and maintenance of the structure, or at least of the chancel. The new owner became the rector, and usually discharged the responsibility for the cure of souls by the appointment of a vicar, paid out of the appropriated revenues, but leaving a substantial surplus. Such a vicar, having the cure of souls, was often known as a curate.

Normally episcopal, papal and royal licences were required for the foundation of a college, and for appropriation of a church. The approval of the bishop of the diocese and of the pope meant agreement that the change could be justified by the consequent advancement of religion. There should be no loss to the pastoral care of the parish or parishes concerned, and any conflicts of interest or problems of ecclesiastical politics should have been resolved. Royal licence was in the form of letters patent, an open letter that carried a legal validity. Following an Act of 1279 under Edward I, any appropriation to a religious corporation required permission to alienate in mortmain (pronounced 'morte-main', meaning 'dead hand'). Whereas property held by living owners was subject to the payment of feudal dues on their deaths, this could not apply if a corporation was the owner: this was land held in mortmain. In subsequent years, further measures, known as the Statutes of Mortmain, sought to control the giving of property in this way, and to overcome the evasions that were practised. Normally the Crown required payment of a large fee to give licence for property to be alienated in mortmain.

An obstacle to appropriation might be the need to acquire the advowson or patronage of the church, since the patron's right of presentation of incumbents could no longer apply. There was no problem where the founder was already patron. In other cases the patronage might be purchased. At Sibthorpe (Nottinghamshire) in 1341, Thomas Sibthorpe acquired for his new college the advowson and rectory of the church from the Knights Hospitallers, in exchange transferring substantial lands to the Knights.[29] Often just the advowson would be acquired for the college; this was not the same as appropriation of the rectory, but once it had happened, appropriation usually followed.

Most colleges had a patron. In the case of a college of canons, as we have seen, the patron presented to the prebends or portions, including that of the head of the college; the head would usually be responsible for filling subsidiary positions, such as vicars choral or clerks. In a college of chantry type, without prebends, we have seen that the patron usually presented only to the position of head of the college. In a college founded for chantry priests who belonged to individual chantries, however, there might be no single patron: each chantry had its own patron. Similarly, a college of fraternity priests had no individual patron. Nor did a college of vicars have a patron; it elected its own head.

The founder of a college was naturally the first patron, and made the first appointments to it. If the founder was a bishop, the patronage would subsequently fall to his successors; if the founder was the sovereign, patronage would remain with the Crown. Private founders would identify who would succeed to the patronage: it might be retained in the family or be vested in a bishop. Whereas the patron presented, institution to the positions would be in the hands of a bishop, normally the bishop of the diocese in which the college lay. Where the patron was himself a bishop, he would probably also institute; but in some cases, for example if the college lay in another diocese, institution might be in the hands of another bishop.

The legal identity of a college as a corporation was established by its foundation charter. The statutes, defining the rules for its life, were usually given by the founder. It was the responsibility of the head of the college to ensure that the statutes were observed. The written statutes were to be kept safely, and at episcopal visitations produced, when the faithfulness with which they were being followed would be examined.

3

The End of the Old Order

Colleges in the Sixteenth Century

The state of religion in early-sixteenth-century England has been much discussed, especially with respect to monastic life. There is room for some difference of opinion, but it seems clear that standards in many monasteries had declined and that the life lived in them was comfortable and lacked commitment to the intended ideal. Among the colleges of canons, we have seen that the absence of many prebendaries had been accepted practice for two or three centuries, and that it is reasonable to conclude that this had been accompanied by some loss of zeal in the maintenance of their religious life. This view is supported by the often critical reports of bishops' visitations. But they continued to function, normally with vicars. They were still valuable to their patrons, and their prebends were occupied. However, a few cases occurred of prebends being granted to laymen – clearly an abuse.

When it comes to chantry colleges, it may be that in the sixteenth century a higher standard of religious life was maintained in some than in many monasteries or colleges of canons. This is not to say that they were without problems: the numbers of chaplains serving in many had fallen below those originally intended, and this reflects a falling off of numbers in all types of religious houses. Some ceased altogether, usually owing to the inadequacy of their endowments. This happened too with many individual chantries. However, as we have seen, there were still new foundations in this period, so there does not seem to have been a general disillusionment with them. Individuals were still moved by the chantry motive, and were leaving money for the foundation of individual chantries right into the last decade of the reign of Henry VIII. Much the same could be said of the fraternities.

With the academic colleges, there was no question of a decline. Unlike other types, most academic colleges had been gradually increasing in size through the late medieval era. New colleges continued to be founded, and as evidenced, for example, by Cardinal Wolsey's foundations at Ipswich and Oxford, the academic college was seen as a high ideal. That monasteries were dissolved to fund new academic colleges, both by Wolsey and (just before the century began) by Bishop Alcock at Jesus College, Cambridge, tells us something about the climate of the times. The academic college was a field in which even King Henry VIII involved himself constructively, at both Oxford and Cambridge.

The Dissolution

The dissolution of the colleges came later than that of the monasteries, of which it was in effect a continuation; it cannot be understood without an understanding of the whole. It was, of course, on a smaller scale than the extinction between 1536 and 1540 of all monastic life in England and Wales, which involved the closure of more than 600 houses, owning between them an important part of the wealth of the nation. As is well known, the origins of this event are inseparable from the problems of Henry VIII in seeking a male heir, which led to the break with Rome. Another important cause, however, was the king's need for money, particularly to fund wars against France and Scotland. More generally, Henry and his advisers felt the need for the crown to have financial resources that would allow it to meet its expenses, domestic as well as military, without having resort to punitive taxation which could result in political unrest.

In consequence of the break with Rome, in 1534 the Act of Supremacy made Henry the supreme head of the Church of England. All religious houses, including the colleges, were required to subscribe to the royal supremacy: and though many in them must have felt misgivings, with a very few exceptions they did so. As a result of Acts of 1532 and 1534, payments to Rome of annates (or first-fruits) and tenths had been stopped, and they were diverted to the Crown. Annates were the payment of one year's revenue by holders of ecclesiastical positions on their appointment; tenths were a tenth part of the 'profit' of a church living. Both had long been an established part of the church financial system. With their transfer to the king, commissioners were sent across the country in 1534–5 to establish a new valuation on which they would be based. This, known as the Valor Ecclesiasticus, listed all Church income, and is the source of many of the valuations mentioned in these pages.

Henry made Thomas Cromwell his vicar-general. By order of Cromwell, a visitation of all the monasteries took place during 1535, ostensibly to establish the state of their spiritual life and to consider whether any reform was necessary. For reasons having more to do with the king's desire for money, however, the outcome was that in March 1536 an Act was passed through parliament to the effect that all monasteries with fewer than twelve monks or nuns and an annual income of less than £200 should be dissolved and, with their endowments, be forfeit to the Crown. The expressed justification for this apparently arbitrary selection was that these smaller monasteries were little better than dens of vice and corruption, in contrast to the greater monasteries, where religious life was 'right well kept and observed'. Whilst this criticism perhaps contained a grain of truth, it was certainly exaggerated, and the descriptions of the faults of some individual houses were probably largely fictional. However, this dissolution was carried through with some flexibility, quite a large number of houses that fell within the criteria nevertheless being permitted to purchase exemption. So what took place could reasonably be viewed as at least partly a necessary reform, and there seemed to be no intention that it would go further.

Matters changed, however, in the autumn of 1536 when, starting with a rising in Lincolnshire, the rebellion known as the Pilgrimage of Grace broke out in northern England. Opposition to the dissolution of the smaller monasteries was only one of its many causes; but some recently dissolved monasteries were re-established under the rebels, and several of the greater monasteries allowed themselves to become involved. During 1537, the rebellion was ruthlessly put down, and as well as the reopened smaller monasteries the greater monasteries that had been implicated were dissolved, and most of their abbots or priors and some of their monks were executed. The atmosphere was now different throughout the country. Without any further Act of Parliament, by a ruthless process of coercion, through 1538 and 1539 Cromwell and his commissioners visited and procured the dissolution of the remaining monasteries, supposedly by voluntary surrender. Where the commissioners met with co-operation, the monks or nuns were well treated, and were granted pensions; the pension of the head of a monastery could represent a large income. However, where they met with opposition, the result could be execution: in the autumn of 1539 the abbots of Colchester, Glastonbury and Reading were hanged in their own abbeys. A new Act was passed in 1539 which, though it did not authorize this final dissolution, ensured that all the property of the dissolved monasteries went to the Crown. The last abbey to fall, in March 1540, was Waltham. Meanwhile the friaries had been dissolved in a single operation in 1538; and in 1540 a further Act dissolved the entire order of Knights Hospitallers.

In this destruction of the monasteries, a few signs had suggested that the colleges were not to suffer the same fate. Some of these signs may be seen as part of the king's strategy to make the process palatable to public opinion. At least one college even acquired property from dissolved monasteries.[30] Unlike the other monasteries, the monastic cathedrals (other than Bath and Coventry) were not dissolved but were refounded with a new constitution of a dean and secular canons. Many of their former monks became part of a chapter of secular clergy in the same building in which they had lived the monastic life. Moreover, there were plans that some of the former great monasteries should be re-established as collegiate cathedrals, with the creation of as many as thirteen new dioceses. In the event many of these plans were not realized, but six cathedrals were created from former abbeys, at Bristol, Chester, Gloucester, Oxford, Peterborough and Westminster. There were also promises to convert some dissolved monasteries into colleges, with the prospect of associated public benefits, particularly through their provision of schools.[31] Again, most of these were not fulfilled, but in 1541–2 the former Augustinian abbey of Thornton (Lincolnshire), the Benedictine abbey of Burton upon Trent (Staffordshire) and the Dominican friary of Brecon (Breconshire, Wales) began a new life as colleges (*see* Appendix VIII). The collegiate church of Southwell, dissolved in 1540 for an abortive cathedral proposal, was actually refounded by an Act of 1543.

But the negative signs were stronger. Some threat at least to chantry colleges had come even before the attack on the monasteries, when in 1531 a measure was enacted to restrict the giving of property to provide a stipend for a chantry priest, though this had had little effect. But by 1540, following the dissolution of the monasteries, the tide was running against religious houses of any sort. In addition, Protestantism was gaining ground amongst the population (though not led by the king, who in most matters of doctrine adhered to the Catholic position). Soul-masses for the dead were one of the features of the old church most incompatible with Protestant feeling. Probably most important, however, was the recognition that the process of coercion that had been applied to the greater abbeys could only too easily be applied also to the colleges; those who co-operated would be well treated and would not go wanting, whereas for those who resisted the consequences might be severe. The dramatic and rapid fall of the greater monasteries was not repeated here; but from 1540 to 1545 there was a steady stream of 'voluntary' surrenders of colleges to the king. Similar procedures were followed to those that had been used with the monasteries: the master and clergy were either given pensions or given benefices. As with the monasteries, the pension allotted to the master could be substantial.

The king's desire for money continued, particularly after the renewal of war with France in 1544, and matters were moved forward in 1545 by a new Act for the dissolution of chantries, colleges, guilds, hospitals and similar bodies, and the transfer of their property to the Crown. This was supposed to apply only to those that were already in decay or being wound up by their own initiative; and the revenues were to be applied 'for good and godly purposes'. To implement it, a new body of commissioners was appointed in February 1546 to visit all such establishments. However, its work was far from complete when the king died on 28 January 1547; and the Act had been so framed that it lapsed with his death. Under the new nine-year-old boy king, Edward VI, or rather under his protector, initially his uncle Edward Seymour, Duke of Somerset, not only did the policy of dissolution continue, but the Government was now firmly set on the establishment of Protestantism. So in December 1547 a new Act was passed for the dissolution of all surviving colleges, chantries, guilds and fraternities. Excluded from the Act were the royal college of Windsor and the academic colleges of Oxford, Cambridge, Winchester and Eton; until the passing of this Act, it had not been certain that the academic colleges would be spared. Opposition in parliament caused the exclusion also of the hospitals, the craft and mercantile guilds, and schools run by religious bodies.

To implement this Act, a new body of commissioners was appointed, and most remaining colleges were quickly dissolved in 1548. These included most of the greatest, such as Newarke College at Leicester, and the three great

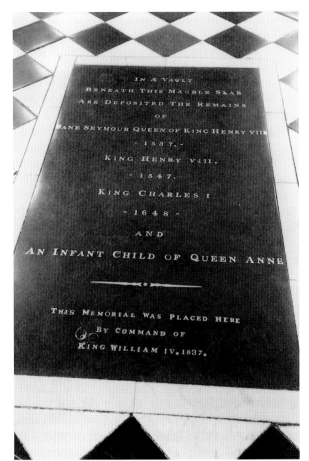

The resting place of Henry VIII in St George's Chapel, Windsor

IN A VAULT
BENEATH THIS MARBLE SLAB
ARE DEPOSITED THE REMAINS
OF
JANE SEYMOUR QUEEN OF KING HENRY VIII
- 1537. -
KING HENRY VIII.
- 1547. -
KING CHARLES I
- 1648 -
AND
AN INFANT CHILD OF QUEEN ANNE

THIS MEMORIAL WAS PLACED HERE
BY COMMAND OF
KING WILLIAM IV. 1837.

colleges of the diocese of York. This process did not have quite the merciless efficiency of the dissolution of the monasteries. A very few were explicitly allowed to continue, notably the recently founded college of Brecon. A few smaller establishments, mostly but not all portionary, seem to have simply been missed, for example Chulmleigh (Devon), Heytesbury (Wiltshire) and St Endellion (Cornwall). During the following reign of the Catholic Queen Mary, who came to the throne in 1553, there was an attempt to reverse the destruction of the previous two reigns and restore some religious life. Since the bulk of the former properties and endowments had been sold and the money spent, this was inevitably on a small scale. Westminster Abbey again became a Benedictine monastery, and the colleges of Manchester, Southwell, Whittington's College in London, and Wolverhampton were restored. Colleges that survived the dissolution or were subsequently restored appear in Appendix VII.

But the queen died in 1558, and in the religious settlement under her successor Elizabeth, most of the changes made by Mary were again reversed, and this time finally. Westminster Abbey, with its unique place in the national life, could not disappear, so it became a collegiate church and royal peculiar, with a dean and twelve canons. Most of the few surviving or re-established colleges continued. In some, the continuation was no more than nominal and there was no collegiate life; but in others, such as Manchester, a moderate religious life was maintained, akin to that of the cathedrals. The chantry function had been completely abolished. The positions in the surviving colleges were literally sinecure – that is, without cure of souls – and with other positions in hospitals and cathedrals they gave rise to the popular meaning of the word as 'an office of profit without duties attached'. Many of their occupants were absentees and pluralists, and they contributed to the impression of the seventeenth- and eighteenth-century Church and its ecclesiastics as too often comfortable and complacent. Major reforms were instituted early in Queen Victoria's reign, and as a consequence most of the surviving colleges and churches of portioners finally ceased by the abolition of the sinecure positions associated with them. The college of Windsor continued, and remains to the present day as a royal peculiar; the same is true of Westminster. More surprisingly, the little College of St Endellion (Cornwall) also survived these reforms, as did a few small portionary churches. At Westminster and Windsor today, a religious life continues comparable to that of the cathedrals, with multiple daily services; they maintain an important musical life, with choirs including boy choristers, and have attached schools.

The secular cathedrals (Chichester, Exeter, Hereford, Lichfield, Lincoln, London, Salisbury, Wells, York and all four Welsh cathedrals) continued largely unaffected by all these changes. They are known as the 'cathedrals of the old foundation'. Prebendaries still exist in them today, but they were rationalized in the nineteenth century as honorary non-resident positions, carrying no income. The formerly monastic medieval cathedrals that were refounded under Henry VIII with a collegiate constitution are Canterbury, Carlisle, Durham, Ely, Norwich, Rochester, Winchester and Worcester. They, with the cathedrals newly established in the same period, are the 'cathedrals of the new foundation', and they remain to this day constitutionally different from those of the old foundation. In them, the equivalents of prebendaries in the cathedrals of the old foundation are called honorary canons. Cathedrals of both types now have only a dean and about three resident canons.

Also largely untouched by the dissolution were the colleges of vicars associated with the secular cathedrals, although no equivalent bodies were established in the cathedrals of the new foundation. In the Middle Ages, vicars choral were required to be at least in minor orders; but minor orders were abolished in the Church of England. The vicars became divided into lay vicars (now often called lay clerks), and priest vicars; there were usually at least two of the latter. This arrangement continues to this day. With the appearance after the Reformation of married vicars, both priest and lay, many wished to live independently: so much of the corporate life of these colleges disappeared, and in time some of their buildings were diverted to other uses or demolished. Nevertheless, important survivals remain. As corporate bodies, they lost most of their financial independence in the nineteenth-century reforms, so their continued existence became little more than nominal. They finally ceased to exist in a further reform of the 1930s. Just the similar Minor Canons' College at St Paul's Cathedral in London survived even this, and maintains a modest corporate existence today. Vicars choral or lay clerks, however, continue in the cathedrals as employees of the dean and chapter.

The dissolution of the colleges was less dramatically destructive of buildings than that of the monasteries. Most collegiate churches had a parochial function, which continued. The church usually remained intact, but in some a part, often the chancel, was demolished or succumbed to neglect. Astley (Warwickshire), Attleborough (Norfolk), St John at Chester, Fotheringhay (Northamptonshire), Lowthorpe (Yorkshire, ER), Rushford (Norfolk), St Edmund at Salisbury, Steyning (Sussex) and Wye (Kent) survive only as fragments of formerly larger buildings. At Howden (Yorkshire, ER) the chancel is a spectacular ruin, as, on a smaller scale, is that of Lowthorpe in the same county. Other churches have completely disappeared, usually demolished shortly after their dissolution. These were mostly chapels of non-parochial colleges, which had no continuing function. Also destroyed were the colleges of 1541–2 at Burton upon Trent and Thornton. A very few collegiate ruins remain, as at Hastings (Sussex), Slapton (Devon) or Wallingford (Berkshire).

As with the monasteries, the buildings, lands and treasures of the dissolved colleges were mostly disposed of by the Crown for what they would fetch. This did not necessarily happen immediately; they were sold in the later years of Henry's reign, throughout Edward's, and some not until well into the time of Elizabeth. Many sales were to peers, courtiers or members of the Privy Chamber. Some were to self-made or rising men such as merchants or lawyers. Sometimes the property was sold to a descendant of the founder of the dissolved house, whose family had retained an interest in it. A small proportion was given away as rewards to those who were in the favour of the monarch. Although the Act of 1547 provided for the reassignment of endowments for the support of the schools, almshouses and other secular functions of the dissolved establishments, in practice this was slow in happening. In some cases the Crown assigned an annual sum to be paid directly to a schoolmaster, to the poor or to an almshouse. Only in the second half of Edward's short reign did some re-endowments take place, and then usually only following active petitioning to the Crown by the communities involved. As a result, some schools and almshouses were permanently lost (as also had been many of those associated with monasteries). Some that now carry the name of Edward VI as founder had in fact previously existed under the patronage of a religious institution, and were fortunate to survive and be re-established under that king.

In this transfer of former ecclesiastical property to the ownership of laymen, the property usually still carried the corresponding responsibilities. Where a college had a parochial function or had appropriated other churches, the new owner or owners had responsibility for the cure of souls. They also had other duties, such as the maintenance of the chancel of the church. A layman possessed of such ecclesiastical property was known as a 'lay impropriator', or simply 'impropriator'; a layman who had responsibility for the cure of souls was a 'lay rector'. A lay rector discharged his responsibilities by the payment of an appropriate sum for the support of a vicar. Lay impropriators did not always carry out their responsibilities adequately, and the consequence could be inadequate provision for parochial clergy, or the neglect and perhaps demolition of a church or part of it. Usually, however, the responsibilities were accepted. This position continued into the twentieth century; for example, at Lanchester (Co. Durham) in 1936, a certain Colonel Cookson was responsible for repairs to the chancel, paid £7 6s 8d annually towards the support of the vicar, and provided six bottles of communion wine each year. In some cases, these responsibilities still exist today. Such situations have sometimes led to disputes, especially over repairs, where the sums involved may be large. The position may have been settled by agreement, the responsibilities being commuted by the payment of a lump sum by the lay impropriator. Among the clergy, the titles vicar and rector continue in use, but no longer carry their former significance: incumbents are no longer dependent on endowments, tithe or payments by individuals.

Developments Since 1558

Although this book is concerned with medieval colleges, the story may be briefly brought up to date. The foundation of non-academic colleges has remained in the past: no new colleges have accompanied the monastic revival of the past 200 years. However, the secular cathedrals have continued in the established church, and from 1836 further cathedrals have been founded. These have usually appropriated important town parish churches; several were formerly collegiate. They have a structure similar to that of their fellows of the new foundation. The revived Roman Catholics have also founded cathedrals, with a comparable organization.

Following the Reformation, academic colleges continued to be founded in Oxford and Cambridge. All the medieval academic colleges have continued, and indeed have grown and evolved so that they are as relevant in the early twenty-first century as they have ever been. Many more colleges have been founded elsewhere, especially in the nineteenth and twentieth centuries, both as schools and as institutions of higher education. In them, the religious aspect has usually been less important than in their medieval predecessors, but many have constructed a chapel, some of which are major buildings. The chapel of Lancing College (Sussex), begun in 1868 to the designs of R. H. Carpenter and only completed in its present form in 1978, is a building of tremendous scale and verve. Its Gothic style is derivative, but by its thrillingly dramatic quality it silences all criticism: it must stand alongside the achievements of the greatest medieval college chapels. Such grand gestures were no longer possible in the twentieth century, but the impetus was not entirely lost. The chapel added in 1990 to Fitzwilliam College, Cambridge, designed by the architects MacCormac Jamieson Pritchard, is a distinctive and exquisite building, and like many of its predecessors represents some of the best architecture of its day.

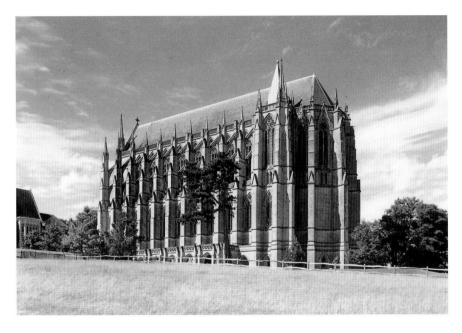

Lancing College (Sussex): the chapel from the south-east

Fitzwilliam College, Cambridge: the chapel from the south

4

The Physical Legacy

Characteristics of Collegiate Churches

Most collegiate churches are sufficiently substantial or interesting that they appear in modern selections of churches most worth visiting, such as those of Simon Jenkins or Sir John Betjeman. One fact which is usually known about a college is its annual income, as given for example in the Valor Ecclesiasticus of 1535. Relating this to the size and ambition of its architecture is interesting, though hazardous. Sometimes founders who were ready to lavish large sums on new building appear not to have committed correspondingly adequate funds for the endowment of their foundation; or it may be that those endowments later declined in value. Conversely, however, sometimes a substantial and adequately endowed college was provided with a surprisingly minor church. Relatively few colleges had an annual income of over £300 a year, and these were major institutions, exemplified by Ottery St Mary (Devon), Southwell (Nottinghamshire) and Warwick, with incomes in 1535 given respectively as £303, £516 and £334. In a college of canons, the prebends normally constituted most of the income, but the prebendaries would be expected to contribute to expenses such as rebuilding schemes. At the other extreme, some collegiate churches were modest. However, there are cases where a college with a small reported income had a remarkably fine church, for example the chantry college of Denston (Suffolk), with its annual income of just £22.

The churches of earlier colleges were usually collegiate when built. Most colleges founded in later periods appropriated an existing parish church. This was then quite often completely or almost completely rebuilt, as at Ottery St Mary (Devon) or Tong (Shropshire). In other cases, either the resources were not available for this, or the existing church was sufficiently large and splendid that rebuilding was not thought necessary. A partial rebuilding or extension might have been carried out, frequently involving the chancel: a large chancel is often a feature of a collegiate church, and may be longer, loftier or broader than the nave. Good examples are Sibthorpe (Nottinghamshire) and Shottesbrooke (Berkshire). In an aisleless chancel, the side walls may be blank, with the sills of its windows set high, to allow for the stalls and the tall canopies with which they were often provided. The chancel of a collegiate church frequently has a medieval sacristy attached.

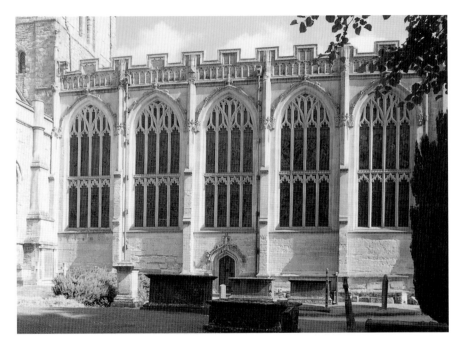

Stratford-on-Avon (Warwickshire): the late-fifteenth-century collegiate chancel, from the south

Such rebuilding or enlargement of a parish church in connection with the establishment of a college did not necessarily take place at the time of incorporation. It may have been undertaken in anticipation of that event, or alternatively not until after the college was functioning. At Tattershall (Lincolnshire), the complete rebuilding of the church did not begin until thirty years after the college was founded. Such factors may help to explain what seems puzzling when relating the architecture to the historical dates.

Churches with many associated individual chantries, which were usually large town churches, frequently show characteristic piecemeal additions of chapels or aisles to house the chantries; they sometimes have double aisles. Such additions almost always date from the fifteenth or early sixteenth century. This is not usually a collegiate characteristic, though a spectacular example may be seen at Manchester.

The chapel of a non-parochial college was usually of distinctive type. There being no lay congregation, no division of the church was needed into chancel, the preserve of priests, and nave, for parishioners. Such a chapel was frequently in the form of an undivided, aisleless hall, perhaps lofty. Examples are Carnary College at Norwich, Noseley (Leicestershire), the College of St Mary at St Davids (Pembrokeshire, Wales) and the College of St Stephen at Westminster.

A similar form was also characteristic of academic colleges, most of which had no parochial connection. In some, the chapel was quite small and simple, forming just part of one side of a courtyard and often attached at one or both ends to other buildings, such as the hall. Others had large and splendid chapels, the form reaching its highest expression at King's College, Cambridge. The range is remarkably wide. It is interesting that, whilst the early Tudor period saw the completion of the enormous chapel of King's College, it also chose at two other newly founded academic colleges in the same town, Jesus and St John's, to reduce the size of the very large medieval churches they had inherited from previous religious houses on their sites.

Almost all the chapels of the academic colleges have at their west end an antechapel, divided from the main space by a screen. The main part of the chapel was filled by stalls (sometimes called 'collegiate seating'); the members of the college occupied these for services, and since there was no lay congregation these chapels had, and have, no pews. The antechapel was not required for congregational worship, but would be available for processions and other activities, such as academic disputations; it often contains memorials. Sometimes it is no more than a room under a west gallery, but it may be a substantial section of the building. Many Oxford colleges, following the lead of New College, adopted a plan in the form of a 'T', effectively a cruciform church without a nave. This provided a very spacious antechapel.

A quite different characteristic of the academic colleges is that, since they continued after the Reformation as thriving and well-funded institutions, many of their chapels were rebuilt, remodelled or lavishly refurnished in the subsequent centuries. Some of this seventeenth- and eighteenth-century work was destroyed in the nineteenth century, but much survives to be seen today.

Collegiate churches of all types often retain some furnishings associated with their function, especially stalls, usually with misericords. These were of course not exclusive to collegiate churches; monastic churches had them, as did some major parish churches. In a collegiate church, the number of stalls may be the same as the number of clergy in the college, but is usually larger. Often, in the church of a chantry college there will be found a memorial to the founder, typically in the form of a tomb-chest with recumbent effigy or effigies. This may occupy an especially privileged position in the centre of the chancel, as at Bunbury (Cheshire), or on the north side of the sanctuary, as at Bere Ferrers (Devon). Later generations of the founder's family often maintained a close connection with the college, and there may be memorials to some of them too. Others who augmented the foundation may also be commemorated.

Tong (Shropshire): the stalls, with misericords

Ludlow (Shropshire): a popular misericord of a mermaid with a mirror, mid-fifteenth century

Bunbury (Cheshire): the chancel, with the tomb of the founder, Sir Hugh Calveley

The visitor to collegiate churches may notice that, whilst in some the collegiate history is described in a guidebook or a notice displayed in the church, others have no such reference at all. Sometimes this may be due to the widespread lack of understanding of medieval colleges: although a church is documented as collegiate in readily accessible sources such as the *Victoria County History*, local historians or writers of guidebooks may overlook or not understand the significance of this. This can also be manifested in misconceptions, confused statements or garbled terminology. A college may be referred to as a monastery, or 'a type of monastery'. One guidebook, in some respects good, refers more than once to the 'collegiate college'!

Collegiate Buildings

The domestic buildings of colleges were far less standardized than those of monasteries. In colleges of canons, as in the secular cathedrals, the early ideal of life in common was usually later replaced by the canons living in separate houses. These might be arranged in a single building, perhaps around a courtyard; but, especially later, they could be substantial, detached houses. Prebendal houses are a feature of the closes of many of the secular cathedrals, and also existed around some collegiate churches. There might be a deanery, larger than the rest. At a church of portioners, the corresponding houses may be known as rectories. In most chantry colleges, the accommodation was in the form of a single house in which all the members lived. This would include a hall for meals to be taken in common; and it often included a small chapel, usually used for devotions separate from the principal work of the college. There was occasionally a separate master's house. A chapter-house survives in a few colleges, as at Howden, Manchester and Warwick. Where there were vicars choral, a separate building was often provided for them. The larger foundations often had their buildings arranged round a courtyard, occasionally with cloister walks. One of the finest surviving collegiate buildings is at Manchester, which includes a small cloister; other cloisters remain at St Stephen's, Westminster, and St George's, Windsor. St George's has an exceptionally large and complete set of buildings, with a deanery, canons' houses, two cloisters and a separate residence for the vicars.

Howden (Yorkshire, East Riding): the chapter-house

Windsor: the Dean's Cloister

Surviving former domestic buildings have found a variety of uses. At Wye (Kent), they again form the nucleus of a college, of agriculture; at Manchester they are occupied by Chetham's School, a specialist music school; at Cobham (Kent) and Coventry, they are used as almshouses; and at Bredgar (Kent), Kirkoswald (Cumberland), Rushford (Norfolk) and elsewhere, they are in use as houses. Those of Higham Ferrers (Northamptonshire) are preserved largely as a ruin, while the buildings of Carnary College at Norwich are part of a school. Even where no collegiate buildings survive, they may have successors; a house called The Deanery may sometimes be found near a collegiate church.

In the colleges of vicars choral at the secular cathedrals, the accommodation would consist of a room or small house for each vicar, perhaps arranged round a quadrangle or down a street. There would also be a common hall and a small chapel. These colleges were usually close to their cathedral, and in several cases had their own covered access to it. Their physical form varied a great deal; at Lichfield (Staffordshire) they were timber-framed, while

Manchester: part of the collegiate buildings, now Chetham's School

Maidstone (Kent): the gatehouse and the hall range

others had architecturally substantial buildings of stone. The most perfect and impressive example is the famous Vicars' Close at Wells (Somerset), laid out down a street. Also very fine is that at Hereford, in the form of a quadrangle with a cloister.

In the academic colleges the typical layout was of fairly regular ranges of two-storeyed buildings round a rectangular courtyard, with the hall and chapel each forming the whole or part of a range. A tall and impressive gatehouse was a frequent feature. Good examples are Front Court of Queens' College, Cambridge, and Front Quad at All Souls College, Oxford.

Unlike the buildings of a monastery, collegiate buildings were often not attached to the church; and even if they were, they were not in that position against the nave and transept that was almost universal among the monasteries. In some chantry colleges, the buildings stood as much as several hundred yards from the church. This apparently surprising fact calls for some comment. Whether the church was appropriated was not a factor. Unlike monks or nuns, who were enclosed and lived in a precinct that did not have free public access, secular priests lived in the world, so they could pass through public spaces on their way to the church. While their observances in the church were central to their lives, they might use much of their remaining time in other ways; on leaving the church they did not have to remain in a 'religious' space. Also, the life did not necessarily require attendance by every chaplain at all the daily masses and canonical hours. The routine of an individual chaplain usually involved celebrating masses at a chantry altar for which he was responsible, and he might arrange a schedule suiting his convenience. Occasionally, some collegiate services might be said in the small chapel in the domestic buildings: at Rushford (Norfolk), it was specified that of the four daily masses, High Mass, Lady Mass and the Mass for the Departed were to be said in the church, but the Mass of the Holy Trinity was to be said in the chapel attached to the dormitory.[32] In all these ways, collegiate life differed from that in a monastery, where the entire community moved between the domestic buildings and the church many times a day for the succession of offices.

Architectural Styles

This book uses the terminology for the periods of medieval architecture first proposed in the early nineteenth century by Rickman, which is widely used and offers a simple framework for describing medieval buildings. The object of the book is not to discuss medieval architecture – for those wishing to know more, numerous studies are available. However, a brief outline may be useful. Fine examples of all periods are to be found among the collegiate churches.

The Anglo-Saxon period lasted from the first post-Roman stone buildings of perhaps the seventh century up to approximately 1066, but most of what is to be seen dates from the late tenth or the eleventh century. Round arches are employed, though triangular heads to doors and windows may appear. Proportions tend to be narrow but tall, both in the buildings themselves and in archways and doorways. There is little ornament. The most common enrichment is narrow stone bands known as 'pilaster strips', projecting perhaps an inch from the wall surface, employed especially on exteriors. These are usually simple vertical bars, but sometimes form more complicated patterns; they also often appear, internally as well as externally, flanking the responds of arches, and may curve round the arch. Quoins (the corners of buildings) often employ a characteristic form of construction known as 'long-and-short', in which long, narrow stones alternate with thin, broad pieces that penetrate far into the wall. Windows (where they survive) are usually very small; they are sometimes double-splayed, the narrowest part of the opening occurring midway through the wall. Surviving work of this period is often on a small scale, but such a church as Bosham (Sussex) demonstrates that the Anglo-Saxons could construct impressively large buildings.

Bosham (Sussex): the Anglo-Saxon tower, early eleventh century, with long-and-short quoins

Chester: St John Baptist. Norman work, probably early twelfth century

The Norman period, approximately from 1066 to 1190, is characterized by massive and heavy masonry, round arches and thick mouldings. Early work is plain and its masonry relatively crude, but as time went on buildings became more sophisticated in their construction and richer in their ornamentation, although no less heavy. Walls are externally reinforced by shallow, flat buttresses. A range of very characteristic ornamental motifs is employed, the commonest being the chevron, a zigzag pattern carved in bold relief; it is often used to make a tremendously lavish display on doorways and arches. Norman work sometimes exhibits a bold but rather barbaric character, with a fondness for grotesque heads, dragons and other powerful but primitive representational carvings. These frequently appear externally on a corbel-table just beneath a roof. Windows are round-arched; in the later part of the period they may be fairly large, and are often enriched with shafts. Capitals may have a regular pattern of scallops, and later there appeared outwardly curving leaf-like volutes; a particular type where the tip of the leaf curls inwards, known as waterleaf, is characteristic of about 1170–90. Blank arcading may appear, and flat ashlar surfaces are sometimes enriched with diaper patterns. The Normans also introduced vaulting, of a simple barrel or groin form in early work, but later with thick ribs, often heavily ornamented.

The period from about 1160 to 1200 frequently shows features of Norman type alongside those of the next period; work of this nature is so often found

Steyning (Sussex), showing
Norman clerestory windows:
late twelfth century

Wimborne Minster (Dorset):
Transitional Norman nave arcade,
with chevron ornament

that it is sometimes referred to as Transitional (Trans.) Norman. Some examples may be of Norman character in their heaviness and their ornamental features, but employ pointed arches; while others may have the character of the following period, especially in their mouldings and ornamental motifs, yet employ nothing but round arches. Many lie somewhere between.

The Early English (EE) period extended from about 1190 to 1280. This is a great contrast to the preceding Norman style, and is characterized by arches which are pointed, often acutely, and long, narrow, pointed windows, known as lancets. The windows are sometimes set in groups of two or three, and occasionally more, those of the larger groups frequently being graduated in size. Pillars are often slender, and externally the walls have slim buttresses of marked projection. Where there are mouldings they are deeply undercut; shafts or rolls may be given keels or fillets. There is a fondness for contrasting dark-coloured stone such as Purbeck marble, especially for shafts. Capitals are often moulded, sometimes known by the self-explanatory term 'trumpet capitals', but sophisticated work may employ the exquisite form known as 'stiff-leaf', a development

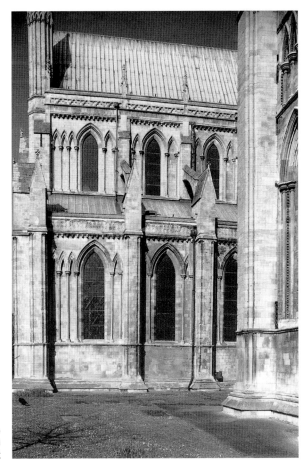

Beverley Minster (Yorkshire, East Riding): the Early English south transept

of the volute. The most characteristic ornament is bands of small cut-away pyramids called 'dog-tooth', often used on arches. Overall design can be of a chaste sophistication, with elegant use of string-courses and blank arcading. In the later part of the period, groups of lancet windows developed by the piercing of the spaces above them with circles or quatrefoils to give what is known as 'plate-tracery'. There followed the development of large arched window openings containing true bar tracery; this first tracery is known as 'geometrical', its design being usually based on circles. Such windows appeared in architecture that is still in most respects Early English in character.

Southwell Minster (Nottinghamshire): Early English blank arcading

The Early English style merged into the Decorated (Dec.) style, which was dominant from about 1280 to 1360. This is a softer style, a period of exuberant delight in new and ever more free and imaginative forms. Windows are large, and often have rich tracery designs, in the later part of the period known as flowing or curvilinear. The ogee or double curve appears, used in window tracery and in small arches such as those above piscina recesses. Arches may be less acutely pointed than earlier. Mouldings are rich, but much less deeply cut than in the Early English style; the sunk quadrant form quite often appears. Ornamentation becomes more luxuriant. The use of contrasting dark marble largely ceases. Capitals in the late thirteenth century went through a period of naturalistic representation of foliage (of which the chapter-house of Southwell (Nottinghamshire)

Beverley Minster: the Decorated nave

Higham Ferrers (Northamptonshire): Decorated windows of ogee form

is a famous example), but later this foliage congealed into more stylised, knobbly patterns. Corbels and hood-stops often show strikingly characterized and animated carvings of human heads. The favourite ornamental device (replacing the dog-tooth) is the 'ball-flower', a small globe with three enclosing petals.

The final style of the Middle Ages was the Perpendicular (Perp.), which lasted from around 1360 until the end of the medieval era; it was unique to England and Wales, with no parallel elsewhere. The curves and flowing forms of the Decorated are now replaced by an emphasis on verticals and horizontals, especially seen in window tracery, which adopts relatively standard forms. Wall surfaces are quite often panelled in a similar manner. Bands of fleurons, each a small square ornament of stylised foliage, are widely used. This was a time in which architecture displayed a confident and suave virtuosity, shown in such features as lofty towers and rich vaults; but it is sometimes criticized for its repetition of standard forms and motifs. Windows are often very large, maximizing the area of glass for use by the stained-glass artists: churches can be veritable glasshouses, with solid wall reduced to a minimum. Straight-headed windows are common, mainly in smaller buildings. Arches are rarely acutely pointed, and the four-centred or depressed arch is widely used. In the second half of the fifteenth century, some changes appeared, and the style is sometimes called Tudor. Probably the supreme feature is the fan vault, in which the form is a series of concave cones. This period has been referred to as the Indian summer of English medieval architecture; two of its most spectacular productions are King's College Chapel, Cambridge, and St George's Chapel, Windsor.

New College, Oxford: the Perpendicular chapel, from the south-east

Ottery St Mary (Devon): early-sixteenth-century fan vault in the Dorset aisle

The Early English, Decorated and Perpendicular styles, all with pointed arches, are together known as Gothic architecture.

After 1540, church building declined to a low level, but against this trend there was considerable new building for the colleges of Oxford and Cambridge. The style employed continued to be Gothic, mainly of Perpendicular character but sometimes with some classical and other elements. From about the Restoration (1660), the classical style finally arrived in ecclesiastical architecture, with its columns, pilasters, architraves, cornices and round arches mainly derived from precedents in classical antiquity. There are three principal orders, known as the Tuscan, Ionic and Corinthian, distinguished by the form of their capitals. Plasterwork could be rich, and colour and gilding might be employed freely. Preaching was now more important than liturgy: in the plans of new parish churches, the chancel was relatively unimportant or even non-existent, and the nave formed an auditorium often filled with galleries. This change, however, did not affect the chapels of academic colleges. Classical styles developed through the eighteenth century; in the early nineteenth century many churches were built in a massive Greek revival style.

From the mid-eighteenth century, a picturesque but often rather superficial revived Gothic style (sometimes called 'gothick') made its appearance. For many years it co-existed with classical styles for new church building, but it developed and its popularity increased until by about 1830 Gothic was fairly universally employed. Then came the Victorian period, in which there appeared a new earnestness in religion and in its architecture. The serious Gothic of the Victorians could range from the reproduction of medieval precedents to the very original and powerful but sometimes harsh and jagged productions of such architects as Butterfield and Street. Much restoration of older churches took place, sometimes good but too often altering existing medieval fabric for the sake of what were considered improvements. Gothic continued into the twentieth century, developing in the 1920s and 1930s a quiet and restrained manner. Only after the Second World War did what might be called 'modern' styles take over.

Notes

1. The word 'college' had one other use, in favour principally in the seventeenth century: this was as a term for an almshouse or hospital. Such are the College of Matrons, founded in 1682 in the Close at Salisbury; Morden College at Blackheath in south-east London, dating from 1695; Morley College, on the edge of the Close at Winchester, of 1672; and Sackville College at East Grinstead (Sussex), founded in 1617. These, however, are outside the scope of this book.
2. Blair, 1985, 115.
3. Ibid., 119–20.
4. Mainly in Yorkshire, it is sometimes used today to mean a collegiate church.
5. Hamilton Thompson, 1917, 142–3, 148–50.
6. Blair, 1985, 124.
7. Martin and Martin, 1999, 42.
8. *VCH*, Staffordshire, iii, 314.
9. Knowles and Hadcock, 1971, 412.
10. Hamilton Thompson, 1917, 151n.
11. *VCH*, Durham, ii, 125; Loades, 1967, 67.
12. Hamilton Thompson, 1917, 170–1.
13. Ibid., 145–6; Harrison, 1952, 23–4.
14. Hamilton Thompson, 1917, 156–66.
15. Ibid., 194–6.
16. cf. Jones, 2000, 110–14.
17. Hamilton Thompson, 1943, 92–3.
18. *VCH*, Northamptonshire, ii, 168.
19. Hamilton Thompson, 1943, 93–5.
20. *VCH*, London, i, 576.
21. *VCH*, Nottinghamshire, ii, 148.
22. *VCH*, Shropshire, ii, 131.
23. Hamilton Thompson, 1917, 189–92.
24. Denton, 1970, *passim*.
25. *VCH*, Staffordshire, iii, 304-5.
26. An exception is De Vaux College at Salisbury.
27. One other type of academic college also came to exist in Oxford and Cambridge; this was the monastic college. Monks too wanted access to

the benefits of learning that were available in the universities, but being monks they did not wish to live with secular students. So about the end of the thirteenth century, the Benedictines made the first moves to establish an academic house in Oxford. Eventually Oxford had five monastic colleges and Cambridge had one; there were also several monastic halls. The monks lived at least a quasi-monastic life. The monastic colleges all came to an end in the dissolution of the monasteries, but most were subsequently refounded as or absorbed by secular colleges. At Cambridge, the Benedictine Buckingham College, which originated in 1428, was in 1542 re-established as Magdalene College. At Oxford, three colleges were Benedictine: Canterbury College, of about 1370, was absorbed by Christ Church; Durham College, established about 1381, was refounded in 1555 as Trinity College; and Gloucester College, which originated in 1283, eventually became Worcester College. The Cistercian St Bernard's College of 1437 was refounded in 1555 as St John's College. However, the Augustinian St Mary's College, founded in 1435, was lost. These were not colleges of priests, so are not discussed further in these pages.

28. Scarisbrick, 1984, 19–39.
29. *VCH*, Nottinghamshire, ii, 151.
30. Arundel: *VCH*, Sussex, ii, 109.
31. Scarisbrick, 1988, 63–4.
32. *VCH*, Norfolk, ii, 458.

Gazetteer

The core of this book is the gazetteer, intended to describe the history and architecture of all the collegiate churches and chapels of England and Wales. Churches are described as they exist today; an attempt to describe only features surviving from the medieval period might be historically legitimate, but they are here treated as buildings that may be visited and enjoyed. Whilst most remain predominantly of the Middle Ages, others are now partly or entirely of later centuries; indeed, every century from the seventeenth to the twentieth is represented, often worthily. Where a church no longer exists, something may be known about it if the site has been investigated archaeologically or if it survived long enough to appear in early illustrations. Standing domestic buildings are also discussed, but in less detail than the churches.

As will by now be appreciated, the boundaries of what was truly 'collegiate' are blurred. The criterion for inclusion is that a church was collegiate at some time between 1200 and 1540. The earlier date excludes most of those former minsters or early collegiate churches that disappeared in the years following the Conquest. Churches that were collegiate but later became monastic are excluded: these are treated in the literature of monasteries, and here appear only in Appendix III. Churches are treated as collegiate if they were used as the church of a college, even though not appropriated. Portionary churches are included where they were more important or probably collegiate in function. The minimum size of a college is taken as three clergy. Associations of chantry or fraternity priests that were not incorporated are excluded. Many churches that fall outside these criteria will, however, be found in Appendix IV.

Colleges of vicars choral, which did not have a collegiate church, appear in Appendix I. Colleges established for chantry priests who served in a cathedral appear in Appendix II. Further appendices list other groups.

Geographical organization is by county. Ever since the local government changes that culminated in the reorganization of 1974, some publications have adopted the new and altered administrative units, while others have adhered to the old counties, sometimes for reasons of sentiment. However, further changes in recent years have led to the dissolution of several new units, the return of some 'lost' counties, and the further complication of the appearance of unitary authorities; as a result, many post-1974 publications that adopted the latest organization are also now out of date. Such problems are here avoided by using the 'traditional' counties. This has the disadvantage that a few places transferred from one county to another here appear in their 'wrong' county: for these, the current organizational unit appears in brackets where, at the time of publication, it is different from that given.

The inclusion of a building in this book does not imply public access. Most formerly collegiate churches are today parish churches of the Church of England. Depending upon local circumstances, many are open to visitors during most normal daytime hours; of those usually locked, an incumbent or churchwarden will often be found who will gladly allow entry to an interested visitor. Chapels of academic colleges are mostly accessible to the public, though a charge may be levied. Some buildings described are the property of other organizations or of individuals; access may be allowed on personal application. The upkeep of an ancient building is expensive and, whatever the arrangements for access, it is appropriate that the visitor make a contribution towards its maintenance.

An asterisk before an entry in the gazetteer is a suggestion of those most worth visiting.

Bedfordshire

This county had one attractive chantry college, at Northill. In addition, the important church of St Paul at Bedford was collegiate in its early days (*see* Appendix III).

* Northill

The Trailly family long held the advowson of the Church of St Mary at Northill. After the deaths of Sir John Trailly in 1401 and his son Sir Reginald the next year, royal licence was obtained by their executors in 1404 to make the church collegiate. The college was founded in 1405, and the church was appropriated to it: it was a chantry college, with a master, four fellows and two choristers. Its annual value was given at the Valor as just over £61; dissolution came in 1547.

The church is mainly of attractive dark brown ironstone. It is stately, tall despite lacking a clerestory, and on a large scale; but there has been considerable renewal. The chancel is early Perp., in three bays, with three-light arched and traceried side windows; though usually dated to about 1370, it is possible it was constructed for the college. The five-light E window in Dec. style is a Victorian amendment. Inside, there is a good Perp. composition of ogee-cinquefoiled piscina and cinquefoiled triple sedilia. On the N side is a medieval sacristy; it has been given a continuation W dated 1862, with a rose window. Also Victorian is the chancel arch. The nave has fine, dignified four-bay Dec. arcades: their pillars are of four major and four

Northill, from the north-east

Northill, looking east

minor shafts, carrying arches of two sunk quadrants. The aisles are tall but narrow, and are battlemented. Most of their windows are Dec., but four have been replaced by a Perp. design, in three lights under a three-centred arch, without tracery. There is a large vaulted S porch with small reticulated side windows; it has a battlemented Perp. upper room which was the chapel of St Anne, used by a chantry founded in 1489. The porch arch and much else are renewed. From the dissolution until 1850, the upper chamber was used as a schoolroom.

The W tower is large and tall, with angle buttresses, shallow battlements and a taller polygonal NE stair turret. Its W window is Dec., as is the renewed arch to the nave; but the belfry stage is Perp., with paired two-light arched openings under a square label on the E and W sides, and single openings to N and S.

Parts of the original stalls remain, with plain poppy-head ends and six misericords, though they have been much renewed. A little old work is incorporated in the tall Victorian chancel screen. A good iron-bound chest is said to be seventeenth century. There are four hatchments and five old benefaction boards. A hand-carried bier is dated by inscription 1663. Unusual and especially fine is the glass set in iron frames inside two of the S aisle windows: heraldic, very rich and mostly bright yellow in colour, it is dated 1664.

Berkshire

The supreme collegiate monument of this county was and is the great College of St George at Windsor, which is unique in still functioning much as its founder intended. Its predecessor, the College of St Edward, is sufficiently distinct, both historically and architecturally, to warrant separate treatment. Berkshire also possesses in Shottesbrooke an outstandingly attractive example of a small chantry college.

* Shottesbrooke

A church was recorded here in Domesday Book. In 1336 Sir William Trussell obtained licence from Edward III, and in the next year established a college in the Church of St John the Baptist, which was appropriated to it. This was a chantry foundation, for a warden, five chaplains and two clerks. About thirty years later, the church and college are reported to have been seriously damaged by fire; during the subsequent period of repair, all but the warden left, and the college apparently never returned to its original numbers. In 1546, there were a warden, two chaplains and a clerk or sexton. The warden was then a layman, and the college was dissolved in the following year, when its annual value was given as £59.

Although historically this was a small and apparently unremarkable college, in architectural terms it is entirely outstanding. The church is not large, with an external length of 88 ft (26.8 m), but it is lofty and of remarkable quality and perfection, a uniform structure of mature Dec. work, almost without later alteration. It must have been entirely rebuilt for the college, and either the damage later in the century did not touch the church or it was repaired just as it had been. Nor may anything be seen of the repairs which followed serious lightning damage in 1757; and little harm was done by the Victorian restoration, of 1852–4 by G.E. Street. Even the setting is special: in the heavily populated E part of Berkshire, it lies in a remarkably quiet and unspoilt enclave of parkland, with a partly Tudor mansion and no village. The church has no electricity; chandeliers are still ready for their original function.

The plan is cruciform, without aisles; collegiate proportions immediately show in that the chancel has three bays whereas the nave has only two. There

Shottesbrooke, from the east

are identical N and S porches. The walls are of knapped flint, with limestone dressings. Over the crossing, the tower has large two-light belfry openings and a hexagonal stair-turret standing out from the NW corner; behind its battlemented parapet rises a splendidly tall stone spire with at its base large blank lucarnes in the cardinal directions. Windows throughout the church have curvilinear tracery, of two lights in the side windows but reaching five in the spectacular E window. Arch mouldings are rich and are mostly continuous. Many ogee arches appear, including small doorways and the little side windows of the porches. Both transepts have a fine ogee piscina recess, and in the chancel is a beautiful composition of piscina and triple sedilia, again employing the ogee form.

The roofs, mostly of crown-post form, are medieval, and the walls have ancient plaster. Furnishings are few, most space being bare; there are a Victorian stone pulpit and a large organ. Glazing is mostly clear, but there are many medieval fragments in the tracery lights. The octagonal font is a noble original piece, without stem, each side having a blank cusped-ogee arch, with finials and relief pinnacles. The stone floors have several excellent medieval brasses, including a large double brass in the centre of the chancel, thought to commemorate the first warden and his brother. An unusual memorial is in the form of an open stone coffin containing an effigy, across the centre of which a bridge of stone carries a brass inscription: this is to a warden who

Shottesbrooke, looking west

died in 1535. Across the full width of the N end of the transept is an extremely rich pair of tomb-recesses, with large lierne-vaulted canopies. They have many image niches now lacking their statues, and much ball-flower. These are the burial places of the founder and his wife, and formerly contained their effigies. The collegiate buildings stood to the S, and had a passage connecting with the S transept.

An unusual Victorian tribute was paid to this church: when in about 1848 the church of Kingswood (Surrey) was rebuilt on a new site, the new building was made in most respects an exact replica of Shottesbrooke. Only the sedilia, piscinas and tomb recesses were omitted. The result could not fail to be beautiful, though the interior startlingly lacks the atmosphere of the original. The architect was Benjamin Ferrey.

Wallingford *(now Oxfordshire)*

This attractive town had one of the major castles of southern England, founded by William the Conqueror in 1067 as part of his strategic series of fortresses. Attached to the Chapel of St Nicholas in the castle, a college was founded about the end of the eleventh century, having royal privileges; it had prebends, but the number is not known. The castle remained royal; it was held by several successive earls of Cornwall, and the college was reconstituted

Wallingford: the ruins from the south

in 1278–80 by Edmund, Earl of Cornwall. He increased its endowments, and it now became a chantry college with a dean, five (later six) chaplains, six clerks and four choristers. Its status as a royal free chapel continued. As described by Leland, a 'fair steeple of stone' was built at the W end of the chapel by John Underhill, dean 1510–36; the 'fair lodging' of the dean was within the castle, timber-framed, with the residence of the chaplains attached. The annual income is given as £147, and the college was dissolved in 1548. The castle declined but was refortified by the royalists in the Civil War; after a lengthy siege and then several years' use as a prison, its destruction was ordered in 1652.

Part of the site is now beautifully laid out as public gardens, and culminates in a lofty mound; a very few scattered fragments of masonry are to be seen, of which the largest is said to be the remains of the collegiate chapel. However, its character is baffling, and appears more domestic than ecclesiastical. It was formerly incorporated in a house, and includes much post-Reformation brick-work. The loftier section is a wall running E–W, standing above a ditch, built of rough clunch, with a considerable batter; it contains a three-light square-headed window of sixteenth-century type. Near its E end is a taller feature which has been improbably suggested as the church tower; the structures at its top are not medieval. From the W end of this wall, a lower wall extends N. It is much patched and altered, but some of its external face is of ashlar, and it has three square-headed two-light windows, all blocked. Near its N end is the one feature which looks ecclesiastical: a Perp. doorway, two-centred in a square label, with a quatrefoil in the spandrels. The remains have not been elucidated, but at the time of writing an archaeological investigation is proposed.

* Windsor: St Edward

Between about 1240 and 1248, a major chapel dedicated to St Edward the Confessor was built in the lower ward of the castle for Henry III. It was served by a college of priests, who did not hold prebends but were paid directly from the royal purse; the chapel had royal freedoms. A surprising degree of uncertainty surrounds the history of this college. It was apparently unaffected by the fire of 1296 which gutted the adjacent royal lodgings, and at this period had eight chaplains and two clerks. Between about 1313 and 1331 it seems to have been reduced in numbers, and during this period we hear instead of chaplains serving in a chapel in the park of Windsor; nothing remains of this chapel, and even its site is unknown. However, after 1331, the chaplains were withdrawn from the chapel in the park, and the College of St Edward returned to its previous numbers.

In 1348, it was replaced by the College of St George. The new college initially used the former chapel of St Edward, which was rededicated, either remodelled or rebuilt, and lavishly refurnished. Only in 1475 was construction begun immediately to its W of a great new chapel for the College of St George. After some years, it was proposed by Henry VII that the older building should become a mortuary chapel for himself and the Tudor dynasty. From 1502 it was again remodelled or rebuilt, but this work was probably never completed as the king transferred his attention to his great new chapel being built at Westminster Abbey. In the 1520s Cardinal Wolsey obtained permission from Henry VIII to make it a mortuary chapel for himself, and further work was carried out. However, with the cardinal's fall from power in 1529, this purpose too was not realized, though the chapel was known thenceforth as the Wolsey Chapel. A plan by Charles II to use its site for a chapel in honour of his father came to nothing. It may have been used for a time under James II as a Roman Catholic chapel. George III too had unrealized plans for it. Finally, after the death in 1861 of the Prince Consort, Queen Victoria had it made into a memorial chapel to him; his body was buried in it before being moved to the new mausoleum at Frogmore. Thus this remarkable building, still including significant work from the time of Henry III, is now rather startlingly known as the Albert Chapel.

Windsor: the Albert Chapel, from the south-east

Although attached to the E end of St George's Chapel, the Albert Chapel is a distinct building. Externally it mostly appears as uniform Perp. work, though of different character from that of St George's; it is a lofty, aisleless structure of five bays plus a polygonal apse. The walls are of limestone ashlar and have boldly projecting buttresses carrying tall pinnacles; the S side has an elaborate openwork parapet, whereas the N has solid battlements. Windows are uniform, in four lights with two transoms, under four-centred arches. Though it is uncertain when most of it was built, its enrichment of crowns and portcullises demonstrates a significant Tudor contribution. Much renewal took place in the nineteenth century.

The surviving thirteenth-century parts may be seen without entering the building. In the Perp. Dean's Cloister on the N side, the lower part of the EE N wall of the chapel remains, with excellent large-scale blank arcading of richly moulded arches on shafts with stiff-leaf capitals. At the W end of this wall, a fine EE doorway opens to a passage, which was the antechapel of St Edward's Chapel and still performs this function for the Albert Chapel. Its panelled tunnel vault and other details are Perp. The W wall of the antechapel remains EE, and its external face now appears in the ambulatory at the E end of St George's Chapel. It has three very fine EE portals, with shafts and richly moulded arches; their curious plain capitals are replacements, perhaps of the late eighteenth century. The central portal possesses its especially fine original doors, their entire surfaces covered in wrought-iron work of sophisticated and beautiful design.

Windsor: the west portals of the Albert Chapel, seen from the ambulatory of St George's Chapel

The interior is dominated by its Victorian purpose. Although the structure remains Perp., its surfaces are entirely covered by Victorian decoration. There is a beautiful lierne vault, and this and all the upper parts of the walls are elaborately painted, with much gilding. Below the windows the walls are lavishly decorated in marbles, with bas-reliefs and pictures in etched marble; at the base is a marble bench. The windows are filled with stained glass. The centre is given over to three great royal memorials. That to the Prince Consort is nearest the altar, in white marble, with a recumbent effigy. That nearest the W end is of the Duke of Albany, who died in 1884, while in the centre is the enormous and extraordinary memorial by Alfred Gilbert to the Duke of Clarence, who died in 1892.

* Windsor: St George

All things considered, St George's Chapel, Windsor, must be regarded as the country's greatest collegiate church. Its claim is threefold. In its status it is unique since, as a result of its close connection with the crown, this college still exists: its dean, canons and other staff still occupy their original buildings, and it continues to function in a manner at least resembling that envisaged by its founder. In its treasures and its historical and royal associations it is outstanding, exceeded among all churches perhaps only by

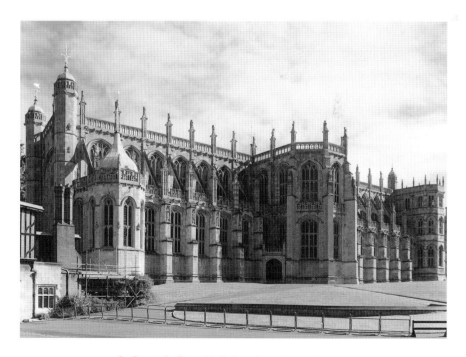

St George's Chapel, Windsor, from the south-west

Westminster Abbey. In its architecture it is superb, one of the three or four finest examples of the last great flowering of Perp. church building. It was founded in 1348 by Edward III, both as a college and as a spiritual home for the order of chivalry which he founded in the same year, the Order of the Garter. His initial plan envisaged a college of a warden and twenty-three canons, with twenty-four poor and infirm knights; the Knights of the Garter were also twenty-four, but were not members of the college. The realization of these plans was held up by the Black Death of 1348–9, but building began in 1350. In 1351 the establishment was revised to comprise a warden (later dean) and twelve canons, with thirteen vicars, four clerks, six choristers and twenty-six poor knights. The Knights of the Garter were now also increased to twenty-six; the poor knights were intended to represent them rather in the manner of vicars. St George's resembled earlier colleges in that the canons held prebends; however, these were bursal and were small: residence was intended, and much larger sums were provided for canons who were resident. As would be expected, it had royal freedoms.

The college at first used the chapel of the previous College of St Edward, which was rededicated to God, the Virgin Mary, St George the Martyr and St Edward the Confessor. It was remodelled, perhaps rebuilt, and was given elaborate new fittings, including an exceptionally large reredos of alabaster, made at Nottingham. In 1475 under Edward IV, however, the present chapel was begun, on a new site immediately W of the old. It was completed in 1528 under Henry VIII. It still had a dean and twelve canons, but the numbers of other clergy were by now even larger, and also included a number of chantry priests. The annual income at the Valor of 1535 was the enormous sum of £1,396. The college was explicitly excluded from the provisions of the 1547 Act, and continued essentially unaltered; an active religious and musical life was maintained. It is interesting that technically chantries were not abolished here, although in practice they were given up. Changes came with the nineteenth-century reforms, and later, and the college now has a dean, four canons and two minor canons, all of whom are resident. There is a choir of sixteen boys and twelve lay clerks, and a choir school of about a hundred boys. It remains a royal peculiar. Religious life in the chapel continues, with at least three services every day. It is still used by the Knights of the Garter.

The chapel magnificently dominates the lower ward of the castle. It is of the highest richness and quality, and demonstrates the distinctive architectural ideals of its period, significantly different from the earlier years of the Perp. style. It is built of excellent limestone ashlar and appears superbly preserved, though this is in part due to extensive but very good restoration. It is cruciform, with aisles throughout, but has no tower (a crossing tower was intended, but never built). The internal length is 222 ft (67.7 m); the high nave and chancel are both seven bays in length. Roofs are low-pitched throughout, with splendid openwork parapets and large panelled pinnacles surmounted by beasts (the King's Beasts); the aisles have buttresses with statues in niches, carrying flying buttresses. The aisle and clerestory windows are

St George's Chapel, Windsor: the vault, looking east

of four lights with two transoms; the enormous E and W windows are of fifteen lights. Arches are mostly of depressed four-centred form. Perhaps uniquely, the ends of the transepts are polygonal apses. At both ends of the church smaller polygonal side chapels project, at the E end of full height, at the W end of aisle height and crowned by leaded ogee roofs. Battlemented turrets flank the centre of the W front.

The distinctive quality of the interior is its breadth, covered by wonderfully rich vaults. Of the high vaults, only that of the crossing (the last work completed) is a fan, the rest being sophisticated lierne vaults, in the chancel with pendants; all are remarkably depressed. Fan vaults cover the aisles. The arcade arches have no capitals and are not emphasized, and the bay spacing is quite small. All internal surfaces are richly moulded, and any flat expanses are panelled. Below the clerestory windows is a rich frieze of angels. Tudor roses appear among the decorative motifs. An ambulatory is beyond the high chancel, forming a physical link with the Albert Chapel. The two E bays of the N chancel aisle are lower than the rest, and have a chapel over: this was Edward IV's chantry, and later became the royal pew.

A great veranda screen surmounted by the organ separates nave from chancel; though convincingly Perp. in appearance, this fine piece in fact dates from about 1790, and is of Coade stone. Several chantry chapels occupy bays in the chancel arcades. The transepts are separated by tall stone screens: they too served as chantry chapels. Most of the glass in the great W window is

St George's Chapel, Windsor: the chancel, looking west

medieval. Especially fine are the stalls, of 1478–85, with tremendously rich canopies, fronts and ends, and with superb carved misericords. There were fifty; four more added about 1790 match almost undetectably. Above the stall canopies is a remarkable display of banners and helms: these are not ancient relics but represent the Knights of the Garter of today. Mounted on the backs of the stalls are 670 small brass or copper heraldic stall plates: these alone remain here after the deaths of their knights, the earliest being of about 1390. Of very great interest is the outstanding series of memorials, of which many but not all are royal. Two are perhaps especially moving. In the centre of the chancel floor, a simple ledger of 1817 marks the vault in which Henry VIII, the instigator of the dissolution of the monasteries and colleges, is buried together with Jane Seymour, Charles I and one other. Projecting from the N chancel aisle is a tiny, low chapel, the burial place of George VI and the Queen Mother.

The buildings of the college are mostly still in existence, though considerably rebuilt and altered. Most were originally constructed in the 1350s. To the NE is the Dean's Cloister, with walks of good early Perp. work; the extensive deanery is on its E side, incorporating what was originally the Garter chapter-house. N of the Dean's Cloister is the Canons' Cloister, with the houses of the canons, mostly timber-framed. W of the chapel is the large Horseshoe Cloister, the name of which describes its plan. It was built in 1478–82 to accommodate the vicars, and is timber-framed and very much restored; the vicars' hall is now the chapter library.

Buckinghamshire

The sole collegiate church in the traditional county of Buckinghamshire is that of the great academic college of Eton.

* Eton *(now Berkshire)*

The college of the Blessed Virgin Mary at Eton was founded in 1440 by Henry VI, then aged eighteen, four months before his foundation of King's College, Cambridge. The two colleges were conceived as a related pair, in this and in other aspects being modelled on William of Wykeham's earlier foundations of Winchester and New College, Oxford; indeed Henry visited Winchester early in 1441 immediately before laying the foundation stone of the chapel at Eton. The first charter envisaged a provost and ten priest fellows with four clerks, six boy choristers, a master of grammar and twenty-five poor scholars; there were also to be twenty-five poor and infirm men. Over the first few years, the king developed his ideas: the relationship between the two colleges was formalized, and their intended scale greatly increased. At Eton, the planned numbers were scaled up to include ten clerks, sixteen choristers and a further ten priests, with seventy scholars; there were also to be ten commoners, who were to board in the town and pay for the education they received. The main purpose of the education was seen as preparation for the priesthood.

Eton College: the chapel, from the north-west

In its constitution, the chantry motive was as important as the academic. Much of the endowment came from property formerly belonging to alien prior-ies, the last of which had been dissolved in 1414. The parish church of Eton was appropriated, and for a time functioned also as the college chapel. Work on the new chapel for the college seems to have been quite advanced when, in 1449, the plans for it were changed to be even larger, apparently involving the demolition of much or all that had already been built. Building proceeded rapidly, but then in 1461 the king was deposed by Edward IV, after which many of the endowments were removed; work stopped, and indeed in 1463 the new king obtained a papal bull for the dissolution of the college. But it survived the crisis, and building was resumed in 1469, though the hospital function of supporting poor men was given up. The 1449 plans had envisaged the present chapel as just the chancel of a vast cruciform building. These were modified: what had been begun was completed, and in 1479–82 the W end was finished off by an antechapel. The old parish church, which had stood close to its S side, was demolished about 1477, so (despite its apparent unsuitability for the role) the new building served as parish church as well as college chapel. Construction of the college buildings continued into the sixteenth century; further building began in the late seventeenth century, and has continued in every century since.

The chapel is one of the great ecclesiastical buildings of the late Perp. era. It is essentially a lofty, aisleless rectangle of eight bays with at the W end, looking the change of plan that it was, the rather lower antechapel making the plan a 'T'. Both exterior and interior are faced in ashlar. It is built over an undercroft, which makes it seem especially tall externally. It has very deep buttresses and is battlemented throughout, with big crocketed pinnacles; the angles at the E end have taller polygonal turrets carrying pretty timber cupolas with ogee tops. The side windows are of five lights, and transomed; the E window has nine lights. The antechapel is itself an impressive structure, also with large windows; attached to its N and S ends are large entrance lobbies, containing stairs up to the floor level. That on the N, attached to a range of college buildings, has a good moulded plaster ceiling and a beautiful late-seventeenth-century staircase.

The interior makes a splendid effect. It has much finely moulded stonework, with, in the four E bays, stone panelling continuing below the windows to the floor, while in the remaining bays the lower parts of the walls are plain. The most surprising feature is the broad, depressed fan vault. This is in fact of 1956–9, replacing a late-seventeenth-century timber roof, and is not a true vault at all, being of stone-faced concrete suspended from steel trusses. Its design is purged of the cusping and curves that would have been expected in a late-fifteenth-century fan vault; but it seems visually satisfying, and there is little doubt that a vault (though not necessarily a fan vault) was originally intended. Three bays on the N side have a group of relatively low attachments: a porch, a vestry (now used as a chapel) and the chantry chapel of Provost Lupton. The last was added about 1515 and opens to the main chapel by an arch containing a fine stone screen; it has a charming fan vault with a big central pendant.

Eton College: the chapel, looking east

An elaborate Victorian stone screen carrying the organ separates the chapel from the antechapel. The Victorian main seating is in collegiate plan. The large brass lectern is fifteenth century, a double desk on a heavily moulded thick stem, with a tripod base. An outstanding possession is the late-fifteenth-century wall-paintings in the W half of the main chapel, which were uncovered from 1923 following removal of the stall backs and canopies. They are remarkable for being mainly monochrome (grisaille), and have texts above and below; what survives is well preserved and is enjoyable. The floor of the antechapel has many indents for brasses, most of the brasses themselves being now mounted on the walls. Most striking among the many other memorials is a late-eighteenth-century statue of the founder. The Snetzler chamber organ is of 1760. There is much later-twentieth-century glass, mostly by John Piper, replacing glass destroyed by a wartime bomb.

The early college buildings are arranged round two courtyards, mostly of brick but far from uniform. An impressive tall gatehouse, Lupton's Tower, opens to Cloister Court, which has cloister walks. The extensive later buildings are mostly across the road to the W. The chapel remained parochial until 1875, though a chapel of ease was first built in the town in 1769. An important religious and musical life continues here, though after much controversy the choir school first established in 1441 ceased in 1968. The term 'conduct', often used in the Middle Ages, is still the name for the chaplains here.

Cambridgeshire

With one exception, this is entirely the story of the academic colleges of
Cambridge, of which there were fourteen in 1540. Most still exist today,
but King's Hall and Michaelhouse were both in 1546 absorbed in the newly
founded Trinity College. The medieval Buckingham College (now represented by Magdalene) was monastic and so does not appear. The chapels of
the Cambridge colleges are very varied; some are small, but the famous
chapel of King's College is by far the greatest of any academic college.
Several of the colleges have in their histories used more than one chapel, the
earlier often a parish church, so they may have two church buildings to be
described.

Cambridge: Christ's College

The origin of this college was an establishment for the training of teachers of
grammar, known as God's House, founded in 1439 by a London priest,
William Byngham. It stood close to Clare Hall, and when in 1446 its site was
needed for Henry VI's King's College, a new site was found for it and it was
made a full college; its charter of 1448 names William Byngham and Henry
VI as joint founders. This small college continued for over fifty years, and
buildings were gradually constructed, including a chapel. Then Lady
Margaret Beaufort came on the scene. She was the mother of Henry VII, and
three times widowed. Her confessor was John Fisher, previously Master of
Michaelhouse and now Bishop of Rochester and chancellor of the university,
and it was probably he who suggested this as an object for her interest. Her
charter of refoundation, renaming it as Christ's College, is dated 1505.
Building went ahead rapidly, including the present fine gate tower and the
replacement or enlargement of the chapel, which was consecrated in 1510.
Lady Margaret took a personal interest in the college, and spent some of her
time here in rooms that are now part of the master's lodge.

The chapel projects E from the NE corner of First Court. Only the W part,
containing the antechapel, appears in the court: it presents a classical appearance, with sash windows at two levels, a tall parapet and a fine arched
doorway with a dentilled architrave on Ionic pilasters. This is part of a
remodelling of the court of about 1760. However, the framework of the
chapel remains early sixteenth century, a broad and quite substantial building. Its N exterior (mostly in the master's garden) is rendered and
battlemented. The NW corner has an octagonal turret which rises quite high
and carries an attractive glazed cupola of 1722. The chapel windows have
depressed four-centred arches and are of three lights, without tracery; the E
window has five lights. On the N side are early-sixteenth-century attachments, now used as vestries and organ chamber; part may originally have
been a chantry chapel. The flat chapel ceiling is original, with moulded
beams, small arched braces and wall-posts on foliage capitals.

Christ's College, Cambridge: the chapel, looking east

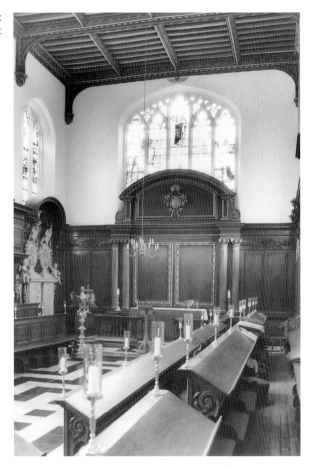

The antechapel has early-eighteenth-century panelling, Corinthian columns and a ceiling of moulded medieval beams. The room above has always been walled off from the chapel. Also early eighteenth century is the fine panelling of the chapel, especially rich in the E part, and the reredos, which has an open segmental pediment and beautiful restrained gilding. There are charming three-sided communion rails, some of their balusters plain and some twisted. Incorporated in the panelling on the N side is a linked pair of standing wall memorials, of 1684. Openings in the panelling reveal several original doorways, one on the S side connecting with the master's lodge. Also opening from the master's lodge is a timber oriel window, now of 1899 but representing an original feature. The N windows have considerable early-sixteenth-century glass. A battered medieval chest is in the antechapel. The finest thing here is the splendid late-fifteenth-century brass eagle lectern.

* Cambridge: Clare Hall

The site of the present college was acquired by the university in 1298, with two houses which were probably used as hostels. In the 1320s it was decided to make this into a college, and the chancellor of the university, Richard de Badew, in 1326 obtained licence for its foundation as University Hall. However, the new foundation got into difficulties, mainly because its endowments were inadequate. In 1336, Lady Elizabeth de Clare, granddaughter of Edward I, three times widowed and possessed of great estates, took an interest in and helped it. Her involvement continued, and in 1338–40 the college came under her control; its name was changed to Clare Hall in 1346. In 1359, Lady Clare was responsible for new statutes, which were the first in either university to give a place to undergraduates as well as master, fellows and graduates. She died in 1360.

The college initially used the nearby Church of St John Zachary. A small chapel was built in the college in the late fourteenth century, but use of St John's continued. When in 1446 this church was demolished to make way for the chapel of King's College, Clare Hall moved to the church of St Edward (*see* Trinity Hall), where the N chapel was built for it. In 1521 there was a fire in Clare Hall; a new chapel was completed in the college in 1535, with a library above it. From 1638, the college was rebuilt in a splendid campaign which was completed in 1715 except for the chapel, which was left projecting E from the NE corner of the court. This was finally rebuilt in 1763–69, on the same site, the architects

Clare College, Cambridge: the chapel, from the south

being Sir James Burrough and James Essex. It is approached from the court through a fine late-seventeenth-century doorway with a large stone shell-hood, leading into a stone-faced passage. From this, entry is to an octagonal antechapel occupying the corner of the court: this is a superb stone-faced room, with blank arches all round, supporting a dome decorated with panels containing delightful enrichment. It is top-lit by a large octagonal lantern, charming both internally and externally, carrying a small dome with pineapple finial. The chapel itself has five bays plus a bay which internally appears as a semi-elliptical apse. Windows are large and round-arched. The S exterior is of ashlar, with a large Corinthian pilaster between each bay and a rich cornice surmounted by a balustrade; the whole stands on a rusticated basement. The little-seen N side, however, is of yellow brick and has a plain parapet. Externally the E end is square, pedimented and divided by pilasters into three, the centre having a blank window, the flanking sections a classical niche. It was probably inspired by Wren's chapel of Pembroke College.

Clare College, Cambridge: the chapel, looking east

Internally, pairs of unfluted Corinthian columns articulate the walls between the windows. The semi-elliptical coffered plaster ceiling is exquisitely enriched, while the half-dome of the apse has a different ornamental pattern. Glass is mostly clear. There are many beautiful fittings of oak, fairly light in colour, almost all original to the building. The W wall has a fine screen, its central arch having Ionic pilasters and a pediment, flanked by niches with Ionic columns and segmental pediments. Tall, dignified panelling runs the length of the chapel, and there are excellent stalls. In the apse, the great pedimented reredos stands forward on paired Corinthian columns. This chapel, although not particularly large, is one of the finest in Cambridge. The crypt is now used as the Junior Combination Room.

* Cambridge: Corpus Christi College

Corpus Christi College is unique among academic colleges in having been founded by a fraternity. About 1350 the Guild of Corpus Christi and the Guild of the Blessed Virgin Mary determined to establish it, and merged, with Henry, Duke of Lancaster, agreeing to become alderman of the united guild.

Cambridge: St Bene't.
The tower

The advowson of the Church of St Bene't (or Benedict) was obtained, and in 1352 royal licence was granted for the foundation of the college and appropriation of the church. The association of the college with the church was close, and for the first 350 years of its existence it was commonly known as Bene't College. In the event, however, appropriation did not take place until 1578. Initially the college was for just a master and two fellows, but by the sixteenth century there were eight fellows. All were to be in priest's orders; they were to celebrate some masses also in St Botolph's Church (previously associated with Gonville Hall), which adjoins the college on the S side. Architecturally, the college is notable for retaining its fourteenth-century Old Court little altered, the oldest court in Cambridge.

Apart from one striking feature, the Church of St Bene't has no collegiate character. It is notable principally for its W tower, an exceptionally good example of Anglo-Saxon work. This is of rubble, with two offsets, and has long-and-short quoins to its full height. The belfry openings are twins divided by a midwall shaft; a pilaster starts above them and rises to the straight top of the tower. Small round-arched and circular openings here seem to be sixteenth-century insertions. Most interesting and impressive is the tower arch, which is thick, constructed of through-stones, with unmoulded responds and arch. The responds are of long-and-short form, but two pilasters run up beside them, and there are huge imposts of complex mouldings, with a beast above. A round-arched doorway is higher up. Some long-and-short quoins of the former Anglo-Saxon nave are also visible, all now internal.

After this, the rest of the church seems dull. It is of medium size, with aisles embracing the tower, which is a little skew to the nave. The broad N aisle and N porch are of 1853, while the S aisle is of 1872. However, the three-bay arcades are Dec., on pillars of four major and four minor shafts, with Perp. clerestory windows and a low-pitched roof. The chancel is short, and is mostly Victorian. Its S side, however, is medieval, showing various altered and blocked features, a cusped-ogee piscina and an ogee sedile recess. Attached here is a two-storeyed block of red brick built by the college about 1500, with square-headed windows: the lower part is a sacristy but the upper part appears to have been a chapel. This continues in a narrow range running S to connect with Old Court of the college, including a formerly vaulted gateway in its lower level. This interesting arrangement resembles that at Peterhouse. The few old contents of the church include a small iron-bound medieval chest; the plain baluster font is eighteenth century.

A separate chapel for the college was built about 1579. This, however, was swept away in the rebuilding campaign of 1823–7 that produced New Court, by the architect William Wilkins. A new chapel was built roughly on the previous site, and presents to the court a W facade of ashlar in enriched Perp. style, with four-centred arches, openwork parapets, niches containing statues, and tall panelled octagonal turrets with spirelets. Entry is to a dark antechapel hardly larger than a porch. The chapel has windows in Perp. style, and internally the walls have stone panelling. It was extended E by two bays in 1870, by Blomfield, in Dec. style, with some display. Of this time is the high-pitched timber roof throughout, replacing a plaster vault. The windows contain some sixteenth-century Rhenish glass. Parts of the stalls are Elizabethan and parts are early sixteenth century, with misericords.

Cambridge: Gonville Hall

Gonville Hall was founded in 1347–8 by Edmund Gonville, a priest of extensive means who also founded a college at Rushford in Norfolk. His original site was between what is now Free School Lane and St Botolph's Church; the college was to use that church, of which it held the advowson, and occupy existing buildings for its accommodation. Gonville died in 1351, and the work was continued by his friend and executor, William Bateman, Bishop of Norwich, who was at the same time involved with his own foundation of Trinity Hall. In 1353 he moved the fledgling college to the site of the present Gonville Court, close to Trinity Hall; the original site became part of Corpus Christi College, which also took over the advowson of St Botolph's Church. From this time, the college used the N aisle of St Michael's Church (*see* Michaelhouse). Bateman died in 1355. Construction of a chapel in the college was licensed from the beginning on the new site, but it was not consecrated until 1393. In 1557, the college was refounded on a larger scale by Dr John Keys or Caius, giving it its modern name of Gonville and Caius College.

Gonville and Caius College, Cambridge: the chapel, from the south

The medieval chapel was remodelled and lengthened to the E about 1637. Further changes of 1718–26 were its ashlar facing, dentilled cornice, panelled parapets and large buttresses (originally carrying flaming urns). An E apse was added in 1868–70, when a turret was also built at the SW and the antechapel was shortened to give more space in the chapel. The resulting building is long but still on a modest scale. Windows have segmental arches and are of three lights without tracery or cusping. The SW turret is circular, and carries an attractive arcaded stone belfry with a dome. Entry is from a passage through the range which continues to the W.

A beautiful feature of the chapel is its canted timber roof of 1637, panelled and gilt, with as its principal motif a cherub in an oval sunburst. The fine stalls and panelling are mainly early eighteenth century. The W gallery over the antechapel contains the organ and has a front that was originally part of an early-eighteenth-century reredos. A medieval piscina high in the S wall was in a previous longer W gallery, which served as the master's oratory. The apse has mosaics. There are two late medieval brasses, and the walls have a good series of memorials. Most remarkable, however, is the enormous memorial to Dr Caius, who died in 1573: it is entirely classical, with a splendid sarcophagus set under a great canopy. It originally stood on the floor but in 1637 it was set in a large raised recess on the N side, rather like a theatre box.

* Cambridge: Jesus College

About 1130, a priory of Benedictine nuns dedicated to St Radegund was founded here. Its church was begun in the late twelfth century but mostly built in the thirteenth, as were its buildings. In 1496–7, the Bishop of Ely, John Alcock, obtained licence to suppress it and use its buildings and endowments for the establishment of an academic college. At this time, there were only two nuns, and the royal licence alleged factors such as the dissolute disposition and incontinency of the nuns; but these may be excuses, as Alcock appears to have been working towards its suppression since 1487, when there were eleven nuns. Whatever the rights and wrongs of this, Alcock has earned our gratitude for the establishment of this fascinating and beautiful college. It was dedicated to the Blessed Virgin Mary, St John the Evangelist and the Glorious Virgin St Radegund, but the present name was used almost immediately. It was initially small, for a master and six fellows; there was also until 1570 a grammar school for boys.

The nunnery church became the college chapel; its greatest interest must be as a monastic survival, but it is instructive to see what was thought appropriate in converting it for collegiate use. It was reduced by shortening the nave from seven bays to two and a half, and removing its aisles and the chapels E of the transepts and flanking the chancel. It is still large. Entry is by Perp. doorways in the nave and N transept, opening from the cloister, which is on its medieval site though the present walks are of about 1500, altered in 1768. The buildings all round are monastic in origin but much remodelled;

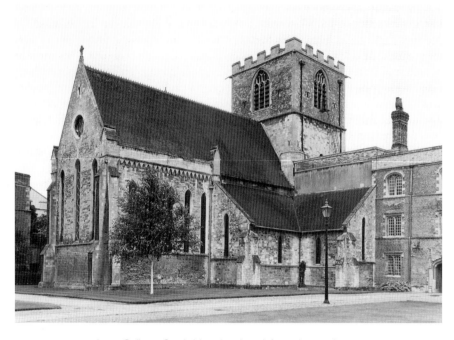

Jesus College, Cambridge: the chapel, from the north-east

the refectory is now the hall. The splendid tripartite EE entrance to the chapter-house has been exposed. Much of the W part of the nave still exists, divided into rooms which are mainly used as the master's lodge.

The nave and S transept appear to be mainly Perp., though a few earlier features are visible. Their windows are mostly of three or four lights under depressed four-centred arches; the S transept main window has five lights and a transom. Late-twelfth-century work appears in the N transept. Its N wall has three tall blocked round-arched windows and another above, all outlined by a continuous roll. The E side has a two-bay EE arcade (now containing Victorian stone screens), but above this is a passage behind paired colonettes carrying round arches, again with a continuous roll. Both transept roofs are of Alcock's time, with excellent moulded timbers. The crossing is EE, its tall arches having large-scale dog-tooth. The EE lower stage of the tower is internally open, with a wall passage behind paired arches of very rich mouldings resting on quatrefoil pillars. Externally, there is a Perp. top stage probably added as part of Alcock's alterations, with battlements and three-light arched openings.

Most spectacular is the mainly EE chancel, though its perfection is partly due to the restoration from 1844 by Pugin, which included the pitched roof, the reinstatement of the noble E triplet of lancets in place of a Perp. insertion, and the restoration of the former N chapel and N transept E aisle to provide vestry and organ accommodation. The N chancel arcade has two large bays. Opposite them are two Perp. windows, set within two perhaps Dec. blocked arches which are visible externally. E of these, both sides are of the most sophisticated EE work. On the S there is a range of four large lancet windows set above a string-course, with very fine mouldings and double shafts carrying shaft-rings. Below are six trefoiled arches on shafts above a bench, continuing with a wider trefoiled arch containing two stepped seats. There is a specially fine double piscina, its arches formed of intersecting round arches in open-work, set in a rectangular frame with dog-tooth. It has stiff-leaf capitals. The N side has five lancets, like their partners but longer; interestingly, the EE N arcade interrupts this work, showing that there were two distinct EE phases.

Jesus College, Cambridge: the chapel, looking east

The nave and transepts form a very large antechapel. Some notable Victorian work is to be seen throughout the chapel. The low-pitched nave roof is by Bodley, and has admirable painted decoration by William Morris. Most windows have stained glass, some designed by Pugin and many others by Morris and Co. The rich screen and lavish stall canopies are by Pugin, though some details of the stalls are reused medieval work.

* Cambridge: King's College

King's College originated in February 1441, when the young Henry VI, probably under the influence of John Langton, Master of Pembroke Hall and chancellor of the university, issued letters patent for the college of St Nicholas, for a rector and twelve fellows. A court was begun on a constricted site E of Clare Hall, and building pressed ahead rapidly. But by 1443, the king's ideas had developed and he now refounded it on a vastly greater scale, to have seventy fellows with ten chaplains, six clerks and sixteen choristers. It was linked to his other great academic college at Eton, in a similar way to William of Wykeham's New College, Oxford, and Winchester. Henry greatly increased the endowments, using property that had belonged to alien priories, which had finally been suppressed in 1414, and other revenues from the Duchy of Lancaster. For this plan, a much larger site was identified immediately S of the old. This contained streets, houses, wharfs, the church of St John Zachary and much else, of which the purchase and clearance was quickly taken in hand. The college was now named the King's College of Our Lady and St Nicholas in Cambridge. In 1446 the king laid the foundation stone of the chapel. Meanwhile the original buildings had been hastily completed and were in use, including a chapel, which stood between the court and the site of the new chapel. In March 1448 the king wrote a lengthy document known as his 'will and intent', in which he described in remarkable detail the planned layout of the college. Building on the chapel was pressed ahead, completing the foundations and wall-bases of the whole, and then building from the E end.

King's College, Cambridge: the chapel, from the south-east

In 1461, however, with nothing finished, the king was deposed by the Yorkist Edward IV. The Duchy of Lancaster funds disappeared, and most of the endowments were confiscated. For a time it seemed that the college might be extinguished, but the new king allowed it to continue, though it was reduced to twenty-three fellows. By about 1477, building work resumed on the chapel, and continued under Richard III. But with Richard's death in 1485 at Bosworth Field and the accession of Henry Tudor as Henry VII, building was halted again, this time for twenty years. It is probable that, by this time, the five E bays were roofed (without their vaulting). In 1506 Henry visited Cambridge and, perhaps under the influence of his mother, Margaret Beaufort, he allocated large funds for the completion of the chapel, which continued under Henry VIII; this final stage occupied the years 1508–15. There followed the installation of the glass and furnishings, and the chapel was finished about 1536. Meanwhile, no other buildings had been constructed, and the college continued to be confined to the cramped premises of Old Court; nor had it yet returned to the numbers planned by Henry VI. In 1724–30 one splendid block of a projected three was built to a classical design by Gibbs. Finally, in 1824–8, to a Gothic design by William Wilkins, the bulk of the college was constructed on Henry VI's site; the college then sold Old Court to the university.

The chapel is one of the supreme achievements of medieval England, and arguably the last. It is of twelve bays, a single aisleless space, the external length being approximately 317 ft (96.6 m); internally the height from floor to vault is 80 ft (24.4 m). Interior and exterior are of the finest regular ashlar; the difference in the stones used in the three phases of construction is just detectable. The ends are flanked by tall octagonal turrets with ogee tops. There are superb openwork battlemented parapets with tall pinnacles. The great side windows are of five lights, with tracery and a transom; the end windows have nine lights. Very deep buttresses stand out from the walls; other than in the end bays, the space between them is filled by low chapels or, at the W, the entrance porches. These chapels have very broad windows of eight lights under depressed arches.

There is only one departure from uniformity: in the last, Tudor, phase of construction, extensive carved decoration was introduced, all based on badges of political significance to the Tudor dynasty. The completion of the chapel, begun by the saintly Henry VI, was seen as playing a role in legitimizing the Tudors. The portcullis was the badge of the Beaufort family; the rose, or Tudor rose, was a symbol of Henry VII's marriage to Elizabeth, the Yorkist heiress; and so on. Externally this means the appearance, on the buttresses of the W half, of crowns, roses, portcullises and heraldic beasts, all large and richly carved, and of lavish carving around the porches and W doorway. Internally, the W part has an amazing virtuoso display of carving, all employing these symbols; they also appear on the high vault throughout. This is a wonderful fan vault, at over 42 ft (12.8 m) the broadest ever constructed; it is of a quite depressed four-centred form, with considerable

King's College, Cambridge: the vault of the chapel

emphasis on the transverse arches separating the bays. Some of the side chapels have fan vaults, but many have lierne vaults. In the W part, the chapels open from the main space through screens of stone tracery; in the E part they mostly do not communicate with the main space at all, but only connect to each other. The lower parts of the walls in the E section of the main chapel are the only plain surfaces in the interior.

The glazing of the chapel could be a major study in itself: almost uniquely, the complete medieval scheme is preserved. It dates from 1515–31, and was the work of glaziers mainly from the Netherlands; the style has a good deal of the Renaissance. Even more Renaissance in style is the woodwork, remarkable at so early a date, especially the enormous screen of dark oak. It has many monograms of HR and HA, referring to Henry VIII and his second wife Anne Boleyn. The stalls are of similar character and quality; they reach the remarkable total of 118, and have misericords. It is not known whether the workmen responsible for this woodwork were English. Some other woodwork is seventeenth century, including the case of the organ on the screen. A notable possession is the great brass lectern, a double-sided desk, given about 1515. Memorials are confined to some of the side chapels. One other treasure which cannot be ignored is the altarpiece, the great Adoration of the Magi by Rubens; it was given in 1961, and for it the sanctuary area was extensively refitted.

King's College, Cambridge: carving in the chapel

As we listen to the broadcast of that essential part of Christmas, the Festival of Nine Lessons and Carols, we may reflect that both the choir and the building in which it is singing were founded by Henry VI. The choir still has its sixteen choristers, who are educated at King's College School.

* Cambridge: King's Hall

This college originated in about 1317 under Edward II as a place for the education of boys destined for royal service ('the king's childer'). It was at first unendowed, being supported directly by payments from the royal purse. In 1337, under Edward III, it was enlarged and put on a regular endowed basis as the Hall of the King's Scholars, for a warden and thirty-two scholars. Buildings were gradually constructed, and were complete about 1438. Its royal association continued, and it became wealthy. In 1546, as one of the last acts of his reign, Henry VIII dissolved it and used it, with Michaelhouse, as the nucleus of his new very large Trinity College, the greatest college of the university. The royal connection has remained, and several members of the royal family spent time as students at Trinity College during the twentieth century.

Substantial parts of the buildings of King's Hall remain, especially the early-sixteenth-century Great Gate, which is the main entrance to Trinity College. For well over the first hundred years of its existence, it had no chapel; it used the parish Church of All Saints, which belonged to St Radegund's nunnery. The church was latterly mainly of the fifteenth and sixteenth centuries; its W tower stood on arches across the pavement. It was demolished in 1865, though the site opposite the Great Gate remains as a garden, with a tall stone memorial cross. A replacement church of the same dedication was built in 1863–4 in Jesus Lane; the architect was G.F. Bodley, and it is an important and distinctive building, now in the care of the Churches Conservation Trust. Its proportions are unusual: long and lofty, but relatively narrow. The nave has a N porch and a lofty S aisle under a pitched roof, with an arcade of five bays. The chancel is the base of the tower, with a tall chapel on its S side. Beyond the tower is only a short sanctuary. Externally the tower is the dominant feature, tall, battlemented and crowned by a splendidly tall stone spire with an unusual total of five tiers of lucarnes. Windows are varied, in Dec. styles; most have stained glass, that in the E window being very fine work by Morris and Co. Also notable is the stencilling and painting of the walls and roofs, again by Morris, now newly restored. From the old church come the octagonal Perp. font, a fine moulded Royal Arms and many memorial tablets set high up behind the organ in the S chapel.

A substantial chapel for King's Hall was consecrated in 1499; it served the new Trinity College in its first years. Queen Mary took a great interest in the college, and under her influence a great new chapel was begun in 1555; its E

Trinity College, Cambridge: the chapel, from the south-west

end, occupying the site of the previous chapel, was completed last, in 1567. It is on a very large scale but architecturally fairly simple, an aisleless building in twelve bays, 205 ft (62.5m) long internally. Much of it is of brick, but the N side is rendered and the S and E sides were ashlared in the nineteenth century. It has regular buttresses, battlements and large crocketed pinnacles; the side windows are long, of four lights under four-centred arches, transomed but without tracery. The nine-light E window has tracery. On the N side towards the W end is a tall octagonal turret, with crocketed ogee top; beside it projects a small Victorian chapel. A broad battlemented S porch in rich Perp. style is of about 1870. Immediately W of the chapel, set slightly skew to it, is a fine large gate-tower built for King's Hall in 1428–32; remarkably, it was moved here in 1599–1600, blocking the chapel W window.

The spacious interior is impressive. A flat roof runs right through, its beams decorated with foliage trails enhanced with colour or gold, resting on short wall posts with shallow arched braces. The four W bays form the antechapel, very light owing to clear glass; the outstanding feature is six pedestals carrying statues of Trinity College worthies: Tennyson, Bacon, Barrow, Whewell and Macauley are seated, but Newton (by Roubiliac) is standing. There is an enormous veranda screen of oak on fluted Tuscan columns, of about 1700, carrying the organ in a splendid case of similar date. The main chapel is more subdued in its lighting, owing to Victorian stained glass. It has beautiful, rich panelling with fluted Corinthian pilasters and a boldly projecting cornice. All this too is early-eighteenth-century work, as is the enormous reredos of baldachino type, standing forward as a tremendously enriched arched canopy. For it the E window was blocked; it is glazed for external appearance only. In the antechapel are the stalls probably of the 1560s: unlike the building their design is of Renaissance character.

* Cambridge: Michaelhouse

Licence for the foundation of this sometimes forgotten college was obtained in 1324 by Hervey de Stanton, who was Edward II's chancellor, and the absentee holder of many prebends and other positions. In 1323 he had acquired the advowson of St Michael's Church, which was subsequently appropriated and gave its name to the college. The college was for a master and seven fellows, who were all to be priests or to take priest's orders within a year. Its annual value in 1534 was £125. The college has the distinction of having had a saint as master: John Fisher, master for a few years from 1497, was executed in 1535 for resisting Henry VIII's assertion of royal supremacy over the Church. He was canonized by the Roman Catholic Church in 1935. In 1546, the college was dissolved in order to become part of Henry VIII's new Trinity College, founded in that year by the amalgamation and augmentation of Michaelhouse and King's Hall.

The buildings of Michaelhouse occupied the SW part of the present Trinity Great Court. A few remnants remain incorporated in the court, but the principal

Cambridge: St Michael, from the south-east

relic is St Michael's Church, which was entirely rebuilt on being made collegiate, and is a most attractive uniform Dec. building, structurally little altered. It has a nave of two bays and a chancel of three (a distinctively collegiate proportion), both with aisles under low-pitched lean-to roofs; the E bay on the N side is separated as a sacristy. The tower occupies the SW corner; it is modest, in three stages, with angle buttresses, a straight parapet and a small spike. It contains the S doorway. There is a Victorian N porch. Windows in the aisles are mostly of two lights, with reticulated tracery; the main E and W windows are of four lights and have elaborate flowing tracery. Most of the exterior is rendered.

The arcades have octagonal pillars carrying arches of three chamfers, the central chamfer being hollow; the chancel arch conforms. Arches of three continuous chamfers open to the tower. The E bay of the chancel has solid side walls; there are triple-stepped sedilia, ogee-trefoiled, with rich crocketing and relief pinnacles. The S chapel is known as the Hervey de Stanton Chapel, with large enriched ogee image niches set diagonally in its E corners; a tiny squint opens to the chancel. W of this is a remarkably lavish ogee Dec. archway with finials and pinnacles, probably the remaining fragment of a former stone screen.

Most roofs are plain replacements which followed a fire in 1849. Long out of regular ecclesiastical use, and from the 1960s used mainly as a parish hall, in 2002 the church was restored and beautifully adapted under the name

Michaelhouse mainly as an exhibition space and café. The chancel remains in ecclesiastical use and contains a set of thirty-six medieval stalls, some having plain misericords: these seem to have come from King's Hall. A cinquefoiled medieval piscina recess is curiously set in the modern blocking of the sacristy doorway. Some memorial tablets have been set on the modern infill of the chancel arcades.

* Cambridge: Pembroke Hall

Royal licence for the foundation of Pembroke Hall (known since the 1830s as Pembroke College) was granted in December 1347 to Mary de St Pol, Countess of Pembroke, the extremely wealthy widow of Aylmer de Valence, Earl of Pembroke. The earl had died in 1324, less than three years after their marriage, when the countess was twenty. She never remarried; in the years before 1347 she had involved herself extensively with other religious houses. She was a friend of Lady Clare (*see* Clare Hall), and the idea of founding a college may well have come from this friendship. For a short period the newly established college used a parish church, probably St Mary the Less; but licence was granted in 1355 for the construction of a chapel, which with the rest of the original small court was probably completed well before the end of the century. The framework of this modest chapel remains, forming the W part of the range of buildings along Pembroke Street, but in the late seventeenth

Pembroke College, Cambridge: the chapel, from the north-east

century it was completely remodelled to become the library (now known as the Old Library), with new windows, external facing and internal decoration including a spectacular plaster ceiling. This could be done because a new larger chapel had been constructed in 1663–5, for which £5,000 was given by Matthew Wren, Bishop of Ely, who had been released only in 1659 after seventeen years of imprisonment in the Tower of London. The new building was probably the first to be designed by his nephew, Christopher Wren, then a scientist.

Wren's chapel is the first true classical building in Cambridge, fine and already showing the sophistication typical of the architect. It is a lofty rectangle of medium size, its side walls of red brick (originally rendered), with a cornice and round-arched windows set in stone frames with an entablature. The walls below the windows have panels outlined in stone. The W front, facing the street, is of ashlar and makes an impressive (and much illustrated) architectural display. It has four Corinthian pilasters and a large round-arched window flanked by classical niches; the whole is crowned by a

Pembroke College, Cambridge: the chapel, looking west

pediment carrying urn finials and containing an elaborate cartouche with garlands. Above is a charming large hexagonal glazed cupola. The entrance doorway at the NW corner opens from a short classical cloister constructed a few years after the chapel. The interior, four bays long, has a superb ceiling of rich plasterwork, with a large coved rectangular panel in the centre and partly circular designs at each end. There is fine plasterwork on the walls, too. There are good seventeenth-century stalls and stall-backs. The W bay contains the original gallery, its centre standing forward on Corinthian columns, with the beautiful organ dating from 1707; the space beneath is beautifully panelled, and has another rich plaster ceiling.

In 1880 the chapel was sympathetically enlarged to the E, the architect being Gilbert Scott the younger. Externally this is of ashlar, with features comparable to those of Wren's W front; the E wall, with its Venetian window, is the original re-erected in its new position. Internally the extension forms a sanctuary, opening by a great round arch resting on massive paired Corinthian columns. Very startlingly, it has in its S side a medieval multi-cusped arched piscina recess: this was removed from the old chapel.

* Cambridge: Peterhouse

Peterhouse was the earliest Cambridge college. It owes its origin to Hugh de Balsham, Bishop of Ely, who in 1280 introduced some scholars into the existing Hospital of St John the Evangelist. However, sharing with the brethren of the hospital was not a success, so in 1284 the bishop moved the scholars to two existing hostel buildings immediately S of the church of St Peter. This he founded as a college, taking as a model the rule of Merton College, Oxford; the church was appropriated (causing further problems with the Hospital of St John, to which it had previously belonged), and gave its name to the college. The growth of the college was slow; in the sixteenth century it had a master and fourteen fellows, with an annual income of £125.

In about 1340–52, the church was rebuilt on a large scale and with a strongly collegiate character. Surprisingly, its dedication was now changed to the Virgin Mary, and to distinguish it from the other Cambridge church of this dedication it became known as St Mary the Less. It is a fine, lofty and spacious vessel of six bays, though somewhat mutilated and restored. Its external ashlar facing has been much renewed, and the S side is extensively patched in brick. The fine large side windows have four lights while the E window has six, all with rich late Dec. tracery. The E wall has several canopied image niches, both outside and in. There are remains of a piscina and large triple sedilia, with their canopies hacked away.

The W bay seems to be a Perp. addition; its W wall is rough, with a modest Perp. window, and clearly was not intended to terminate the building; transepts or a nave were probably planned. Outside the W end is now a low twentieth-century choir vestry. In its N side, now forming the entrance, is a fragment of a former tower, giving access to the church by its small Norman

Cambridge: St Mary the Less, from the north-east

arch, set off-axis: this arrangement is of 1891. Midway along the chapel, each side has an enriched but restored four-centred opening with a doorway beside it: these formerly opened to small Perp. chantry chapels, now demolished. That on the S side now gives access to a small but beautiful chapel in classical style, added in 1931. Attached to the S side of the sanctuary is a small vaulted chapel, formerly a charnel-house, with a sacristy over. Adjacent to this is a room containing stairs which rise to a gallery, connecting with the buildings of the college: this arrangement is of about 1350, but was later partly rebuilt in brick.

With mostly clear glass, the church is very light. Its usage is High, and it has some fine modern fittings. There is a very large octagonal Perp. font, with its partly seventeenth-century cover suspended from the roof. The dignified oak pulpit with tester is of 1741. The striking organ of 1978 is mounted on the S wall near the E end.

St Mary the Less served the college until the construction in 1628–32 of its present distinctive and charming chapel. It is a striking example of Laudian Gothic, a mixture of Gothic and classical styles, built under the mastership of Dr Matthew Wren, later uncle of the architect (and encountered at Pembroke College): but the architect of this building is unknown. It stands in the centre of the open E end of the court, with galleries on arches (rebuilt in the eighteenth century) connecting with the ranges each side. It is a rectangle four bays in length, with polygonal buttresses and polygonal turrets at its E corners. Its gables have extraordinary curly shapes, showing Flemish influence. The side

Peterhouse, Cambridge: the
chapel, from the west

windows have three lights under four-centred arches, with tracery of approximately Perp. type. It is of brick, but was ashlared later in the seventeenth
century. The W wall is rusticated and has a pair of niches of mostly classical
character. The interior has a broad, low-pitched roof with short hammerbeams, pendants and panels containing oval sunbursts. A gallery containing
the organ occupies the W end. There is much fine, dark woodwork, partly of
the seventeenth and eighteenth centuries but with alterations of 1821–2. The
windows throughout have pictorial stained glass, in the E window seventeenth
century but elsewhere nineteenth-century German, making an unusual and
attractive ensemble.

Cambridge: Queens' College

The principal mover here was Andrew Dockett, Rector of St Botolph's Church
and principal of the quite important St Bernard's Hostel. In 1446 he obtained a
charter for the establishment of the College of St Bernard, to be a small college

of a president and four fellows. It was to stand on Trumpington Street, opposite his hostel; but in 1447 he obtained a larger site near the river. In a new charter of 1448, the young queen, Margaret of Anjou, probably by Dockett's initiative but also no doubt as a response to her husband's foundation of King's College, was named founder of what was now called the Queen's College of SS Margaret and Bernard. The foundation stone was laid on 15 April in that year by her chamberlain, Sir John Wenlock. Dockett was the first president, a position he retained until his death in 1484. He must have been astute in promoting the college, for in 1465, by which time Henry VI was imprisoned in the Tower of London and his queen was in exile, he obtained the patronage of Edward IV's queen, Elizabeth Woodville. She is named as joint founder in the statutes of 1475, by which time the college had increased in size to a president and twelve fellows. Thus the name of the college is Queens' in reference to its two royal founders. Two courts were built in the fifteenth century, the only Cambridge college so equipped before the Reformation.

The original chapel forms the E part of the N range of Front Court; it was built in 1448–9 and like the rest of the court is faced in red brick. It has traceried Perp. windows under four-centred arches, of three lights to each side and five lights to the E. The W end has smaller windows at two levels to light the gallery and the antechapel below. Entry is from a passage through the range, above which is a pretty octagonal cupola of 1910. This is a modest building;

Queens' College, Cambridge: the former chapel, from the south-west

in 1952 it became part of the college library and, with subsequent refurbishment, now has an intermediate floor and good late-twentieth-century fittings.

In 1889–91 a much larger chapel was provided further to the N, for which the architect was Bodley. It too is of red brick, and is very lofty, with window tracery in a style between Dec. and Perp. Externally it has battlements, a quite rich S doorway, and several image niches. The side windows are tall and set high, and the E window is of seven lights, internally flanked by tall niches containing statues. The pointed wagon roof is painted, as is the E wall. A rich Gothic screen carrying the organ separates the W end as a rather cluttered antechapel. A few memorials from the old chapel are here, including, set up against the wall, four fifteenth- and sixteenth-century slabs with brasses.

Cambridge: St Catharine's Hall

This began in 1473 as a modest foundation for a master and three fellows; the founder was Robert Wodelarke, who was provost of King's College, and his first plans had been made as early as 1459. The numbers gradually increased; there were six fellows in 1515, but its annual income in 1535 was still only £39, less than half that of any other Cambridge college. Not until 1860 was its name changed to St Catharine's College. Of the buildings constructed in the early years, none now remains; they included a chapel, which stood in the centre of the

St Catharine's College, Cambridge: the chapel, from the south-east

present lawn. Principal Court as it now appears is due to a great rebuilding scheme begun in 1674. The chapel occupies the E part of the N range, and was the last part built, in 1694–7, but not fitted out and consecrated until 1704. It is in four bays, with large windows of mullion-and-transom cross form; its external appearance is very domestic, and as an ecclesiastical building will surprise some. Like the rest of the court, its walls are of beautiful pinkish-red brick, with rusticated stone quoins and a cornice. The windows are pedimented and have rectangular panels below, and there is a fine entrance doorway with unfluted Ionic columns and pilasters. Pedimented dormers appear in the roof. The E wall is much enriched; it has a pediment and its window, which is blank, has a mullion and transom, a segmental pediment, and pedimented shell niches to each side.

Internally the chapel is a very lofty room, but short in proportion. Occupying the W bay is a gallery carrying the organ, and beneath it is a gracious room forming the antechapel, with fine panelling and a great standing wall memorial of 1705. The flat plaster ceiling of the chapel is divided into plain panels, but has a little enrichment on its cornice. Most of the fittings are original and form a fine set, with high panelling and finely dignified stalls. Extra richness in the sanctuary includes Corinthian pilasters, and the E wall has a very large and tall reredos, with fluted Corinthian columns, segmental pediment and four urn finials. Equally rich is the W wall below the gallery. Three of the windows have been given Victorian stained glass.

* Cambridge: St John's College

Founded about 1200, the Hospital of St John the Evangelist was an important almshouse, its brethren following the Augustinian rule. In 1280–4, scholars were introduced in an unsuccessful experiment by Bishop Balsham of Ely (*see* Peterhouse). It was then not until about 1505 that the hospital was considered for suppression and replacement by a college: the movers were Lady Margaret Beaufort, mother of Henry VII, and her confessor John Fisher, Bishop of Rochester, chancellor of the university and former Master of Michaelhouse. Lady Margaret had already refounded Christ's College. The foundation here was not complete when she died in 1509, but Fisher continued, overcoming the difficulties of the death of the king and the fact that Lady Margaret had not addressed this new project in her will. The College of St John the Evangelist was established in 1511, when the last brethren of the hospital left; it opened in 1516, and First Court was splendidly completed by 1520. In 1535 it had a master and twenty-seven fellows, and its annual income of £507 exceeded all other Cambridge colleges except King's.

The college kept the chapel of the hospital, which had been a substantial building 121 ft (36.9 m) long, built about 1280 probably as part of Bishop Balsham's collegiate experiment. It formed the N side of First Court. Also kept was a building immediately N of this known as the infirmary. The chapel had originally been long and narrow, without transepts but with crossing arches which probably carried a tower. It was heavily remodelled, with large Perp.

St John's College,
Cambridge: the chapel,
from the south-east

windows throughout; the tower and the E crossing arch were removed, and part of the nave became a short antechapel, while its W section became part of the master's lodge (as in the similar remodelling at Jesus College). However, in 1866–7 all this was demolished, and a large and ambitious new chapel was built, for which the architect was Sir George Gilbert Scott. The new chapel stands further N than its predecessor, and the foundations of the latter have been left visible in the grass.

Scott's chapel has a body of seven bays with a five-sided apse and a crossing with shallow transepts, making this the only Cambridge example of the 'T' plan. The windows have tracery of early-Dec. type; enrichments include shafts, an openwork parapet with pinnacles, blank arcading below the windows, and buttresses with elaborate niches containing statues. The original plans envisaged only a flèche, but Henry Hoare, a former member of the college, offered £3,000 down and £1,000 a year for five years to build a tower. As a result there is now above the crossing a massive structure 163 ft (49.7 m) in height, with three tall two-light openings in each side; its design was inspired by Pershore Abbey. Unfortunately, Hoare died in a railway accident two years after the acceptance of his offer, so the college was left with a large debt for its tower! The W front is sheer, with a window of seven lights; along its base runs a brick cloister of the 1930s. The principal entrance to the chapel is by a splendid portal in the E side of the S transept.

The interior is a rich example of Victoriana. A painted timber tunnel vault with ribs covers the chancel, and there are lavish fittings; an elaborate timber screen separates chapel from antechapel. The early-sixteenth-century stalls occupy the three E bays. A very fine thirteenth-century double piscina is incorporated: its two pointed openings are formed from intersecting round arches, resting on shafts; this came from the former infirmary, which was probably the first chapel of the hospital. The lower stage of the tower forms a lantern; tall two-bay arcades open to the transepts, which are vaulted in stone. In the S transept are three large recesses with Perp. panelling, their arches four-centred

St John's College, Cambridge: the chapel, looking east

in a square label: these are partly from the sixteenth-century chantry chapel of Bishop Fisher in the old chapel. Iron railings surround a fine early-sixteenth-century memorial to Hugh Ashton, an early fellow. It has a coloured praying effigy on a tomb-chest, which is open to reveal a cadaver below; the whole has a canopy with cresting and pinnacles. Also here are a beautiful seventeenth-century chest and two seated effigies on plinths. The college is noted for its musical tradition, maintaining sixteen choristers: these originated only in the 1670s. It also has a school, originally just for the choristers but now large.

* Cambridge: Trinity Hall

Trinity Hall was founded in 1350 by William Bateman, Bishop of Norwich; it was intended for the study of civil and canon law. It was from the beginning a small college, and has remained so, but it is also most attractive. Its court was built during the second half of the fourteenth century, and includes a chapel, dating probably from about 1366. The chapel is small, today the smallest in an old Cambridge college, and must have been used only for subsidiary purposes: for its principal functions the college used the nearby parish Church of St John Zachary, as did the adjacent Clare Hall. In 1446, this church was demolished to make way for the chapel of King's College, and its parish was merged with that of St Edward, to which Trinity Hall and Clare Hall moved and which was now

Trinity Hall, Cambridge: the chapel, from the south

appropriated to Trinity Hall. The college chapel was consecrated only in 1513; this may mark the time when the use of the Church of St Edward ceased.

The chapel forms half of the S range of the principal court. With most of the court, it was remodelled on this side in the early eighteenth century, in fine golden-brown ashlar, with a straight parapet and a pedimented doorway. Its S side however is more obviously medieval, rendered, with three buttresses. It is only two bays long, plus a third bay at the W which forms the antechapel and since 1922 has had an organ gallery above, and a half bay at the E end, which until 1864 was a separate room. It has large round-arched windows, and the antechapel has two small circular windows in its S side.

The antechapel has attractive seventeenth-century panelling, and also has a blocked medieval doorway. The chapel itself has a shallow plaster tunnel vault of 1729–30, coffered and richly decorated, with much heraldry; but the nineteenth- and twentieth-century extensions have flat ceilings. It is a beautiful interior, with much mellow oak. The big reredos has fluted Ionic pilasters and a broken pediment, and incorporates a large painting as altarpiece. A door in the panelling opens to reveal a probably fourteenth-century ogee-cinquefoiled piscina. There are some attractive memorials, including several brasses.

The exterior of St Edward's Church is pleasant, but it consists largely of Victorian restorations, which are responsible for all of the windows. Also renewed are most external details of the W tower, which has three stages and is rendered except for its brick battlements. The tower arch and an internally

Cambridge: St Edward, looking east

authentic lancet window demonstrate that it is EE The nave has arcades of four short but tall bays, of elegant early-Perp. work; the pillars are of four hollows and four polygonal shafts, the faces of the latter concave. The roofs continue over the aisles, and have some old timbers. In the E bay of the nave, the aisles widen in the manner of transepts. These, however, are the W bays of the broad chapels added soon after 1446, on the S for Trinity Hall and on the N for Clare Hall. Four-centred arches demarcate the transept bays, and the chapels have four-centred arches to the chancel: there are two of these for Trinity Hall but one broad arch for Clare. The Perp. windows are renewed, but probably original are the blank Perp. tracery continuing below two S windows, and several low cinquefoiled recesses of puzzling purpose. The timber roofs here are again largely ancient.

The pulpit is a notable possession. It is of about 1510, hexagonal, quite small and simple, with linenfold panelling; it is known as 'Latimer's pulpit' from its connexion with that Protestant notable and bishop martyred in 1555, and is also associated with Cranmer. Almost matching it is a tall seat, also with linenfold, but this is made up, and was given in 1947. The octagonal font in Perp. style appears to be Victorian, but is in fact an authentic piece drastically restored by the Camden Society.

Newton

Licence for this small chantry college was obtained by Sir John Colville in 1406. He rebuilt an existing chapel, picturesquely known as St Mary-on-the-Sea, and provided buildings for the accommodation of a master or warden, three priests and three clerks; it was also to have an important hospital function supporting twelve almsmen. In 1411, the parish Church of St James was appropriated, and was henceforth to be served by one of the chaplains. In the statutes provided by Sir John in 1446, the number of almsmen is reduced to ten. However, it seems that the endowments were not sufficient for these numbers, for in 1454 it was reconstituted by Bishop Bourchier with just three poor men and one woman, though the other numbers remained the same. By 1525, there seem to have been three priests but no one else, and by twenty years later it seems that all chantry function had ceased since, surprisingly, it was explicitly exempted from the 1547 Act. However, this did not save it from soon falling into disuse and ruin. Nothing remains; it stood in the grounds of the former rectory, about 500 yds SE of the parish church. The village is now 8 miles (13 km) from the Wash, but close to the college site is the Roman bank, to which the sea once came up. The full name of the benefice today is still Newton in the Isle with St Mary in the Marsh.

Cheshire

Of Cheshire's two collegiate churches, one was a college of canons, the other a chantry college. Both are excellent examples of their type, and that of Chester is particularly fascinating both in its history and its structure.

* Bunbury

Sir Hugh Calveley was a knight of whom colourful stories were told; he was much involved in the French wars of the reigns of Edward III and Richard II. In his old age, he turned his resources to the establishment of a college in the Church of St Boniface; he acquired the advowson and was granted royal licence for the foundation in 1387. It was a chantry college for a master or warden and seven chaplains, the master having responsibility for the cure of souls; there seem also to have been at least two choristers. The college was dissolved in 1548; its annual value was given as £48.

The church is fine and very large, and makes a splendid display. Sir Hugh Calveley is thought to have been responsible for its complete or largely complete reconstruction: but despite the late date, it seems to have been entirely in the Dec. style. Sir Hugh was in his seventies in 1387, so perhaps his taste in architecture was conservative. The church has a W tower, a long aisled nave, and a chancel with on its S side the broad late-medieval Ridley Chapel and on the N a medieval sacristy. The lower part of the tower is Dec.; it has W buttresses, a fine three-light W window, and an arch of continuous mouldings. It is large; the upper of its two stages is Perp. and has battlements with corner and intermediate pinnacles. Also largely Dec. is the S porch. The very spacious nave was otherwise remodelled in the late fifteenth century. Its six-

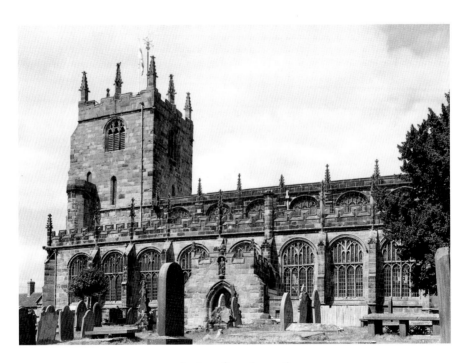

Bunbury, from the south

bay arcades have lofty slim pillars of four shafts and four hollows, with polygonal capitals to the shafts only. Surprisingly, the clerestory is a Victorian
addition, in respectable style; so are the battlemented parapets of the aisles.
The excellent nave and aisle roofs, however, are of 1950, the church having
sustained major damage by a land-mine in 1940. The very large aisle windows
are late fifteenth century, in four lights, with almost round arches. Two further
bays of the aisles extend W to embrace the tower.

Also large and noble in effect is the chancel, and here the panelled roof is late
medieval. Its windows are all Dec., with rich flowing tracery, in three lights to
the N and five to the E. There are an ogee tomb-recess, a cusped-ogee double
piscina recess and cusped-ogee triple sedilia. The E window formerly had glass
dated 1343, but archaeological investigations in 1952–3 suggested that a chancel of about that date was extended in the late-fourteenth-century rebuilding,
this window being reset in the new E wall. A three-bay arcade opens to the
Ridley Chapel, with pillars of many shafts, four-centred arches and no capitals;
it is one bay shorter than the chancel. The chapel was added about 1527 and
has very large windows, the E one flanked by large pedestals for images.

The church has some splendid contents. Foremost must be the magnificent
memorial to the founder of the college, who died in 1394. Standing in the
centre of the chancel, it was installed in 1416, and is considered the finest
medieval tomb in the county. It is an alabaster tomb-chest with recumbent

Bunbury, looking east

effigy of the same material, and is surrounded by its original wrought-iron railing or hearse, a rare survival (*but see* Warwick). Other fine memorials include
several further medieval effigies and the large monument to Sir George Beeston,
commander at the age of 89 of the *Dreadnought* in the defeat of the Spanish
Armada. The shapely 1741 standing effigy of a lady so disturbed a subsequent
vicar that he had it buried; it was rediscovered in 1882 and returned to the
church. The octagonal font with crisp, simple designs is dated 1663, while the
excellent communion rails are of 1717. The fine rood screen dates from 1921.
Mounted murally is a striking series of medieval painted panels, restored in
1988, from parclose screens removed in 1865. A splendid brass chandelier is of
1756. A very fine original stone screen fills the arcade to the Ridley Chapel, and
retains much original painting, showing Renaissance motifs. Its doors are
carved with linenfold and in their upper parts a curious imitation of wicker-
work. Most glass is clear, but there is some post-war stained glass.

Nothing remains of the collegiate buildings, which stood SW of the church.
However, the timber-framed house provided for the chantry priest who served
the Ridley Chapel is still to be seen in the lane which runs to the S.

* Chester: St John Baptist

A foundation in 689 by Ethelred, King of Mercia, is suggested, but the evidence
seems little more than legend. Similarly doubtful is its founding or refounding
between 901 and 911 by Ethelred, Earl of Mercia. More certainly, however, it
was repaired and refounded as a college of canons in 1057 by Leofric, Earl of
Mercia. It was important, with a dean and seven canons, numbers it retained
throughout the medieval era. In 1075, under the Norman policy that bishoprics
should be in major towns, Bishop Peter of Lichfield moved his seat to this
church, which thereby became a cathedral. In 1095 or 1102, however, his
successor Robert de Lymesey removed the see to Coventry. Chester continued
as a college, and indeed retained a special status as almost a third cathedral in
the diocese of Coventry and Lichfield till the Reformation; the title Bishop of
Chester was still sometimes used. Church and college were still in existence
when the new diocese of Chester was formed in 1541: but the Benedictine
Abbey of St Werburgh (*see* Appendix III) was chosen to be its cathedral. The
College of St John was dissolved probably in 1547. Its annual income was in
excess of £100, and it had seven vicars, two clerks, four choristers and others
in addition to its dean and seven canons. The survival of the church appeared
unlikely, its roofs being stripped of lead; but about 1574 walls were built delim-
iting the part that remained to the parish, and that section was repaired.

What is to be seen today is predominantly Norman, though it is truncated
in all four directions. This extraordinary condition is the result not just of
mutilation following the dissolution of the college; towers have collapsed, and
there was even damage in the Civil War. The Norman work is relatively early,
and an interesting question is whether it was begun during the cathedral
period. Judgements differ, but it seems more likely that building started in the

Chester: St John Baptist, looking east

early twelfth century, just after the see moved away. It was a very large cruciform building, its character entirely that of a great church; but its scale is not
quite that of a cathedral. Unlike St Werburgh's, it is set just outside the city
walls. It appears as a massive, towerless hulk, with ruins prominent at both
the E and W ends. Unfortunately, the external appearance is predominantly of
the restorations by R.C. Hussey, 1859–66, but looking earlier.

The ruin at the W end is of the former NW tower. Its upper parts first
collapsed in 1574, but it was rebuilt, and as shown in old photographs was
very tall; but it collapsed again on Good Friday, 1881. Its remaining base has
angle buttresses and a large W window with an ogee hood-mould. Just E of it
stands the very impressive N porch, which was destroyed in 1881 but rebuilt
in replica the following year. It was EE, and its outer arch has the spectacular
total of eight orders; it covers a doorway of seven orders which is genuine EE,
though its shafts are renewed. The W part of the nave has gone, and the doorway opens into a Victorian passage outside the present W wall.

Unlike the exterior, the interior is very authentic. In the nave, the four remaining bays have thick cylindrical piers, circular scalloped capitals, and arches of
three unmoulded orders. The triforium and clerestory are EE, both having a wall
passage and four richly shafted openings per bay. An oddity is that in most of
the clerestory, only every second arch opens in a lancet window, which can never
give a symmetrical bay. The S aisle wall is Victorian, but the N is ancient, with

broad shafted lancets. The wide and lofty crossing arches are of very impressive Norman work, again in three unmoulded orders, with scalloped capitals. Above them, the main roof runs through; a crossing tower collapsed about 1468, doing much damage to the chancel. Both transepts now project just to aisle width, their walls externally cut off to form crude buttresses.

The high chancel had five bays, with a bay spacing smaller than that of the nave; just one bay survives, its arcade arches enriched with rolls. On the N side the Norman triforium remains, an undivided arch of three unmoulded orders. The S chancel aisle has blank arcading; in place of the N chancel aisle there is now a small tower of 1886–7, its frilly pyramidal top scarcely higher than the main roof. Outside, the S aisle wall continues, with more blank arcading and a Norman window. Attached here is a large square late-thirteenth-century building, vaulted from a central column, with narrow paired lancets; this is said to be the chapter-house. Its W wall was part of the S transept. The E wall of the chancel stands, and has a large three-order Norman arch: this must originally have opened to an apse, but the apse was later replaced by a long chapel of unknown extent. Chapels were also built flanking this, and much remains of these. That on the N is of fine Perp. work; that on the S is a largely complete shell, of noble Dec. work, with many details remaining, including its vaulting springers.

One pillar of the nave retains a probably fourteenth-century painting of John the Baptist. What remains of the S transept and S chancel aisle forms the

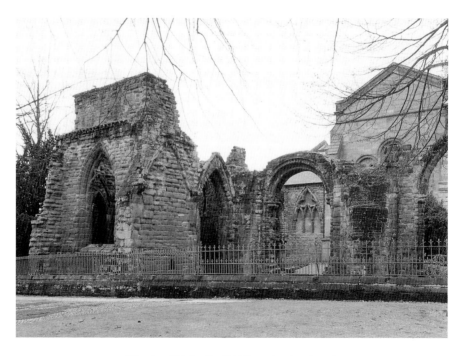

Chester: St John Baptist. The ruined east end

Lady Chapel, with a fine screen and gate of 1660 and a reredos of 1692 with scrolly pediments. In the NW corner of the church are many interesting relics: pre-Conquest cross-heads, several coffin-lids with foliated crosses and other motifs, and three damaged medieval recumbent effigies. An effigy of 1347 to a lady shows just her upper part in relief, the lower half being flat and carved with rich foliage patterns.

Cornwall

Medieval Cornwall was well provided with colleges, several of them pre-Conquest in origin. Most were small, and though they are all of interest few of the churches are more important than the larger parish churches of the county. Penryn, had it survived, would have been a different matter. The churches of Cornwall are distinctive architecturally: usually Perp., low, without clerestories, normally with wagon roofs continuous from end to end, lacking a chancel arch but having aisles of the same width and height as the central vessel. Also characteristic of the county is the dedication of churches to local saints, often unknown elsewhere, who have frequently given their names also to their villages or towns.

Crantock

The church is dedicated to St Carantoc, one of those half-legendary Celtic saints who are said to have made their way from Ireland to Cornwall about the time of St Patrick; he landed in the Gannel estuary, above which the church now stands. A college was attached to the church in pre-Conquest times; it was refounded, probably in about 1236, by Bishop Brewer of Exeter, for a dean or provost and nine prebendaries. Later it also had seven vicars choral. It was reconstituted under Bishop Grandisson in 1351, with only four vicars, two of whom served the cures of Crantock and St Columb Minor. There were also two clerks and several boys being educated. The annual value soon before its dissolution is given as £89.

The church is distinctive and, by having a chancel taller than the nave and furnished with a chancel arch and lean-to aisles, it is of a character unusual for Cornwall; however, it is not large, and though interesting some of the architecture is surprisingly rustic. It is cruciform; collegiate character is evident in that the chancel is loftier and on a larger scale than the nave, giving curious proportions to the building. There has been much restoration; the tracery of the mostly square-headed Dec. or Perp. windows is almost entirely renewed, and there is ugly internal stripping of plaster round windows and arches. A former central tower collapsed in the early fifteenth century, apparently doing much damage to the nave and transepts. It seems that following this the present W tower was built. It is, however, elementary in its details; it has three stages, short angle buttresses and battlements projected out on a corbel course.

Crantock, from the south

The masonry of the nave and transepts is of rubble, rough and heavy in construction; the S porch has a rather similar character but dates from the seventeenth century. Two clearly Norman features remain: in the W wall of the N transept, blocked and only visible internally, is an unmoulded Norman doorway; and almost hidden behind the rood screen there are the remains, about 4 ft (just over 1 m) high, of the fine twin-shafted E responds of two of the former tower arches. The present chancel arch, of two continuous chamfers, is larger than the Norman arch must have been. Other features of the nave and transepts, such as the rough segmental transept arches, could be of almost any date.

A little, probably nineteenth-century sanctus bell turret stands between the nave and the chancel. The externally rough-cast chancel has aisles under its roof slopes, and is Dec.: its tall two-bay arcades have large chamfered arches on piers of an elongated octagonal plan. Its E window of five lights is quite fine. The rood stair remains in the N respond of the chancel arch; its rich door in Jacobean style incorporates some old work.

Under the tower are fragments of several late medieval alabaster statues, a Virgin and Child being recognizable. They are displayed in a frame attractively made up from pieces of a screen and bench-ends. The font appears to be of the Norman type, characteristic of Cornwall, that has a circular bowl with four projecting heads, resting on a cylinder and four shafts; a double line of small zigzag runs round its rim. However, in relief across its E face is the date 1474 in black-letter Roman characters, implying either retooling at that time or its manufacture in an anachronistic style. The interior is dark. Its principal beauty is its very rich High Church fittings, dating mainly from 1897–1907. They include a splendid screen with coving, loft and rood, which incorporates a few medieval parts. There are fine parclose screens, rich sanctuary panelling, reredos, timber sedilia, and lavish stalls including four modern misericords. The pews have good carved ends in the late medieval manner. The largely renewed roofs have fine colouring above the rood and the sanctuary.

In the churchyard is a shelter containing the parish stocks, with an entertaining inscription describing their last use in about 1817.

Penryn

Penryn, or Glasney, College was founded in 1265 by Bishop Walter Bronescombe of Exeter, for a provost and twelve canons, with thirteen vicars. According to the story written down two centuries later, the bishop had been told three times by St Thomas of Canterbury in a vision that it was God's will that he should do this. The college was dedicated to the Blessed Virgin Mary and St Thomas of Canterbury. It was not a chantry college (though it later included four chantries). The canons held prebends, although these were bursal; residence was intended. It was non-parochial, the parish church remaining that of St Gluvias, just outside the town. Glasney was by far the most important college in Cornwall, valued in the sixteenth century at £205. Alas, after its dissolution in 1548 it was completely demolished. Part of the site is today a public playing field (Glasney Field), with a memorial stone. The site has never been excavated, but some architectural fragments from the college are displayed in Penryn Museum. One fragment of masonry standing about 10 ft (3 m) high (at the time of writing extremely overgrown) is said to be part of the NE corner of the church. Medieval sources give a considerable amount of information. The church was cruciform with a central tower, over 200 ft (60 m) in length as paced by William of Worcester in 1478, and the chancel was vaulted. Chantry chapels and an eastern Lady Chapel were added in the fourteenth and fifteenth centuries. There seem to have been cloisters and a chapterhouse. In the sixteenth century the precinct was fortified for the defence of the harbour, with three strong towers and guns; but nothing is visible of this either.

* Probus

St Probus is said to have lived in the fifth century, and to have come from Dorset. A monastery is thought to have been founded here by King Athelstan (ruled 924–40); it had secular canons in 1086. It was given by Henry I in the early twelfth century to Exeter Cathedral, and was then a college for a dean and five prebendaries. Its revenues came from the tithe in its large parish, and the prebends were perhaps of portionary character. From 1268 it ceased to have a dean, the revenues of the deanery being transferred to Exeter. However, the five prebendaries continued, and there was a vicar to undertake the

Probus, looking east

parochial responsibilities. Two chaplains probably served the chapels of Cornelly and Merther in the parish.

The church of SS Probus and Grace is large, Perp. throughout, and of typical Cornish type, with its walls of rough slate with granite dressings, three equal pitched roofs and absence of any division between nave and chancel. There are engagingly rustic small N and S porches, the latter with an inscription apparently dating it to 1637. The arcades are of seven bays, unusually lofty for Cornwall, their pillars of a section with four shafts and an intermediate wave carrying richly moulded arches on capitals each having four blank shields. The side windows are mostly of three lights, arched, with tracery; two of the E windows have five lights. An elegant rood stair is on the N side. In the chancel is a much-repaired Norman pillar piscina. The two E bays on the S side, with their arcade and a transept-like attachment for organ and vestry space, though matching well are in fact an early-twentieth-century addition.

Open timber roofs have replaced the old wagon roofs other than over the chancel and N aisle. Some old woodwork, principally many bench-ends, has been incorporated in the screens to the chancel, chapels and tower. A large early-sixteenth-century brass is in the floor; the few mural memorials include a fine piece of 1766. There are a good example of the 1643 letter of Charles I to the people of Cornwall and a very large Royal Arms painted on boards, unusual in being of James II, dated 1685. In the N porch are the parish stocks.

In all this, the church is attractive. It is made outstanding, however, by its great

W tower. This is of the sixteenth century, and was not completed until the reign of Elizabeth. It is of ashlared elvan, an igneous rock similar to granite, which here is of beautiful grey-green colour. At approximately 125 ft (38 m) high, it is the tallest medieval tower in the county, but more importantly it is of superbly sophisticated and rich design, often considered as a remote member of the great Somerset family of towers. It is divided into three tall stages, with bands of quatrefoils between the stages and elsewhere; the belfry has pairs of arched three-light transomed openings, containing stone grilles. Above these is elaborate blank arcading. Further enrichment is applied to the battlements, and there are large corner and intermediate pinnacles, all octagonal and accompanied by further pinnacles around their bases. The buttresses are slightly set back from the corners, and are enriched with long pinnacles in relief. In the lowest stage, the N and S sides have three very large canopied image niches. Inside, it opens to the nave by a lofty panelled arch, and there are springers for a vault which was perhaps never completed. It is certainly the finest medieval tower in Cornwall.

Probus: the tower from the south

* St Buryan

The name is pronounced 'berian'; St Beriana is said to have come from Ireland in the fifth century. A college was apparently established about 930 by King Athelstan. It was refounded in 1238 by Bishop Brewer of Exeter, for a dean and three prebendaries; its value in the sixteenth century was £65. In the reign of Edward I it was claimed, on dubious grounds, as a royal free chapel, a claim that was contested by the Bishop of Exeter. The dispute went on for many years through the fourteenth century, at law and in other ways. In one episode, Bishop Grandisson excommunicated the clergy and parishioners; following this, he apparently achieved victory, visiting the parish in 1336 to absolve the people from the excommunication. But this was not the end, and eventually St Buryan remained as a royal free chapel, in the gift of the dukes of Cornwall. There were four vicars and also curates serving the cure at St Buryan and its dependent churches of Sennen and St Levan. Although non-residence of canons was not unusual, St Buryan seems to have acquired a bad reputation, exemplified by the remark of Leland in 1534 that it had a dean and three prebendaries who 'almost never be there'. The prebendaries were abolished after 1545, but for some reason the deanery continued, normally with an absentee dean, and still a royal peculiar. The last dean was notorious: Fitzroy Stanhope was an army officer who lost a leg at the Battle

St Buryan, looking east

of Waterloo. He applied to his commander, the Duke of York, for a pension; the duke referred him to his brother, the Prince of Wales and Duke of Cornwall, who gave him the deanery of St Buryan. Before Stanhope could receive this, however, he had to be ordained. Most bishops were unwilling to do this, but eventually the Bishop of Cork, a friend of the Duke of York, agreed to do so when visiting London: Stanhope became dean in 1817. He seems to have visited St Buryan only once. The deanery was abolished in the Victorian reforms, but not until Stanhope's death: he received the revenues until 1864, totalling about £60,000 during his years as dean.

The building is fairly large, and is dignified and fine. It was almost all rebuilt in the late fifteenth or early sixteenth century, and is of ashlared granite; most windows are straight headed, with austere uncusped arched lights. A polygonal turret for the rood stair projects on the S side, and there is an ambitious S porch, tall, with buttresses, battlements and pinnacles. Both the porch arch and the doorway are four-centred in a square label; internally it has a stoup recess,

St Buryan: the tower from the south

and the upper parts of its walls have blank quatrefoils. The W tower is lofty and stately, in four stages, with set-back buttresses, battlements with corner pinnacles, and a higher battlemented polygonal stair turret at the NE corner.

The spacious and light interior is noble in effect, though it is not lavish. There has been some restoration. Its plain plastered wagon roofs include some old work. The arcades are almost uniform, of six bays, with moulded four-centred arches, tall pillars of four shafts and four hollows, and imposts with multiple rings of mouldings. The sanctuary projects beyond the aisles. Its N and E sides are externally partly of rubble masonry with obvious patching and alterations, and internally the N wall shows one and a half blocked and very battered bays of Norman arcade; a small chapel here was finally demolished in 1750.

The dominant feature is the splendid rood screen, with good carved panels, coving and a front beam with rich foliage trails including heads, birds and animals; it is extensively restored but about half the work is original. It also has some original colouring. There are four medieval stalls with plain misericords. A reading-desk has been made up from old pieces including two bench-ends, one with a mermaid. Set in the floor is a large thirteenth-century coffin-lid with an inscription in Norman French. The granite font is of a local Perp. type with a circular bowl having shield-bearing angels projecting in three positions, and a cross on a shield in a fourth.

Recent campanological enthusiasm here has not only restored the bells, which before 1990 had been unringable for most of the century, but also increased their number from four to six. They are claimed as the world's heaviest peal of this number.

* St Columb Major

This is quite an attractive small town, set high, and its Church of St Columba, Virgin, is fine and on a large scale, although spread out and in the usual Cornish way internally low. It was long in the patronage of the Arundell family, who regularly appointed to it younger sons or close associates of the family. In 1427 Sir John Arundell founded a chantry college of a warden and four priests, with a clerk, to serve in the Chapel of Our Lady on the S side of the chancel. The church was not appropriated. Also serving in the church were two other chantry priests. The annual value of the college is given as £53; it was dissolved in or after 1545.

The church has a W tower and a cruciform body of irregular slate masonry in which the transepts are partly but not completely absorbed by the broad aisles and chapels. In 1676 a supply of gunpowder kept in the church was ignited by some youths, who were killed; extensive repairs were necessary, though it is not clear what changes these may have involved. The tower is tall, Perp., with buttresses set back from the corners; it is rendered except for the topmost of its four stages, which is of ashlared granite. It has battlements with hexagonal corner pinnacles and at the NW corner a rectangular stair turret carrying an amusing granite spirelet. In its base, the tower has broad arches to allow a

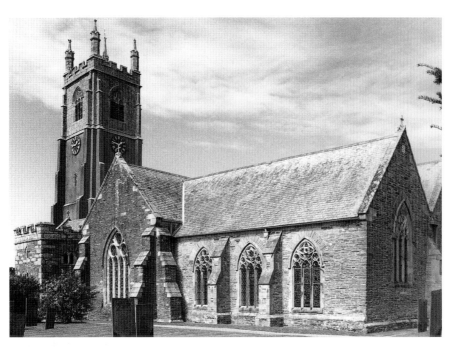

St Columb Major, from the south-east

passage through. Two worn coffin-lids are set up against the wall in here. The college building is said to have stood immediately to the W, but nothing remains.

Unusually for this county, the framework of the church is largely Dec., including the S chapel, which must have existed before the establishment in it of the chantry. Both sides of the church have a two-storeyed porch. The S doorway is a fine Dec. piece, with rich mouldings and ballflower decoration, in limestone. There is striking Dec. tracery in a window in the S aisle, in the large window of the S transept and in all those of the S chapel; but they are mostly renewed. All other windows are Perp., arched and traceried; they include one of three lights unusually opening from the nave to the ringing chamber of the tower. The nave arcades are of three very large bays, of limestone, with pillars of four shafts on a square core carrying well-moulded capitals and arches with two orders of sunk quadrants; the chancel has arcades of two smaller bays, similar on the S side to those of the nave, but probably later on the N. Further Dec. arches open from the transepts to the aisles and chapels. Ogee piscina recesses are in the chancel and S chapel.

There are fine early-twentieth-century fittings, especially the very rich screen with coving and rood. With this go parclose screens, a richly carved pulpit dated 1905 and an elaborate lectern. The church is High in usage, and the chancel is normally inaccessible. There are ancient wagon roofs in the W part of the church, with richly carved ribs; the chancel roof is finely coloured. The broad S chapel is rich in effect; it has a carpet and modern fittings. An

St Columb Major, looking south-east

ancient iron-bound chest is here. The pews are mostly nineteenth century, of deal, but many have good medieval ends with tracery and motifs including the instruments of the passion. Two brasses are sixteenth and seventeenth century. There is a large letter of Charles I to the people of Cornwall, painted on canvas. Again Dec. but of rather extraordinary character is the font: its octagonal bowl rests on a cylinder and four quatrefoil corner shafts; three of its sides have geometrical designs, but the others have elongated quatrefoils containing curious or grotesque carvings of faces.

* St Endellion

St Endelienta is believed to have been one of the many daughters of the sixth-century Welsh prince, Brychan; several of her sisters, such as Minver and Tetha, also have the dedication of Cornish churches. The first record of the church as collegiate is in 1288, when there were four prebendaries. Although the prebends of St Endellion are sometimes referred to as portions, each possessed an independent endowment, and so they are probably correctly regarded as prebends. Two were in lay patronage, and two were in the patronage of Bodmin Priory; one of the latter was the rectorial prebend, with responsibility for the cure of souls.

The very remarkable fact about this delightful collegiate church is that it still has four prebendaries today. For no obvious reason, the college survived the 1540s; equally remarkably, it survived the reforms of the nineteenth

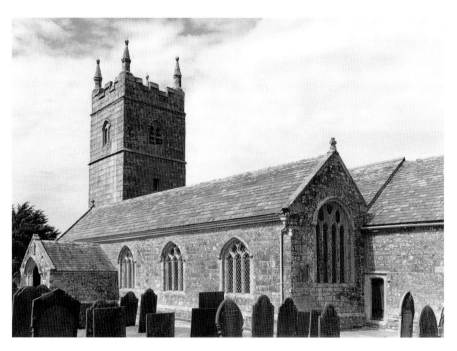

St Endellion, from the south-east

century. Throughout its post-Reformation existence there was probably no active collegiate life; the patrons continued to present to the prebends, which were sinecure but provided income. The holder of the 'Bodmin' (or 'Kings') prebend in the 1880s was involved in the building of a chapel in Port Isaac in the parish, and when that became a separate parish in 1913 the prebendal revenues were transferred to it. However, the college did not disappear, and in 1929 it was rehabilitated by the initiative of Walter Frere, Bishop of Truro. Under the statutes then issued, which are still in force today, only the rector (or holder of the rectorial prebend) is resident; appointment to the other prebends is an honour, carrying a spiritual but no financial element. The prebendaries are to pray for one another, to visit the church at least annually, to assist the rector when required, and to celebrate Holy Communion with a special intention for the college at least once a year. An annual chapter meeting is held. The survival or preservation of the college in this form is unique.

The church has always been remote from the centres of population in its parish. Just E of the churchyard stands the former prebendal house of Trehaverock, and just to the N is the rectory; neither now has any obvious medieval structure. Another former prebendal house near the church was demolished in about 1960.

The church is most attractive, though not particularly large. It is of typical Cornish form, fairly low, undivided E-W, with a W tower, aisles under pitched roofs, and the chancel extending a bay beyond the aisles; it is of uniform Perp.

work in rather irregular granite ashlar. The tower is of finer ashlar, unbuttressed, in three stages, with battlements and corner pinnacles; most of its details are modest, but it has the sophistication of a frieze of quatrefoils on its plinth. There is quite a large S porch, covering a round-arched doorway with continuous mouldings containing a series of fleurons. The aisles have three-light arched and traceried side windows; the E window of the chancel has five lights under a depressed arch. The arcades are of five bays, with four-centred moulded arches on monolithic granite pillars of four shafts and four hollows, the capitals having imposts with varied foliage motifs. A section of the N aisle wall stands forward as a shallow projection, part of which contains the rood stair, while the rest internally forms a recess perhaps once used as a small chapel. There are excellent old wagon roofs.

In the S chapel is an exceptionally fine altar-tomb, which is probably the shrine of St Endelienta. It is of beautiful black Catacleuse stone, the sides having miniature buttresses and big recesses with multifoiled ogee arches and miniature vaults; the top has its five consecration crosses. Of similar sophistication and in the same stone is a stoup recess by the S doorway, ornamented with acorns and carrying shields with carved coats of arms. The plain tub font on a cylindrical stem is Norman.

A 1933 drawing is displayed showing 'the Church in pitch pine days', and a remarkable feature is the 'de-Victorianization' which was carried out mainly in 1937–40. The result is most lovely. All glass is clear, and the floor is of slate.

St Endellion: the probable shrine of St Endelienta

The walls have some rough plaster, and are painted grey: this replaces a former stripped surface. There are excellent thick, plain pews of light oak, most of those in the centre block having good medieval ends, straight-topped, with typical carved motifs. The attractive part-polygonal pulpit with baluster sides is made up largely from sections of late-seventeenth-century communion rail. Also of about 1940 are four massive stalls with misericords, each inscribed with the name of its prebend: Rector, Marnays, Bodmin and Trehaverock.

* St Michael Penkevil

In the early fourteenth century, this church was remodelled and enlarged by its patron, Sir John de Trejagu, and in 1319 he converted it into a chantry college of four chaplains. It was entitled an archpresbytery, and the head chaplain, who was responsible for the cure of souls, was called archpriest. It seems that the endowment was inadequate; an indulgence was obtained in 1335 from Pope Benedict XII with which it was hoped to attract funds, but the prospects

St Michael Penkevil: the tower from the south-east

of the college continuing were probably brought to an end by the Black Death of 1349. Certainly it had ceased to exist by 1426, when the church was again a normal rectory.

The church, cruciform without aisles, is unconventional for Cornwall; it is an impressive and bulky building. Part of the present structure is apparently thirteenth century, a now almost illegible inscribed stone in the chancel being said to record its consecration by Bishop Bronescombe in 1261. Sir John's enlargements probably included the transepts and the massive W tower. It is a beautiful church, but alas the predominant impression is Victorian, due to the severe restoration of 1862–5, by G.E. Street. Comparison with old illustrations shows that the general plan and elevation are little altered, but externally virtually nothing appears old. Internally, a few features are clearly medieval, though even these are much renewed: they are in the transepts, including the transept arches, and in the tower, where the arch rests on head corbels with large image niches; the broad interior of the tower is continuous with the nave. Windows are all in Dec. style. The tower has set-back buttresses, large belfry openings with three-light intersecting tracery and a prominent polygonal turret. Particularly Victorian in appearance is the tower top, with its straight parapet and high pyramidal roof. The S porch is tall and has an upper room.

The roofs are Victorian. Some features in the transepts, in so far as they represent medieval work, are remarkable. Both end walls have a broad tomb-recess containing a plain tomb, and adjacent to it a set of cinquefoiled sedilia.

St Michael Penkevil: the north transept

In the N transept these are triple and turn the corner so that one sedile is in the E wall, whereas in the S transept they are double. A cinquefoiled piscina is in each transept E wall, that in the N transept being ogee in form. Both transepts have a doorway giving on to a shallow vaulted cupboard, and at a higher level are what may be blocked doorways associated with the rood. Each transept has a rectangular reredos recess containing elaborate tracery; they are dissimilar, that on the N probably being fifteenth century. The N transept altar has an ancient stone mensa with its consecration crosses. These transepts are regarded as two of the chantry chapels served by the chaplains of the college, a third being in the second stage of the tower, where there are the remains of an altar and piscina. The fourth was the chancel.

This is now effectively an estate church to the nearby great house of Tregothnan, home of the Boscawen family, since 1720 viscounts Falmouth. A broad, low mausoleum extends E from the chancel. There are many fine mural memorials, mostly to Boscawens, and notable standing wall memorials of 1559 and 1763, the latter by Rysbrack. Two late medieval brasses remain. In the porch is a font bowl probably of the thirteenth century. The Victorian furnishings are of high quality and include fine pews and stalls, but the ubiquitous stained glass makes the church dark.

Cumberland (*now part of Cumbria*)

Both collegiate churches of Cumberland are set in the lovely undulating countryside around Penrith. They are attractive late-medieval foundations of chantry type.

* Greystoke

The College of Greystoke was planned by William, 14th Baron of Greystoke, of Greystoke Castle, who in 1358 obtained licences for its foundation from the king and the bishop. However, he died the next year, and it was not until 1374, when his son Ralf was of age, that the licence from the king was renewed. There were then lengthy delays while a commission appointed by the bishop made its investigations, and considerable opposition had to be overcome before in 1382 the college was established. This was a chantry college for a master or provost and six chaplains. Its annual income was given in the sixteenth century as £82, and it was dissolved in 1548. As at the county's other college, there was here a challenge to its dissolution, in this case claiming that the church was not truly collegiate (i.e. appropriated), and so was not subject to confiscation. A court upheld the claim so, although the college was dissolved, the church continued as a rectory, held by the last provost. Surprisingly, the surrender of the chantry college was not the end of the collegiate story of Greystoke, because in 1958 an experimental pre-theological college was established here. However, this too is now past history, for it closed in 1979 owing to lack of candidates.

Greystoke, from the south

The Church of St Andrew is attractive and impressively massive; it is notably broad but not lofty. Most of it appears to be Perp., but it is suggested that some of this is seventeenth-century work; there has also been much nineteenth-century restoration. The W tower is very solid but low, in two stages, with battlements and diagonal buttresses; it was largely rebuilt in the nineteenth century. The exterior is all of good grey ashlar, but internally much of it is deprived of plaster, and some surfaces are scraped. Roofs are good quality Victorian work, in the nave of hammerbeam form; the very wide aisles have low-pitched roofs. Externally there are straight parapets throughout, and the chancel has pinnacles. Most windows are of three lights with Perp. tracery, cusped in the chancel, uncusped elsewhere; the large E window has five lights. The arcades have six bays, but the E bay is broader and is EE, former transepts having been taken into the aisles; the remaining bays are mainly or entirely of 1817–18. A large blocked squint passes from the N aisle to the chancel. The Perp. S porch covers a round-arched doorway which is probably also Perp. Another round-arched doorway opens from the S aisle to a large two-storeyed attachment, externally battlemented, with two-light square-headed windows; a squint in its lower level gives a view of the aisle altar, and at the upper level two four-light square-headed windows look into the aisle. The chancel arch is probably EE; it retains its ancient rood beam with a few carved motifs, though almost all of the screen beneath is relatively recent.

The chancel is spacious and light. Entirely of 1848 are its triple sedilia,

Greystoke, looking south-east

piscina, and a deep arched recess on the N side set in an external projection. This recess contains old artefacts, including the damaged alabaster effigy of William, 14th Baron of Greystoke; also here is a tablet commemorating the two colleges. The ancient stalls survive, with twenty carved misericords; one shows St George and the dragon. Much of the glass in the E window is of the fifteenth century; a few other windows have old fragments too. There are several small sixteenth-century brasses, one of which is to the provost John Whelpdale, who died in 1526.

* Kirkoswald

Established by Thomas, Lord Dacre, about 1523, this was the last chantry college founded in England. The founder was patron of the church, which was appropriated. The collegiate establishment consisted of a provost and five chaplains, with a vicar to serve the cure of souls. Its income in 1535 was given as £78. When commissioners arrived on 20 April 1547 to dissolve it under the Act of 1545, the provost and chaplains refused, which it seems was possible at this time, after the death of Henry VIII. However, its reprieve lasted only until the next year, when it was dissolved by authority of the Act of December 1547. Despite their earlier resistance, the provost and chaplains received pensions.

As its name implies, the church is dedicated to St Oswald; it is unusual and charming, though not large. It is approached by a pretty path curving round

Kirkoswald, from the south-west, with the belfry visible on the hill beyond

the base of a hill, away from the village; it is set with its chancel burrowing into the steep hillside. The church seems towerless, but in fact the tower, or rather belfry, stands on top of the roughly conical hill. It is in a single stage, with battlements and a turret; it was originally built in 1743, but in its present appearance is of 1892, though none the less engaging for that.

The church was altered in about 1523, and the chancel completely rebuilt. This is uniform and aisleless, externally of irregular ashlar; its windows are all large, square-headed, of three uncusped arched lights in the side windows and five to the E. Four steps rise in the chancel arch, which is curiously tall in relation to its width; this is probably EE, but its base is Norman, showing the battered remains of shafts. It is flanked by image niches of dissimilar sizes. The nave has a modest late-Perp. clerestory, externally concealed by the pitched roofs of the aisles. Its arcades are of three bays, the E two being round arched: on the N side these are of two unmoulded orders, and are Norman; on the S they have chamfers, and must be a little later. After a double respond, the W bay on each side is later again, with double-chamfered pointed arches on grotesque corbel heads. The windows in the aisles are varied, though several are square-headed with uncusped lights; there is a blocked EE S doorway with good mouldings, formerly shafted. The N aisle wall appears largely Victorian, but it has a very humble partly ancient porch, of stone and venerable timbers. Both aisles end to the E in a depressed double-chamfered arch, presumably once

Kirkoswald, looking east

leading to a chapel which was removed when the chancel was rebuilt; they now open only to recesses of Victorian work.

The tall baluster communion rails are of the eighteenth century. There are some attractive mural memorials in the chancel, and in the nave is a decayed medieval recumbent effigy. Set up against the N exterior is a striking series of carved coffin-lids: most have foliated crosses, and two have swords. Outside the base of the W wall is St Oswald's Well, the water of which rises from a spring under the E end and flows under the length of the church to emerge here; there are steps down to the water, and a metal cup on a chain. The present arrangement is probably Victorian.

Several hundred yards away, closer to the village, the fine mansion known as The College was indeed the domestic building of the college. It has work of about 1523 and also incorporates part of a late-fifteenth-century tower house. Most of its appearance today is due to alterations and enlargements in the seventeenth century and later.

Derbyshire

The county's principal collegiate church is now Derby Cathedral. Also in Derby, St Alkmund's is remarkable for the very interesting early relics which the site has yielded.

* Derby: All Saints

All Saints was a pre-Conquest collegiate church, perhaps founded by King Edmund about 943, and it possessed the freedoms of a royal foundation. In the early Norman period it had a dean and seven canons. At the beginning of the twelfth century, Henry I gave it to Lincoln Cathedral; this came to mean that the Dean of Lincoln was also Dean of All Saints, Derby, while one of the canons was acting head, with the title of sub-dean. It continued with a sub-dean and six canons; by the thirteenth century most canons were non-resident and there were also seven vicars. Despite the gift to Lincoln, it was still a royal free chapel and, as with others in the diocese of Coventry and Lichfield, this status caused disputes; it was one of those whose freedoms were finally accepted by the bishop in 1281. The annual value in 1535 was just £38 14s, excluding the substantial sum that went to the dean. The college was dissolved in 1548.

Derby Cathedral, from the south-east

College Place to the N, which now has eighteenth- and nineteenth-century buildings, is probably the site of the canons' houses. The church was the principal parish church of Derby, and in 1927 became the cathedral of a newly created diocese. It seems well worthy of its new status: it is a superb building, and its tremendous W tower, 212 ft (64.6 m) high, dominates the city as a cathedral should. The surroundings are also pleasant, with an attractive landscaped area of grass and trees to the E where, shockingly, a power station formerly stood; since its removal, the church has been cleaned and redecorated.

The tower was built about 1510–30, and is outstandingly fine and majestic. There are three major stages, divided by bands of panelling; angle buttresses are slightly set back from the corners, containing large canopied image niches and higher up having pinnacles in relief. An unusual feature is a long inscription running along the N and S sides. The higher stages have much sophisticated enrichment, while the belfry openings are large, four-centred, in four lights with a transom; above are panelled battlements with large corner and smaller intermediate pinnacles. The fine W doorway, flanked by further image niches, is the main entrance to the church; eighteenth-century gallery stairs curve elegantly up both sides of the tower interior.

The church was otherwise rebuilt in 1723–5 to the design of James Gibbs. It is a large and splendid structure of ashlar, with a single tier of large windows, round-arched with keystone and intermittent rustication. It is six bays long, with paired pilasters at the corners and between the bays, surmounted by a

Derby Cathedral, looking east from the gallery

cornice and balustraded parapet. Internally it has aisles of full height covered by plaster groin vaults, while the central space has a plaster barrel vault; they have restrained enrichment, and are exquisitely decorated in white, pink and a little gold. The tall Tuscan columns carry square pieces of entablature, with round arches hardly distinguished from the ceiling. There was formerly no chancel but one was provided in 1965–72, the architect being Sebastian Comper: it is of two broad aisleless bays, with its E end obtusely pointed. Its style reproduces most of the motifs of the eighteenth-century work, but the external surrounds of the windows are simply moulded. Also introduced at this time was a great baldachino over the altar. One can feel that this is work worthy of the noble building to which it has been added.

The glass is clear throughout except for two windows of bright abstract glass. There is a splendid deep W gallery on fluted Ionic columns, elegantly recessed in the centre where the organ stands; there have never been side galleries. Outstanding is the great wrought-iron screen, which extends the full width of the church and incorporates the Royal Arms in its centre. It is original to the building, and is by the famous smith Robert Bakewell; there is other work by him, too, including a sword-rest on the mayor's pew. A timber former consistory court dates from 1634. There are many notable memorials. A late medieval recumbent effigy of oak rests on an oaken tomb-chest (better preserved than the effigy) with small figures along its side. A fifteenth-century incised slab commemorates John Lawe, sub-dean. The famous Bess of Hardwick, who died in 1608, has an appropriately enormous standing wall memorial, incorporating her recumbent effigy. It is surprising to learn that the exquisite font of white marble was made in 1974, but it is to a design by Gibbs. Other modern fittings too are excellent and appropriate.

Derby: St Alkmund

This was probably the first church of Northworthy (later renamed Derby by the Danes), and was important from an early date. St Alkmund, a prince of the royal house of Northumbria, died in battle soon after 800 in circumstances that led to his being regarded as a martyr; he was buried initially at Lilleshall in Shropshire, but about 820 his body was moved to Northworthy, where his tomb in the church became a place of pilgrimage. The church was collegiate and had six canons at the time of Domesday. By this time, however, the Church of All Saints was also collegiate, and St Alkmund's declined in importance as All Saints grew to be the principal church of the town; by 1253 its college had apparently been absorbed by that of All Saints. St Alkmund's remained parochial, and still possessed the shrine of the saint. The church was entirely rebuilt in 1844–6, as a large and elaborate building with a tall stone spire. It was, however, demolished in 1967–8, when a major archaeological investigation showed the sequence of buildings from the eighth century. An outstanding discovery was a sarcophagus with elaborate and sophisticated interlace carving, almost certainly that provided in about 820 for the saint. Together with other Anglo-Saxon fragments from here, it is now displayed in Derby Museum. The site was deeply quarried away for the Inner Ring Road (known as St Alkmund's Way); a memorial stone was set up in a surviving corner, which is about 200 yd N of All Saints.

The demolished church was, however, replaced by a new building constructed in 1970–2, standing on the suburban Kedleston Road ½ mile away. This is large, mostly of brick inside and out; the main space is a flat-roofed auditorium of irregular shape, the W part approximately semicircular while the S wall has a

Derby: St Alkmund. The entrance side

saw-tooth form with full-length windows in the facets aligned towards the altar. Fittings include a massive pulpit of concrete, an organ, and band facilities with an electronic control console. Also here, however, is the modest Perp. font, its octagonal bowl having panelled sides. In the large glass-walled lobby area are some mostly eighteenth-century mural memorials. Also here is a Jacobean tomb-chest with recumbent effigy, of which the head is curiously under-sized (why?). The most striking external feature of the church is its conical spire, made of blue fibreglass. It stands on eight concrete pylons above a side part of the lobby, and beneath it has been set another notable discovery from the excavation, a twelfth-century shrine base, its sides ornamented with blank arcading. This almost certainly supported a shrine of the saint which in Norman times replaced the earlier sarcophagus; it is a moving sight here.

Devon

This county had an unusually large number of collegiate churches. Those of Crediton and Ottery St Mary were major establishments, and have correspondingly outstanding churches. The others were all much less important, and two have been largely or wholly destroyed. However, Bere Ferrers and Tiverton in particular are notably fine buildings, while Haccombe is visited for its fine memorials.

* Bere Ferrers

Only the Norman font tells us that there was a church here in the twelfth century. It was probably partly rebuilt in the mid-thirteenth century by the lord of the manor, Sir William de Ferrers. More rebuilding is suggested about 1300. Some of the structure, however, seems to be due to another Sir William de Ferrers, grandson of the former, who in about 1330 made it into a chantry college, known as an archpresbytery, with an archpriest, four chaplains and a deacon. This college continued until dissolution in about 1546; its value in the sixteenth century is given as just £24. As also at Haccombe in this county, the rector continues to hold the title archpriest, which confers a few archaic privileges such as the right to walk beside rather than behind the bishop at a visitation.

The church, dedicated to St Andrew, is beautifully set, close beside the estuary; but at first sight it seems a disappointing building. It is covered in dour dark grey roughcast, and it has a poor, thin W tower, almost without features other than its corbelled-out parapet with battlements and corner pinnacles. But this is a large and quite complex church, and its scale and some of its qualities soon become apparent. In plan it is cruciform, added to which are a S aisle and a S chancel chapel under pitched roofs. The cruciform basis is mainly Dec., though confident dating of the parts is not easy; it has good windows including an E window of five lights with intersecting tracery and a striking four-light S transept S window of reticulated tracery. Other windows, both in the S side and else-

Bere Ferrers, looking east

Bere Ferrers: the north transept

where, are Perp., of good-quality work. There is a two-storeyed Perp. S porch, containing an excellent timber ceiling and a pillar stoup. Despite its plainness, the W tower is medieval, perhaps of the thirteenth century.

Internally, the church is immediately very attractive and full of interest. It is light and quite lofty. Open timber roofs renewed in 1985–6 cover the nave and chancel, but the others have plaster barrel ceilings. Unusually for this region, there is a chancel arch. The fine nave arcade has tall monolithic granite pillars of four shafts and four hollows, carrying well-moulded four-centred arches; it has three bays, then a wider bay for the transept. Two more bays follow to the chancel. The blocked rood stair remains. In the chancel are twin stepped sedilia, simple work in granite; more elaborate is the trefoiled piscina with shelf. A vestry at the NE was formerly a chantry chapel; beside its doorway it has a very rich Dec. opening to the sanctuary of limestone, with tall pinnacles, a crocketed gable and cusps carrying heads. This forms a canopy over two fine recumbent effigies, probably of Sir William de Ferrers, founder of the college, and his wife Matilda.

The arch to the N transept has typical Dec. mouldings, and beside it is a large squint. This transept is strikingly long and contains much of interest. It has an ogee-cinquefoiled piscina with shelf, three of its Dec. windows are shafted, and in the N wall is a Dec. arched tomb-recess containing a tomb with a fine effigy of a knight, recumbent but in the act of rising and drawing his sword; this is probably Sir Reginald de Ferrers, father of the founder of the college. Another tomb-chest here is early sixteenth century, and there is a puzzling large slab finely carved with a regular pattern and three rose window designs, probably late medieval. A late Perp. fireplace probably dates from the use of the transept as the squire's pew.

Most of the base of the rood screen remains, with foliage trails and tracery, retaining some colour. The pews are almost entirely late medieval, and are well preserved; their straight-topped ends mostly have a uniform tracery design which also appears on the pew fronts and backs. In the sanctuary floor is another curious late medieval carved slab. The font is an extraordinary Norman example: it is square at the base and roughly circular at the top, with giant volutes at the four angles. A notable possession is the original glass of the E window, fairly complete and very fine.

Chulmleigh

The small college in this church is thought to have been established in the thirteenth century, probably by a member of the Courtenay family, who held the patronage. It had five prebends (some early records suggest seven, but this certainly did not apply later), as well as a rector; it is sometimes regarded as a church of portioners. The annual value in 1535 was reported as £24. Its main historical interest is that it survived the period of the dissolution, and prebendaries continued to be appointed until it was dissolved under the Act of 1840.

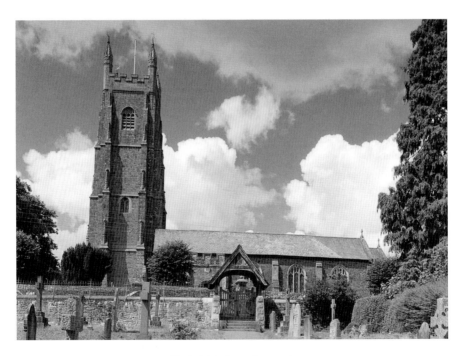

Chulmleigh, from the south

The Church of St Mary Magdalene is of typical Devon character, and is attractive but not outstanding. It is all Perp., mostly of irregular slate masonry, and has a W tower and a body undivided E-W, with aisles under pitched roofs one bay shorter than the chancel. There is a battlemented S porch with a round arch, a band of quatrefoils, and an image niche. The windows in the aisles are of three lights, arched and traceried. The E end was rebuilt in the nineteenth century, though retaining the Perp. style; a nineteenth-century priest's door is attractively set diagonally in a corner. Most impressive externally is the tall tower, in four stages, with set-back buttresses, battlements and octagonal corner pinnacles. Below its W window is a band of quatrefoils, and its buttress offsets are enriched by diagonally set pinnacles.

Above the S doorway is a small roundel of the crucifixion, thought to be early Norman. The arcades have five large bays, with pillars of four shafts and four hollows, simple capitals and rather irregular arches which, on the S side, are four-centred or in one case not pointed at all. The N arcade leans noticeably. Curiously the arcades stop about 6 ft short of the tower arch, the intervening blank section having a barrel vault. There are plastered wagon roofs with bosses throughout; in the central vessel, angels are set above the wall-plates.

The octagonal font is Perp., with round its bowl a band of small quatrefoils and relief cresting. The former Jacobean pulpit is now in the Congregational church. There are four large benefaction boards and just one splendidly elaborate mural memorial, of 1706. The great feature is the screen, running the full width, which is largely authentic. It has tracery in four-light divisions, traceried base panels and splendid ribbed coving with bosses, its front surmounted by three bands of foliage. It is in excellent condition and retains a little colour.

* Crediton

The earliest reported historical event at Crediton was the birth in about 680 of the boy who was to become St Boniface, the evangelist of Germany. In 739, King Aethelheard of Wessex gave land here to Bishop Forthere of Sherborne for the establishment of a monastery. At the beginning of the tenth century, the diocese of Sherborne was divided, and Crediton became the seat of a bishop for Devon. For this a new church was built, with a charter from King Athelstan in 933. In 1050, Bishop Leofric moved his seat from Crediton to Exeter. Crediton remained important, however, with secular priests. In the early twelfth century Bishop Warelwast gave it a charter, in which its eighteen poor prebends were reorganized into twelve adequate ones. Some of these were true prebends, but others seem to have been bursal; the precentor was head of the college. Its charter was confirmed in 1235 by Bishop Brewer. Bishop Grandisson in the fourteenth century added four choristers and four singing men; there may also have been vicars choral. Its annual value in 1535 is given as the large sum of £332.

At the dissolution, the parishioners raised £200 to purchase the complete church; they also purchased the living of Exminster, to provide a substantial income. By a charter of Edward VI, renewed in 1560 by Elizabeth, the church

Crediton, from the south-east

and its affairs were vested in a corporation of twelve governors. These charters also provided for a grammar school, replacing a school that had been provided by the college. The governors were granted a seal by Charles II in 1674; they still exist today. Similar bodies of governors exist at Ottery St Mary and at Wimborne Minster (Dorset).

The Church of the Holy Cross is a magnificent and very large cruciform building, with a central tower and eastern Lady Chapel; the external length is about 225 ft (68.6 m). It is mostly Perp., but the crossing and transepts retain some twelfth-century work. The relatively low crossing has Norman pillars with shafts and scalloped capitals, carrying pointed arches of two unmoulded orders, which may be an EE alteration. Externally, the lowest stage of the tower has small round-arched openings to N and S, but the main part of the tower is EE, with two lancet openings each side flanked by blank trefoiled lancets; above are later battlements and big octagonal corner pinnacles. The transepts are lower than the nave and chancel; the N transept has Norman flat buttresses, but they otherwise appear Perp., with large end windows of six lights. On their W sides both have a lobby and a pretty battlemented turret, an early-nineteenth-century addition for access to former galleries. The Lady Chapel, projecting two bays beyond the flanking chapels, served from the sixteenth century until 1860 as the grammar school; it was restored as part of the church in 1876–7. A few details show its thirteenth-century origin, but it has Perp. windows.

The nave and chancel are uniform Perp. work, built probably from about 1410; the nave has six bays, the high chancel has five. Both have battlemented parapets, low-pitched roofs and large four-light traceried aisle windows; the clerestory windows are similar but in the nave are of only three lights. Internally the windows are all shafted. The arcades have two-centred arches on pillars of four shafts and four large waves, with capitals only to the shafts. Above is a string-course with fleurons, and shafts rise to support the roof. The battlemented S porch of two storeys is probably an early-sixteenth-century addition; it has a good vault with large foliage bosses. On the S side of the chancel is a large attachment in three storeys, now with nineteenth-century windows but basically thirteenth century; it shows traces of two arches to the chancel aisle, perhaps implying that its two lower storeys replace a former chapel. The top storey is thought to have been the chapter-house, and is now the governors' room; it is full of interesting and surprising artefacts, including armour and several old chests.

The roofs are Victorian, but are good; however the stripping of the plaster in the same period is unfortunate. Covering the E wall of the nave is an assertive display of canopy work, statuary and mosaics, a memorial of 1911 to Sir Redvers Buller: this seems regrettable. There are large, remarkably elaborate triple sedilia, richly vaulted and retaining much original colour, but they have been severely mutilated. The back of this structure is panelled, with a

Crediton, looking east

broad, finely vaulted tomb-recess; this too has colour. In the Lady Chapel, a fine thirteenth-century double piscina was in 1921 curiously set up in front of the wall. Good memorials include a fourteenth-century tomb-chest with recumbent effigies, and on the N side of the sanctuary two large early-seventeenth-century monuments. In the S transept are three coffin-lids with foliated crosses. The font is of the Norman table type, with four blank arches on each side, resting on nineteenth-century supports.

Exeter

Rougemont Castle, the castle of Exeter, was royal, founded by the Conqueror. Its Chapel of St Mary was collegiate, with four prebendaries. It is thought that it was given by the Conqueror to Ralph Avenil; in the early twelfth century it went to Plympton Priory, and later it was held by the earls of Devon. No deans are known, and it is possible that the prebends were really portions. Despite the royal connection, it was not a royal free chapel. It does not seem to have been a thriving establishment, and when in 1322 Bishop Stapeldon undertook a visitation, he found it ruinous and apparently abandoned. He ordered repairs, which seem to have been carried out, but whether any collegiate life resumed is not known. The chapel remained in existence and roofed until it was demolished in 1792.

The impressive walls of the inner bailey still stand, but all the medieval buildings inside were demolished in the eighteenth century, and the circuit of the walls now contains the large classical law courts of 1774. Standing alongside the present eighteenth-century gateway is the original early Norman gatehouse; the chapel stood a little way NE of this, its site now partly occupied by a nondescript Victorian building of red brick. Old illustrations show it as a very modest structure consisting of a nave and short chancel, with a small timber belfry on the nave roof.

* Haccombe

This church, with its rare dedication to St Blaise, is thought to have been founded by Sir Stephen de Haccombe on his return in 1233 from the Crusades. In 1328, Bishop Grandisson consecrated an extension to the church built by Sir Stephen's grandson, another Sir Stephen. The latter planned to make the church collegiate, but died before he could do so; however, licence was granted in 1335 to Sir John de L'Ercedekne, husband of Sir Stephen's grand-daughter Cicely, to establish it as a chantry college for an archpriest and five chaplains. The foundation was confirmed by Bishop Grandisson in 1337; the church was appropriated, and it also at some time became a peculiar of the archbishops of Canterbury. The sixteenth-century income of the college was given as £25 per annum. It was dissolved in the 1540s, but curiously the rectors of the church retained the title of archpriest, which was confirmed by King George V in 1913, and they still have this title today. This entitles the holders to certain obscure privileges, including the right to wear special vestments. A similar situation applies at Bere Ferrers. Haccombe remained a peculiar of Canterbury until the nineteenth century.

The church stands close to the large but plain late Georgian mansion, which is now divided into flats; there is no village, but the church is used and well cared for. Despite its collegiate status, it is a small and architecturally very modest building. It has a nave and chancel without structural division, apparently thirteenth century, with a N aisle under a lean-to roof, stopping short of the sanctuary: this aisle must be the extension which was consecrated in 1328, built no doubt with the college in mind. The walls are of rubble, and there are a little nineteenth-century W belfry, a small plain S porch and a shallow W porch with a pointed barrel vault and a holy-water stoup outside. It is over-restored: the lancet windows, mainly in pairs but with triplets to the E, are entirely nineteenth century, though an old picture demonstrates that they represent the original form. Just the three-light W window of simplest bar tracery has original stonework.

Haccombe, from the west

The four-bay arcade has thick octagonal pillars, plain renewed capitals and unmoulded pointed arches, surprisingly elementary for their date. All four bays of the aisle wall have a plain arched tomb-recess, and its E wall has another, with curiously set in front of it a crocketed ogee structure of limestone. In the chancel are a further tomb-recess and plain triple sedilia. Both the S and W doorways have ancient doors. Most furnishings are indifferent, but the stone screen of 1822 is attractive, as is the reredos probably of the same time. Some fragmentary but interesting fourteenth-century glass remains. A quite large floor area has medieval tiles. There are two hatchments.

It is its outstanding medieval memorials that make this church special. Two tomb-recesses contain thirteenth-century recumbent effigies of ladies. An effigy of a knight, between the chancel and the chapel, is of a similar period and is thought to represent the earlier Sir Stephen de Haccombe: it retains remarkably well-preserved colour. A nineteenth-century tomb-chest carries the restored effigies of Sir Hugh Courtenay, who died in 1425, and his wife Philippa. Perhaps the finest, however, is a miniature recumbent effigy of alabaster, an exquisite late-fourteenth-century piece, probably marking a heart burial. There are also several late brasses.

* Ottery St Mary

In 1061, Edward the Confessor granted the manor and Church of St Mary at Ottery to the cathedral of Rouen in Normandy. There seems later to have been dissatisfaction with the management by Rouen, and in 1280 Walter de Lechelade, Precentor of Exeter Cathedral, who was responsible on behalf of Rouen for the exactions from Ottery, was murdered as he left the cathedral. It is to John de Grandisson, bishop from 1327 to 1369, that the establishment of a college here is due. In 1334–5, he negotiated the purchase of the manor and church from Rouen. Royal licence for the college was granted in December 1337. The college was very large, with an annual value in the sixteenth century of £303; it had a warden and eight canons who held prebends, which however were small, since residence was intended. The total strength was forty, including at least eight vicars, ten clerks, eight boy choristers and a master of grammar. It was surrendered to the Crown in 1545. Four governors were appointed by letters patent in the same year, as a corporate body responsible for the maintenance of the church, increased to twelve in 1552. This arrangement, existing elsewhere only at Crediton and at Wimborne Minster (Dorset), continues to this day.

A consecration is recorded in 1259, but the church was largely rebuilt on the establishment of the college. It is a large and magnificent structure, though of idiosyncratic design: it is curiously hard to distinguish between EE and Dec. contributions, since the latter avoids tracery altogether and seems still to employ some lancet windows. It may be that the outer walls of the chancel and transepts are EE, and most of the rest new construction of the fourteenth century. It is cruciform with transeptal towers, a feature unique but for Exeter Cathedral, and it has an external length of 172 ft (52.4 m). There are straight parapets with a few pinnacles, and the aisles are narrow. The E limb is longer than the nave, and has an eastern Lady Chapel; a suggestion of double transepts (another echo of Exeter) is given by a pair of two-storeyed vestry blocks flanking the chancel. The towers have angle buttresses, and in their E sides have five narrow lancets grouped under a projecting gable; the belfries have three narrow lancets each side. Their attractive openwork battlemented parapets with openwork corner pinnacles are renewed Perp. work, and the N tower has a short lead-covered spire.

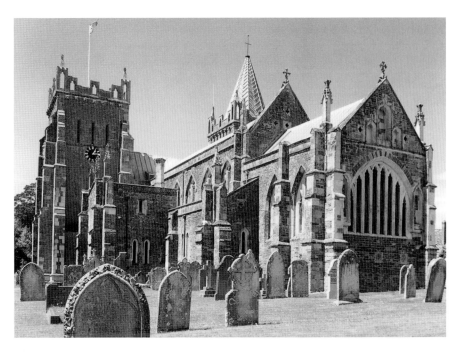

Ottery St Mary, from the south-east

The church is vaulted throughout, and these vaults are its greatest distinction. Those over the aisles and nave are the simplest, while the transepts, crossing and Lady Chapel have lovely and sophisticated lierne vaults, with fine bosses. The two-bay transept vaults ignore the external distinction of the parts which are towers. The chancel vault is supreme, basically a tunnel vault with the ribs applied purely as decoration, in a curved form of net-like appearance. Startling but effective colouring was in the 1970s applied to the vaults. Structurally the chancel is of six bays; its pillars have four shafts and complex mouldings between, with capitals only on the shafts towards the arches. In place of a triforium there are nodding-ogee image niches (much restored), and squeezed below the vault are three-light clerestory windows. One bay short of the chancel E wall is a great stone reredos, its front largely restored but with original Dec. panelling on its back. On the S side is a fine free-standing pinnacled compo-sition of triple stepped sedilia; on the N is a large canopied Elizabethan tomb-chest. The Lady Chapel is of three bays; it has an eight-light E window, quadruple sedilia, and across its W end a veranda screen or gallery of stone, with pretty details, original though much restored.

The nave has five bays, in their design a simplified version of the chancel. In one bay, each side has a large and very rich Dec. canopy above a tomb-chest with recumbent effigy. These are Sir Otho de Grandisson, brother of the founder, and his wife, who were great benefactors. There is a tall battlemented

Ottery St Mary, looking east

Perp. S porch; this is possibly post-dissolution work, since a cloister originally stood on this side, with a chapter-house and other buildings. Attached
to the N side is the Dorset aisle, a spectacular addition of the first years of
the sixteenth century. It is of ashlar, battlemented, with regular arched and
traceried windows, that to the W of six lights, and an enriched N porch of
three storeys. Its supreme feature is again its vault, in this case a delicious
fan vault, with openwork pendants, each given a different twist.
Representations of an owl and an elephant are entertaining features of the
aisle arcade.

It is regrettable that it was thought right in 1919 to strip the interior of plaster. Medieval stalls, some with misericords, are now distributed between the
chancel and the Lady Chapel. A few original bench-ends and some screenwork remain. In the S transept is a splendid astronomical clock, possibly
fourteenth century, which is still running. The fine hexagonal pulpit is eighteenth century. In the Lady Chapel is an eagle lectern of gilded oak;
remarkably, this was a gift of Bishop Grandisson.

Slapton

The de Brien family were lords of the manor and patrons of the parish church from before 1250. Sir Guy de Brien, born probably about 1307, was a notable figure, among his positions being that of standard bearer to Edward III at the battle of Crécy in 1346. In 1370 he was made a Knight of the Garter – his stall plate is still in St George's Chapel, Windsor. He died in 1390, and his fine tomb may be seen in Tewkesbury Abbey. At Slapton, he founded a chantry college, for which he obtained licence in 1369; it was fully established in 1372–4, and he added further endowments in subsequent years. The college was for a rector, five priests known as fellows and four clerks; it was to serve not in the parish church of St James but in the manor chapel of St Mary, which was no doubt rebuilt for the purpose. The parish church was appropriated to the college, and was served by one of its priests. In 1535, the annual income of the college was given as £63; it was dissolved in 1545. Among those pensioned were four poor people of Slapton, so the college apparently also had a small hospital function.

Slapton, from the east

The principal surviving relic, ruinous but almost complete and still dominating the village, is what must have been the W tower of the chapel. It is massive, about 80 ft (24 m) high, on a much larger scale than the parish church 100 yd away. It is of coursed slate rubble, with diagonal buttresses and at the SW corner a boldly projecting octagonal stair turret. Most of the stonework of the windows has gone, but a few details remain to confirm the Perp. date. Inside, it retains the springers of a vault. Its arch to the former nave is large but unmoulded, and above it remains the weathering for the nave roof. The most surprising feature of the tower is the bold machicolations at its summit, though the parapet they must have carried has gone. These machicolations also appear round the stair turret, which carries a stone spirelet.

Nothing remains of the body of the chapel, and the site has not been excavated. The tower stands in the garden of the substantial and romantic house called The Chantry, which now appears to be mostly early nineteenth century. This house incorporates some probably medieval walling, and almost certainly represents the domestic accommodation of the college. Ownership of the house still carries the position of lay rector.

* Tiverton

In 1146, the revenues of this church were given by Baldwin, Earl of Devon, to the Cluniac Priory of St James at Exeter. But in subsequent years the revenues were in part returned to the earls of Devon, and by 1291 the living had been divided into four portions, of which three were in the patronage of the earls of Devon, the Courtenay family, while the fourth was held by the Priory of St James. This was unambiguously a church of portioners, though it may have been collegiate in its function. In 1444, the patronage of the prior's portion was given to the newly founded King's College, Cambridge. No change took place at the Reformation, King's College and the descendants of the Courtenays continuing to present to their portions. The system was finally abolished in 1889.

Standing close to the partly ruined castle, once a seat of the Courtenays, the Church of St Peter is a proud and noble building. Of particular interest is its S exterior, whereas much of the rest, though it makes a fine impression, is nineteenth century. The style is Perp. throughout, with low-pitched roofs; it is all on a most generous scale. The large and tall W tower is in four stages, with set-back buttresses having big beasts on their offsets. It has battlements and eight pinnacles; broad canopied image niches flank the large W doorway. Inside, its tall arch has panelled responds. The nave is of six large bays, with broad aisles; the chancel has two rather smaller bays with flanking chapels, and the sanctuary projects a bay further. The N side is all of 1853–6, by E. Ashworth, when the aisle was rebuilt wider. A surprise here is a reset Norman doorway of two continuous orders, with orthogonal chevron. The nave arcades have four-centred arches, excellent capitals with foliage and many other motifs, and tall pillars of complex section distinguished by each incorporating a large canopied image niche; above is a clerestory of three-light windows. All this, however, is rebuilt, though the

Tiverton: St Peter, from the south-east

arcades reuse their original capitals and apparently follow the original form. Unusually for Devon there is a chancel arch. Also largely rebuilt is the chancel, but its arcades are original, with pillars of four shafts and four waves and arches four-centred on the N side and two-centred on the S.

The S aisle and S chapel were rebuilt about 1517 by several Tiverton merchants, with large windows of four lights under four-centred arches. Limestone is employed for the buttresses, battlements and pinnacles, with rich panelling and motifs including ships, anchors and wool-packs. The climax is the porch and the specially tall chantry chapel E of it, which were due to the greatest of these merchants, John Greenway. They are externally entirely of limestone, and are a riot of elaboration; the names or initials of John and Joan Greenway appear frequently. The exterior of the porch has been much renewed, but the chapel is authentic, and was admirably restored in 1985–6. It has a tall stepped battlemented parapet of openwork, with pinnacles. Its most memorable decoration is a frieze representing the sea, with a range of merchant ships sailing on it. Internally the porch has a barrel vault covered in continuous reticulations containing fleurons, anchors and other motifs; the round-arched inner doorway is flanked by image niches, and above is a large carving of the Assumption flanked by the donors. The chapel too has a barrel vault, in this case charmingly moulded as if it were a fan vault, with pendants. The tall two-bay arcade to the church has a partly original stone screen, cut down and altered in 1825.

Tiverton: St Peter. Carvings on the Greenway Chapel

The organ is very splendid, its rich case and much else dating from 1696. An exceptionally magnificent brass chandelier is of 1707, with the initials AR for Queen Anne; ejected in 1856, it was reinstated in 1941. In the chancel are tomb-chests of 1579 and 1613, and in the Greenway chapel are the large brasses which were once on the Greenways' tomb. There is an iron-bound medieval chest. Nothing is left of a former detached chapel just NE of the church, which held important memorials to the Courtenays.

Dorset

Dorset has only one collegiate church: but this is one of the major buildings of the class.

* Wimborne Minster

This church is of early origin: at the beginning of the seventh century a nunnery was established by Cuthburga, sister of King Ine of Wessex. Initially dedicated to the Virgin Mary, it was afterwards rededicated to St Cuthburga. In later Anglo-Saxon times this was a double monastery, with separate cloisters for men and women; it was important, and a brother of Alfred the Great was buried here. It seems, however, that it was destroyed by the Danes about the end of the tenth century, and was later re-established perhaps by Edward the Confessor, for secular canons. In the late thirteenth century, it had a dean and four canons; it was a royal free chapel, and in contrast to others its freedoms seem never to have been a subject of dispute. In later years there were also four vicars, four deacons and five singing men. In 1496 a chantry was attached to the college by Lady Margaret Beaufort, mother of Henry VII, the priest of which was also to teach grammar in a school. The annual value of the college in 1535 is given as £131. It was dissolved in 1547, when the commissioners recommended that the school continue. In 1562, under Queen Elizabeth, some of the former property of the college was returned; the school became the grammar school, and twelve governors were appointed to manage the minster's affairs. This body, similar to those at Crediton and Ottery St Mary (both in Devon), still exists. The church continued to be a royal peculiar until 1846.

This is an impressive and beautiful church, very large, with an external length of 197 ft (60 m), dominating the town as a great church should. Its title

Wimborne Minster, from the south-west

of 'minster' has also been taken by the town. It has two bulky towers, engagingly distinctive in character and also colour, the stone of the W tower being green and that of the central tower red. The earliest clearly dateable work is Norman, but it is suggested that the core is pre-Conquest. Significant restoration has taken place and all the roofs have been replaced, but for the most part renewal is not obtrusive. The very fine central tower is early twelfth century, mainly constructed of the local ironstone, with sophisticated external detailing including nook-shafts, openings enriched by shafts with volute capitals, and intersecting blank arcading. Above a corbel-course, it now carries an assertive but perhaps clumsy embattled parapet of 1608 with large obelisk corner pinnacles, erected after the fall of the medieval spire. Inside, it has fine rather depressed round arches of two unmoulded orders which, however, are rather low for the lofty nave. Above is a lantern, with a finely detailed gallery and above this two very large shafted windows on each side. The addition to the nave of a clerestory of large square-headed Perp. windows has produced a three-storeyed elevation; the Norman former clerestory windows now open inside the lean-to aisles. The arcades have six bays in total. The bay against the tower is narrow, with single-step arches, pointed but contemporary with the tower. Then come three larger late Norman bays, with cylindrical pillars, scalloped capitals and pointed arches sumptuously decorated with chevron, some of it orthogonal. The last two bays are Dec. work, simple though displaying a little ball-flower ornament. Also in the Dec. period, the aisles were widened, and there are a small S porch and a spacious vaulted Dec. N porch with a room over. The impressive and stately W tower was added in the mid-fifteenth century. It is in four stages, with twin two-light transomed belfry openings and polygonal buttresses rising to become pinnacles. Its lofty interior is vaulted.

Both transepts are partly Norman but extended in the Dec. period; in the N transept a large Norman altar recess has been exposed, revealing bright but indecipherable remains of later medieval painting. On its W side, this transept has a stair turret which is convincingly of early work, possibly pre-Conquest. Flanking the chancel are broad aisles under pitched roofs, their details largely Dec., but much renewed and partly rebuilt. The chancel opens to them by three arches, all dissimilar, separated by pieces of wall. The first is early Norman, pointed as in the nave, the next is Dec. and the third is very rich EE work, beyond which is an aisleless sanctuary, also EE. Above is a clerestory of small lancets, much restored. The EE work is superb, with very fine detailing including much use of Purbeck marble; the E window is a noble enriched triplet of lancets with very rich mouldings, dog-tooth, double shafting and a foiled circle above each lancet. The side lancets too are specially enriched. There are very lovely Dec. sedilia and piscina. This E end is raised high, twelve steps up from the nave. From each chancel aisle, broad steps lead down into an exquisitely beautiful vaulted crypt or Lady Chapel: this is a Dec. insertion below the earlier E end, with windows of spherical triangle form. Some of the vaulting arches have large cusps.

Wimborne Minster, looking east

Standing E of the S transept is a vaulted medieval sacristy, with a room over which contains a remarkable late-seventeenth-century chained library. There are many splendid memorials. Perhaps the finest is the Perp. tomb-chest with effigies of John Beaufort, Duke of Somerset, and his wife Margaret, grandparents of Henry VII. In the N chancel aisle are three ancient chests, one of which, convincingly attributed to Anglo-Saxon times, is a massive squared tree-trunk, hollowed out for no more than a small storage recess. The stalls are unusual in being largely Jacobean, with misericords and much characteristic carving. The brass eagle lectern is dated 1623. In the W tower is a remarkable early-fourteenth-century astronomical clock; its mechanism is in the belfry, and on the quarter hours drives a quarter jack outside. The impressive octagonal font is EE, with two trefoiled blank arches on each side; it rests on a central support and eight shafts. No collegiate buildings remain, but 250 yd to the S is the very fine early-eighteenth-century Dean's Court, probably on the site of the medieval deanery.

Co. Durham

Under the domination of the great cathedral monastery of Durham, with its powerful prince-bishops, this county was almost devoid of other monasteries (the only house independent of Durham was the vanished Benedictine nunnery of Neasham). By contrast, this is an important county for collegiate churches, and the foundation of five of the total of six was due to the bishops; indeed three were founded or refounded by Bishop Anthony Bek. The remaining college was of chantry type. All six are very fine and interesting churches.

* Auckland: St Andrew

The church is often referred to as St Andrew Auckland, and the place as South Church; it is a good mile (1.6 km) from the town of Bishop Auckland which it serves. The town stands at the gates of the great castle of the bishops, still their residence today. The origins of the college are said to go back to 1083, when it received some of the canons who had to leave Durham Cathedral when it was made monastic in that year. Auckland certainly had prebends, or more probably portions, in 1226 when, during a vacancy in the bishopric, a canon was presented by the king. However, it was refounded in 1292–4 by Bishop Anthony Bek, for a dean, twelve canons and the same number of vicars. Five of the canons were to be priests, four to be deacons and three sub-deacons; the corresponding vicars were to be of the same orders. The college was further reconstituted by Cardinal Langley, Bishop of Durham, in 1428, when the prebends were reorganized to make their values more equal, and new statutes were introduced. Its annual value was given at the Valor as almost £180, when it had a dean and ten prebendaries; it was dissolved in 1548.

Auckland: St Andrew, from the south-east

The church is as important as the size of the college might lead one to expect: it is impressive and very large; the length is given as 157 ft (47.9 m). Internally it is grandly spacious, broad as well as long and lofty. It is almost all basically thirteenth century, but with Perp. alterations which have given it low-pitched roofs throughout, with battlemented or straight parapets. In plan it is cruciform, with an aisled nave and W tower. The chancel is notably long; it has a string-course round both the exterior and interior, and its S side has four regular lancets (the N side is interrupted by a Victorian organ chamber). Strangely, however, between these lancets are two-light windows of uncusped Y-tracery; internally all share the same linked hood-moulds, but only the lancets are outlined by a roll. The explanation seems to be that the present church or at least chancel was built around 1260–70, and that the Y-tracery windows replace lancets or blank arcading and were inserted under Bishop Bek. The many other Y-tracery windows throughout the church probably also date from the latter time. There are beautiful double sedilia, with well-moulded arches on shafts of trefoil section; a third sedile seems to have been cut away for the priest's door. Also impressive is the N transept, with an internal string-course and two long E lancets again with an internal roll. The S transept is largely a Victorian rebuilding, to the original design.

The nave has arcades of five large bays, of which the E bays serve the transepts; the pillars alternate between octagonal and a plan of four major and four minor shafts, and the arches have very rich EE mouldings. Above is a simple Perp. clerestory. There is a large two-storeyed S porch, vaulted in two

Auckland: St Andrew, looking east

bays, each bay having a two-light side window, and with a finely moulded doorway and outer arch. Also EE are the three lower stages of the tall tower, which has angle buttresses, another buttress on the W side, and lancet openings. The fourth stage is Perp., with battlements and large two-light openings. A rather clumsy stair turret is at the SW corner. A Victorian vestry extends the S aisle alongside the tower.

The stripping of the plaster and the insertion of a Victorian chancel arch have done little damage to this glorious interior. The chancel contains a fine set of twenty-four stalls, known to have been given by Cardinal Langley in 1416–17, with beautiful traceried fronts, poppy-head ends and carved misericords. Otherwise the church is lightly furnished, mainly with nineteenth-century work. The few mural memorials include one of 1637 painted on boards in lozenge form; there are also a large fourteenth-century brass and two hatchments. In the NW corner are many interesting architectural fragments and two fine fourteenth-century recumbent effigies: one of a lady in stone, and one of a knight in oak. In front of the tower arch stands a large cross, put together in 1931 from fragments found in 1881 in the foundations of the S transept: it may be of around 800, and is especially fine.

Several hundred yards away, reached by a bridge across the river, stands what is known as the East Deanery; this was the residential accommodation of the college, set around a courtyard. A few parts go back to the thirteenth century. It has been renovated for modern use.

* Chester-le-Street

This is a place of uncommon historical interest, for the predecessor of the present church of St Mary and St Cuthbert was a cathedral from 883, when the monks of Lindisfarne moved here as a result of the attacks of the Vikings, bringing with them the body of St Cuthbert. They left in 995, again taking the body of the saint, which subsequently reached its final resting place at Durham. The church was then parochial until 1286 when, a legal dispute between two claimants to the rectory being in progress, Bishop Anthony Bek intervened, ejecting both claimants and establishing instead a college of a dean and seven prebendaries, with seven vicars. Its revenues came from the tithe of the very large parish, and its constitution was almost identical to that of Lanchester, which had been founded two years previously. Residence was not demanded of the prebendaries, but they were to provide vicars, who in three cases should be priests. Most responsibilities were with the dean, including the cure of souls and provision for the two chapels in the parish. The college continued in this form throughout its life, although there were four occasions in the early fifteenth century when Bishop Langley had to rebuke the canons for their neglect of divine service and of the fabric and possessions of the church. Its sixteenth-century value was given as £77. Dissolution came in 1547.

The church stands in the centre of the site of the Roman fort that once stood here. As befits the successor to a cathedral, the church is large-scale, impres-

Chester-le-Street, from the north-west

sive and important. It is mainly thirteenth century, of ashlared sandstone. It has a long and spacious nave of five very large bays, unclerestoried, with aisles under low-pitched lean-to roofs. The arcades have double-chamfered arches on tall cylindrical pillars with moulded capitals; extension is indicated by double responds instead of pillars three bays from the chancel arch. The W tower stands on quite slender pillars and arches such that internally it reads almost as a sixth bay of nave; its pillars have multiple shafts. Externally this W end is impressive, with the broad tower turning octagonal immediately above roof level, where it has long, cusped Y-tracery bell-openings. It carries battlements, pinnacles, and a very tall, plain stone spire added about 1400, 158 ft (48.2 m) in height. The windows in the aisles are varied but mostly renewed; the N and S doorways are EE. The elaborate S porch of ashlar in gothick style is of 1742. At the E end of the N aisle is an attachment built of smooth ashlar: this is the Lambton Pew, dating from 1829. It replaces a larger medieval attachment, of which the arcade of two large bays is visible in the aisle, the W bay blocked, the E bay open only above impost level.

The chancel is aisleless and not particularly long. It too is thirteenth century, and though it has a Victorian E window, two S windows are original, each a lancet-pair with a pierced spandrel. The beautiful triple sedilia have deeply-moulded trefoiled arches resting on quatrefoil shafts. The much-restored piscina goes with them. A large sacristy and organ chamber on the N side are both partly late medieval in their structure.

Chester-le-Street, looking east

Plaster has been removed from the interior, and the roofs are Victorian; it is very dark, with Victorian stained glass. However, most architectural detail is authentic. The chancel fittings are a rich nineteenth-century ensemble; nothing medieval remains. Most remarkable among the contents is the set of recumbent effigies in the N aisle: there are fourteen, and they rest on a continuous plinth extending the length of the aisle, with two at the W end beginning a second row. They all commemorate Lumleys, and are known as the Lumley Warriors; they were assembled about 1594, and are identified by Elizabethan tablets on the wall behind. Five are genuinely medieval (two of these were brought from Durham), but most are Elizabethan, in imitation of medieval effigies: the whole is a remarkable expression of family pride. Elsewhere are a further medieval effigy and a fifteenth-century brass. The font is fine, with a curved concave-octagonal bowl, each face having a shield carrying carved heraldry.

This church has another unusual and interesting feature: in the late fourteenth century the N tower arch was blocked, and the aisle here was converted into a cell for an anchorite, with a room on two levels. It has a very narrow squint aligned on the N aisle altar. After the Reformation, it became an almshouse, with two more rooms added on the N side. It is now an excellent small museum, with Roman relics, fragments of early carved crosses and many other interesting artefacts.

* Darlington

As at Norton and Auckland, it is said that some of the secular canons of Durham came here when that cathedral was made monastic in 1083. More certainly, it was either founded or reconstituted by Bishop Hugh le Puiset (or Pudsey) in the late twelfth century for a vicar and four canons; though often referred to as prebendaries, they were really portioners. The college was in a bad state in the early fifteenth century, when no canons were resident, nor had they provided any deputies. Bishop Neville about 1439 altered the constitution with the intention of correcting these failings; the vicar was given the title dean, and additional endowment was provided for his support. The portions became normal prebends, and canons failing to provide a vicar were to forfeit five marks to the dean. The annual value in 1535 was given as £53, and dissolution is reported not to have taken place until 1550.

The church, dedicated to St Cuthbert, was rebuilt under Bishop le Puiset, probably from about 1190. It is an exceptionally magnificent and noble large

Darlington, from the west

structure, very lofty and of 'great church' character. Its plan is cruciform with a crossing tower and spire. It has a two-storeyed elevation throughout, and is rich but of classic EE perfection and sophistication. The nave is in four bays, with lean-to aisles, while the aisleless chancel has three bays; a low late medieval sacristy is attached to the S side of the chancel. The church is faced both externally and internally with dark grey ashlar; the considerable restoration carried out in the 1860s (which included the windows of the E wall) was generally good. There are only two significant medieval alterations to the EE ensemble, both Dec. The aisle walls were raised, with low-pitched roofs, straight parapets and large two-light square-headed windows; however the rich EE N and S doorways remain, set in shallow projections. The Dec. tower has on each side five two-light arched forms with reticulated tracery, only the central of which is open. Above are shallow battlements with small corner pinnacles and the tall stone spire, which reaches 151 ft (46 m); the spire lost some height and its spire-lights during rebuilding in 1752. Much patching and blocking of windows has been necessary near the crossing in response to problems caused by the weight of the spire. As a great EE structure with a lofty Dec. tower and spire, Darlington is strikingly reminiscent of Salisbury Cathedral, albeit on a much smaller scale.

The exterior has shallow pilaster buttresses, and two string-courses run all round the chancel and transepts. Polygonal turrets flank the chancel and transept ends. The windows are large lancets; many are enriched with shafts and have deep arch mouldings. Internally they have similar enrichments, but many also have shaft-rings, nailhead, dog-tooth and stiff-leaf capitals; one in the chancel rather startlingly has chevron. They are set in shafted blank arcading inside and out. Much of the blob-like nutmeg ornament also appears, for example on the crossing arches. There is considerable variability, and the S transept is noticeably more lavish than its partner. In the nave, the clerestory is of single lancets, and the internal blank arcading is given up after half a bay, though the external continues. Following a rich first bay, the arcades employ relatively simple arches of three large chamfers, with cylindrical or octagonal pillars. Above a very finely moulded and shafted portal in a steeply gabled projection, the W front has two large lancets set in blank arcading; there are square flanking turrets.

The open timber roofs are mostly ancient, but that of the chancel is Victorian, replacing a low-pitched Perp. structure. A large and surprisingly plain stone screen fills the E tower arch, with a central archway; it carries the organ and is a major obstruction. It is late fourteenth century, and must have been intended as reinforcement for the tower. Probably at the same time, the E crossing pillars were crudely covered in thick masonry. The chancel has fine stepped triple sedilia of Dec. workmanship, ogee-trefoiled in a square frame. Opposite is a Perp. Easter Sepulchre recess, with a four-centred arch. There are fine fifteenth-century stalls, eighteen in all, with traceried fronts, heavy poppy-head ends and eleven surviving carved misericords. In the S transept is the plain fourteenth-century octagonal font; above it rises a great spire-like cover, entirely medieval in style although it is of 1662: this is one of the pieces inspired by Bishop Cosin of Durham. Formerly suspended from the roof, it now rests

Darlington, looking east

on a rather startling steel structure of 1972. There is a damaged late-thirteenth-century recumbent effigy. Since the demolition of a power station which formerly adjoined, the church has an attractively spacious and green setting.

* Lanchester

Lanchester is a large village, once a Roman station, lying just outside the industrial area of the county. This was one of Bishop Anthony Bek's three collegiate foundations, established in 1283–4 for a dean and seven prebendaries. Its support came from the revenues of the very large parish. In its constitution, it was almost identical to Chester-le-Street, which had the same numbers; the prebendaries were each to provide a vicar, of whom three were to be priests but the others could be deacons or sub-deacons. The dean was to provide two chaplains or vicars. He had responsibility for the cure of souls, and also had to ensure adequate service at the three chapels in the parish. In 1378 and again in 1418 enquiries by bishops disclosed a bad state of affairs, with an absent dean, no vicars, and the church and buildings decaying. The income of the college in 1535 was given as only £49, but in 1548 as £73. It was dissolved in 1548.

The church is now dedicated to All Saints, but was apparently originally dedicated to St Mary; it is fairly large, and is very unspoilt and interesting. It is mainly of cream-coloured limestone. The W tower is Perp., with short, shallow diagonal buttresses, battlements and small corner pinnacles; inside, it has

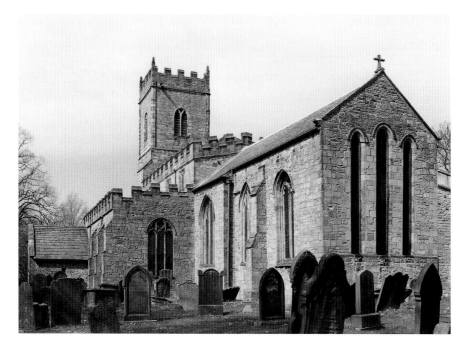

Lanchester, from the south-east

a rib vault. The nave is splendid: tall, with fine uniform arcades of four bays, dating from about 1200. They have slender cylindrical pillars carrying pointed arches of two orders, the inner chamfered, the outer with a keeled roll, under an enriched hood-mould. On the N side the pillars are monolithic to just below their tops, and are almost certainly reused Roman pieces. The aisles and clerestory are externally battlemented, with low-pitched roofs; they have two-light square-headed Perp. windows, those in the aisles very long. There is a S porch with an EE arch, but the twin demishaft responds with cushion capitals are Norman; the segmental arch of the doorway to the church has a zigzag hood-mould and also must be rearranged Norman work. Another reused Norman piece forms a tomb-recess in the S aisle, its depressed round arch heavily loaded with chevron; the top has been shaved off for a window. An early-fourteenth-century recumbent effigy of a priest is here.

The chancel arch is a splendid Norman piece: tall, with three orders of uniform chevron, resting on large shafts carrying cushion capitals and imposts with diaper. The chancel is particularly beautiful. It is EE, as witness its lovely graduated triplet of long E lancets; several further blocked lancets are in the N side. All these lancets have shouldered rere-arches. Also EE is the trefoiled piscina. Alterations were made to the chancel from 1284 for its collegiate function. Two large two-light S windows were put in, and W of them a large three-light window was set in a projection, internally forming a recess for the

Lanchester, looking east

stalls; this recess has a high pointed arch of four big chamfers, curiously set on squinch-like corbels. On the N side a massive low segmental arch, similarly of four chamfers, was provided to open to a new chapel, which is now filled by the organ. E of this chapel is a medieval sacristy, now altered and incorporated in a twentieth-century parish extension. This sacristy is approached by a remarkable and beautiful EE priest's doorway, cinquefoiled, with a tympanum having sophisticated if damaged carvings of Christ and two angels.

Six stalls remain (there were more); they have misericords, though most have been mutilated. The S door is probably thirteenth century, with some original ironwork. The communion rails are restored seventeenth-century work, with knobs. Also perhaps of that century is a beautiful round-topped chest (the 'parish kist'). There are three hatchments. On the W wall is an excellent Royal Arms of 1767, painted on canvas; above this, most unusually, is a clock face, perhaps of the same date (consultation of this by members of the congregation during sermons must be rather obvious!). The excellent plain oak pews are of 1939, by Robert Thompson of Kilburn (well known for the mouse with which he 'signed' his work). In the S porch, together with architectural fragments and four medieval coffin-lids, is a most impressive and perfect Roman altar, with sophisticated decoration and a large inscribed dedication to the goddess Garmangabis.

* Norton

Set in a beautiful, large village which is now a suburb of Stockton-on-Tees, the college belonged to the bishops of Durham. Its foundation date is not known; it was first mentioned in 1227, but this is one of the three churches to which it is suggested that canons came from Durham in 1083, when that cathedral was made monastic. It had a vicar and eight canons, in the presentation of the bishops of Durham; the vicar was head, and the canons were portioners, receiving equal stipends from the tithe of the large parish. The portions were £6 per annum in 1291; they seem later to have been sometimes used for the support of those studying at university. Dissolution took place in 1548. The church, dedicated to St Mary the Virgin, is cruciform with a central tower, but it is not large. Its particular interest is the survival of Anglo-Saxon work: this is principally the tower, but also includes much of the rubble walling of the transepts, and perhaps the walling above the nave arcades. The N and S tower arches are original, unmoulded and without normal capitals, but they are mutilated, a former inner order having probably been removed. This may have been done at the time, around 1190, when larger E and W arches were put in; these are round, with good multiple mouldings including keeled rolls. Internally the tower is open to quite high up, and each side has a large triangular-headed opening, internally shouldered: these were originally doorways opening inside the former high-pitched roofs. Two small round-headed windows higher up each side were external. Above

Norton, from the south-west

these, there are now simple Perp. square-headed openings and battlements.

The present roofs are all low pitched, with battlemented parapets. The nave has arcades of three bays, similar to the E and W tower arches except that they are pointed; they have cylindrical pillars with on the N side moulded capitals but on the S scallops and waterleaf. Above is a string-course and a clerestory of round-arched windows, no doubt of the same date as the arcades (one on the S now has a Perp. replacement), with external flat buttresses. The aisle walls and S porch are of 1876, replacing wider aisles that had been built in 1823; they are battlemented and pinnacled and now have Edwardian windows. Also nineteenth century are the large W window and the S end of the S transept. The chancel is an EE enlargement. Its S and E windows are Perp. or Victorian, but one N lancet remains (now internal), and to the E there are exposed shafts with shaft-rings which belonged to a former lancet group. Details on the S side are strangely mutilated, but there are the remains of sedilia showing fine shafts and dog-tooth. A large attachment housing the organ and vestry is on the N side.

All internal plaster has been stripped, and few old contents remain. There are many twentieth-century furnishings, including excellent oak pews by the 'mouse-man' Robert Thompson. Two old chests are in use. Set on a large modern plinth is a well-preserved recumbent effigy of a knight, with an ogee-trefoiled canopy at his head: this is a fine early-fourteenth-century piece, but its heraldry shows that it was appropriated to someone else in the sixteenth century. Another recumbent effigy is of similar period, and there is a coffin-lid with foliated cross.

Norton, looking east

* Staindrop

Unlike the other colleges in the county, Staindrop was of chantry type. Ralph Neville, 1st Earl of Westmorland, of the great castle of Raby which stands 1 mile from the village, was in 1408 granted licence for its foundation. It had a master, six chaplains and two clerks; however, it also had much of the character of a hospital, since up to eighteen poor or decayed persons, usually former servants of the Nevilles, were also included as brethren. Its annual value in the sixteenth century was given as £126; it was dissolved in 1548. At this time, although there were fewer chaplains and almspeople, it also had two singing men and two choristers.

The village is large and attractive, and the church of St Mary is very impressive. It is also very interesting and mostly authentic, despite some renewal of window tracery and the loss of plaster from the nave and aisles. Roofs are low pitched throughout, with straight parapets. The building history is complicated. The remains of early windows exposed in the nave are regarded as pre-Conquest, but the walls have been cut through by Trans. Norman arcades of round double-chamfered arches on quite slim cylindrical pillars with capitals having varieties of scallops or leaves. They are of four bays, a double respond showing that the W bay is an addition to the early nave. Above is a Perp. clerestory of square-headed windows. The W tower is embraced by the aisles, and stands on noble, slender EE arches. It is large, with a W lancet and little

Staindrop, from the south-east

twin EE openings higher up; above this it is corbelled out for a large Perp. belfry stage, with battlements. A startlingly large square stair turret is at the NW corner.

The church has remarkably broad aisles. The S aisle is clearly the width of a former transept. It was the Lady Chapel, and has fine Dec. windows with reticulated tracery, but its W window is an EE lancet triplet. Its plain Dec. S doorway is covered by a porch vaulted on transverse arches. A trefoiled piscina is in the aisle E wall, near which a door opens to a tiny vaulted sacristy; externally, this sacristy looks like a much-overgrown clasping buttress. The aisle, moreover, has triple sedilia, with fine but damaged trefoiled arches. W of these are two tomb-recesses, one of which has a large crocketed gable and rich Dec. detailing. The N aisle is equally wide, but the transept extends still a little further and has to the N a fine triplet of large equal lancets, internally shouldered. Most windows in this aisle are Perp.

The chancel is of three large bays. It appears mostly Perp., with large three-light arched S windows. However, its structure is basically EE, seen in the chancel arch and the excellent triple stepped sedilia, which have finely moulded trefoiled arches resting on corbels of stiff-leaf. The N side has a very large sacristy with an upper room, forming an impressive block rising the full height of the chancel. Most of its openings are Perp., but its upper level has two lancet windows and a squint towards the altar; it was perhaps occupied by a priest.

Impressive too are the contents. There are twenty-four stalls with misericords, which also have their ancient fronts, with traceried poppy-head ends, and

Staindrop, looking east

their back panelling. They probably date from the foundation of the college. With these goes the screen, which has simple tracery. The font has a concave-octagonal stem and bowl, with blank shields. There is a large medieval chest with heavy ironwork. On the walls are some good memorials, five hatchments, and a helm. At the W end, wrought-iron railings surround a group of exceptionally fine monuments. Outstanding is the alabaster tomb-chest of Ralph Neville, founder of the college, with recumbent effigies of himself and his two wives; it has many fine details. A tomb-chest to an Elizabethan Neville also has three recumbent effigies, but they are of oak, very dark in colour. Two other tomb-chests, also with beautiful recumbent effigies, are nineteenth-century work; one is by Westmacott. Three further effigies in the S aisle are of the thirteenth and fourteenth centuries.

Essex

Only one collegiate church of Essex appears below. Another foundation, at Halstead, never exceeded two chaplains (*see* Appendix IV).

Pleshey

Pleshey is a picturesque village attractively situated in a rural part of Essex, and is interestingly set within the very large circular outer line of fortifications of a castle which is now reduced to earthworks, although these remain impressive. The college was founded in 1394–5 by Thomas of Woodstock, Duke of Gloucester, who was the seventh son of Edward III; Pleshey Castle was his principal residence. The college and its Church of the Holy Trinity were built on a new site; the church also served the parish, the previous parish Church of St Mary being appropriated to the college and demolished. In 1397, the duke was murdered, allegedly on the orders of King Richard II, and his lands, including Pleshey Castle, became forfeit to the Crown. These were the turbulent last years of the Plantagenets, and only two years later, Richard II was deposed. The House of Lancaster in the person of Henry IV came to the throne, and in 1400 Richard was himself probably murdered in Pontefract Castle.

Despite these events, the college continued as planned: it was a substantial chantry foundation for a master and eight chaplains, with two clerks and two boy choristers. The founder's grandson, Humphrey, Duke of Buckingham, who died in 1460, by his will left money for a chapel to be added to the church, and provided endowments to increase the college by three further priests and to support six poor men. These changes may, however, not have been fully implemented. The annual value of the college in 1535 was £139, when there were a master and six chaplains. It was dissolved in 1546, the property going to Sir John Gates, Chancellor of the Duchy of Lancaster. The buildings of the college and the chancel of the church were demolished; the nave is said to have collapsed in the seventeenth century. The church was reconstructed with a new

nave and chancel in about 1720, but what is seen today is the result of a further almost complete rebuilding of the 1860s, for which the architect was Frederick Chancellor. It is of flint and pebble, cruciform with a central tower and windows in geometrical Dec. style; it is lofty though not large, and quite attractive. The tower is fairly tall, with a straight parapet stepping up at the corners; a very obviously Victorian polygonal turret projects from its NE corner, and a curious flying buttress of questionable structural value leans on it at the SE. The side walls of the chancel are windowless.

Internally, too, all appears Victorian, with the exception of the crossing. The N and S crossing arches are quite tall, double-chamfered, with their inner order resting on corbels, while the W arch, also in two orders, is rather lower but is enclosed on its W side within another order which rises higher. These arches are of the original building period; the E arch is Victorian but conforms. Flanking the W arch are two large medieval indents of brasses. A good group of mural memorials can be seen in the chancel, including a large standing memorial of

1758 with two flaming urns and a bust of the deceased. Set in the wall of the N transept is a slab with a large black-letter inscription 'Ricardus Rex II', supposedly a relic of the castle and related to the events there in 1397–9.

Gloucestershire

This county was home to an important and interesting college of canons at Westbury-on-Trym. More modest later colleges were at Bristol and Tormarton.

* Bristol: All Saints

The Guild of Kalendars in Bristol probably existed before the Conquest. In the thirteenth century it was the most important religious guild in the city. The name refers to its practice of holding meetings in church on or near the calends

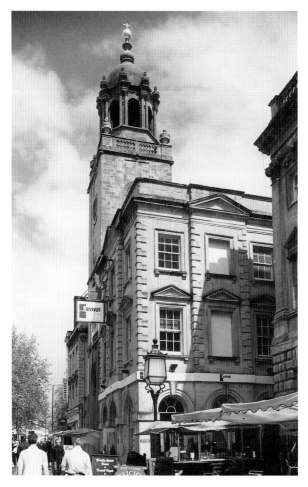

Bristol: All Saints, from the west, showing the successor to the Kalendars' building

(or first day) of each month. From the late twelfth century it used the Church of All Saints. The guild became wealthy, and owned much property. By the 1370s it supported four priests, who maintained the canonical hours and served in the S aisle of the church; the principal priest was head of the guild, and was known as prior. The church, which belonged to the city's abbey of St Augustine (now the cathedral), was not appropriated, but the guild was a welcome guest. The accommodation for the prior and priests was built against the NW corner of the church, and indeed encroached into it. From about 1443, this building was reconstructed, together with much of the N aisle of the church, with further accommodation extending the length of the aisle at a high level. The S aisle was also rebuilt. In the same period, by the initiative of Bishop John Carpenter (also encountered at nearby Westbury-on-Trym), the guild was reorganized. The number of chaplains was reduced by one, but the prior was to be a bachelor of theology or master of arts, with the intention that the Kalendars should play a significant evangelical role in the city. As part of this purpose, the guild acquired the function for which it is best known, providing in its building a public library, open for four hours each weekday. Clergy were probably the intended users. In 1535, the guild's endowment income was £35 5s; it was dissolved in 1548.

This city-centre church is quite large, but it remains remarkably hemmed in by buildings. The Kalendars' building at the NW corner is now represented by a beautiful classical structure of 1782, in three storeys. Similarly occupying the SW corner was the vicar's house, and this remains partly original, though much altered in Elizabethan times. Between these structures appears the large six-light Perp. W window of the church. The nave, which is lofty, is in two very dissimilar parts: it begins with two bays of Norman arcade, having low arches of two unmoulded orders on cylindrical piers with square scalloped capitals. Both aisles here are narrow, with low flat ceilings, above which the adjoining houses still extend; the walls dividing the houses from the church have no openings. The three E bays are large-scale Perp. work, rebuilt after 1443, with arcades of moulded two-centred arches on tall pillars of four shafts and four wave mouldings, the shafts carrying foliage capitals. The chancel arch goes with the arcades. The N aisle (lying along the street) has large four-light windows and much panelling inside and out; the S aisle is plainer, with three-light windows. No trace remains of the former room above this section of the N aisle, thought to have been the library, which was probably of timber.

The lofty, aisleless chancel has been considerably rebuilt, but remains partly Perp.; its N and E sides are hidden by further buildings. It has a rich ensemble of triple sedilia and very large piscina, all with ogee arches, crockets, pinnacles and finials. The E wall is of 1850, and has a curious arrangement of three enriched arches opening to a low vaulted space behind the altar. On the N side stands the tower: it was rebuilt in 1711–16 and is a fine, tall classical structure, in four stages, with a balustrade and corner urns. Its first stage faces the street, with a large blank arch of rusticated masonry. It carries a large octagonal stone cupola, with a dome and gold ball, which has twice been rebuilt.

Bristol: All Saints, looking east

The interior is attractive, though most plaster has been stripped and no medieval fittings remain. There are many large mural memorials; a large and fine standing wall memorial of 1729 has a semi-recumbent effigy by Rysbrack. All Saints is one of the city's redundant churches, but it has found a good alternative use principally as a diocesan resource centre. Most of the nave has bookcases and other office fittings, but the chancel retains its full ecclesiastical furnishings.

Tormarton

The Church of St Mary Magdalene was made collegiate in 1344 by its patron and lord of the manor, John de la Riviere. His foundation was a chantry college for a warden (who had the cure of souls) with four chaplains, two clerks (specified as a deacon and a sub-deacon) and three choristers. In the early fifteenth century, the inadequacy of the endowments led to the number of chaplains being reduced by one. No further history of the college seems to be documented, suggesting that it ceased altogether at some time in the following years.

The church is attractive, of medium size, set in a fine churchyard with many table-tombs. It has Norman origins, as can be seen in the fine chancel arch of three orders, with chevron on its arch and capitals having varieties of scallops. Also Norman is the chancel, as evidenced by the striking external string-course with a large billet motif, but its windows are later. The W tower is of about 1200, internally spacious, with a lancet window each side. Its low pointed

Tormarton, from the south-east

arch to the nave is in three orders, of which the inner rests on capitals of a curious Trans. Norman form. It has two stages and then a recessed Perp. belfry stage with battlements and square-headed two-light openings, of which unusually there are three in the E and W sides. Attached W of the tower is a surprising porch-like attachment, said to have been rebuilt in the seventeenth century; it once had an upper floor, and curiously shows a small blocked doorway in each side. Three two-light reticulated Dec. windows are in the N side of the nave. There is a S aisle, said to have been added for the college; its W window is reticulated, but the others are Perp. The three-bay arcade has pillars of four shafts and four hollows, moulded capitals, and arches of two hollow chamfers. A passage squint opens from the aisle to the chancel, in which medieval image niches flank the Victorian E window.

There is a good polygonal Jacobean pulpit. The font, under the tower, is a distinctive and fine piece of about 1200: its square bowl has scallops on the lower part, where it reduces to rest on a slim stem of complex mouldings. In the chancel are two large indents for brasses, one of which was to John de la Riviere; he was in armour and holding a church. Another brass of 1493 remains intact.

* Westbury-on-Trym

This place is now part of the northern suburbs of Bristol, but it was of ecclesiastical importance before the city existed; it eventually became an important

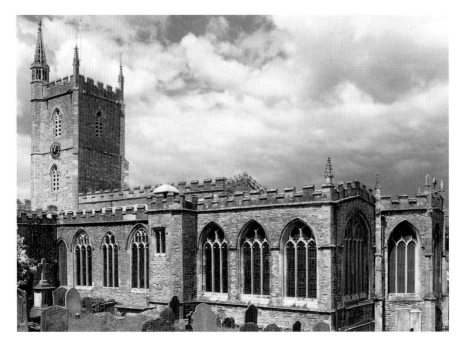

Westbury-on-Trym, from the south-east

college, and has a very interesting history. An early monastery existed here, perhaps founded in 716. About 962, by the initiative of Archbishop (later St) Dunstan, this was reformed under the Benedictine rule, with the aid of monks from the French abbey at Saint-Benoît-sur-Loire. However, in 974, most of the monks moved to Ramsey, and Westbury became less important; it was not even mentioned in the Domesday Survey. In 1093 Bishop Wulfstan of Worcester revived the monastery, which was dedicated to St Mary; however it was altered, perhaps to house secular canons, by his successor Sampson. This period is confused, but it seems that in 1194–5 it was established as a collegiate church of a dean and five canons; at this time the tithe was simply divided so that strictly the canons were portioners. Most canons were soon non-resident, and the church also had four priest vicars and one sub-deacon vicar. From 1286, Bishop Giffard took a great interest in the college and planned to make it a second cathedral of his diocese, with a chapter of secular canons to balance that of monks in the cathedral at Worcester. To this end, he converted nine churches in his patronage into additional prebends of Westbury. However, the scheme was opposed by the prior and monks of Worcester; the quarrel was taken to the king, who supported the Worcester view, and after Giffard's death in 1301 nothing more is heard of this scheme, or of the additional prebends.

This, however, was not the end of the idea. It was revived much later by Bishop Carpenter, who in 1455 reorganized and enlarged the college, rededicated the church to the Holy Trinity, and began to use the title 'Bishop of

Worcester and Westbury'. The reorganization added a sub-dean, to whom was given responsibility for the cure of souls, a treasurer, a schoolmaster to teach grammar, six priests, perhaps with a chantry function, twelve choristers and an almshouse for six men and six women. Bishop Carpenter also added to the church and built new collegiate buildings. However, after his death in 1476, there was no further suggestion of Westbury as a cathedral; indeed, the college was still in existence when the new diocese of Bristol was formed in 1542, but there is no suggestion that Westbury was considered. The college was dissolved in 1544, when its annual value was given as £232.

The church is impressive and very engaging; it is large but by no means uniform, and it must be said that none of it approaches cathedral stature. It has a W tower, a nave with broad aisles, and a chancel flanked by chapels; the roofs are low pitched and there are battlements throughout. Windows are mostly Perp., large, with tracery. Substantial EE work remains, however. Externally this is seen mainly in the S aisle, which is especially broad and has as its W window a fine large triplet of lancets. Its S doorway (much renewed) has two orders of shafts, stiff-leaf capitals and an arch of rich mouldings; there is a large trefoiled recess above. This aisle has stepped triple sedilia, with deeply moulded EE arches on broadly filleted shafts, also a large EE piscina, now impossibly high up. Both nave arcades are of this period, in three large bays, with double-chamfered arches on cylindrical pillars. On the S they have octagonal imposts and some charming, sparing stiff-leaf decoration; the N arcade is a little

Westbury-on-Trym, looking east

later, with slimmer pillars and circular moulded capitals. Also EE is the chancel arch.

All else is Perp., but of several campaigns. The tower is tall, in four stages, with diagonal buttresses, battlements, corner pinnacles and two image niches; its polygonal stair turret was in 1851 given a very distinctive openwork top carrying an openwork spirelet. There is a S porch, originally with an upper floor accessed by a square battlemented stair turret on its W side. The N aisle wall is Perp., and extends W to embrace the tower. Above the nave arcades is a clerestory of two windows per bay; its last windows before the chancel arch are much larger, no doubt to light the rood.

The E limb is set S of the axis of the nave, and droops yet further S. Its most distinctive feature is a polygonal apse (very occasionally adopted in the Perp. period), with pinnacles and buttresses with relief pinnacles; internally it has a real nobility of effect. The two-bay N chapel is shorter than the chancel, with an arcade of two-centred arches on pillars of four shafts and four waves. At its junction with the aisle is a square rood-stair turret. The S chapel is of three bays, later and markedly loftier than its partner; its very tall arcade has depressed four-centred arches. At its W end it too has a square projection for a rood stair, in this case particularly large and with exits in two different positions.

Hardly any medieval contents remain. There are many mural memorials. Between the sanctuary and the S chapel is a tomb-chest in good Perp. style, with openwork sides; this is of 1853, but contains the original cadaver effigy of Bishop Carpenter. The collegiate buildings due to him survive in part, 100 yd away in College Road. They originally formed a quadrangle, but much was lost when they were burnt in the Civil War. Still intact is its four-storeyed gatehouse, battlemented, with a passage rib-vaulted in two bays. Attached to this is a mainly Georgian block, but two circular corner turrets of the former quadrangle survive, with ogee stone tops giving a surprising and distinctive character. The building was vested in the National Trust in 1907, and is now mostly used as a parish centre.

Hampshire

All of Hampshire's three very different colleges were situated in or near to Winchester, and all were founded by bishops. Two have disappeared, but the great academic college of St Mary at Winchester continues as an outstanding institution.

Marwell

Founded by the famous Bishop of Winchester Henry de Blois at some time during his long episcopate (1129–71), the college of Marwell is remembered mainly as the first college that, in both purpose and organization, was of chantry type. Dedicated to SS. Stephen, Lawrence, Vincent and Quintin, it was a small non-parochial college for four priests, who were each to receive a stipend of 60s (£3) annually. The priests were to be permanently resident and to pray continuously for the souls of the king, the bishop of Winchester, other benefactors and all faithful Christians, both living and dead. A new charter was given in 1226 by Bishop Peter des Roches, in which a deacon was added to the college; the priests were now each year to elect one of their number as head, with the title of prior. As time went on, the value of the endowments declined, and in 1535 there were only two priests, supported by an income of £12. Dissolution took place in 1548.

Also established here by Henry de Blois was a substantial residence for the bishops. The large moated site is now Marwell Manor Farm; the farmhouse is mainly of post-Reformation construction, but it incorporates some medieval walling with a few minor features: these are possibly remains of the college. Nothing is known of the site or nature of the chapel, though the fact that William of Wykeham once conducted sixty ordinations here in one day might suggest that it was large.

Winchester: St Elizabeth's College

This college was founded in 1301 by Bishop John of Pontoise; building was begun in 1302, the chapel being completed in 1304. It was a chantry college for a provost and six chaplains, with three deacons, three sub-deacons and seven boy choristers; it was a substantial foundation, with an annual value in 1535 of £112. The dedication was to St Elizabeth of Hungary. Its site was in the water meadows immediately outside the gates of the bishop's castle of Wolvesey; it thus stood just E or SE of the location where, about eighty years after its establishment, the College of St Mary was built. Within its precinct and among the property appropriated to it on its foundation was a church of St Stephen; this remained in use, but the college conducted its services in its own chapel of St Elizabeth. After the establishment of the College of St Mary, a few commoners from there lodged in St Elizabeth's College. Dissolution took place in March 1544, and the site was granted to Thomas Wriothesley, who shortly afterwards sold it for £360 to St Mary's College. Its chapel contained three altars and considering the size of the college was probably substantial. However, together with the other college buildings and the church of St Stephen, it has vanished completely; the site is mostly meadow and has not been excavated.

* Winchester: St Mary's College (*now Winchester College*)

The foundation of this famous academic college was due to William of Wykeham, twice Chancellor of England and Bishop of Winchester from 1367 to 1404. He was also the founder of New College, Oxford, and he conceived the two colleges together as a comprehensive scheme for the education of boys intended for the priesthood, who would enter Winchester aged between eight and twelve and then pass on to Oxford. This dual foundation was a very important innovation; moreover, the scale and the meticulous planning of the two colleges had not been approached by any previous academic foundation. Wykeham had first begun a school in Winchester in 1373, but after this he fell into disgrace under Edward III. With the accession of Richard II he returned to favour, and there were scholars here again by 1379; the foundation of the college is usually dated to the royal licence of 1382. The site was obtained and building began in 1387; the college was opened in 1394 and the buildings were completed in about 1402.

The foundation was for a warden and ten priests known as fellows, with seventy poor scholars. At the beginning up to ten commoners were also admitted: these were boys from more wealthy backgrounds whose families paid for their education, and unlike the scholars they were expected to find accommodation outside. A remarkable aspect of the college today is that the number of scholars has remained unchanged (though the nature of the requirements and the significance of the scholarships have inevitably altered), whereas the number of commoners has greatly increased. Also part of the establishment

Winchester College: the chapel, from the south-east

were three chaplains, three clerks and sixteen boy choristers: alongside the educational aspect of the foundation, it also fully maintained the function of a chantry college, the statutes requiring the daily maintenance of the canonical hours and the saying of masses for the dead. This function was an important part of the work of the fellows, and also required the choristers and others; the scholars and commoners, however, were only obliged to attend chapel on Sundays and feast days. The musical aspect has continued, and today there are still sixteen boy choristers, known as 'quiristers'.

The chapel forms the E part of the S side of Chamber Court, with the hall continuing the same roof line to its W. It is a lofty, aisleless rectangle six bays in length, of fine ashlared limestone, with deep buttresses, a straight parapet and large transomed windows of three lights under two-centred arches. The E window has seven lights, and the gable above is crowned by a large pinnacle containing an image niche, now empty. At the W end is a passage or antechapel, approached from the court through doors of glass and metal dated 1966, and opening to the chapel by a large doorway which has its excellent original doors. Internally the chapel windows have attached shafts and moulded rere-arches. Two windows at the NE are blank, since the E side of the court abuts here, with a tower of three storeys, the lowest a vaulted sacristy; a polygonal stair turret here rises higher to a battlemented top. The chapel is covered by its original vault of timber, which in its design approaches the fan form. Originally a tower with a timber spire stood at

Winchester College: the chapel, looking east

the SW corner. This was demolished and in its place was constructed, mainly in 1473–85, a fine two-bay chapel, Thurburn's Chantry, covered by an excellent tierceron vault of stone with good bosses; above its W bay was built a tall and beautiful tower, with angle buttresses, a straight openwork parapet, panelled corner pinnacles and square-headed openings throughout. From the first this tower gave trouble, and it was rebuilt from the foundations in 1862–3, reusing most of the original stones and adhering largely but not completely to the original design.

In 1680–1 the chapel was lavishly refitted, with splendid classical panelling; this was removed in 1874, and only the sumptuous altar rails remain. Restoration work by Butterfield in 1874 included the reinstatement of the very rich triple canopied sedilia and the elaborate reredos which had been added about 1470, both of which had been hacked away for the panelling. The present furnishings of the chapel are excellent early-twentieth-century work and include a W gallery, high oak panelling and pews with carved ends and armrests. The stalls are partly original and have nineteen misericords, with interesting carvings. Until 1822–3 the chapel retained a remarkably complete original scheme of glazing; but now it is almost all a copy dating from those years, though even as such it is fine. Some original pieces have been recovered and are in Thurburn's Chantry and elsewhere. In the floor of the E part are what appear to be six fine and exceptionally well-preserved late medieval brasses. They are not entirely what they seem, however; the originals were lost, and they were reinstated in 1882 from rubbings made long before.

The original college buildings remain complete and little altered, arranged around two courts. Also dating from the original construction is a beautiful cloister with fine traceried openings and high wagon roofs, not directly attached to the other buildings; it contains many memorials. In the centre of the cloister stands a battlemented building in two storeys of which the lower level is another chapel, Fromond's Chantry, vaulted in two bays; this was built about 1430. The college has grown greatly in post-medieval times and has spread mainly to the SW, with many buildings of the seventeenth century and later.

Herefordshire

Herefordshire had no true collegiate church, but contained the two significant portionary churches of Ledbury (*see* Appendix IV) and Bromyard. The county's finest medieval college is the vicars' college at Hereford (*see* Appendix I).

* Bromyard

A record of about 840 indicates the early presence of a minster here. In Domesday Book, two priests and a chaplain are stated to have held land at Bromyard. This situation continued, and in 1384, an inquiry ordered by the bishop found that the church had three portioners and a vicar, the last having

Bromyard, from the south-east

responsibility for the cure of souls. The portions were stated to be equal shares: this was a classic example of a church of portioners. Its portions survived the sixteenth century, and were only abolished in the Victorian era.

The Church of St Peter is large and cruciform, with central tower. It is attractive and likeable, though most of its architecture is modest. Its origins are late Norman, and its finest features are the well-preserved N and S doorways, which are both reset in the walls of the aisles added probably quite soon after their original construction. That to the S is in three orders, with shafts, good capitals and an arch having motifs including orthogonal chevron; a patterned tympanum has been largely cut away. Above it is a panel with an excellently preserved carving of St Peter, with book and keys: its date is uncertain but it is probably eleventh century, either before or after the Conquest. The N doorway is comparable, but its tympanum is a restoration. A smaller doorway in the N transept, in two orders, is of similar character and has its tympanum complete.

The external surfaces are largely of rubble masonry in the local sandstone, and much of the interior has been stripped of its plaster. Most of the church was rebuilt or remodelled in the early fourteenth century, with modest windows of intersecting or Y-tracery. The chancel is aisleless and quite long. There were quite extensive alterations in 1805, in which the cylindrical pillars of the nave were made taller, though the other features of the arcades seem to remain largely authentic. They are of five bays and both have pointed arches: the S arcade is of about 1200, with sophisticated scalloped capitals, octagonal imposts and arches

Bromyard, looking east

of two unmoulded orders, while the N is rather later and has double-chamfered arches on quatrefoil imposts with stiff-leaf capitals. The aisles are of the same width as the transepts; they and the nave have plain plaster ceilings with very large coves, no doubt in their present form dating from 1805. The crossing arches are Dec., of two chamfered orders; with these goes the battlemented tower, which is mainly distinctive for its taller battlemented circular stair turret.

The church has an unusually large number of arched tomb-recesses, mostly Dec.; there are six inside and another two outside. None contains a tomb. The excellent circular font is Norman, with decoration arranged in two bands; its cylindrical stem is a replacement. The attractive Victorian pulpit incorporates some eighteenth-century work. A curiosity is the 'Bromyard Bushel', a circular bronze tub on four feet, of 1670.

Hertfordshire

The county's one collegiate church is a modest example.

Stanstead St Margaret's

Anciently known as the Church of St Margaret, Thele, but now dedicated to St Mary the Virgin, this church has the smallest parish in Hertfordshire; in the early fourteenth century it was said to offer so poor a living that hardly any priest would accept it. Its patron, Sir William Goldington, determined to resolve this and do more, and in 1316 he established a chantry college of a warden and four chaplains, to celebrate at the altar of St Mary in the church; the church was appropriated to the college. In addition to land and property, the endowments included the church of Aldham in Essex. Despite some further endowments in subsequent years, it seems that the property was not well managed, and by the early fifteenth century the college supported only one priest. In 1431 licence was granted by Henry VI to the Bishop of London for its dissolution, and the transfer of its remaining endowments to the hospital of Elsing Spital in London; the hospital was to provide two regular canons to maintain religious life at Thele.

This is a charming church, but for one of collegiate status it is remarkably small, consisting of a nave and chancel without structural division. The exterior is of rubble masonry, with some remains of old rendering; its early origin may be seen in a small blocked Norman window on the S side. An aisle and chapel added along the N side for the college have been demolished, but three blocked arches which opened to them are visible outside; a fourth arch W of these is not now visible. The church was remodelled as well as extended when the college was established; most striking is the fine Dec. E window, which is of four lights, with complicated curvilinear tracery. The S side has two-light reticulated windows and an entrance doorway with good Dec. continuous mouldings; but

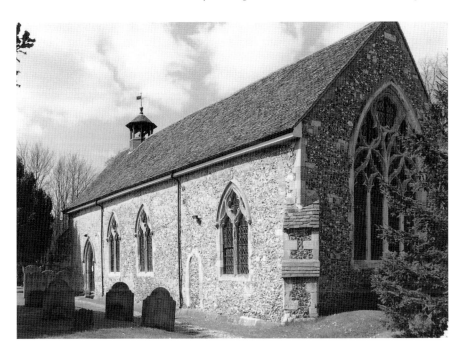

Stanstead St Margaret's, from the south-east

the W window is Victorian and the Y-tracery windows in the N side, set in the blocking of the arcade, are probably early nineteenth century. Over the W end is a tiny octagonal open belfry of timber.

Much of the attractiveness of the interior is due to a refitting of about 1810. This provided oak box pews, plain with curved corners; corresponding panelling runs round the walls. The modestly Gothic oak pulpit is perhaps rather later. There is a W gallery, with good classical panelling on its front; it contains more contemporary seating and a small organ of about 1830 in a very attractive mahogany case of gothick design, which is equipped as a barrel organ and has fourteen barrels. Each end of the N side has a small early-nineteenth-century attachment, the E one a vestry, the W one containing the gallery stairs. The church has a plaster barrel ceiling, but shows its ancient tie-beams and crown-posts. Tall ogee-cinquefoiled image niches flank the E window. Set up against the wall is a large tomb slab with worn foliated cross and part of an inscription.

Huntingdonshire (*now part of Cambridgeshire*)

This small county had no medieval college.

Isle of Wight

The Isle of Wight had no medieval college, though there was an interesting marginal establishment at Barton (*see* Appendix IV).

Kent

Following the unsuccessful attempt of the archbishops of Canterbury to establish a major college at Hackington (*see* Appendix IV), they did later found a college of canons at Wingham. The remaining six colleges of Kent were all of chantry type, forming an attractive and varied series; that of Maidstone has a very large church, while the small college of Bredgar was of unusual character.

* Ashford

In 1467, Sir John Fogge, lord of the nearby manor of Repton, obtained licence from the king to found in the parish Church of St Mary a chantry college for a master, two chaplains, and two clerks. Being already appropriated to Horton Priory a few miles away, the church could not be appropriated to the college. Sir John was responsible for much rebuilding of the church, which now appears as a mainly Perp. structure. He was a prominent figure and had served Henry VI, but later took part in the uprising against him that put Edward IV on the throne. He was subsequently involved in an unsuccessful attempt to overthrow Richard III, and was impeached and deprived of his possessions. He returned to favour under Henry VII (crowned 1485), but, perhaps as a result of these fluctuations of fortune, it is not clear that the college was established as planned. Its third master is mentioned in 1503, so it achieved some existence; but it seems to have ceased soon after.

The church is stately and large, and externally appears uniform, with three-light windows under depressed pointed-segmental arches as its characteristic feature. In fact almost the whole exterior of the W part is Victorian, matching the old work and in its stonework now deceptively worn: the aisles were rebuilt in 1837 almost to double their original width, and the whole was in 1860 extended W by one bay. The plan is cruciform; chapels of full height flank the chancel, and the transepts have E aisles: all these are battlemented. The large E window has five lights and is transomed; beneath it outside is a niche containing a worn seated figure, probably the Trinity. Some earlier rubble masonry is visible in the W walls of the transepts, the S one showing a

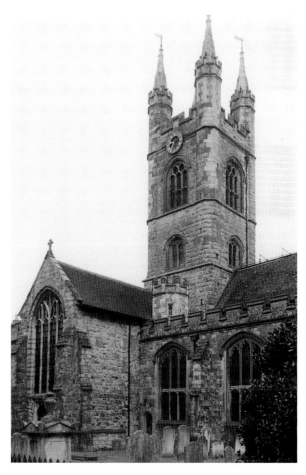

Ashford, from the north-west

blocked window of ogee form. Rising two tall stages above the roofs, the impressive crossing tower is 120 ft (36.6 m) high. Its belfry openings are of three lights and transomed, and it has polygonal angle buttresses which continue above the battlements as massive and tall pinnacles.

The interior is dark but makes a fine impression. All the arcades are similar: tall and quite slender, with double-chamfered arches on cylindrical pillars, probably fourteenth century throughout. There are three bays to the chancel, three to the transepts and three old bays to the nave. The axis of the chancel deviates to the N. The tall crossing arches are of obviously Perp. type, though they probably encase earlier work. A striking barrel ceiling of moulded plasterwork covers the nave; the plasterwork continues high on the wall above the W crossing arch, where it is dated 1638. There are a W gallery and galleries in the aisles, standing well back behind the arcades; their attractive panelled fronts are seventeenth and eighteenth century. The stalls are partly ancient, with fourteen original misericords, mostly with foliage designs; two more are Victorian. On the walls are a fine moulded Royal Arms of Charles II and many good memorials. The Perp. font is concave-octagonal in plan, its bowl ornamented with quatrefoils. There is an iron-bound medieval chest with a round top. On the N side of the sanctuary is the large and very fine tomb-chest of Sir John Fogge, who died in 1490; though damaged, its top retains part of its brass. Nearby is his large helm. There are several other medieval brasses, most notably a beautiful effigy of a lady, of about 1375. Especially rich in monuments

Ashford: the south transept

is the S transept, which has three major Elizabethan and Jacobean standing wall memorials, enclosed by their original iron railings.

The churchyard stands most attractively in a compact square, with old houses all round. In the SE corner is a timber-framed house known as The College: this is indeed part of the building erected for the college in the fifteenth century, and is today the vicarage.

Bredgar

This interesting small chantry college of the Holy Trinity had an apparently unique constitution, in that an important part of its purpose was the education of two of its members. It was founded in 1392–3 by Robert de Bredgare, with others, to serve in the Church of St John the Baptist, which was not appropriated. It was to consist of a chaplain master and two clerk scholars; the latter were to be studying for the priesthood, taking the order of sub-deacon in their twentieth year, and were not permitted to remain beyond the age of twenty-four. From 1398, two further clerk scholars were maintained on behalf of the college in the almonry school at Canterbury Cathedral. At the Valor of 1535, the annual value was given as £27; the college had been dissolved by 1542.

Much of the attractive church is of the Perp. remodelling carried out on the establishment of the college, though in size it is no more than a typical village church. It is externally mostly of knapped flint. The W tower has a modest

Bredgar, from the south-east

Norman W doorway, of two orders, with orthogonal chevron. Otherwise the tower appears later; it is unbuttressed, in three stages, with battlements and a polygonal stair turret at the SE corner. The nave is aisled and the chancel is flanked by single-bay chapels; the S aisle is fairly narrow and has a low-pitched roof, while the broader N aisle has a high-pitched roof, internally showing its very rough crown-post trusses. Other roofs are old too, and most are ceiled. The nave has three-bay Perp. arcades with arches of two hollow chamfers resting on octagonal pillars; the chancel arch and the arches from the chancel to the chapels conform. There is a Victorian S porch. The windows are Perp. except for a few of the Dec. period in the N aisle. In the S wall is the rood stair, which is externally half-octagonal and continues as a surprisingly tall battlemented turret. The N chapel was used by the college.

In the tower arch is an attractive seventeenth-century screen with thick balusters, and in the tower are two large framed benefaction texts and a ringers' rhyme of 1751. There are two hatchments, an enormous Royal Arms on canvas and a small brass to Thomas Coly, master of the college, who died in 1518. Among several worthy mural memorials, one of 1618 has Corinthian columns and obelisks. Just a few fragments of medieval glass survived the wartime explosion of a flying bomb nearby.

A hundred yards to the NW, on the opposite side of the road, the domestic accommodation of the college remains complete, and is known as Chantry House. Formerly divided into four small cottages, it was restored about 1973 as a very beautiful single house. It is a long, relatively narrow building of flint, in two storeys; the main alteration has been the eighteenth-century modernization of most window openings.

* Cobham

This is a notable and very attractive example of a chantry college, still complete with its buildings alongside the church. It is therefore the more surprising to realize that, when Sir John de Cobham, 3rd Baron Cobham, obtained the royal licence in 1362 and founded the college, the parish Church of St Mary Magdalene was not appropriated, and this remained the case. Other churches were appropriated as part of its endowments, which were successively increased until in 1389 there were a master and ten chaplains, six more than planned in 1362. The annual value in 1535 was £128. It was dissolved earlier than most, in 1539, by voluntary surrender approved by Act of Parliament, to George, 9th Baron Cobham, descendant of the founder. This, however, was not the end of the life of this college. His son William, 10th baron, who died in 1596, by his will gave the collegiate buildings together with materials and endowments for the founding of an almshouse for the accommodation of twenty poor persons, to be called the New College of Cobham. This was established in 1598, and still exists today.

The church is partly EE and partly of Perp. work dating from the foundation of the college. It is large, with an internal length of 128 ft (39 m), but

Cobham: the church tower seen from the courtyard of the college

its external appearance is less impressive than might be expected, partly because of its low-pitched roofs hidden behind straight parapets. The chancel is especially large, but preceded the college: it is a pure EE structure, five bays long and very broad, with large regular lancet windows in the side walls and three equal lancets to the E. Externally the side lancets are outlined by a slim roll. Internally, a string-course runs round, the lancets are all shafted and the side ones have linked hood-moulds. A large damaged double piscina with twin trefoiled arches and much dog-tooth is original but not *in situ*, having been reassembled from its pieces. In its former position is now a Perp. piscina of the most lavish richness, with much delicate canopy work. Of almost equally rich Perp. work are the tall triple sedilia. Near the SE corner are the remains of a spiral staircase, a curious feature which may have led to a loft above a reredos. The large chancel arch is Victorian, replacing a smaller predecessor.

The nave, though wide, is less so than the chancel; it has four-bay EE arcades, with arches mostly of two hollow chamfers on cylindrical pillars. Above is a small Perp. clerestory (externally invisible from ground level). Both aisles are broad, that on the N particularly so; they have Perp. windows, mostly square-headed and traceried. Also Perp. is the W tower, in four short stages, with angle buttresses, battlements and a higher polygonal stair turret. It is embraced by the aisles, and internally has tall arches on three sides. Entry is through a two-storeyed N porch with a quadripartite rib vault.

Cobham: the chancel, looking west

The fame of this church lies in its collection of medieval brasses, perhaps the finest anywhere. They are mostly fourteenth and fifteenth century, and fifteen of them form a spectacular group in the centre of the chancel floor, with a few more close by. They are in excellent condition, partly the result of careful nineteenth-century restoration; one is to the founder of the college, and is believed to have been laid down in 1367, although he did not die until 1407 at the age of 92. Most brasses commemorate members of the Cobham family, but three are to masters of the college. The chancel resembles a museum, since the whole central area is normally roped off for the preservation of the brasses. Moreover, directly in front of the altar is the exceptionally lavish tomb-chest of the 9th Baron Cobham, erected in 1561, with fluted Ionic columns and recumbent alabaster effigies of himself and his wife Anne. It is surrounded by medieval tiles. Other ancient contents of the chancel include eighteen stalls, very much renewed and retaining only one misericord, and four helms mounted on hooks (now repre-sented by copies, the originals being in the Tower of London). The font is EE. Part of the former rood screen now surrounds a vestry area in the N aisle.

S of the church, separated from it only by a passage 2 or 3 yd wide, stand the college buildings, constructed around a rectangular courtyard. The hall and the outer walls are largely original, but most windows and the walls facing the courtyard are of 1597–8. There are the remains of former connections to the church. Further S are ruins of the medieval kitchen, which was part of a second quadrangle. The accommodation was internally much modernized in

1981 to form thirteen self-contained flats, and close by is a group of sixteen further flats completed in 1994.

* Maidstone

The Church of St Mary at Maidstone was important before the Conquest. During the late-twelfth-century episodes in which the archbishops of Canterbury attempted to establish a great collegiate church at Hackington or Lambeth (*see* Appendix IV), Archbishop Walter at one stage considered founding it at Maidstone; but nothing came of this. Later, in 1239, Archbishop Edmund Rich attempted the foundation of a college for fifty canons at Maidstone; but this too was thwarted. It was not until 1395 that Archbishop Courtenay obtained papal and royal licences to found here a chantry college for a master, twelve chaplains and twelve clerks. It was established in 1396, and approval was given for it to absorb the thirteenth-century Hospital of SS Peter and Paul, which had originally supported ten poor, but latterly only had five. The foundation was

Maidstone, from the
south-east

confirmed by the pope in 1398, after the archbishop's death, when his executors stated that the full staff had already been appointed. The parish church was completely rebuilt, presumably on the earlier site, and was rededicated to All Saints. Building continued into the fifteenth century. At a visitation in 1511, there were apparently only a master, sub-master and five fellows, together with some clerks. The net annual income in 1535 was given as £159 7s 10d. Five poor were still supported by the hospital function. The college was dissolved in 1547; it was purchased in 1549 for £1,082 by George Brooke, Baron Cobham.

This is a major church, consistent throughout and on a very large scale, though remarkable for its breadth rather than its height. Externally, it is mostly battlemented, but it is quiet and without display. The large tower forms the S porch; it is in three stages with big angle buttresses, battlements and a higher polygonal turret. It carried a timber spire until this was brought down by lightning in 1730. Inside, it shows springers for a vault which was removed in the seventeenth century to allow bells to be raised. There is a N porch of 1927.

The nave has six bays, with exceptionally broad aisles; the fairly low-pitched roofs are good work of about 1886 by Pearson. Windows are arched and traceried, those of the aisles having four lights while the main W window has six. The tall arcade pillars are of a complex section having shafts in the E–W direction, which alone carry capitals; the arches are two-centred. Above is a clerestory of modest square-headed windows. The N aisle has a tall battlemented rood-stair turret, but curiously it is one bay W of the site of the screen. There is a very broad chancel arch, and the chancel continues at the same height, with arched clerestory windows. It is of three bays, which are larger than those of the nave; its aisles are less than half the width of the nave aisles, but their windows have five lights. On the S side is a two-storeyed medieval sacristy.

In the sanctuary bay of the S chancel arcade is a splendid free-standing composition in five parts, four being sedilia and one a double piscina. Each section is vaulted, and the central three carry elaborate crocketed spirelets. The back of the structure, facing the aisle, has a vaulted recess with the tomb of John Wotton, the first master, who died in 1417; the tomb may have preceded the structure above. The recess retains much painting. There are parclose screens mostly of the nineteenth century, but one bay is medieval, with coving. The E window is largely obstructed by a tall early-twentieth-century stone reredos. In the centre of the chancel floor is the indent of the very large brass of the founder; originally it was on his tomb-chest in this position. Still in place and very authentic are most of the fine stalls, with stall-fronts and poppy-head ends: there are eighteen, with carved misericords. However, the Victorian chancel screen has been removed to the W end of the N aisle, taking with it the six ancient return stalls, but these are in poor condition and lack their misericords. The octagonal font is Jacobean. A notable seventeenth-century monument has four life-size standing figures in their shrouds, and close to it a large marble table. There are some very good mural memorials and many benefaction boards. Late-nineteenth-century painting covers the chancel walls.

Maidstone, looking east

To the S, large parts of the collegiate buildings survive and are among the most impressive in existence. Most prominent is the massive, rectangular gatehouse, with a broad vaulted passage. Running W from this is a fine two-storeyed range, which includes the refectory and, on the upper floor, four priests' rooms; it ends in a battlemented tower above the river. Further buildings run S from here, a good deal altered, with a large block which was probably the master's house. A wooden cloister walk connected these parts. Still further S are more remains, including another gatehouse. The church and these buildings are only part of a remarkable medieval group, for N of the church much remains of the former archbishop's palace, now used for civic purposes. Across the road, the former stables of the palace are now a museum.

* Ulcombe

At the request of its patron, Ralph St Leger, a small college was founded in the Church of All Saints in about 1215–20 by the Archbishop of Canterbury, Stephen Langton. The college was for an archpriest, two canons, a deacon and a clerk; it was an early example of a chantry college. It ceased before the end of the medieval era, though the date is uncertain. The church is quite large, of ragstone rubble; it is irregular in its plan, but the E part of the chancel is a fine extension dating from the establishment of the college. It is set high on a ridge, and close to the N side stands Ulcombe Place, which incorporates the much-altered domestic accommodation of the college.

The W tower is modest, in three stages, with diagonal buttresses, battlements and a higher polygonal stair turret; it has Perp. features. The nave has a S aisle under a low-pitched roof, continuing as a S chapel. A Perp. S porch with small side windows covers a Dec. doorway, containing its ancient door. On the N side are an aisle and chapel, but the aisle extends along only the E part of the nave; windows here are mostly straight-headed Perp. work, but the E window of the chapel is a graduated triplet of lancets. Most other windows in the church are Dec., some with reticulated tracery.

The nave has a S arcade of three bays, and on the N side a single similar arch: both are of perhaps 1200, with pointed slightly chamfered arches, undercut imposts and slightly chamfered rectangular pillars and responds. These pillars must be pieces of pre-existing wall cut through by the arches; three blocked Norman windows are exposed in the N side. Also in the N side is a rood stair. The S chapel has a two-bay arcade which is probably a little earlier than the nave arcades, with unmoulded pointed arches and a thick, short cylindrical pier with a scalloped capital. In contrast, its partner on the N is elegant late Perp. work, also of two bays, with finely moulded four-centred arches on a slim pillar of four shafts and four hollows. The EE sanctuary extends one bay further, its side walls internally enriched by a large blank arch with a hood-mould. Its E wall has a large graduated triplet of lancets, with

Ulcombe, looking east

bold shafts and shaft-rings, deeply moulded rere-arches and unusual circular flowers set in a hollow of the mouldings. Also unusual are the two broad segmental recesses below this window, one containing a piscina basin.

The arch to the N aisle has striking remains of painted decoration contemporary with its construction, mainly big zigzags in red, yellow and black; there are also red lines imitating ashlar. On the S arcade, several painted scenes include two thirteenth-century crucifixions, rather decayed but still beautiful in their mellow colour. A mutilated crag of masonry on the E respond is interpreted as a hacked-away statue. Both chancel arcades contain well-preserved parclose screens: that on the N is late, and has linenfold panelling, while that on the S is Dec., with mouchette wheels in its tracery. Against the latter are five stalls with misericords, three of them carved. In the N chapel are three medieval tomb-chests: two are plain, but the third carries a brass of a knight under a canopy, dated 1419. Another worthy memorial is a brass of 1470 to a knight and his lady; he was a St Leger.

* Wingham

The Church of St Mary the Virgin was made collegiate in 1287 by Archbishop John Pecham of Canterbury, completing a process begun in 1273 by his predecessor Robert Kilwardby. The delay was caused by the resistance of the existing rector, whose agreement Kilwardby had failed to secure. Pecham finally obtained arbitration at the papal court, which allowed the foundation to go ahead. Kilwardby had intended a provost and ten canons, but it was now for a provost and six canons, who were two each of priests, deacons and sub-deacons. Their prebends were derived from the tithe of the very large parish, which had previously supported four portioners. Residence was not obligatory, and from the first the canons were expected to appoint vicars to take their places in choir. At a visitation by Archbishop Warham in 1511, many irregularities were found, and there were only four vicars. The college was dissolved in 1547, its annual value shortly before being given as £170. A canon, John Haile, who objected to the king's divorce from Catherine of Aragon, was executed at Tyburn in 1535 for 'maliciously slandering the king'; and in the reign of Mary, John Blande, a former canon, was burnt at Canterbury for his Protestant beliefs: so Wingham has the sad distinction of canons having been both Catholic and Protestant martyrs.

The church is impressively large and dignified, though alterations have left it irregular and given it the surprising feature of a timber arcade. It has a nave and S aisle of equal width, which were largely rebuilt in the mid-sixteenth century; both have crown-post roofs, and between them are five bays of plain, tall octagonal timber posts, with small braces at their tops. The S side has regular untraceried three-light windows under depressed arches. There is a battlemented S porch with two-light side windows; it formerly had an upper room. The early Perp. W tower of flint and rubble has angle buttresses, battlements and a quite tall recessed timber spire.

Wingham, from the south-west

Wingham, looking east

The chancel, taller than the nave, is impressive and spacious late-thirteenth-century work dating from the foundation of the college, with windows of early Dec. tracery; but the chancel arch and E window are Victorian. A string-course runs round its interior, and there are triple sedilia with shafts and round arches, set very low. A single large arch with rich mouldings opens each side, on the S to a large chapel or transept of the same period, with a fine three-light E window set in a projection of the wall. Its very large S window has shafts and deep mouldings, but is partly blocked in perhaps seventeenth-century brickwork, containing a smaller Perp. window. Its acutely pointed W arch is of about 1200. The corresponding N chapel has been rebuilt longer, perhaps in the eighteenth century, with a hipped roof; one of its N windows has three wooden mullions while the other is of Venetian type. Externally this chapel has much patching and buttressing in brick, and its W wall shows a blocked arch similar to that on the S side. The nave has lost a N aisle, as shown also by an external piscina, of good Dec. design.

The chancel contains fourteen stalls with carved misericords, though only seven of the latter are old. Part of the base of the screen remains *in situ*, with Perp. tracery. A rare possession is the reredos, a large stone panel with two tiers of scenes in relief, including the Last Supper: it was given in 1934 and is thought to be fifteenth-century French work. The S chapel has very fine late-seventeenth-century wrought-iron screens, going with the very large and splendid memorial of 1682 in the form of a square pedestal which stands in the centre; its corners are enriched with scrolls, heads of oxen and cherubs, and it is crowned by an obelisk with garlands of fruit. There are several more fine memorials on the walls here, and more in the N chapel, now used for the organ and vestry.

SE of the church, three fine timber-framed houses in a row were canons' houses; they seem to be mostly of the fifteenth century.

* Wye

John Kempe was born in the parish of Wye in 1380. He rose to be Archbishop of York, and it was as such that in 1432 he obtained licence from Henry VI to found a chantry college in the Church of SS Gregory and Martin. It was not until 1448 that the first provost was appointed to the new college. The church had long been appropriated to Battle Abbey, but in 1449 agreement was reached whereby it was transferred to the college. In 1452, Kempe became Archbishop of Canterbury. The establishment was stated as a provost, two fellows, a parochial chaplain, seven choristers and two clerks; there was also a master of grammar. In 1535, its net annual income was given as £93; dissolution came in 1545.

The church was remodelled and probably extended on the foundation of the college, and was very large, of cruciform plan. Today, it remains very attractive, but externally presents a curiously truncated appearance; this is due to the collapse in 1686 of its central tower, which did so much damage that nothing is left of the former chancel and transepts, and only four of the five bays of its aisled nave remain. Externally the nave appears as Perp. work, fine and upstanding, the aisles battlemented, with low-pitched roofs and square-headed windows, the central space with a high-pitched roof and a clerestory of three-light windows under depressed arches. Earlier work shows only in the fine W doorway, which is EE though much renewed, with three orders of shafts. Internally the arcades are EE in their large arches of deep mouldings, but their pillars of four shafts and four hollows must be Perp. replacements. The fine nave roof incorporates the arms of Archbishop Kempe. There is a large battlemented S porch with a room above; its front, with rusticated pointed arch and quoins, is of 1787.

Wye, from the south-west

E. of the S aisle stands the tower, massive but not tall. Its general aspect appears medieval, with diagonal buttresses, battlements, corner pinnacles and a battlemented polygonal stair turret; however it is entirely of 1701–6, as evidenced by its modest round-arched openings partly of brick. On its N side is what seems externally an insignificant battlemented chancel with shallow apse; N of this the old fifth bay of the N aisle remains (now used as vestry). Internally, however, this chancel is a delight: it does not seem small, and it is a perfect and unspoilt early-eighteenth-century ensemble. Its side walls are windowless, but the apse has three large round-arched windows; the walls rise to a cornice and a canted plaster ceiling. It is fitted with beautiful high panelling, raised in the apse as a reredos with texts; there are stalls, a reading-desk each side and elegant baluster communion rails. The whole is exquisitely decorated in black and grey, the panels outlined in white and gold, with a dark blue ceiling.

An attractive series of mural memorials enlivens the chancel walls, the latest being of 1995. There are eight hatchments in the nave, and a late medieval brass is mounted murally. The excellent Perp. font is concave-octagonal in both stem and bowl, with a quatrefoil on each face of the latter.

Immediately E of the spacious churchyard the college buildings still stand, of modest but attractive fifteenth-century work; they comprise a hall and three ranges around a courtyard. The upper storey was timber-framed, but was rebuilt in brick in the eighteenth century, when the charming brick cloister was also

Wye, looking east

constructed, replacing a timber structure. A separate single-storeyed range was probably the grammar school, which continued after the dissolution. The buildings survived in domestic use; since 1884 they have been an agricultural college, now part of London University, and there are large later extensions. The library and information technology department is known as the Kempe Centre.

Lancashire

The county's one collegiate church is a notably magnificent example, and is now Manchester Cathedral.

* **Manchester** (*now in Greater Manchester*)

In 1421, Thomas de la Warre, Rector of Manchester, obtained licence from Henry V, from the bishop and from Pope Martin V to establish a college in the parish Church of SS Mary, George and Denys. It had a chantry function, and the church was appropriated. The founder was also lord of the manor of Manchester, and he gave his nearby manor house to become its domestic accommodation. The college was established in 1422 and had a warden, eight priest fellows, four clerks and six choristers. This was a large foundation, valued in the sixteenth century at £213 per annum. It was dissolved in 1547, but was refounded under Queen Mary. Under Queen Elizabeth, the endowments were mostly alienated, and prospects were uncertain until in 1578 the queen granted a new charter, and it continued on a somewhat reduced scale, with a warden, four fellows, two chaplains, four boy choristers and four singing men, under the name Christ's College. A real religious life was maintained. It was again dissolved in 1646, but restored under Charles II. Under the Cathedrals Act of 1840, it was not dissolved but its staff were made into a dean and canons, in preparation for becoming the cathedral of the new diocese of Manchester in 1847. Subsequent proposals for building a new and larger cathedral came to nothing.

The church is a very large and very splendid building; its external length, excluding the post-medieval W porch, is over 220 ft (67 m). It was completely

Manchester Cathedral, from the north-east

rebuilt after it became collegiate, the choir under John Huntington, warden from 1422 to 1458, the nave and other parts following. The building remains essentially of this period, but it has suffered much nineteenth-century restoration and rebuilding, and its external ashlar surfaces are totally renewed. The Victorian work maintained the Perp. style, but also increased the richness; it included the splendid two-storeyed N and S porches, which are vaulted, and the upper part and all the external details of the W tower, which has much panelling in Perp. style, set-back buttresses with image niches and an openwork battlemented parapet with many pinnacles. Also Victorian are the elaborate openwork parapets with pinnacles throughout the church. The roofs are low pitched. The whole is consistent in its effect, though closer examination shows that it is far from uniform. The interior is splendid too, and here, although major parts have been rebuilt, there is much that is authentic. However, it is dark, an effect accentuated by its dark-coloured sandstone, and its old woodwork is almost black.

The nave and chancel are of the same height, and both have six bays. Their arcades have pillars of a complex shafted section with capitals on the shafts only, carrying finely moulded two-centred arches. The spandrels are panelled, and above are a richly crested string-course and large five-light clerestory windows. In the nave the arcades have been rebuilt, but in the chancel everything is authentic. Rood stairs climb each side of the lofty chancel arch, which has panelled spandrels and responds; externally the stairs continue as turrets with crocketed spirelets. The tall tower arch is original, surrounded by damaged Perp. panelling; the fan vault in the tower is Victorian.

A particular feature of the church is the ranges of chantry chapels added late in the medieval era, giving it double aisles almost throughout. The outer aisles are broader than the inner. Their large windows are mostly of four lights, arched and traceried. They have many irregularities, and on the S side sections are Victorian. A single-bay chapel, the Ely Chapel, formerly projected even further northwards near the E end, but this section was flattened by a bomb in 1940, and in the subsequent restoration the Ely Chapel was omitted. On the S side near the E end, instead of the outer aisle there is a small but charming octagonal chapter-house; it has a fine entrance arrangement, with two richly moulded four-centred doorways set within a larger panelled arch. Beneath the E window, a rich arch with flanking image niches opens to a short Lady Chapel: this had been largely rebuilt in the eighteenth century, but was destroyed in 1940; it has been rebuilt to a new, rather austere design. Extensive early-twentieth-century attachments providing cathedral facilities are S of the chancel. A large and lavish W porch with flanking vestries is of 1898–1900.

The chancel is the finest part of the building, and indeed is magnificent by any standards. Moreover it displays the superb medieval woodwork which is the greatest glory of the church. Outstanding are the thirty stalls, with exceptionally fine carved misericords and tremendously rich and lofty canopies; they date from about 1505–10. The great veranda rood screen is much restored but basically original. Further very distinctive screens occupy the arcades E of the stalls, with wrought-iron work below big ogee arches, an engaging eighteenth-

Manchester Cathedral, looking east

century modification of medieval work. The splendid chancel roof is panelled, with cusped braces springing from shield-bearing angels. Other roofs, including that of the nave, are also authentic and of fine workmanship. Several original parclose screens are in the outer aisles, and even the screen to the Lady Chapel survives, with interesting carved figures. The large eighteenth-century font has a gadrooned octagonal bowl on a baluster stem. There are some good memorials, including two medieval brasses. The Victorian glass was all destroyed in 1940, but much modern stained glass has been put in since.

The city-centre surroundings of the cathedral are not attractive, but 100 yd to the N the collegiate buildings remain intact, and are beautiful: an almost miraculous survival. The former manor house was entirely rebuilt in the years following 1422. After 1547 they became the town house of the earls of Derby, and then during the Commonwealth, by the initiative of Humphrey Chetham, they were purchased and in 1653 became a school. Since 1969, Chetham's School has been a specialist music school. The buildings are remarkably well preserved, and constitute one of the finest survivals of collegiate domestic buildings. They are two storeyed and consist of a long narrow range with a gatehouse attached to its E end, and at its W end a block laid out around a small rectangular courtyard. On the E side of the courtyard is the hall, and the other three sides have cloister walks, with three-light openings under depressed arches.

Leicestershire

Two of the standing collegiate churches of Leicestershire are very fine examples. Altogether greater, however, would have been the now vanished church of Newarke College, at Leicester.

Leicester: Newarke College

This college, the full name of which was the College of the Annunciation of Our Lady of the Newarke, was founded in 1353–6 by Henry, 4th Earl and 1st Duke of Lancaster. It was a very large foundation, for a dean, twelve canons, thirteen vicars and several others. In its constitution, with canons holding small bursal prebends in the gift of the patron, it closely resembled Edward IV's recently founded colleges at Windsor and Westminster. It was of chantry function, essentially a place of prayer for the House of Lancaster, of which the founder's grandson in 1399 became king as Henry IV. It was closely associated with a major hospital which had been founded in 1331 by the duke's father, Henry, 3rd Earl of Lancaster, for fifty poor, with four chaplains: this was enlarged to accommodate 100 poor and sick people. The college and hospital stood in the Newarke, or New Work, a large, semi-fortified walled area immediately adjoining the castle; its impressive early-fifteenth-century Magazine Gateway remains intact, occupied by a museum but alas isolated on an island in a dual carriageway. Each of the canons had a house in the Newarke; the

All that remains of Newarke College, Leicester

vicars were also to live in these. The church was not completed until after 1414, and had a cloister. During the fifteenth and early sixteenth centuries, several individual chantries were established in the church, and three further houses were constructed for the priests who served them. The annual value in 1535 was the very large figure of £595. By one of Henry VIII's schemes of the late 1530s, it would have been made a cathedral, but this did not happen; instead, the college was dissolved in 1548, and demolition followed.

The church must have been a major building. Its site is occupied by a very large structure erected between 1896 and 1937, now part of De Montfort University. Inside this, in an area known as the Science and Engineering Research Centre, a railing surrounds the only surviving fragment: two moderate-sized arches running E–W, of two large continuous chamfers, Dec. in character. A notice states that they were removed during construction of the building but in 1937 replaced in their original position. Disappointingly, there seems to have been no excavation or recording, and nothing is known of the size of the church or the role of these arches; it is not even certain that they were part of the church. No canon's house survives, but something may be seen of the later houses constructed for the chantry priests. One is only a fragment, but the Newarke Chantry House of 1511–12 is a substantial building of stone in three storeys; it is now a museum. At the dissolution, the hospital was allowed to continue. In the seventeenth century it was renamed Trinity Hospital, and from 1898 to 1902 it was largely rebuilt, but its chapel remains, albeit heavily restored. The scale of what remains of the hospital accommodation conveys something of the importance of the foundation. It is now used by De Montfort University.

* Leicester: St Mary de Castro

This church may have been a pre-Conquest foundation; it is even possible that it is the successor to the cathedral which Leicester possessed from the seventh century until 874. But the first firm fact is its establishment within the castle in about 1107 by Robert de Beaumont, 1st Earl of Leicester, as a large college for a dean and twelve canons. However, in 1147 the founder's son, Robert le Bossu, transferred most of the endowments to his new foundation of the Augustinian abbey of Leicester. This was part of the widespread trend at this time of converting houses of secular canons into monasteries of canons regular; in this case, however, an arrangement was made (either immediately or a few years later) whereby the college continued on a more modest scale, with a sacrist and seven others. These were later referred to as a dean and prebendaries, but the prebends were bursal and were small; the holders were all appointed by the Abbot of Leicester, and there were no vicars choral. The abbey provided a vicar for the parochial function. The college remained on this scale, with an annual value in 1535 of £24; it continued after the end of the abbey, and was dissolved probably in 1548.

The church is on a very large scale, which it had from the first and which, despite the curtailment of the college, was maintained in later additions. It has

Leicester: St Mary de Castro,
from the south-east

much that is exceptionally interesting or impressive, but as a whole it is strangely muddled so that its effect, especially internally, is extraordinary rather than beautiful. Much of this is due to the character of the later medieval alterations, but extensive nineteenth-century interference (mostly by Sir Gilbert Scott) has also contributed. The basis is a Norman church which was aisleless but of striking length and very ambitious character. It was constructed in two phases. The first, from about 1107, is most clearly seen at the W end, which shows blank arcading or the remains of it both inside and out. In the late Norman period the chancel was remodelled and extended by 20 ft (6 m), and chapels were constructed E of the transepts; it is not clear whether the transepts themselves were of the first or second phase. The chancel is lavish, having large windows with chevron on their arches and shafts both internally and externally, some of the shafts enriched with spiral or zigzag. There is a corbel-table of grotesques and some striking diaper enrichment of the wall surface. In the two E bays the buttresses are in the form of paired demicolumns, and the very large windows have orthogonal chevron. However, there is considerable restoration, and the E wall is a Victorian imitation. Further remains of Norman work can be seen in various places along much of the length of the interior; plaster has been removed throughout, to ugly effect. The N side now has a Victorian arcade in rich EE style, with lean-to aisle, N transept and vestry. Reset in this aisle are two good late Norman doorways, with much chevron. Previously, however, this part had been quite different, and attached to it was a timber-framed domestic range extending from the adjacent Castle House.

Also remarkable are the mainly late-thirteenth-century extensions on the S side, which have given the church an extremely broad and lofty aisle, much wider than the nave and chancel; the width was probably determined by the Norman transept which it absorbed. This aisle seems to have been set aside for

Leicester: St Mary de Castro. The Norman sedilia in the chancel

parochial use. It has large S windows, of which the three-light geometrical tracery is unfortunately a Victorian alteration; above are three-light Perp. clerestory windows and a straight parapet. The exceptionally broad, low-pitched roof is Perp. work, with fine enrichments including some tracery. This aisle opens to the chancel by two very large Perp. arches. To the nave, there are now three Victorian bays in rich EE style. Two further bays at the W, however, are genuine EE work (from which the Victorian bays are largely copied), with richly moulded arches on quatrefoil pillars; above appear the remains of Norman windows, set in blank arcading, and above these is an exquisite clerestory of lancets, internally outlined by a roll and externally set in shafted blank arcading. The most extraordinary aspect of this work is that its formerly external face is hardly visible, since the tower, itself begun in the later thirteenth century, stands on its three arches within the aisle, with just a narrow gap on each side. This tower is externally splendid, the dominating feature of the church. It is very large, in four stages, with shallow diagonal buttresses; the belfry is of two-light Y-tracery openings set in fine blank arcading. Above are a band of panelling, battlements with corner pinnacles and a splendidly tall and slender crocketed spire with three tiers of lucarnes. The spire reaches 179 ft (54.6 m); it has several times had to be at least partly rebuilt.

The extensive Victorian stained glass makes the interior very dark. The late Norman triple stepped sedilia are rare and very fine, with arches thickly encrusted with chevron, resting on paired shafts with elaborate capitals. With them goes a Norman piscina, but this is restored. Also fine are the EE sedilia in the aisle, with dog-tooth ornamentation and stiff-leaf capitals. Most furnishings are typical town-church Victorian work in oak. Some old work remains in screens and other pieces; a medieval vestry door is finely ornamented. There are many mural memorials. The striking circular EE font has many decorative motifs including trefoils, shields and angels; it rests on a cylinder and four shafts. The immediate setting of the church remains beautiful, with trees, parkland, the castle mound and several surviving structures of the castle.

* Noseley

This was a small chantry college, founded in the chapel of the manor house. The first moves were made in 1274 by Anketin de Martivall; his son, Roger, continued with the foundation of the college in 1303, and the royal approval is dated 1306. It was for three priests, one of whom was warden. Further endowments were added later; in 1335 the advowson of the parish church of Noseley was acquired, and in 1338 the church was appropriated. In the sixteenth century the annual value was given as almost £25; in 1526, in addition to the three chaplains, there were two deacons, two clerks and a curate who had responsibility for the cure of souls in the parish. Regular services ceased in the parish church perhaps from 1338; the village declined and all but disappeared, and by the sixteenth century the church was in ruins. It has since vanished, though its site is known. The college was dissolved in 1547. Parochial responsibility remained, the owners of the manor house being lay rectors. In the absence of the parish church, services continued to be held in the chapel.

The chapel built for the college probably from about 1274 remains today, and is most unusual and lovely. It is dedicated to St Mary. It is aisleless but has the remarkable undivided length of nine bays. There are regular buttresses and a large two-light Y-tracery window in each bay, except that the W bay instead has a doorway each side (blocked on the N). The present low-pitched roof is a Perp. remodelling, together with the battlemented parapets and the five-light E and W windows, which both have a depressed

Noseley, from the south

Noseley, looking west

arch but differ in their designs. The W window is externally flanked by trefoiled niches and has the principal entrance doorway beneath. Irregularities towards the E end on the N side mark the location of the former tower, which was connected to the church by a two-storeyed attachment; it was demolished probably in the early nineteenth century following damage by lightning.

Internally, the chapel is spacious, noble and exquisite. Its internal surfaces lack plaster but are not unattractive. The side windows are surrounded by a filleted roll. The roof is largely authentic, and has tracery above its arched braces. Halfway down the chapel, each side has an arched piscina with a ledge for a shelf; there was originally a screen at this point. In the sanctuary is a fine composition of triple sedilia and double piscina; there is stiff-leaf, and the piscina has twin trefoiled arches. The stalls are largely late medieval, and have some tracery in their fronts and notably fine ends with rich tracery and lavish poppy-heads carrying cockerels. Their seats, however, are replacements. There is extensive though fragmentary medieval glass in the E window. The font is a fine Dec. piece, octagonal, each side having a different two-light tracery design under a crocketed gable. In the floor are several ledgers with incised effigies. There is a good series of mural memorials, the finer ones being towards the E end and culminating in two seventeenth-century wall memorials with tomb-chests carrying effigies; almost all are to the Hazlerigg family, who own Noseley Hall to this day.

In status this remains a private chapel and it stands on private land, on the lawn near the eighteenth-century and later Hall. It is maintained in excellent condition, and about three services are held each year.

Sapcote

The Bassett family was important here from at least the twelfth century, and its heads were patrons of the parish Church of All Saints. It was Ralph Bassett who in 1361 obtained licence to establish a small chantry college, to serve in the Chapel of St Mary in the church. His initial foundation was for two priests, but in the early 1370s he increased it to three, of whom one was warden. The church was not appropriated. After Bassett's death, the endowments were in 1385 further increased, and a new charter obtained from Richard II. The subsequent existence of the college was uneventful; its annual income in the sixteenth century was just £16 10s, and it was dissolved in 1547.

The church is medium sized, attractive but of no special distinction. It has a W tower of cream-coloured ashlar, tall, with shallow diagonal buttresses, battlements and modest Perp. openings, carrying a good stone spire with two tiers of lucarnes, reaching about 120 ft (36 m). The church is otherwise of rubble masonry: a chancel with a nineteenth-century N vestry-organ chamber, and a nave with a N aisle under low-pitched roof and a Victorian N porch. There has been considerable nineteenth-century renewal, and features such as windows may have been altered. Windows on the S side of the nave are long,

of varied Dec. and Perp. designs, and the S doorway is Perp. The aisle was the Chapel of St Mary, probably added by Ralph Bassett. It has windows in Dec. style, at least one being entirely Victorian; the N doorway has two continuous chamfers. The four-bay arcade has double-chamfered arches on cylindrical pillars. Above is a clerestory of two-light Perp. windows.

The windows in the chancel are also in Dec. style. The chancel arch is good, double-chamfered on demicolumn responds, and on its N side is a squint with a quatrefoil front opening. In the chancel are an ogee-trefoiled piscina and an enriched ogee-trefoiled credence recess with finial; but the sedilia are Victorian. Perhaps the best feature of the chancel is its oak roof, though it is partly nineteenth century; its closely spaced tie-beams have solid braces from their wall-posts, central bosses and tracery above. The font is an attractive Norman piece; it has a cylindrical stem and a circular bowl with leaf and other motifs.

Lincolnshire

This county possessed two chantry colleges, of which that of Tattershall was a major establishment and has left us one of our most important collegiate churches.

* Spilsby

The Church of St James at Spilsby was originally a chapel of ease to nearby Eresby, where the Willoughby family owned the great house or castle. It was Robert, 1st Lord Willoughby, who planned to establish a college dedicated to the Holy Trinity in the chapel of Spilsby. Papal approval was obtained in 1347 and royal approval in 1349, but, the founder having died in 1348, the actual foundation took place in 1351 under his son, the 2nd lord. As part of its endowment, three churches including that of Eresby were to be appropriated to the college, which was intended for a master and twelve chaplains. It seems that this ambitious scale was never fully achieved, but in 1378 there were a master and eight chaplains. However, decline soon followed: in 1422 there were a master and five chaplains, in 1443 a master and only two. Soon after this, it may have ceased altogether; but it was revived by Sir William Willoughby, who died in 1503, and from then until its suppression in 1547 there were a master and three chaplains. The annual value at the dissolution was given as almost £41.

Spilsby, from the south-east

Spilsby: the Willoughby Chapel

At first sight, the church appears mostly Victorian: the parts of the exterior which were not newly built by W Bassett Smith in 1879 were given the same rock-faced texture of Ancaster stone. Only the large, early-sixteenth-century tower was exempt. This has a plinth with shield-enclosing quatrefoils, polygonal buttresses and three-light belfry openings with straight-shanked arches; it is divided into five stages and has battlements with large corner and intermediate pinnacles.

Internally, much more is old, but the plan is confusing. The tower stands W of what was originally the nave, with four-bay early-fourteenth-century arcades of double-chamfered arches on octagonal pillars, their capitals having a band of tiny ball-flowers. Its N aisle is narrow and has three-light arched Perp. windows. In place of a S aisle, however, there is a very broad space which is now the nave. This appears entirely Victorian, which is true of its clerestory, its extension W to embrace the tower, and its S arcade of five bays with another aisle. However, this space was created probably around 1350 on the foundation of the college, together with the equally broad Chapel of the Holy Trinity to its E, which is now the chancel. This too seems all Victorian, but its five-light reticulated E window may possibly represent original work.

It is the state of the original chancel that is startling and makes the church memorable. At what date it ceased to be the chancel is uncertain. However, its Dec. chancel arch is now completely filled by a great memorial of about 1582, the W side forming a solid screen, the E side having a tomb-chest and extraordinary features, including three large standing figures, two of them wild men. This is now the Willoughby Chapel, separated from the present chancel by a two-bay arcade containing iron railings, and filled by a remarkable display of monuments. Three are fourteenth-century tomb-chests with effigies, one probably to the 1st Lord Willoughby, the others to the 2nd and 3rd. Two large brasses are in the floor. There are other post-medieval memorials too.

* Tattershall

Ralph, 3rd Lord Cromwell, became Treasurer of England in 1433, and in the following year began the massive rebuilding of his castle at Tattershall (now owned by the National Trust). In 1439, he obtained licence to convert the parish church into a chantry college for a warden, six chaplains, six clerks and six choristers, with attached to it an almshouse for thirteen poor people. The college at first functioned in the existing Church of SS Peter and Paul. New statutes were given in 1501 by Bishop Smith of Lincoln. In 1536, during the Lincolnshire uprising, the warden was accused of giving supplies to the insurgents; despite this, he and the college seem to have avoided retribution. This was a very large college; before it was dissolved in 1545 its annual value was given as £348.

Surprisingly, it seems that not until thirty years after the foundation of the college did the building of a new church begin, under Cromwell's executor

Tattershall, from the south

Bishop Waynflete. Then, however, it was apparently completed quickly, and is on a magnificent scale; in character it is reminiscent of Fotheringhay. The new building was dedicated to the Holy Trinity. It is uniform throughout, faced inside and out in ashlar, and 188 ft (57.3 m) in external length. Outside, but not inside, a certain austerity may be felt; though sophisticated, it has little enrichment, the parapets are mostly straight and the arched windows, though all traceried, eschew cusping. However, some parapets are enlivened by pinnacles (often now missing); the tower has a straight parapet and four large pinnacles. Many arches are four-centred. It is lofty, and with its large windows is of 'glasshouse' type. The aisled nave has four bays, with a large W tower embraced by the aisles; there are transepts of full height though narrower than the nave, which have tall arches but no true crossing; and the aisleless chancel has five bays, and is a little less lofty than the nave.

The tall windows of the chancel are of three large lights, with transoms. The E window has seven lights, with above it outside a large pinnacle containing a

Tattershall: the north side of the nave

canopied image niche. In the aisles, the windows are of four lights, while the clerestory has two large three-light windows to each bay. This clerestory continues in the sides of the transepts; their end walls have very large six-light windows. The tower has big belfry openings of three lights. Blockings and patchings low on the S exterior of the chancel show where a long sacristy was once attached. Four-centred in a square label are the moderate S doorway, the large enriched W doorway and the N doorway, the last covered by a relatively low porch. All have their original traceried doors.

Roofs are low pitched, with good moulded timbers, mostly original; there are no vaults. Other than in the lower part of the E window, all medieval glass has been lost, so the church is very light. The arcades have very tall pillars of four shafts (triple to E and W) and four hollows; their finely moulded arches are two centred. Arches open from the tower in three directions; that to the nave is panelled. In the chancel is a fine composition of piscina and triple sedilia, all equal in size, with four-centred arches and much enrichment. Large piscinas in the transepts have miniature vaults. There is a chancel screen of stone, now carrying the organ: it is early sixteenth century. Its W side has three arches, the side ones blank, and much panelling; the passage has a four-centred barrel vault. Few old fittings remain, and much of this great space is unfurnished. In the chancel, a nineteenth-century polygonal pulpit of timber incorporates a few reused Perp. fragments, and some other decayed pieces are displayed in a case. The octagonal oak pulpit on a tall panelled stem is original, however. A Jacobean tester is above. The octagonal font has a plain bowl and stem, but its base has blank arcading: it may pre-date the present church. In the N transept is a good series of brasses, three of them to clergy of the college; like much else here, they have to be covered because of bats living in the church. A clock mechanism probably of the early seventeenth century is displayed.

The collegiate buildings stood NE of the church, and were of brick. Nothing remains, but a roofless building in the village, now cared for by English Heritage, was connected with the college. The almshouse run by the college survived its dissolution, and still stands just N of the church: it is a row of small single-storeyed houses, now dating from the seventeenth century.

London

London had many colleges, though most were minor; there were also several marginal cases, which appear in Appendix IV. The two major establishments were the colleges of St Martin le Grand and St Stephen at Westminster, which were both royal. Of the eight churches or chapels here accounted collegiate, only four today have standing representatives, of which only one is a complete medieval fabric. A good deal more was to be seen at the beginning of the nineteenth century.

* Garlickhythe College

The name of the Church of St James Garlickhythe refers to an early trade of the city. First mentioned in the twelfth century, the church was rebuilt in the early fourteenth century, and seems to have been large. Later in that century several chantries were established, and by the late fifteenth century there were seven chantry priests here. In 1481, a building was provided for their accommodation and they were formed into a college; this did not involve the appropriation of the church. The college was dissolved probably in 1548. The church was destroyed in the Great Fire; a new one was constructed on the site by Wren from 1676, with the steeple completed in 1713–17. Some damage was suffered in both world wars, but it was not severe: this, however, was only by good fortune, since in 1941 a high-explosive bomb fell through the roof and buried itself in the floor near the SE corner, but failed to explode and was later removed. The church was damaged again in 1989, when a tower crane collapsed on to the centre of the S side; it has once more been restored.

London: St James Garlickhythe, from the south-west

London: St James
Garlickhythe, looking
north-east

This is one of the larger Wren churches, and among the finest; it also retains extensive contemporary fittings, some of them brought from the nearby church of St Michael Queenhythe, demolished in 1876. Much of the exterior is of brick or has lined rendering; there is a clerestory of brick. The W tower, formerly mainly of coursed ragstone, was largely refaced in Portland ashlar following external wartime fire damage. It is in three stages, crowned by a balustrade within which rises a charming steeple of three stages, square in plan but with paired Ionic columns projecting diagonally from the corners of the lowest stage. Beneath a beautiful clock originally of 1682 projecting from the wall, entry is through a fine pedimented W doorway, opening through the base of the tower to a mellow, low lobby with a stone floor, original panelling and gallery stairs each side. The church itself is a lofty rectangle five bays long; very unusually for a Wren church, it has a sanctuary projecting a bay further, narrow but of full height. Tall slim Ionic columns separate the aisles from the main space, carrying a rich entablature and a great coved ceiling with a beautifully enriched central area. There are large round-arched main windows (some of them blocked); smaller segmental clerestory windows penetrate the coving. As in many of Wren's finest designs, the planning is of subtle sophistication; the central bay differs from the others, being slightly wider and of full height, implying transepts. The original tall windows of this bay have been replaced by smaller circular openings.

This is a particularly light interior, thanks to its large windows and the destruction of Victorian stained glass. There is a deep W gallery with a beautiful front, containing a magnificent organ of 1697 by Bernhardt Schmidt. The walls are panelled, and the columns have tall panelled octagonal bases. The stalls have rich high backs and twisted baluster fronts. Particularly splendid is the large hexagonal pulpit, from St Michael Queenhythe, with an enormous tester and a very elegant stair. Other fine period work includes the reredos and the communion rail. A large oil painting of 1815 is used as altar-piece. The beautiful, slim font has a gadrooned octagonal bowl with four cherubs; its cover, also original, is of ogee form. There are two moulded Royal Arms, one of which came from St Michael Queenhythe. The first register begins in 1535, and is said to be the oldest in England.

Guildhall College

The Guildhall has been the seat of the government of London probably since the twelfth century. A Chapel of Our Lady, St Mary Magdalen and All Saints was built there at the end of the thirteenth century. In 1368, a chantry college was established for a warden, four chaplains and a clerk, to serve at the altar of Our Lady in the chapel; this had been proposed over ten years earlier by Adam Fraunceys, twice Lord Mayor, with Henry Frowyk and Peter Fanelore, but only the two former lived to see it become reality. Presentation of the chaplains was in the gift of the mayor and corporation. From about 1430 the chapel was rebuilt, being completed in the early 1450s; the accommodation for the chaplains was also demolished and a new building provided. In 1449–50, two more chaplains were added by the Guild of St Nicholas. The annual value of the college in 1535 was given as almost £34. Following a visitation, new statutes were provided as late as 1542 by Bishop Bonner. Suppression took place in 1548.

In 1550 the chapel was purchased by the Corporation of London, and continued in use. The splendid early-fifteenth-century Great Hall of the Guildhall survives today, but alas the chapel was demolished in 1822. Many pictures remain to tell us what it was like. It was a fine uniform Perp. structure of five bays, about 90 ft (27 m) long, with aisles stopping one bay short of the E end. Its roofs were low pitched, with straight parapets. The W front had Perp. panelling and a large main window of seven lights; this front stood just to the right of the still-existing Guildhall porch. There was a clerestory, both the aisles and clerestory having three-light arched windows. The arcades had arches of many mouldings, two-centred and only slightly pointed, resting on shafted pillars longer on their E–W axes. Plaster ceilings had been added, and the chapel latterly had fittings for its function as the Court of Requests.

Guildhall College, London: the chapel, from the north-east. Watercolour
by R.B. Schnebbelie, 1820

Pountney College

About 1333–4, John Pulteney, Lord Mayor of London, added to the Church
of St Laurence, Candelwyk Street, a chapel in honour of Corpus Christi and
St John Baptist. To serve in it, he established a chantry college of a master
and six chaplains. The advowson and the church were appropriated to the
college, since when the church has been known as St Laurence Pountney. In
1344, Pulteney increased the foundation to the large number of twelve chaplains in addition to the master, with four choristers. All were accommodated
in the building provided for the college. The statutes were not drawn up
until after 1346. It had an annual value of £80 at its dissolution in 1547, but
there seem to have been only the master, three chaplains and four conducts,
to whom pensions were granted. The church was destroyed in the Great Fire,
following which it was not rebuilt, its parish being united by the Rebuilding
Act of 1670 with that of St Mary Abchurch. The churchyard, however,
remains to this day.

St Martin le Grand

This church is said to have had early origins. The college was founded shortly before or after the Conquest by a royal chaplain called Ingelric and his brother Girard. Ingelric held positions under both Edward the Confessor and William the Conqueror, and the latter added to the endowments of the college, and took the first steps to free it from episcopal authority. Its endowments were steadily increased through the next century, and it became very large and important; a papal letter of 1176 confirmed its status as a royal free chapel, and during the thirteenth century these privileges were fully established. In 1158, the college was reconstituted with prebends, which were for a dean and nine canons; two more canons were added in 1240. There were at least seven vicars in 1235, and two chantries were established in 1254; in 1304 four boy choristers were added. The deanery and prebends were normally held by clerks

London: St Martin le Grand. Remains of the crypt, with plan and artefacts, exposed during demolition work in 1818. Etching by Bartholomew Howlett, 1825

in royal service; some prominent names appear, for example, Henry de Blois, Bishop of Winchester, who was dean for a period in the mid-twelfth century. Substantial building operations took place in the early twelfth century and again in 1258–61, when Henry III gave quantities of stone, Purbeck marble and finished statues. When William of Wykeham was dean, about 1360–3, he put in hand repairs to the nave of the church and the rebuilding of the cloisters and chapter-house, the latter with a stone vault. In the fifteenth century, the precincts had the right of permanent sanctuary, which caused many problems with common criminals taking refuge there and continuing to be a menace to the city.

In 1503, most of the revenues, including the prebends for all but two canons, were given to Westminster Abbey as a part of the endowment of its new Chapel of Henry VII. The Abbot of Westminster nominally became Dean of St Martin le Grand. On 1535 figures, the college retained £91 out of an annual income of over £400. However, its life seems to have been little altered except that it was no longer supporting absent prebendaries, and it continued with eight vicars, six clerks and four boy choristers. It was dissolved in 1542. The church and other buildings were demolished about 1547, and the site was built over. During site clearance in 1818, crypts which had survived as cellars were exposed and drawn; there seems to have been a crypt of massive early Norman character beneath the nave, and another of elegant EE design beneath the chancel. The length of the church is said to have been about 200 ft (60 m). Although the buildings have been lost, the ownership of the college by Westminster Abbey has led to the survival of its extensive documentary archive.

* St Peter ad Vincula (Tower of London)

In the early twelfth century, this was a parish church standing just W of the Tower of London. In the thirteenth century it was taken within the enlarged circuit of the walls of the Tower; it was rebuilt under Edward I in 1286–7. At this time it had at least one chantry chaplain. In 1354, Edward III increased it to a rector and three chantry chaplains, and a further two chaplains were added in 1356. Being within a royal fortress, it had the exemptions from episcopal authority of a royal free chapel. In February 1483, Edward IV issued letters patent for its enlargement, with a normal collegiate constitution; but his death later that year prevented this from happening. It therefore continued as established by Edward III. It is doubtful whether it was incorporated, but authorities led by the *Victoria County History* assert that it was 'practically collegiate', and treat it as such. This position is accepted here. The chapel is of unique historical status and interest. It was destroyed by fire in 1512, following which it was completely rebuilt. Dissolution took place in 1548. Despite changes in status since then, it remains today a royal peculiar, and is one of the three chapels royal. It is well used, serving a good congregation, many of whom live within the Tower.

The chapel is a free-standing building of moderate size, and is an attractive example of Tudor architecture. It is five bays in length, undivided E–W, with

London: St Peter ad Vincula, from the south-east

a broad N aisle one bay shorter; there are straight parapets. The attractive low-pitched roofs are original, of chestnut, with excellent mouldings. All the windows have four-centred arches and their lights are cusped but without tracery; most are of three lights, but the E window is of five. The arches of the arcade are also four-centred, beautifully moulded, on pillars of four shafts and four hollows. There is a thin, very plain W tower, old in origin but Victorian in its hard flint surface. Its straight top carries a square cupola containing one bell. The chapel appears attractively unspoilt, though it was in fact much restored in Victorian times. It was considerably 'de-restored' in the 1970s, when Victorian pews, pulpit and stone reredos were removed, modern oak seats introduced and the Victorian flint facing of the S wall replaced by the present appropriate rendered surface.

A very moving aspect of this chapel is the many burials of important historical figures that took place in it in the sixteenth, seventeenth and early eighteenth centuries, mostly with severed heads. Unsurprisingly they have no memorials from the period, but their names are listed on a relatively recent brass plate; they include Anne Boleyn, Catherine Howard, Lady Jane Grey, Sir Thomas More and James Stuart, Duke of Monmouth. There are also some very fine memorials to others. On the N side of the sanctuary is a very long double standing wall memorial to Sir Richard Blount and his son Sir Michael, of the seventeenth century. Opposite is the much smaller but most beautiful Payler memorial, of similar period, with effigies in oval niches. Under the arcade is a tomb-chest of the 1540s carrying recumbent effigies of Sir Richard

Cholmondeley and his wife; remarkably, when opened in 1876, it was found to contain the octagonal Perp. font, which had presumably been hidden there. Most impressive of all is the very large and lavish canopied tomb-chest of about 1447 to John Holland, Duke of Exeter, his wife and (probably) his sister: this was originally in the great chapel of the Hospital of St Katharine, which stood a little way E of the Tower (*see* Appendix IV). The large organ is a notable instrument by Bernhardt Schmidt, commissioned by Charles II for the Banqueting House, Whitehall; it was moved here in 1890. Communicating with the church on the N side are some much-altered late medieval vaults, of secular origin; they contain several recent memorials, particularly beautiful being that erected about 1970 to Sir Thomas More.

Walworth's College

The church of St Michael Crooked Lane seems to have been first mentioned in 1291. About 1366–8, with the involvement of John Lovekyn, four times Lord Mayor, a complete rebuilding of the church was begun. About ten years later,

London: St Michael Crooked Lane, immediately before demolition in 1831. Watercolour by P.W. Justyne, 1831

a S aisle and a chapel dedicated to St Peter were added by William Walworth, Lord Mayor at the time. Walworth had been Lovekyn's apprentice: both were also connected with college foundation at Kingston upon Thames (Surrey: *see* p. 359). In 1381, Walworth obtained royal licence to suppress several chantries in the church, of which the endowments had become inadequate, and to replace them with a chantry college of a master and nine chaplains who were to celebrate for the founders of the original chantries, for William Walworth and his wife Margaret, and for John Lovekyn. A house for the collegiate accommodation was constructed close to the church, but the church was not appropriated. In the sixteenth century, the significant annual income of £126 is reported; the college was dissolved in 1548.

The church was gutted in the Great Fire, and was rebuilt under Wren in 1685–98, with the steeple added to the tower in 1711–14. It was one of the simpler Wren churches, an undivided rectangular auditorium of slightly irregular layout, suggesting the reuse of earlier foundations. The tower projected from the N part of the W wall, and was tall. Its steeple was of timber covered in lead, a striking structure in four stages. This was the earliest of the many nineteenth-century losses among the City parish churches, being demolished in 1831 to make room for the approach road to the new London Bridge, which was built just upstream of its predecessor.

Westminster: St Stephen

It was in the early eleventh century that the kings of England made Westminster their principal residence, and it continued in that role until 1532. Technically it remains a royal palace today. Since Norman times, the greatest building on the site has been Westminster Hall; a chapel was no doubt constructed at the beginning, and Henry III spent much money on it. At this period, it had four chaplains. In 1292, under Edward I, a complete rebuilding of the chapel was begun, which was interrupted by a fire in the palace in 1298, work on the chapel being resumed only in about 1321. It was built above a lower chapel, which was finished by 1327. The upper chapel was structurally complete by 1350, but its decoration was not completed until about 1365. Edward III was closely involved with the project, and in 1348 he founded in the chapel a college of a dean, twelve canons, thirteen vicars, four clerks and six choristers. Also in this year, he founded the College of St George at Windsor; both colleges were of closely similar size and constitution. Unlike most foundations of this period, they had canons holding prebends, though the prebends were small compared to the sums provided for being in residence: canons were expected to reside. In 1349, the pope confirmed its status as a royal free chapel. This position later resulted in a major dispute between the college and Westminster Abbey, which considered that it had jurisdiction over any chapels within the parish of St Margaret; it lasted from 1375 to 1393, for much of which period the members of the college were excommunicated. In the fifteenth century, many chantries and obits were established in the chapel. The annual value in 1535 is given as £1,085; this enormous sum seems to

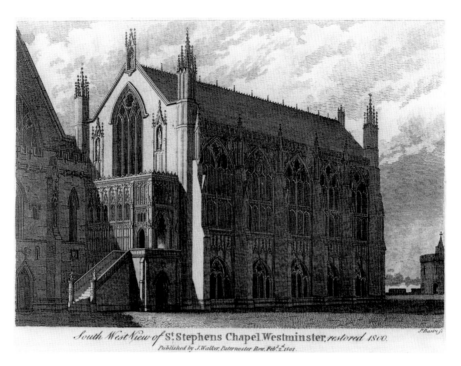

South West View of St Stephens Chapel Westminster restored 1800.
Published by J. Walker, Paternoster Row. Feb.ʳ 2. 1801.

St Stephen, Westminster: the chapel (then the House of Commons) from the south-west, as restored in 1800. Engraving by James Basire, 1801

have been necessary at least partly to support the hospitality the college was required to offer to those visiting the Court.

The original design of the chapel under Edward I almost certainly owed much to the famous Sainte-Chapelle in Paris, the chapel of the kings of France, built in the mid-thirteenth century. Both were built above a lower chapel, were lofty and of great sophistication, but relatively moderate in their overall dimensions. The fourteenth-century work at Westminster has been much discussed; the style of the upper chapel was Perp., very richly detailed, and it may have been the birthplace of this style. It had a timber vault, very large arched windows and a polygonal turret at the corners. Its decoration was extremely lavish: especially splendid were the wall-paintings and the glass.

The college was dissolved in 1547 and the chapel was converted to secular use as the House of Commons, a role it performed for almost 300 years. It was refurnished, and later its structure was considerably modified by Wren; further alterations or restorations took place in the early nineteenth century. But on the night of 16 October, 1834, most of the Palace of Westminster was destroyed by fire; the chapel was gutted. In the reconstruction of the palace by Barry and Pugin, begun in 1836 and not completed until the 1870s, the upper chapel was demolished and in its place was built St Stephen's Hall. This is on the plan of the chapel, and must approximately

St Stephen, Westminster: the chapel, cloister and part of Westminster Hall, immediately following the fire of 16 October 1834. Lithograph by John Taylor, 1835

represent its form; it is a lofty, vaulted room with very large windows. It is lined with statues of past statesmen and forms the very impressive approach usually traversed by visitors to the central lobby of the palace.

The lower chapel was restored after the fire, and is known as the Chapel of St Mary Undercroft. It is extremely rich, in Dec. style, its surfaces covered in gorgeous coloured decoration. However, the restoration was drastic, and the only part that can confidently be said to be authentic is the splendid tierceron vault with its large bosses. This rests on groups of dark marble shafts, with moulded capitals. The windows are in four lights, with cusped rere-arches and shafts with foliage capitals. Rich Victorian fittings include a fine wrought-iron screen, a marble dado, stone altar rails and elaborate arcading on the window-less E wall. Several small Victorian attachments include a rich polygonal baptistery at the SW corner.

Another heavily restored survivor of the fire is the cloister, which stands on the N side of the chapel; it had to be much restored again after bomb damage in 1941. It dates from 1526–9, and very unusually is in two storeys, though the restoration of the upper level amounted almost to rebuilding. Its openings are of four lights, with tracery, and it has a fan vault, with bosses carrying Tudor symbols; much of this vault remains original. Projecting into the garth from the W side is an oratory with a polygonal end. The cloister is glazed, and is now used as office space for the resource centres of the Labour and Conservative parties. Neither the chapel nor the cloister is normally accessible to visitors.

* Whittington's College

The church of St Michael Paternoster Royal derived its curious name from Paternoster Lane (now College Hill), probably where rosary makers lived, and La Riole (now College Street), the names of which referred to the import of wine from La Reole, near Bordeaux. Richard Whittington, four times Lord Mayor (and remotely connected to the pantomime story) lived close to the church, and in about 1411 determined on rebuilding it and making it collegiate. This project

London: St Michael Paternoster Royal, from the south-east

was not complete when he died in 1423, but the college was established by his executors the next year. It was a chantry college, dedicated to the Holy Ghost and St Mary, for a master, four chaplains, two clerks and four choristers. The church was appropriated, and William Brooke, the rector, became the first master. A building for the accommodation of the members was built immediately E of the church. The charter particularly specified that the chaplains should be well educated in letters, and it is perhaps as a reflection of this that the last master, Richard Smith, appointed in 1537, became the first Regius Professor of Divinity at Oxford. The college was dissolved in 1547, and Smith's religious views obliged him to go into exile at Louvain. However, the college was one of the few revived under Queen Mary, and Smith returned and again became master, but it was once more dissolved under Elizabeth.

The church was gutted in the Great Fire; it was one of the last to be rebuilt, in 1685–94, and the steeple was added to the tower in 1713–17. It was again severely damaged by a flying bomb in 1944, though the tower remained intact and the church was not burnt. It was restored in 1967–8 (rainwater heads are dated 1690 and 1967!), and is now used as the headquarters of the Missions to Seamen. Though generally regarded as a Wren church, this is one that may well have been designed by Robert Hooke.

Externally, the church is a broad rectangle six bays long; the S and W sides are of Portland ashlar, but other parts are of red brick or are rendered. The W wall is a little skew, and the tower is in the SW corner, projecting slightly from the rectangle. It is in three stages, with circular openings in the second stage, two-light rectangular openings in the third, and an openwork parapet. Its relatively short but very elegant octagonal steeple also has three stages, the lowest having Ionic columns standing outside its angles. The body of the church has a balustraded parapet. The entrance doorways at the S and W have a segmental arch beneath a cornice. The windows are large and round-arched, with moulded surrounds having a winged cherub at the head; the E wall has three, the central one larger than the others. Attached to the E wall is an original vestry, now incorporated in a post-war building; other buildings are attached on the N side.

Internally, this is one of the simpler Wren churches: the main space is a broad undivided rectangle. Originally it was five bays long, but in the restoration it was reduced to four, the W end being filled by offices. The ceiling has very large coving and just two bands of ornament. Some furnishings are basically authentic, including the excellent large reredos with fluted Corinthian columns, the octagonal font cover, and the hexagonal pulpit on a very slender stem, with inlay, carved fruit and a fluted pilaster supporting its tester. Also of the seventeenth century are three large wrought-iron sword-rests and a very large brass chandelier. Many of these pieces came from the church of All Hallows-the-Great, which was demolished in 1894. Much else dates from the restoration, including the good but plain panelling and the very shallow W gallery on large Tuscan columns, the centre standing forward to carry the organ; there is frankly modern glazed infilling below. Some attractive mural memorials survived the destruction of 1944. Several windows have brightly coloured abstract glass.

Middlesex

Other than in the area that in 1888 was absorbed into the new county of London, there were no colleges in Middlesex.

Norfolk

Norfolk possessed many collegiate churches, of which most were late foundations of chantry type. Following the dissolution of their colleges, two of the churches were mutilated and three totally destroyed. The finest of the survivors are probably Attleborough and Thompson, but all are rewarding to visit.

* Attleborough

Sir Robert de Mortimer, who died in 1387, left by his will instructions to his trustees to accumulate the income of several of his manors, and when the total reached 2,000 marks to use it for the establishment of a chantry college. This was to be in the Chapel of the Holy Cross in the Church of St Mary and have a master and four chaplains or fellows. His instructions were carried out, royal licence being obtained in 1405, and the first master appointed in 1417. The number of clergy declined in later years, there being a master and three chaplains in 1493,

Attleborough, from the north-west

and in the sixteenth century usually only a master and two. The annual income in 1535 was £21 16s 3d. In 1540, it was one of the first voluntary surrenders of a college. The S chancel aisle was the Chapel of Holy Cross; following the dissolution of the college, this Chapel and the entire E limb of the church were apparently demolished. Since the church had not been appropriated to the college, this is surprising; a possible explanation is that the loss of the chancel was caused by the fall of the spire, which took place in the seventeenth century.

Standing in a spacious churchyard, the church is impressively large, beautiful and interesting; it was originally cruciform. The E arch of the central tower is now blocked, as is the arch to the former S chancel aisle. The tower is earliest, its arches being Norman. They are excellent, quite low, with sophisticated scalloped capitals on triple shafts; the W side has extra enrichment, and the E side externally shows the remains of vaulting shafts for a former Norman chancel. Higher up, the tower is EE, with two-light openings of plate tracery

Attleborough, looking east

(but on two sides the tracery has been removed). There are plain brick battlements built after the collapse of the spire.

The rest of the church is splendid, large-scale work. It seems at first to be all of uniform Dec. character, with fine windows of flowing tracery, many showing a four-petalled flower motif. However, some features suggest the Perp. style, and the arcades could easily be Perp. The date of this work is problematical; it may all be late fourteenth century, but an alternative view is that it dates from about 1340 and was remodelled and given new arcades in the early fifteenth century. Although Sir Robert has been credited with it, it seems unlikely that its construction was directly associated with the college. However, the S chancel aisle and perhaps the chancel may have been rebuilt for the college in Perp. style, from which survives a four-light Perp. window amusingly bodged into the blocked arch from the S transept. There are straight parapets and low-pitched roofs throughout. The arcades are of five bays, with richly moulded two-centred arches on tremendously tall, slim pillars of a complex section, longer on their N–S axis. Above the spandrels are clerestory windows with four-centred arches but tracery rather of Dec. type, in three lights. Also of three lights are the large, regular windows of the aisles; above the S doorway (which now leads to a flint-faced parish room erected in 1992–4) there is instead of a window the engaging substitute of a tracery design in flushwork. Internally, the aisles have the distinction of large blank arcading, enclosing the windows and matching the arcades. The five-light W window is splendid. There is a fine two-storeyed N porch, with side windows and a tierceron vault; externally it has statues on its parapet, three nodding-ogee image niches and a little flushwork. Both transepts have large Dec. windows; the S transept is longer than its partner. The roofs are largely ancient, with good moulded timbers.

The fame of the church, however, is the great oak screen which extends across its full width. This has single-light divisions with frilly ornamentation instead of tracery; it is complete with large coving and the rich parapet of its loft. It is one of the finest in East Anglia, and has much original colour; the panels in the base have figures. It was moved to the W end in 1842, being restored and replaced in its original position in 1931. Above it, the lofty wall has two windows with regrettable neo-Norman detailing of 1909, but large areas are covered by late medieval wall-painting, in quite good preservation. In the S aisle a painting of St Christopher may be seen, and there are the remains of several painted consecration crosses. The space under the tower forms a small chapel; the N transept is filled by the organ, the S being partitioned into modern offices. An ancient offertory box has heavy ironwork. Also iron-bound is a splendid large medieval chest. A stone coffin-lid has a cross of curious form, both ends resembling a double axe-head. The hexagonal pulpit is an excellent piece of around 1700, with its original base and a charmingly enriched stair. The extraordinary lectern, with handrails in the form of serpents, is of cast-iron and dates from 1816. It came from elsewhere, as did the pulpit and the octagonal Perp. font. There are many fragments of medieval glass in the W window.

Herringby

This is sometimes regarded as a hospital, but categorization as a college seems to be warranted. It was founded in 1447 under the will of Hugh atte Fenne, for a master and three priests; it also had two servants and gave accommodation to eight poor men. It was alternatively known as God's House. The existing parish Church of St Ethelbert was appropriated, and served the college. The endowments were substantially increased in 1518; its annual value in 1535 was given as £69. Dissolution took place probably in 1545. Herringby is a depopulated village; the parish was amalgamated about 1580 with that of Stokesby, and the church was demolished in 1610. Nothing is now to be seen except a few architectural fragments built into a garden wall of the Hall.

* Norton Subcourse

As a college this had a curious and short history. The church was among the endowments of the nearby chantry college of Raveningham (*see* p. 238), which was founded in 1350. From 1371 there were several proposals for the removal of the college to a new site, either at Norton Subcourse or at Mettingham Castle in Suffolk, which was also relatively close by. Sir John de Norwich, grandson of the founder of the college, by his will of 1373 bequeathed £450 for the rebuilding of the church of Norton Subcourse, where he wished to be buried, and to which eventually, in 1387, the college moved. By this time, it had a master and twelve chaplains. However, it did not stay long here, and in

Norton Subcourse, from the east

Norton Subcourse, looking east

1394 the previously proposed move to Mettingham Castle (*see* p. 352) took place, and Norton Subcourse returned to its previous status.

The Church of St Mary is a mellow and beautiful building, externally covered in ancient render. It is aisleless and undivided E–W, but it is strikingly long and on quite a large scale. The round W tower is EE, with small lancet windows elegantly outlined by a roll; the belfry openings of uncusped Y-tracery are later, as is the straight parapet of brick. It is set very much off-centre to the nave, where the W wall shows a small blocked EE arch and a blocked doorway over. All the other details of the church are entirely Dec., and some question attaches to its date. Contracts of 1319 for new roofs survive, a date which seems to fit the architecture, so was anything done with the money bequeathed by Sir John de Norwich? The windows are in two lights, of uniform size but with varying tracery, while the excellent E window has reticulated tracery in five lights. The N and S doorways (the former blocked) have good continuous mouldings. A shallow projection in the N wall contains the rood stair, and there is an ogee-trefoiled piscina in the S wall opposite. A string course runs round the chancel both internally and externally; interestingly, the external string-course steps up to reflect the position of the sedilia inside, while the internal string-course simply stops for them. These sedilia are small scale but charming: there are three seats divided by shafts, together with an excellent double piscina, all having cinquefoiled ogee arches with finials. On the N side is a very depressed ogee tomb-recess. The windows of the chancel have the refinement of internal shafting.

The church has a canted plaster ceiling; its decoration is superb, with the walls yellow and the ceiling white, making a simple but exquisite interior. Most windows have clear glass, but a few fragments of medieval stained glass survive. Between nave and chancel stands a white-painted beam, with eighteenth-century pilasters against the walls. There is a pretty chamber organ. The octagonal font is EE, with two shallow pointed arches on each face, resting on a cylinder and eight shafts.

* Norwich: Carnary College

This was a chantry college for four priests, dedicated to St John the Evangelist, founded in 1316 by Bishop Salmon. Its priests were to celebrate for the bishop, his parents, and his predecessors and successors as Bishop of Norwich. It was

Norwich School: the chapel, from the south

to be under the control of the prior and convent of the cathedral. The chapel of the college stands just 50 yd from the W front of the cathedral. It was perhaps the 1330s before the chapel was built; its furnishings were not paid for until 1337. The college was probably dissolved in 1548, following which the chapel and buildings were purchased by the Corporation of Norwich to become the grammar school, a function they still perform today under the name Norwich School.

The chapel is superb, a lofty, aisleless Dec. building of four bays, externally all of ashlar. It stands over quite a tall undercroft, which has a vault with thick chamfered ribs and no capitals. The windows of the undercroft are circular, with multiple cusps and very rich external mouldings. Above, the chapel windows are large, in three lights with tracery of a fairly simple type; they are internally shafted, with leaf capitals and richly moulded arches. The enormous window of the E wall is now partly blocked and contains a four-light window of plain intersecting tracery, a late-eighteenth-century amendment. Enriched polygonal turrets mark the corners of the chapel, turning square higher up and terminating in a large pinnacle. The external stonework of the S side is much renewed and the window tracery is all restoration, but the N side is largely original. W of the chapel extends a large block of building now mainly of nineteenth-century appearance, but incorporating the domestic accommodation of the college. This was originally separate from the chapel, but further building filled the gap in the late fifteenth century, as part of which, immediately W of the chapel, is an enriched porch. This has a lierne vault coming very low over the steps as they climb and turn inside to give access to a doorway into the chapel.

The sanctuary has a large piscina recess under a tall gable with finial and flanking pinnacles. A simpler ogee-trefoiled piscina is halfway along the S side. Several doors at the W end are of ancient woodwork. A spiral stairway gives access to a W gallery, which has an attractive baluster front and a room beneath; this gallery was inserted in the sixteenth century for the school – a function illustrated by its numerous graffiti! The building was returned to use as a chapel early in the twentieth century, and most furnishings are high-quality work of the 1930s, in oak. The interior is light and beautiful.

Norwich: St Mary in the Fields

Also known as Chapel-in-the-Fields, this college began life as a hospital founded by John le Brun, a priest, standing then in open fields SW of the city. It rapidly gained in importance, and after 1248 became a college, with a dean and ten prebendaries. Its patronage soon came into the hands of the bishops. Six chantry chaplains were later added to the foundation, and there were others who celebrated in the church but were not members of the college. A cloister was built in the late fourteenth century, and there seems to have been much rebuilding of the church in the fifteenth century. It had an annual value of £86 in 1535, and on its dissolution in 1544 it was purchased by the last dean, Miles Spencer, a pluralist who held many other preferments in East Anglia. He seems to have been responsible for the demolition of the church. The buildings became a mansion, largely rebuilt in the mid-eighteenth century as the Assembly Rooms. This incorporates an undercroft and a few other fragments of the college buildings. Excavations have revealed much of the layout of the college; the church was large, about 190 ft (58 m) in external length, and had an aisled chancel of three bays, a crossing with transepts not projecting beyond the aisles, a nave of four bays with a N aisle and a W tower. The cloister was on its S side.

* Raveningham

This chantry college was founded in 1350 by Sir John de Norwich, for a master and eight chaplains or fellows. The Church of St Andrew was appropriated to it. Its subsequent history was curious. In 1371, licence was obtained to move the college to Norton Subcourse, a nearby church which was one of the endowments of the college. This, however, did not happen. Sir John's seat had been Mettingham Castle (Suffolk), which by now belonged to his grandson, another Sir John, who was the last male heir of the family. When he died his cousin, Catherine de Brewse, inherited his properties. In 1382, after her death, her trustees, Sir John Plays and Sir Robert Howard, obtained licence to increase the college to a master and twelve chaplains, and to move it to Mettingham Castle. However, this encountered difficulties, so instead, in 1387, the trustees moved it to Norton Subcourse (*see* p. 234). The college thus had a life at Raveningham of only thirty-seven years, the church then returning to being simply parochial.

The church stands deep in the grounds of Raveningham Hall, with almost no village. It is well maintained and interesting, but there has been considerable nineteenth-century alteration. It has a Norman round W tower, which like the rest of the church is covered in recent rather unattractive render; it has three elementary round-arched openings to the W. An octagonal EE top stage has been added, and there are Perp. stepped battlements and pinnacles, with simple flushwork. The church has nineteenth-century slated roofs of relatively low pitch. It has a nave with a lean-to N aisle and a chancel with a N vestry.

Raveningham, from the north

Raveningham, looking west

The S side of the nave has large traceried Perp. windows with depressed pointed-segmental arches; two are in two lights but the other, though of the same size, is divided into three lights. A tall, plain S porch covers a mutilated S doorway mostly of brick, which still contains its ancient door with excellent, probably thirteenth-century ornamental ironwork. Above the aisle is a clerestory of shallow square-headed windows, perhaps early nineteenth century. The chancel has several large raking buttresses, and its priest's door and side windows of lancet or Y-tracery form are blocked.

The interior is attractively light. The small tower arch is round and plastered, with simple imposts. Internally as externally the nave seems Perp.; its low four-bay arcade has short, roughly plastered octagonal pillars and plain triple-chamfered arches, also plastered; they lean outwards. One pillar is stripped to show its brick construction. The chancel, the axis of which deviates to the N, has its walls covered by much-enriched blank arcading, the arches set within gables with pinnacles and finials. This striking work is filled with memorial inscriptions to the Bacon family of Raveningham Hall, and is beautifully decorated in cream and white. It must be of the early nineteenth century, but it takes its inspiration from one bay on the S side, which is a very elaborate Dec. tomb-recess, at least partly genuine though much restored. This now contains a low tomb of 1708. There is an arched piscina, its jambs unusually continued down to the floor.

The fine octagonal font has carved subjects on its faces, with four saints and the symbols of the evangelists; it rests on a stem surrounded by four lions. The chancel floor is finely laid out with a regular array of ledgers, and also has a late medieval brass to a lady. There is a coffin-lid with a foliated cross. At the W end is a large white free-standing square memorial of 1815, carrying an urn. A chest has its date of 1683 in iron figures.

Rushford

Edmund Gonville was both patron and, from 1326, rector of the Church of St John the Evangelist at Rushford (formerly known as Rushworth). In 1341–2 he established a chantry college in the church, which was appropriated to the college. He did not wish to become master, and in 1342 moved on and became Rector of Terrington; he is best known for his foundation in 1347–8 of Gonville Hall in Cambridge, now Gonville and Caius College. His college at Rushford was initially for a master and four fellows; the statutes required the maintenance of the canonical hours together with four masses daily. In 1485, Lady Anne Wingfield increased the college by two further chaplains, and in 1490 added a grammar school for thirteen boys, later fifteen. In 1535 the annual value of the college was assessed as £85; it was dissolved in 1541. It went to the Earl of Surrey, who destroyed most of the church, the rest being put to agricultural use. Only after 1585, when the estate was purchased by the Buxton family, was the surviving part of the church patched up and restored to its parochial function.

The church is Dec. and was probably built for the college, though an earlier date has been suggested. It must have been a very large and fine building, but what remains is no more than a mutilated fragment: its nobility has gone, but enough is left to be highly interesting and evocative. Its E end outside has broken-off walls and the fine responds of the former chancel arch, together with vaulting shafts; between them is now a small and mean polygonal apse of 1904, roughcast, its string-course and lancet windows constructed of timber. The site of the chancel remains visible as a long, slightly raised area; its length is reported to have been 59 ft (18 m), and it had a S chapel. The nave remains, of four bays; the E bay formerly opened to transepts, and on the N side the responds show outside, again with a vaulting shaft. Internally, the responds of both transept arches are visible, the S ones now opening to a Victorian organ-chamber; the arches are cut off just above their springing, the whole nave having been reduced in height. The present roof is of thatch; the mark of the former roof may be seen on the E wall of the tower.

A lancet-pair is set in the blocked N transept arch, and similar windows occupy the other bays, except for those containing the N and S doorways of continuous mouldings; the windows are set within a larger external feature of which the arch just begins to curve in below the roof. Some of these lancet-pairs are of stone, some of yellow brick, and some of red brick: are they all post-dissolution insertions replacing former traceried windows, or can some represent the original form? Internally the walls retain bold moulded shafts that, when complete, formed large blank arcading, as at nearby Attleborough. The interior is, however, dominated by a remodelling of 1904, with a flat panelled timber

Rushford, from the north

ceiling, a quite elaborate screen, tall wooden panelling and stencilled decoration. This is poor work; it is dark, and the effect is of a small, cheap Victorian church.

There is a Perp. S porch, in flint with some brick, formerly possessing an upper room; it has blocked square-headed side windows and enrichments including carved panels and a little flushwork. The W tower stands complete, tall and stately but plain, with diagonal buttresses and a straight parapet. In its W side are two small trefoiled lancets, and the belfry has large two-light openings of cusped Y-tracery.

The village today is very small, but the church is maintained and has regular services. Part of the domestic building of the college still stands 75 yd to the S, now a private residence. It is of flint and quite impressive, but there are many Victorian alterations. It was formerly a quadrangle, of which two ranges, one of them a chapel, have disappeared. Until 1850, the grammar school building stood just S of the churchyard.

Thetford: St Mary, Bailey End

The Fraternity or Guild of the Blessed Virgin Mary at Thetford became important in later medieval times. About the end of the thirteenth century, by the munificence of Sir Gilbert de Pykenham, a chapel was built for it, in what was then the market-place of the town; the name derives from the area, which was part of the bailey of the castle abandoned 100 years earlier. In 1389, the chapel was served by a master and two priests, and in 1443 endowments were given for a further two priests. It seems to have been incorporated at some time early in the fifteenth century. Its annual value in 1535 was £23, at which time there were a master, two priests and two clerks. In 1538, the Corporation of Thetford sold most of the guild's property, including all the plate of the chapel. The continued existence of the college was presumably largely nominal, but it lasted until dissolution in 1547, when the chapel and other buildings were promptly demolished. There are no remains, and the site has not been excavated.

* Thompson

A small chantry is said to have been established in the Church of St Martin in the late thirteenth century. Perhaps as an enlargement of this, a chantry college for a warden and five priests was founded in 1349 by the patron of the church, Sir Thomas de Shardelowe, with his brother John. This was the year of the Black Death, by which the foundation may have been prompted; it is thought that the founders' mother Agnes died earlier in the year. The church was appropriated, and the college took responsibility for the cure of souls without appointment of a vicar. As specified by the foundation deed, the master was to have an annual stipend of 12 marks and the chaplains 11 marks. The nephew of the founders, Sir John de Shardelow, on his death in 1391 left 100s to the college and 7 marks for a chaplain to celebrate for him there for a year. In the late fifteenth and early sixteenth centuries, the college had a

Thompson, from the north-east

master and only between two and four chaplains. Its annual value was given as £52 in 1534; dissolution came early, in 1541.

The church is aisleless but on quite a large and stately scale. It is almost entirely Dec., and its date is suggested as between about 1300 and 1340, though it is possible it was built for the college. The fine W tower has diagonal buttresses, a plinth with chequer of flint and stone, and battlements with flushwork. Its W window is in three lights with elaborate flowing tracery, while the belfry has simple two-light Y-tracery openings. There is a spacious S porch with long single-light side windows and a blocked three-light window over its arch; it covers an impressive S doorway of three orders of continuous sunk quadrants. The nave has three-light windows of uncusped intersecting tracery; the rood stair climbs up from the reveal of the NE window. In the chancel all windows have splendid flowing tracery, that to the E being of five lights while each side has two windows of three lights. A composition of ogee-trefoiled piscina and triple ogee-cinquefoiled sedilia is set under a square label, three of the spandrels containing a green man. A Perp. addition to the nave, opening by a tall depressed arch, is a broad, shallow S chapel.

This church is outstanding and memorable in that it seems wonderfully unrestored and its contents are almost entirely ancient, of mellow unvarnished oak. It is all in sound condition: its present state is the result of an admirable conservative restoration in 1910–13. The roofs are plain original work. Several painted consecration crosses are visible. The fine S door is original, with a foliage trail running all round. The pews, with poppy-head ends, are

Thompson, looking east

surely late medieval, but the dates 1625 and 1632 are surprisingly inscribed on the two pew fronts: these presumably refer to alterations, perhaps at the time when the attractive Jacobean family box pew was put in adjacent to them. There is a splendid three-decker pulpit of Jacobean work: the octagonal top deck rests on a baluster stem and has a back plate and tester; a rectangular middle deck is below, while the lowest deck in front seems to be made up of earlier parts. At the W end are three ancient chests, one being of dug-out construction. The octagonal font is fine Dec. work, each face having a different design and the stem having cusped-ogee panels. A low screen to the S chapel, with tracery and shields, is probably contemporary with its structure.

The chancel screen is also original, with Dec. tracery in two-light divisions. It has much medieval paint, consisting of decorative patterns in red and black. There are original stalls, of which four retain their carved misericords; the stall fronts too are partly ancient. The charming if rather decayed baluster communion rails are of the seventeenth century. The N windows of the chancel are blocked, as is just the tracery of the others, though their design remains visible inside and out: this must be a seventeenth- or eighteenth-century economy measure (such blocking was common before nineteenth-century restorers got to work: long may it remain here!). All the glass is clear, and the chancel is very light.

The college buildings stand about 500 yd to the S, and are known as College Farm. They are of flint, and most of the basic structure is of the early fifteenth century, although the internal arrangements have been completely altered.

Northamptonshire

This county has a fine series of five collegiate churches. All were varieties of the chantry type, and all are impressive architecturally. Outstanding among them is Fotheringhay, even though it is incomplete.

* Cotterstock

This attractive chantry college was founded by John Gifford, who had been rector of the parish church until 1317: he was one of those medieval clerics whose work was primarily as a servant of the crown, but who obtained a large income from multiple church appointments held simultaneously as a pluralist. From 1313 he was in the service of Queen Isabella, becoming steward of her lands beyond the Trent; later he served the king, one of his appointments being Deputy Justice of South Wales. Gifford made his first moves to establish a college at Cotterstock in about 1335, and purchased the manor and the advowson of the church in 1336. The royal charter was granted in 1338, the episcopal licence in 1339, and the church was appropriated in 1340. Gifford himself died of the Black Death in 1349. His college was large, for a provost, twelve chaplains and two clerks. However, litigation by one Simon Norwiche at the end of the fifteenth century, involving ownership of the manor, resulted in the impoverishment of the college. In 1535 it had only a provost, three priests and three clerks, and its annual value was given as nearly £43. Its dissolution took place early, in 1536.

Cotterstock is a small village, and the Church of St Andrew appears correspondingly modest, except that it has a splendid chancel on a strikingly larger scale. The church otherwise comprises a W tower, aisled nave and S porch, mostly of irregular stone, with low-pitched roofs. The tower has a late Norman W doorway with shafts and a depressed round arch with chevron, both normal and orthogonal. Otherwise the tower is mainly EE, with belfry openings of two lancets under a shafted containing arch, the tympanum containing a blank or pierced motif. Its panelled battlements and diagonal

Cotterstock, from the south-east

buttresses are Perp. The arch to the nave is good EE work. There are two-bay EE arcades, similar but not identical, with quite tall cylindrical pillars. Both the clerestory and the aisles have Dec. two-light square-headed windows, a modification of John Gifford's time. More ambitious than all this is the Perp. S porch, of ashlar, with side windows and a battlemented parapet on the front of which stand three beasts. It contains a tierceron vault with fine bosses, easily seen because they are so low.

The chancel was entirely constructed for the college, and is a fine example of Dec. work. It is in three bays, externally of ashlar, with a straight parapet, gargoyles and regular buttresses; the side windows of three lights and the E window of five all have excellent flowing tracery. Its interior is light, spacious

Cotterstock: the piscina and sedilia

and sophisticated, in contrast to the relative darkness and small scale of the nave. A string-course runs round, and there is an excellent grouping of piscina and triple stepped sedilia, all under crocketed ogee canopies; an engaging refinement is that one sedile is cinquefoiled, the next trefoiled, and the next unfoiled, while the piscina again is cinquefoiled. An ogee aumbry is opposite. The stair for access to the rood opens from the N aisle, but unusually emerges on the chancel side of the wall. An ogee squint passes from the S aisle to the chancel.

The restoration of 1876–7 stripped the plaster from the interior, replaced the roofs except that of the chancel, and was responsible for most of the furnishings. The octagonal font is Perp., with quatrefoil and mouchette designs on its faces, a panelled stem and a charming foliage trail round its base. In the tower are two stone coffin-lids, one with a mutilated thirteenth-century effigy. A very fine brass in the chancel commemorates Provost Wyntryngham, who died in 1420. A vestry is attached at a skew angle at the NE corner; it is now mainly Victorian but originated as part of a range connecting to the domestic accommodation of the college; the site of the latter is now occupied by a farmhouse a few yards further N.

* Fotheringhay

This very beautiful small village has two special claims to fame which make it much visited: the site of the castle where Mary Queen of Scots was executed, now reduced to earthworks but still evocative; and the great collegiate church.

Both have a strong association with the House of York, and the castle was the birthplace of Richard III, the last Yorkist king. In the late fourteenth century, Edmund, fifth son of Edward III and 1st Duke of York, founded a chantry college in the chapel of the castle, which was intended to have the large staff of a master, twelve chaplains and four clerks. Edmund died in 1402, and his son Edward planned to enlarge the college further, and to move it from the castle to the parish church. For this he obtained letters patent in 1411, and papal sanction in 1412; the king, Henry IV, was made principal founder, and the new college had royal freedoms. Its dedication was to St Mary and All Saints. The church was appropriated in 1415; the college had a master, twelve chaplains known as fellows, eight clerks and thirteen choristers. Part of its endowment came from former alien priories, which were finally dissolved in 1414.

Building began in 1414 of a magnificent new chancel for the college, replacing that of the parish church. Construction also started on the domestic buildings, which were on a large scale and laid out around a cloister, sited on land which had for a short period in the twelfth century been occupied by a Cluniac nunnery. Edward was killed in 1415 at Agincourt, but work continued, and the chancel was complete by 1434. In that year, a contract was established by Richard, the 3rd duke, with William Horwood, mason, for the construction of a new nave, which was to be on the same scale and pattern as the chancel. It was completed about 1441. In 1460, Richard was killed at the battle of Wakefield, and his son, having in 1461 become king as Edward IV,

Fotheringhay, from the south-east

refounded and further endowed the college. Its chantry purpose was for the members of the House of York; the statutes specified a life that was almost monastic in character. Its annual value in 1535 was given as nearly £420; it was dissolved in 1548. The chancel and buildings went to Dudley, Earl of Northumberland, who removed the lead from the roofs; the roofless chancel was demolished in 1573. Only the nave of the church remains. The site of the domestic buildings is visible as a rough platform in the field immediately to the S, with traces incorporated in the churchyard wall; the S wall of the church near its E end shows the remains of its former connection to the buildings.

The surviving nave is a noble and exceptionally fine Perp. structure of ashlar, on a very large scale. There were no transepts. The length of the former chancel is not known. The nave is of seven bays, the two W bays embracing the tower, with even the battlemented clerestory parapet continuing. The clerestory windows are of four lights under four-centred arches, and the tall aisle windows too are of four lights, with transoms; the aisles are battlemented

Fotheringhay, looking west

and have buttresses carrying tall pinnacles. Slender flying buttresses arch across to the clerestory, though since they are curved they must contribute more to elegance than to support. There is a very broad, battlemented N porch; alongside the entrance passage is a room, formerly the treasury, and above is a chapel. The present E wall of the church has a five-light window high up which originally opened W from the chancel before the present nave was built, and is 'inside out'. This wall is much patched, and shows traces of the earlier parish church.

The massive tower has a broad but relatively low eight-light W window and a very large W doorway in a square label. Above clerestory level are two stages with clasping buttresses, the upper having very broad four-light transomed belfry openings. There is a straight parapet with battlemented octagonal corner turrets, above which is a very tall octagonal stage with long three-light transomed openings (now largely filled in), rising to its own battlements and pinnacles. Such spectacular octagonal top stages of towers are a Northamptonshire speciality; there is another at Irthlingborough.

The interior is stately and strikingly broad. Its arcades have two-centred arches on tall pillars of complex section, with capitals on their E and W shafts only; the narrower E bay has no arcade opening. The beautiful low-pitched timber roofs are original; surprisingly, the only vault is under the tower, a splendid fan vault dated 1529. Beneath it, on a tall stepped pedestal, the very fine octagonal Perp. font has quatrefoils on its bowl and large grotesques and fleurons below. The excellent hexagonal timber pulpit is fifteenth century; it carries the arms of Edward IV and has a canopy with rich vaulting, which rather confusingly is covered by a much larger Jacobean tester. It has recently been repainted. In 1573, Queen Elizabeth visited, and seeing in the ruined chancel the desecrated tombs of her York ancestors she ordered their reburial in the church. Edward, the 2nd duke, and Richard, the 3rd duke, with his wife Cecily, now have a tomb on each side of the sanctuary, massive, tall and dignified, with paired Corinthian columns. There are excellent oak box pews, with brass knobs, dating from 1817; they stand on probably medieval pew platforms. Parts of the former stalls are now in three nearby churches. A relatively recent addition is the furnishing of a chapel as a memorial to the House of York, dedicated in 1982.

* Higham Ferrers

Henry Chichele was born in Higham Ferrers in 1363; from 1414 to 1443 he was Archbishop of Canterbury and, in addition to foundations in his home town, he founded All Souls College, Oxford. In 1422 he obtained royal licence for a chantry college at Higham Ferrers, for a master, seven chaplains and eight clerks, with six choristers. One chaplain or clerk was to be grammar master, and another choir master. The college was fully established by 1425. The parish Church of St Mary was already exceptionally large and magnificent, but it belonged to Newarke College, Leicester, and was not available for appropriation. However, it was used as the principal church of the college, and an agreement was reached whereby the master of Higham Ferrers would automatically be nominated by Newarke College to the vicarage of the church.

Archbishop Chichele's legacy here is a remarkable set of medieval buildings. Close to the W front of the church stands an exquisite small Perp. chantry chapel, established by the archbishop and long used as the grammar school. He also built or rebuilt a bedehouse for twelve poor men aged over fifty years, with a woman attendant, which was made subject to the college. This still stands on the S side of the churchyard, though it is no longer used for its original purpose. Two hundred yards NW of the church, with the main street between, are the buildings of the college, which are in the care of English Heritage. Though largely in ruins and in part reduced to foundations they are an impressive example of collegiate domestic buildings, laid out around a quadrangle. The E front facing the street has a fine gateway, with a large four-centred arch under a square label, and three canopied image niches above. A range along the S side remains roofed, and its E part is thought to have been a chapel, though it has been much altered.

The size of the church may reflect the importance of the town as a centre of the estates of the earls, later dukes, of Lancaster. Its structure represents two main phases, EE and Dec. The W tower is EE, tall and massive, with set-back buttresses, image niches and much-enriched belfry openings. Above these is a Dec. openwork parapet with corner pinnacles from which openwork flying buttresses leap to the splendid, very tall crocketed spire, which has three tiers of lucarnes and reaches 170 ft (51.8 m). The spire and part of the tower

Higham Ferrers, from the east

collapsed in 1631; creditably, they were promptly rebuilt, to the original design. A remarkable feature is the W portal, deeply recessed into the tower wall, with a ribbed barrel vault above blank arcading. It has twin doorways, their jambs and arches carrying a continuous series of small figures, while the tympanum is covered with scenes in roundels. There are also image niches; but a statue of the Virgin and Child is recent.

The church has low-pitched roofs throughout; the S side is all battlemented and has pinnacles. It consists of twin naves and chancels (the N chancel is liturgically the Lady Chapel); the naves are flanked by lower aisles. There are no chancel arches. Much of the S side, including the battlemented S porch, was conservatively rebuilt during the Victorian restoration. The arcades are of four large bays; the S arcade is rebuilt EE work, with pillars of quatrefoil form, while the other two are in a relatively simple Dec. style, with octagonal pillars. Above is a modest Perp. clerestory. Both aisles have Dec. windows, on the S side arched, on the N square-headed. The chancel and Lady Chapel are long, and have tall three-light side windows of bold ogee form, with reticulated tracery. The very large E windows are in five lights and are again ogee, externally both surmounted by a canopied image niche. Two arches open between the chancel and the Lady Chapel, the E of which is smaller but has splendid Dec. enrichment; it contains a large tomb-chest, contemporary with the structure. This tomb carries a specially fine large brass dated 1337 which, however, does not belong to it; it was placed here in 1633.

Higham Ferrers: the south nave, looking east

There is a great screen, mainly old in its lower parts and due to Archbishop Chichele. Its upper part is of 1920, by J. N Comper, with a rich loft and rood. Also of the fifteenth century are several parclose screens. The chancel has an impressive set of twenty stalls with carved misericords, for the use of the college; they carry the arms of Archbishop Chichele and of the see of Canterbury. There are medieval tiles here too. In the Lady Chapel are brasses to the archbishop's parents and to his brother with his wife. The font is EE, octagonal on a quatrefoil stem, with characteristic decoration on alternate faces. Other furnishings are Victorian, but the screen and ringing gallery in the tower are striking modern work.

* Irthlingborough

In 1353 the manor of Irthlingborough was acquired by John Pyel, a native of the town who had become a wealthy mercer (cloth-merchant) in London, where he was Lord Mayor in 1372. In 1375 he obtained royal licence to found a chantry college in the parish Church of St Peter. However, he died in 1376 and it was not until 1388 that his widow Joan completed the foundation, and several more years passed before it was actually functioning. As a chantry college, it was unusual in that its priests were known as canons, and held prebends; it had a dean and five canons, with four clerks. The church was appropriated. Its annual income in 1535 was almost £71; dissolution took place in 1547.

The basis of the church is EE, but there is a good deal of Dec. work; the latter was probably due to the Pyels and built after 1353, though how late the contributions in this style can be is a matter for debate. It is a large church with some fine features: but it seems at first most peculiar, largely because of its massive tower, which stands some way W of the nave and out of axis with it. It is connected to the W doorway by two sections of building; the one closer to the church has N and S doorways and functions as porch, but the other section (now used as a vestry) is narrow, much patched and altered, and was clearly formerly of two storeys. On the N side of this and the tower are two low, rib-vaulted undercrofts. All these are remaining fragments of the collegiate buildings, of which most unusually the tower formed the nucleus. The tower formerly leaned and was taken down and rebuilt accurately in 1887-93; it is Dec. in style, very tall and distinctive, though perhaps more extraordinary than beautiful. Much is made of the contrast between brown and cream stone. It has four stages, with set-back buttresses and belfry openings of paired traceried single lights flanking an image niche. Above are battlements and polygonal battlemented corner turrets, within which are two further octagonal stages, rising to battlements containing arrow-loops, and an ogee spirelet of timber. Fireplaces in the upper storeys of the tower show that they were used as part of the collegiate accommodation.

The church itself has a battlemented nave with a clerestory of quite large three-light Perp. windows under depressed arches; the aisles and transepts have straight parapets. Also embattled is the chancel, which has a clerestory of

Irthlingborough, from the south-east

Irthlingborough, looking east

straight-headed Dec. windows and is flanked by broad chapels; its axis deviates to the N. All roofs are low-pitched throughout. The main windows are varied, mostly Dec. or Perp., but there are also a few lancets. The W doorway is impressively flanked on each side by an ogee-trefoiled stoup recess surmounted by two canopied image niches. Internal surfaces of the church have lost their plaster. The nave arcades are of four bays and ignore the transepts. They are EE, with double-chamfered arches on quatrefoil pillars, though they are not identical; the effect of contrasting stone colours is used here too. On the S side is the rood opening. Beneath the S transept is a vaulted crypt or charnel-house. A modern glass screen separates the N transept as a parish room, which opens by a massive arch on its E side to a further room of 1988; previously, this arch was a blank recess of puzzling purpose. Externally the new extension matches the old work quite convincingly, having a panelled Perp. parapet which was reset from the N chapel. The two-bay chancel arcades resemble those of the nave. In the N chapel is a remarkably elaborate aumbry, in an enriched ogee setting; it was reassembled in 1934 from its rediscovered fragments. The S chapel has several image brackets and a squint to the chancel with a battlemented cinquefoiled front. In the sanctuary are a double piscina with a pendant double arch, and a richly trefoiled Easter Sepulchre recess and tomb.

Most furnishings are good-quality nineteenth-century work. From the collegiate days there remain eight stalls with poppy-head ends and some misericords. The octagonal Perp. font has a bowl with battlemented edges and panelled sides, on a panelled stem. There are several medieval memorials including, in the S chapel, the tomb-chest with recumbent alabaster effigies of John and Joan Pyel. The altar in this chapel is a rich Perp. tomb-chest, with a panelled front and canopy.

* Northampton: All Saints

This was a very large and important medieval parish church. In the mid-fifteenth century as many as sixteen chaplains served in it, belonging to the fraternities of the Holy Trinity, the Virgin Mary, Corpus Christi, St George, the Rood, St John the Baptist and St Katharine. In 1460, the vicar of the church, William Breton, was granted royal licence to found a college, with the purpose of establishing in perpetuity a common life for the vicar and these priests. A common residence was constructed; the vicar was warden, and the other priests were known as fellows. The church was not appropriated. The independent income of the college was very small, as the chaplains continued to be supported by their fraternities. Dissolution took place probably in 1548.

The church was burnt in a great fire which in 1675 destroyed much of the town. Its replacement is of 1676–80, the architect probably being Henry Bell. It is a very large and splendid building, externally all of brown ashlar, in a rich classical style. It is one of the few churches built outside London at this period that may be compared with Wren's work. The tower of the former church was retained, internally showing small and low N and S arches of multiple pointed

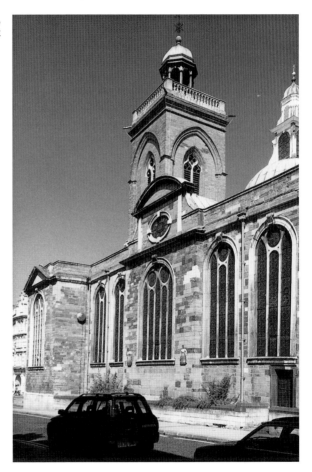

Northampton: All Saints, from the south-east

orders; there may be a Norman core here, but these arches are work of the early seventeenth century, when the tower was strengthened. The upper parts are Gothic, but were probably altered in the seventeenth century; they are surmounted by a balustrade and an octagonal open cupola of 1704. It is now a W tower and forms the main entrance, but it was central in the medieval church, which had a nave extending an unknown distance across the square to the W; the present large church occupies the site of only the medieval E limb. The narthex areas flanking the tower are wider than the church itself, and represent the former transepts. Across the W front is a very impressive portico of Ionic columns, eight wide and two deep, added in 1701. It has a balustraded parapet, and in the centre stands a statue of Charles II, in Roman costume: this is of 1712, commemorating his assistance in the rebuilding.

The nave is of three very large bays, with full-height aisles of the same width as the bays, the whole thus forming a square; it has great Ionic columns, and the centre has a coffered dome carrying a beautiful lantern, externally in two stages.

Northampton: All Saints, looking east from the west gallery

A large chandelier with four tiers of branches hangs from here. There are splendidly enriched plaster ceilings, which in the central bays of both axes are in the form of shallow coffered tunnel vaults. Externally the church has straight parapets; the central bay projects slightly, and has a gable with an oval window and segmental pediment. The very large windows are round-arched in moulded surrounds with a scrolled keystone; their division into multiple lights, with curious tracery, is original. Galleries resting on fluted Ionic columns of timber run round three sides; they have fine panelled fronts, but they stand back behind the main columns, to rather curious effect: this is an amendment of 1865. There is a large chancel, also of the seventeenth century, though much additional enrichment was applied here in 1888, including a great mahogany reredos with columns, pilasters and much gilding. Contrasting on its S side is a low two-bay chapel in late Perp. style, added as a Great War memorial. Beneath the chancel is a second medieval survival, a rib-vaulted crypt perhaps of the fourteenth century.

Though the furnishings were much altered in the nineteenth century, a good deal of seventeenth-century work remains, including the beautiful enriched baluster communion rails, the marble font with gadrooned circular bowl and original cover, and the rich hexagonal pulpit with gilding. The pews are made from the materials of the old box pews. There is an elaborate mayor's pew. A structure with a raised reading platform and moulded Royal Arms was formerly a consistory court. There are many mural memorials.

This remains today an important and active church, and it is used for the civic services of the town. It has a musical life of cathedral type. The name of College Street to the NW is a reminder of the site of the collegiate building.

Northumberland

Only one church in this county has a place here. Also of much interest, however, are the remains of the intended college at Warkworth, which was almost certainly never completed (*see* Appendix IV).

* Ponteland

The name of this place is pronounced 'ponteeland'. As shown by a charter of not later than 1155, the rectory of the Church of St Mary was already at that time divided into three, all in the gift of the same patron: this was a church of portioners, though they were also referred to as prebendaries. In 1240, by a decision of the papal legate, one of the portioners was responsible for the cure of souls, while the others were 'to serve the church fittingly for the prebends'; if absent, they were to provide vicars. This implies that the function was collegiate. About 1270, the patron of the time, Peter de Montfort, granted the church to the newly founded Merton College in Oxford. This action, however, was opposed by the bishops of Durham, leading eventually to an appeal to Rome by the warden and scholars of Merton. As a result, in 1302 a bull of Pope Boniface VIII confirmed the grant of Ponteland to Merton College, and in May 1303 the pope rejected an appeal against this decision. In consequence, the portions disappeared, and Ponteland became a vicarage in the patronage of Merton College, as it remains today.

Ponteland, from the south

The church is attractive and enjoyable, although it has suffered considerable restoration, including the removal of all plaster and the replacement of its roofs. It is cruciform, built mainly of squared sandstone. The unbuttressed W tower is in three stages, of which the two lower are Norman; the W doorway is original, with a lintel and an arch with chevron. The top stage is Perp., with a straight parapet; it has been given a rather curious twentieth-century ogee finial or spirelet of metal. A big SW buttress seems to have been provided for structural reasons; a Victorian stair turret has been added at the NE corner. Inside, the tower arch is EE. The nave has arcades of four bays, the E bay corresponding to the transepts; they have double-chamfered arches dying without capitals into octagonal pillars. On the S side this is Perp. work, but on the N it is a nineteenth-century rebuilding, except for its perhaps Norman W respond. The S aisle and S transept windows are Perp., mostly with depressed arches. The aisles have straight parapets and low-pitched lean-to roofs, and the S side has a little clerestory of trefoiled circles. There is an attractive S porch, vaulted on transverse arches; this is regarded as EE work reset in its present position.

Differing markedly from the rest, the impressive N transept and chancel date from an EE building campaign. The transept has a fine graduated lancet triplet in its N wall, and three good uniform lancets in its E side; internally, all the lancets are shouldered, the N ones surprisingly with lintels, and there is an arched piscina. This is an excellent EE ensemble. The chancel is long, in three bays. Externally it has regular buttresses and a string-course. Two of its lancet windows remain, internally shouldered, but most of its windows are now Dec. The inner order of the double-chamfered chancel arch rests on strikingly carved (but restored) corbels representing Adam and Eve.

The fittings are relatively undistinguished; disconcertingly, the modern seating in the chancel faces W, towards the nave altar. There are some attractive mural memorials. Above the tower arch is a Georgian Royal Arms on canvas. The font is perhaps fourteenth century, with a plain octagonal bowl on a square base. A little old glass survives in the chancel S windows.

Nottinghamshire

Of the collegiate churches of Nottinghamshire, that of Southwell is of course supreme, and is now the cathedral. The others were all chantry colleges; most were minor, but Sibthorpe was more substantial, and is a very attractive example.

* Clifton

In 1349, three chantry priests were established in the Church of St Mary the Virgin by Sir Gervase Clifton. In 1476, his great-great-grandson, Sir Robert Clifton, increased the endowments and formed the three priests into a small college of a warden and two fellows, dedicated to the Holy Trinity. After the death of Sir Robert in 1478, the foundation was completed by his son, another

Sir Gervase. The church was not appropriated. The annual value of the college in 1534 was just £20 2s 6d; all three priests remained until the surrender in 1547 or 1548.

The church has an attractive setting close to the large Georgian Clifton Hall. It appears as a substantial village church, cruciform, with a tall central tower. Parts may date from around 1349. The tower is Dec. throughout, including its double-chamfered arches on half-octagonal responds, with the stair incorporated in its large NW pillar. It is battlemented and has three ashlar-built stages above the low-pitched roofs of the church; most of its openings have Y-tracery. The nave appears externally Dec., with mostly two-light windows; it has lean-to aisles, a clerestory of square-headed windows, and W of the S transept a low medieval attachment, apparently a sacristy. A N porch covers a charming Dec. doorway which is simply chamfered but enriched with four-petalled flowers in relief. The arcades are of three bays: the two E bays on the N are fine Trans. Norman work, with cylindrical pillars, capitals having flat leaves, square imposts and slightly pointed arches with a keeled roll and a dog-tooth hood-mould. The S arcade is Dec., with double-chamfered arches on octagonal pillars which have striking capitals of giant knobbly leaves. Also Dec. is the S transept, which has three-light arched windows, with tracery.

The chancel was rebuilt when the college was established; it is of ashlar, with large three-light straight-headed side windows and an arched E window, of five lights with a transom. Its interior also is ashlar-faced; it has an ogee-trefoiled piscina and a fine composition of triple ogee-cinquefoiled sedilia,

Clifton, from the south

with relief pinnacles. The roof is original, and has bosses which have been coloured and gilded to lovely effect. A rich doorway of late Tudor type on the S side is dated 1632, and leads to a low ashlar attachment in Perp. style, perhaps originally a sacristy but now a sealed mausoleum. The N transept has features similar to those of the chancel, and was no doubt rebuilt at the same time.

A large stone-faced parish room has been attached alongside the church on the S. Internally, the church is now effectively divided into two parts. The nave was completely refitted in the 1970s: it has a new roof, which has distinctive sunk timber panels for acoustic purposes, and furnishings of pale oak in a rather aggressively modern style. The altar is beneath the tower, and the Victorian chancel screen has been bleached and glazed. Only one old fitment remains: the plain perhaps fourteenth-century octagonal font. The S transept is used with the nave, mainly as storage. Very different is the atmosphere in the chancel and N transept. The chancel has some excellent nineteenth-century furnishings, also a heavy medieval chest with curved top. An extraordinary small late-medieval timber carving is identified as depicting a spitting Jew. An impressive series of memorials, all to the Clifton family, largely fills the N transept. Of three brasses in the floor, one is to Sir Robert, the founder of the college, and another to his son, Sir Gervase. Two medieval tomb-chests have recumbent effigies of alabaster, and a tomb-chest of 1587 carries recumbent effigies of yet another Sir Gervase, with his two wives. Most remarkable is a large standing wall memorial of 1631, its lower part carrying what appears as a black coffin, below which a stone grated enclosure is open to reveal a most macabre simulated jumble of bones and skulls.

Ruddington

Royal licence for this small and rather odd chantry college was obtained in 1459 by William Babington. A college house was constructed at Ruddington, and the college was to use the Chapel of St Andrew in the S aisle of the parish Church of St Peter; the church was not appropriated. The college was for a warden and four chaplains. However, two of the chaplains were to celebrate not at Ruddington but at the chapel in the manor of Chilwell, another property of the Babingtons. Since Chilwell is almost 5 miles away, on the other side of the Trent, these chaplains cannot normally have lived at Ruddington. The value of the college in 1534 was £30, at which time there were only a warden and two chaplains, one of whom was serving at Chilwell. In 1546 there remained only the warden and one chaplain; dissolution took place soon after.

The church stood at a place known as Flawford, 1 mile from the main village. As early as the thirteenth century, a Chapel of St Mary was built in the village; in the early eighteenth century the chapel was enlarged, and the parish church was by this time scarcely used and was falling into ruin. In 1773, the Archbishop of York came and solemnized the transfer to the chapel of both the parochial status and the dedication of the old church. The latter was then demolished. During the demolition a very fine group of three probably late-fourteenth-century alabaster figures was found under the chancel floor, presumably hidden at the Reformation; they are now in the Castle Museum in Nottingham. The site, still today far from houses, is an attractive open space, with a few scattered gravestones; it has been excavated in recent years, and the plan of the quite large church is marked in the grass. The replacement church was rebuilt in 1825 and again in 1887–8; it is large and quite ambitious. Only the tower, at the NW corner, is in its lower part medieval. In 1887–8, it was given a tall and elaborate upper stage, but, curiously, reset atop this is a modest recessed stone spire of medieval work, with one tier of simple lucarnes. There is even a story that this was originally on the old church at Flawford, and so has been twice rebuilt on this tower.

* Sibthorpe

This is a particularly interesting example of a chantry college. It owes its existence to Thomas Sibthorpe, a member of a wealthy local family who was a priest and also served as a clerk in royal service. In 1324 he endowed a perpetual chantry for one priest, to be established in a Chapel of St Mary which he caused to be added to the parish Church of St Peter. Successive subsequent enlargements of this foundation led to there being in 1335 three chaplains, one with the title of warden, and a clerk as their server; two of the chaplains served in the Chapel of St Mary, the other in a Chapel of St Anne, also attached to the church and built or rebuilt by Thomas Sibthorpe. He continued to increase his foundation: it was incorporated, in 1340 the church was appropriated to

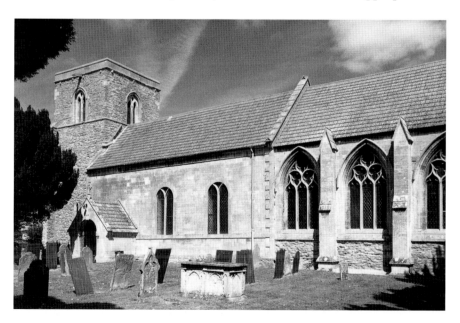

Sibthorpe, from the south-east

it and by 1343 it reached its full complement of a warden, nine chaplains and two clerks. At this stage, Thomas Sibthorpe undertook his greatest building campaign, causing the chancel of the church to be rebuilt on a splendid scale.

The college is interesting for the survival of its very detailed original statutes, describing all aspects of its life, and giving particular attention to the liturgy and to the lights which were to be maintained in the church. It seems unlikely, however, that standards were maintained in later years as Thomas Sibthorpe intended: the number of chaplains in the sixteenth century is not known, but the annual value in 1534 was only £25 18s 8d, and the last warden, Thomas Magnus, was a pluralist who is unlikely to have spent much time here. The college was surrendered in 1545 by Magnus, who then purchased for £197 a life grant of it and its property.

Sibthorpe: the north side of the nave

The present appearance is of a modest village church of a tower and nave, but with a very fine Dec. chancel on a noticeably larger scale. It is a delightful building. The tower is of rubble with minimal dressings, in two stages with angle buttresses and a straight parapet. This is EE work, as seen in the W door-way, a S lancet window and the belfry openings of two lights under a containing arch, with a pierced spandrel. Its small arch to the nave has two chamfered ribs resting on corbels. The nave has lost two aisles: the N was the Chapel of St Mary, Thomas Sibthorpe's first addition to the church. Externally its two blocked arches are visible, with E of them an arched piscina recess, and the blocking contains windows of reticulated tracery, one of four lights, the other of three in its upper part but most oddly stepping out below to five lights. This last feature was probably an amendment made when the aisle was demolished and the windows reset, perhaps in the seventeenth century. The Chapel of St Anne was on the S, but this side is now aisleless and eighteenth century, of smooth ashlar, with plain round-arched windows containing Y-tracery. There is also an eighteenth-century S porch. The nave has a plain flat plaster ceiling. A fine EE arch opens to the chancel, with good stiff-leaf capitals on two orders of attached shafts.

The chancel is slightly higher and wider than the nave. It is of three bays, with regular buttresses and fine three-light side windows of flowing tracery, all to the same design; the E window has five lights. On the N side, there is a coffin-lid with a foliated cross in a low arched tomb recess, which seems Victorian or heavily restored. Above it, however, unrestored and even retaining some colour, is an ogee Easter Sepulchre recess, flanked by panels with carved sleeping soldiers, with above these the risen Christ and censing angels, set in a large crocketed gable. Easter sepulchres of this type are characteristic of Nottinghamshire and Lincolnshire. There is an excellent alabaster tomb-chest of 1590, with a back plate and recumbent effigy. The font is one of many in this area dated 1662; it has a curved octagonal bowl on an octagonal stem, with characteristic simple decoration.

* Southwell

This very important church had early origins, but the first generally accepted date is 956, when lands here were given to Oskytel, Archbishop of York. The college may have been established soon afterwards. With Beverley and Ripon, it was one of the three great collegiate churches of the Diocese of York, which in their regions had much of the influence and independence of cathedrals. Prebendaries were probably established by Archbishop Ealdred, who died in 1069. There were originally seven, but they were increased to sixteen by the 1290s. It then also had sixteen vicars choral, together with sub-deacons, choristers and clerks. In addition there were many chantry priests, reaching thirteen in the fifteenth century. A grammar school was supported, with one of the vicars choral as master, assisted by a chantry priest. In 1302 Archbishop Corbridge laid down that at least two canons should always be in residence. Unusually, the college had no head; the senior canon in residence presided at chapter meetings. In 1535, three canons were in residence; in addition to the vicars choral and chantry priests, there were four deacons or sub-deacons, six choristers, two thuribulers and two clerks.

The history of Southwell from 1540 is surprising. It was one of the churches proposed as a new see under Henry VIII, and with this intention the college was dissolved in August 1540. However, this came to nothing. Remarkably, by Act of Parliament in January 1543, the entire college was reinstated as it had been. In 1548, under Edward VI, it was again dissolved. But this, too, was not the end: in 1557, under Queen Mary, it was decided that it had been exempt

Southwell Minster: south side
of the nave, looking west

from the Chantries Act under which it had been dissolved, and it was again
reinstated, still with sixteen prebendaries. New statutes were given in 1585
under Queen Elizabeth. In this period it had six vicars choral, six choristers
and six singing men. Not until 1841 was the college dissolved, subject to the
life interest of the existing prebendaries. It was raised to cathedral rank in
1884; all the former prebendaries were by then dead, but one vicar choral of
the collegiate church survived to become a vicar choral of the cathedral.

The minster is a glorious building, dominating the little town and fully
deserving its cathedral status. It is remarkably well preserved throughout,
perfect and showing little restoration; it is all of excellent ashlar. Its internal
length is given as 306 ft (93 m). It is not particularly lofty: it is its exquisite
qualities that most impress. The nave, crossing and transepts, with a central
tower and twin W towers, are of a uniform Norman build of the first half of
the twelfth century. Some aisle windows and the great W window are Perp.
insertions, but the transepts have completely unaltered elevations with three

tiers of Norman windows; their gables are remarkably covered in an ornamental pattern. Internally, little chevron is to be seen; capitals are scalloped
and there is much billet and rope-moulding, the latter especially striking on a
very large scale on the crossing arches. Outside, chevron appears on a string-
course all round and on the S transept doorway, the W portal and the splendid
six-order N doorway. The last is covered by an impressive and large barrel-
vaulted porch, with a Norman room above. The W front is very fine; the
towers carry very effective lead-covered pyramidal spires, a Victorian reinstatement of the probable original form. Also entirely Norman is the central
tower, with two stages above the pitched roofs. The aisles are rib vaulted, but
the high roofs are of timber, now renewed. Including the towers, the nave has
eight bays. The arcade has massive and quite short cylindrical piers, while the
triforium is of single arches but has corbels or stumps suggesting an unfulfilled
intention to subdivide; the clerestory has single windows, externally circular.

The E limb is a glorious EE rebuilding. It is vaulted throughout, but the
triforium and clerestory are combined, so the elevations are of only two stages.
It has six aisled bays, with the high chancel continuing for a further two; there
are small E transepts of aisle height. Its windows are uniform large lancets,
mostly in pairs, with filleted shafts. All arches have spendid deep mouldings.
The arcade pillars are of eight equal shafts. There is much dog-tooth and nailhead decoration; capitals are mostly moulded but with stiff-leaf in such
important places as the lancets of the sanctuary. Large arched double piscinas

Southwell Minster: the chancel, looking east

of uniform design appear, also several triangular-headed aumbries. The lavish quintuple sedilia with piscina are an insertion of about 1330; they show some restoration. With these goes the splendid and noble chancel screen, with ogee arches throughout and very rich decoration; its vault has flying ribs. An EE chapel opens off the E side of the N transept. From the N chancel aisle, an arcaded passage leads to perhaps the loveliest and most famous feature of Southwell, the octagonal chapter-house. This is of about 1290; it has large three-light windows of late geometrical tracery, and is small enough that its lierne vault of stone needs no central pillar. Its greatest glory is the wonderful foliage carving of its capitals and other features, which is naturalistic, reproducing with exquisite fidelity many wild species.

There are few old fittings, but they include a superb late medieval brass lectern recovered in the eighteenth century from the pond at Newstead Priory, into which it was doubtless thrown for concealment in 1539. In the S transept is a set of medieval benches with poppy-head ends. Just six carved misericords remain in the chancel. The W door is magnificent original Norman work, with elaborate ironwork, while the N doorway has remarkable fourteenth-century doors covered in reticulated mouldings. There is a little old glass. The lovely octagonal font is dated 1661, and has its original cover. Archbishop Sandys, who died in 1588, has an especially fine alabaster tomb-chest. Other furnishings include many beautiful modern contributions.

Southwell was a favourite residence of many archbishops of York, and the

Southwell Minster: Norman blank arcading in the porch

ruins of their large palace lie to the SE, with a part incorporated in the early-twentieth-century bishop's palace. N and W of the minster there are the successors to many former prebendal houses, some incorporating medieval parts. Although never separately incorporated, common residences were built for both the chantry priests and the vicars choral. The latter, standing to the E, continued in use after the Reformation, and was mostly rebuilt about 1780 as the charming Vicars' Court.

* Tuxford

In 1362 John de Lungvillers, patron of the parish Church of St Nicholas, was granted licence by Edward III to found in it a chantry college of five priests, one being known as warden, with the rectory house becoming the collegiate accommodation. The advowson was to be given to the college. However, his plan does not seem to have taken effect in this form. Instead, six years later he gave the church to Newstead Priory, on condition that the priory maintain three chaplains in it for the chantry purpose originally intended, and two more at Newstead for the same object. As a college, therefore, this was marginal; but despite the ownership by Newstead, it had some independent existence. There were still three chantry priests at Tuxford in 1534, though the annual income was stated to be the very small sum of £9 2s 1d. It continued after the dissolution of the priory, but was surrendered in 1545.

The church is attractive and interesting, though it is only of medium size. It is externally mostly of ashlar. The W tower has diagonal buttresses and is in two stages, with an ogee-trefoiled single-light W window and arched belfry openings, of which the former two-light tracery has for some reason been roughly broken away; it is battlemented and carries a recessed broach spire of stone, with one tier of spire-lights. The tower arch of triple chamfers dying into the responds confirms its Dec. date. All the roofs of the church are low pitched, and all except the chancel have battlemented parapets, producing some surprisingly romantic skylines, especially where they involve the large square battlemented turret of the rood stair S of the chancel arch. The nave roof is fine and has bosses and at the sides winged angels; other roofs have been renewed, and plaster has been stripped from the walls. The nave has four bays; the S arcade is Dec., with octagonal pillars, while the N arcade, with cylindrical pillars and trumpet capitals, is EE. Above is a clerestory of three-light Perp. windows with four-centred arches; the aisle windows are similar. Both sides have a porch, the S much the larger, with its Dec. arch flanked by rectangular niches of dissimilar sizes, which no doubt contained images.

The fine chancel was built around 1495, a gift of the Prior of Newstead. Its E window is of five lights, and the S side has four regularly buttressed bays with three-light pointed segmental windows; all window tracery is uncusped. On the N side is a medieval sacristy. W of this, a two-bay Perp. arcade rather surprisingly opens to a large square room now mainly of the seventeenth century, with two large square-headed N windows and a flat plaster ceiling

Tuxford, from the south

with moulded coving. It also has a Dec. piscina. The walls of this room are mostly lined with memorials, and there are two fourteenth-century recumbent effigies, one of a knight and one of a lady, and a very large but damaged standing wall memorial of 1625 with two recumbent effigies. This is used as a parish room, but the memorials have a dominating effect!

The S aisle has a large head corbel carrying the lower half of a finely draped seated figure, which was probably a Virgin and Child. Beside this, probably originally serving as a reredos, a large square panel with enriched ogee-cinque-foiled arch contains a carving of the martyrdom of St Laurence: he was roasted on a gridiron. St Laurence also appears above in late-medieval glass: presumably this was a chapel dedicated to him. The upper part of the chancel screen is late medieval, with elaborate tracery. An amusing feature in the sacristy is a cupboard made from half of a probably late Georgian pulpit. The font, with an elegantly shaped plain octagonal bowl on a tall octagonal stem, is dated 1662 (a date shared with many others in this area). It has a tall cover dating from this time, with finials and pretty patterning; and, remarkably, it also has a large and rich canopy dated 1673, suspended above on a chain.

Oxfordshire

Every college of Oxfordshire was in Oxford itself, where there were fourteen just before 1540, all but one of academic type. The chapels of the Oxford colleges form a very fine series, those of Merton College and New College being on a very large scale, while that of Christ Church is also the cathedral. Many adopt the 'T' plan, which is almost peculiar to Oxford. Several were built in the first half of the seventeenth century, a period notable in Oxford for a late flowering of the Gothic style. The chapels of the Oxford colleges are also memorable for the extensive survival of their old glass, both medieval and seventeenth or eighteenth century. Some of the colleges in their earlier period used parish churches of the town as their chapels, before building their own.

* Oxford: All Souls College

Henry Chichele, Archbishop of Canterbury from 1414 to 1443, was the founder both of a college in his home town of Higham Ferrers (Northamptonshire) and of the small Cistercian St Bernard's College at Oxford. In 1436 he began moves to establish an academic college at Oxford; building began in 1438, in which year the foundation charter was granted by Henry VI. At Chichele's suggestion, the king accepted the role of co-founder; only a few years later he was to embark on his great foundations at Eton and Cambridge. The college was sufficiently ready for the first members to take up residence in 1442. Statutes were given by Chichele in 1443, shortly before his death, and building was completed in about 1447. This was a major foundation, for a warden and forty fellows. Chichele had been educated at

All Souls College, Oxford: the chapel, from the south

Winchester and at New College, and the influence of the latter is seen at All Souls in both its constitution and its architecture. It had a very strong chantry aspect: it was the College of All the Souls of the Faithful Departed, and prayers for the royal family, the House of Lancaster, were a prominent part of its statutes. When the House of York came to power in the 1460s, it was threatened with the loss of its possessions, but agreement was reached.

Front Quadrangle remains basically as it was built; the chapel forms its N side. As at Magdalen College, it is a somewhat reduced version of that of New College, in 'T' plan, with a body of five bays and an antechapel of two. It is of ashlar, with battlements, pinnacles and boldly projecting buttresses; the windows are of three lights, transomed, under four-centred arches. The W range

All Souls College, Oxford: the chapel, looking east

of the court abuts on to the antechapel, which, however, partly projects into the court. A further small square projection has a doorway opening to an exquisite corridor fan-vaulted in four bays, at the end of which a moulded straight-topped doorway opens to the chapel. Because of the course of Catte Street to the W, the W wall is skew and forces the whole antechapel to be so as well. Its main W window is of seven lights.

Two lofty arches open to each transept, with pillars of four shafts and four hollows. The fine main roof is original, of hammerbeam form, with gilt angels. Perp. panelling appears below the W window and elsewhere. In the sanctuary, the elaborate triple sedilia and other details are mainly restoration by Sir Gilbert Scott in the 1870s, as is the very rich tomb-recess on the N side; a striking recumbent effigy of white marble here is early twentieth century. There is no E window, the hall being beyond, and the E wall forms a reredos, with canopy work in three tiers. Unlike the similar work at New and Magdalen colleges, this is largely authentic and is very fine, though the statuary is Victorian.

There are original stalls with good carved misericords and desks with poppy-head ends. Much of the back panelling, however, is restoration. Separating the chapel from the antechapel, the screen is the one classical piece here, of 1664 and 1716, with Corinthian columns and pilasters, its great central arch surmounted by an open pediment; it is painted dark blue with much gold, a dramatic and rich mixture. Most glass in the antechapel is original work of the 1440s, and is particularly good. There are several fine standing wall memorials, some good mural tablets and, in the floor, a few small medieval brasses. Four bright panels of seventeenth-century painting on boards once adorned the roof above the sanctuary, and are a reminder of a once extensive scheme of decoration of that period.

All Souls remains different from all the other old Oxford colleges in that it has no undergraduates.

Oxford: Balliol College

The beginnings of Balliol were humble, and it only gradually grew in stature. It started in the 1260s as a house for sixteen poor scholars, who were funded by John de Balliol, lord of Barnard Castle (Co. Durham), as a penance imposed on him by the Bishop of Durham. Balliol's claim to be the earliest of the Oxford academic colleges is based on the fact that it has never moved from this first site, but it was not a college at that stage. After his death in 1269, John de Balliol's widow Devorgilla continued the support, and in 1282 gave the house its first charter. In the following years, further benefactions were given, including those of Sir Philip de Somervyle, who in 1340 provided new statutes. Growth continued through the Middle Ages, and further statutes were given in 1507 by Richard Fox, Bishop of Winchester. By these, it had a master, ten graduate fellows and ten scholars, with two chaplains to serve the chapel.

In its early years, the college used as its chapel the nearby Church of St Mary Magdalen, the N aisle of which may have been added for the purpose. It is a short and very broad church, squeezed between streets E and W. Though interesting, it is not very attractive, and it was severely restored in 1841–2, an early work by G.G. Scott. It has an early-sixteenth-century W tower largely embraced by the aisles, in four stages and battlemented; its plinth has two authentic Perp. friezes of shield-enclosing quatrefoils, but all else is renewed. The body of the church has three bays, with arcades partly Perp. but partly Victorian; a Norman chancel arch is reported to have been removed in 1841. The broad N aisle, known as the Martyrs' Aisle, is entirely by Scott; he made its W bay a little wider, with a N–S roof and a rich N entrance. Both aisles have pitched roofs, and another covers an outer S aisle. The latter is Dec. work of about 1330; its arcade has three bays not of equal size, with arches of two sunk hollow chamfers and no capitals. Its windows have reticulated tracery, renewed but supposedly authentic in design, and the enriched S buttresses with large statues in niches also reproduce the original form. W of this aisle is a Perp. porch. All four E windows of the church are Victorian, with rich Dec. style tracery. The font is an elaborate Perp. piece. A chest probably of about 1300 has its front carved with geometrical tracery.

Licence for a chapel in the college was first obtained from the bishop in 1293, and building began in 1309, but owing to difficulties over finance it was not complete until 1327. This chapel was rebuilt on the same site in 1522–9. It was again completely replaced in 1856–7, when the architect was William Butterfield. The approach, however, is by a passage through the medieval range W of the chapel, entered by a splendidly rich Perp. doorway with ogee finial. The chapel is an undivided rectangle, very lofty and with a very high-

Balliol College, Oxford: the chapel, from the south-west

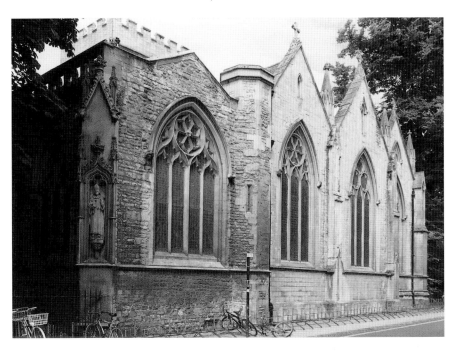

Oxford: St Mary Magdalen, from the south-east

pitched roof; a timber arch distinguishes the two sanctuary bays from the three remaining bays. Externally it is of banded pink and buff stone, and the bays are defined by flat buttresses connected above the windows by moulded arches. The windows are large, in two or three lights, with tracery of late geometrical type, internally shafted; the E window has five lights. At the NW corner is a tall turret of chamfered square plan; its top is open as a belfry, above which is a stumpy spire.

Many of the fittings are classical work from the preceding chapel. The hexagonal pulpit with Corinthian angle columns is Jacobean. There is noble panelling, some of it seventeenth century. A fine screen separates the W end as an antechapel; the organ is impressively cantilevered out from the W wall. The splendid brass lectern, with a crowned eagle, dates from about 1630. Also of metal is the extraordinary long altar table, with five large medallions: it is a war memorial dating from 1927. The windows have extensive sixteenth-century glass, transferred from the previous chapel.

* Oxford: Brasenose College

Brasenose Hall existed from about 1260, and was long owned by University College; it was one of many academic halls in Oxford, which were essentially no more than boarding-houses. The name is believed to have come from its brass door-knocker; the supposed original was recovered in 1890 from

Brasenose College, Oxford: the east wall of the chapel

Stamford in Lincolnshire, and is mounted in the hall of the present college. It was in the early sixteenth century that William Smyth, Bishop of Lincoln, and Sir Richard Sutton, a lawyer, decided to establish a new college, absorbing Brasenose Hall as its basis. The foundation date is usually taken as 1509, in which year building work began on the new quadrangle; the charter dates from 1512. The founders specified that it should have a provost and twelve fellows, but the numbers were at first smaller than this. Brasenose Hall and other previous buildings on the site were demolished, with the exception of a fifteenth-century structure that became the kitchen. What is now called Old Quadrangle was completed by 1518, with a hall and gatehouse. There was no proper chapel, a room on the first floor being used for the purpose.

In the early seventeenth century the college began a second quadrangle. The E side of this has the library standing above what was an open cloister, built in 1657–9; the cloister was converted to rooms in 1807. On the S side is the chapel, begun in 1656 and consecrated in 1666. It is a remarkable and engaging building, perhaps the last of Oxford's buildings distinctively to combine classical and late Gothic styles, and one of the boldest. It again employs the 'T' plan, and is externally all of ashlar, lofty but only of medium size. Its chancel has five bays. The windows have pointed arches and tracery of curious but basically Gothic form; the side ones are of three lights, but the end ones have five and are distinguished by a large oval in their tracery. Externally, the S and W sides are almost Gothic, with buttresses and crocketed pinnacles. By contrast, the N side (facing the court) is largely classical, with Corinthian pilasters, a dentilled cornice and a high parapet carrying elaborate urns. Alongside the chancel, the cloister continues, now forming a vestry and porch, with oval windows in pairs and a stone tunnel vault. The N façade of the transept has a large, totally classical, doorcase with broken segmental pediment, and a shaped gable. Similarly largely classical is the E wall.

Internally, the structure is plain with the exception of the roof which is the supreme achievement here, exuberant and extraordinary. It is a most elaborate fan vault, of plaster; it has pendants at the sides and centre, and stands out from the walls on brackets. The brackets are in fact hammerbeams, and remarkably the basis is a fifteenth-century hammerbeam roof reused from the chapel of the former Augustinian St Mary's College, which Brasenose had bought in 1580. This determined the dimensions of the new building. It has colour added in the nineteenth century.

Brasenose College, Oxford: the plaster fan vault of the chapel

The chapel has much good woodwork, with oak panelling all round, stalls, a pulpit and a splendid balcony screen on Ionic columns, carrying the organ; all this work is seventeenth century in part, but much restored. As elsewhere in Oxford, perspective arches appear on the panelling and pulpit. The restrained reredos of marble, with Ionic pilasters and columns, is of about 1740. Two large brass chandeliers are of 1749. The particularly large and haughty brass eagle lectern was given in 1731.

* Oxford: Cardinal College

Thomas Wolsey, born of humble parents in Ipswich, rose to be Archbishop of York, a cardinal, and from 1515 Chancellor of England – Henry VIII's chief minister. His best-known and most grandiose project was Hampton Court Palace. In 1523, he turned to the creation of an academic college in Oxford, on a scale to overshadow all others. To this end, in 1524 he obtained a papal bull authorizing the dissolution of over twenty smaller monasteries to secure an income for the college. One of these was the Priory of St Frideswide in Oxford (which had once been a college of canons: *see* Appendix III). This was to provide much of the site; further land included the parish Church of St Michael, which was demolished and its parish united with St Aldate's.

Cardinal College was founded in 1525. Building had already begun, and proceeded at a prodigious rate. By its revised statutes of 1527, it was to have a staff of 186, including a dean, a sub-dean, sixty canons of the first order, forty canons of the second order (scholars) and thirteen chaplains. Wolsey also planned that this should be a dual foundation (as at Eton and King's College, Cambridge), with a feeder college in Ipswich (*see* page 350). At Oxford, there were over thirty canons by 1529. But later in this year, Wolsey fell from power. All building ceased. Initially, the king apparently intended to destroy both foundations; in the case of Ipswich that indeed happened, but at Oxford he hesitated. Wolsey died in November 1530 and eventually, in July 1532, the king issued letters patent for the foundation of King Henry VIII College. This was much reduced from the scale of Wolsey's intention, with a dean, twelve secular canons, eight chaplains, some choristers and twelve almspeople. It may be regarded as a holding operation, and it effectively had no provision for an academic function. No further significant construction work took place on the half-finished college. King Henry VIII College had a life of thirteen years.

One concession made during the dissolution of the monasteries was the establishment of six new dioceses, using former monastic churches. One of these was Oxford, and in 1542 its cathedral was established in the great former Augustinian Abbey of Osney (*see* Appendix VIII), on the W side of the town. In 1545, however, a new scheme was devised, which would enable the Crown to regain more revenue from the Church. The cathedral was to be amalgamated with King Henry VIII College, the chapel of which, the former Priory Church of St Frideswide, though little more than half the size of Osney, should serve as the cathedral church. Accordingly, cathedral and college were

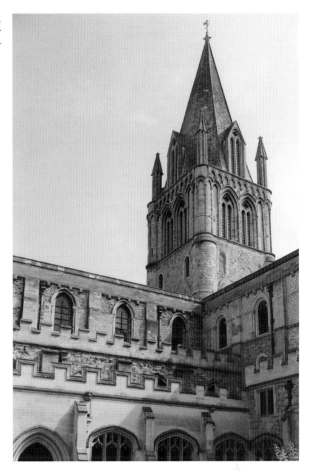

Oxford Cathedral: nave, south transept and tower from the cloister

surrendered to the Crown in 1545, and in November 1546, in one of the last acts of his reign, Henry VIII reconstituted the college as Christ Church. In its two functions, this is a unique combination. Wolsey's educational function was restored, with provision for a hundred students.

In Wolsey's plan, the Church of St Frideswide had not been required, and its W end was demolished immediately to make way for part of his immense new quadrangle. A new chapel, perhaps comparable to King's College Chapel, Cambridge, was to be built on the N side of the quadrangle. But at the time of his fall, this was no more than wall bases. The bulk of the former priory church, which had remained in temporary use, functioned as the chapel of King Henry VIII College, and in 1546 became the cathedral. Its position remains subordinate, outside a corner of the quadrangle, and in scale it is certainly small for a cathedral. Yet it is a sophisticated building of very high quality, surprisingly complicated in its layout, and with notable contents, so arguably it justifies its status. It is cruciform, with aisles even to the transepts

Oxford Cathedral: the chancel, looking east

(but in the S transept the cloister walk replaces the W aisle). The chancel is of five bays, the E bay being aisleless; of the nave, four bays remain, probably three having been destroyed. One bay, without aisles, was recreated by Sir Gilbert Scott in his restoration of the 1870s, with W of this a very large porch connecting by two archways with the quadrangle. Only in the late seventeenth century was the quadrangle completed; the upper part of the great gatehouse (Tom Tower) is by Wren.

The church is basically late Norman throughout, with little change in style; it has striking, large capitals, some of crocket form, and there are many roll mouldings but no chevron. Cylindrical pillars (in the nave alternating with octagonal) carry a three-storeyed elevation, but the triforium, a double opening, is curiously set below the main arcade arch, with therefore a lower arch to the aisle. In the transepts the clerestory is Norman, but in the nave it has turned EE in style. Over the crossing is a Norman lantern, with an arcaded walkway and above this windows set in large blank arcading. The aisles have

Norman rib-vaults, but the high roofs are of timber. The glorious exception to this is the chancel, which in about 1500 was given a fine Perp. clerestory with panelled reveals, and above this a most wonderful vault. This is of unique design, with bold transverse arches that spring from the sides, linked by outer panelled sections; then great pendants intervene, and the transverse arches disappear behind the luxuriant main vault of lierne-star form.

Many aisle windows are Perp., as is the large five-light window of the N transept. However the E wall, in Norman style with a striking rose window, is by Scott. The upper part of the tower is EE, with corner pinnacles and a stone spire, relatively short, with large lucarnes at its base. This, almost the only part of the exterior to make much impact, is important as one of the earliest spires in existence. Two successive three-bay chapels, the Lady and Latin Chapels, extend E from the N transept: they are vaulted, and form a spacious and most beautiful area.

A Victorian balcony screen carrying the organ separates the W end as an antechapel. A massive Victorian stone sacristy fills much of the S transept. The original stalls are now in the Latin Chapel, with poppy-head ends; just two have misericords. In the N chancel aisle is the shrine of St Frideswide, of 1289, destroyed at the Reformation but re-erected from its fragments in about 1889; it still has some exquisite carving. A large and elaborate late medieval structure nearby, its upper part of timber, is probably a watching loft. There are many very fine memorials, including several splendid fourteenth-century tomb-chests with recumbent effigies; the one to Prior Sutton has a rich Dec. canopy. Much good glass is to be seen, most notably some of the fourteenth century in the Latin Chapel.

The priory cloisters were rebuilt in about 1500, with lierne vaults. Their W part was demolished for the college. The chapter-house entrance is Norman, with much chevron, but the room itself is EE, vaulted, with exquisite quintuple lancets in the E wall, doubled internally. The foundation stone of the Ipswich college is reset here.

Oxford: Corpus Christi College

The foundation of this college was due to Bishop Richard Fox of Winchester. We do not know when it started, but building began in 1512. His initial plans were for a monastic college, which was to take monks from his cathedral priory of Winchester; however, in 1514, he was persuaded by Bishop Hugh Oldham of Exeter to change this to a secular college. Bishop Oldham gave the very large sum of £4,000 to the college, which was intended for a president and twenty fellows, with twenty *discipuli* or undergraduates. The chapel was to be served by two priests with two acolytes (the organist and sub-sacrist) and two choirboys. The college statutes date from 1517, in which year the first fellows were elected and came into residence; the full numbers were reached in 1522. Included in the statutes were careful geographical requirements by county for those becoming members.

Corpus Christi College, Oxford: the chapel, looking east

The chapel dates from the original construction period. It is a small, un-divided building, four bays long, continuing E from the library range. Its windows have four-centred arches and simple Perp. tracery, and are of three lights except for the E window of five; over the W end is a tiny lead-covered hexagonal belfry with an ogee top. Entry is from a passage at the W end; the antechapel section contains the large organ, and above is a small glazed gallery connecting with the library. Separating the antechapel from the main chapel is a massive, probably late-seventeenth-century, screen, its large segmental pediment standing forward on fluted Corinthian columns. There are fine oak panelling and stalls, also of the late seventeenth century; the panelling has the motif of perspective arches also met elsewhere at Oxford, and the stall ends have big ball finials. The reredos incorporates a large oil-painting as altarpiece. The brass eagle lectern, with charming little lions sitting on its three feet, is of about 1537, either given by or given as a memorial to the first president. The wagon roof, with bosses, is partly original.

The masonry of the N exterior shows a surprising number of alterations. The S side is covered by a charming classical cloister walk dating from 1706–12; it has heavy round arches and a coved plaster ceiling with beautiful enrichment. Many minor memorials are here. This college is today the smallest in Oxford: its buildings, partly medieval and partly eighteenth century, are modest but most attractive.

* Oxford: Exeter Hall

This college was founded in 1314 by Walter Stapeldon, a Devon man who rose to be Bishop of Exeter and Treasurer of England under Edward II. He planned it for a rector and twelve fellows. Initially he purchased an existing academic hall, Hart Hall, to provide accommodation, but in 1315 the members moved to another, St Stephen's Hall, on part of what became the present site. The college was fully established by about 1325, and was initially known as Stapeldon Hall. It later became Exeter Hall, but did not adopt the name Exeter College until the mid-sixteenth century. The bishop's intention was to improve the provision of educated clergy in his diocese, and for its first few centuries it drew most of its members from the south-west. It was a modest and relatively poor foundation, and grew only gradually. Major growth came in the sixteenth century, when Sir William Petre more than doubled its endowments, and it received a new constitution.

A chapel was built shortly after the foundation, being licensed in 1321 and consecrated in 1326. There was much rebuilding of the college in the seventeenth century; a chapel was built on a new site in 1624, and the old one was made into a library, but destroyed by fire in 1709. As seen in old pictures, the seventeenth-century chapel was a substantial building with a S aisle, entirely in Perp. style. It was, however, demolished and replaced in 1856–9 by a very ambitious new building designed by Sir Gilbert Scott. This stands on the same

Exeter College, Oxford: the chapel, from the south

site, though this had been the subject of much argument in the college, and Scott may have designed it for a different location. Certainly it is out of scale as it stands on the N side of the partly seventeenth-century quadrangle.

The inspiration of the chapel is the Sainte-Chapelle in Paris. It is an extremely lofty single space of five bays plus a polygonal apse. The windows are very tall, of geometrical Dec. type, in three lights, but two for the apse. High on the buttresses are canopied image niches (statues were only ever provided for those on the S side). Above is an openwork parapet and a steeply pitched roof, on the W part of which is an impressively large octagonal flèche carrying a tall spirelet. Entry is by an elaborate S portal under a large gable.

The interior is rich, dignified and lovely. It has a tierceron vault resting on clustered shafts rising from large figure corbels and having elaborate foliage capitals. The windows are shafted, and all have Victorian stained glass. Blank arcading in the apse incorporates the sedilia. An elaborate stone screen, with pink marble shafts, separates the W bay as an antechapel. The organ rests on a shallow balcony projecting from the W wall. There are richly canopied Victorian stalls. In a glazed frame is a tapestry of 1890, by Burne-Jones of William Morris & Co. A few minor memorials in the floor are older than the structure, as are an excellently preserved medieval chest used for offerings and the fine brass eagle lectern of 1637, with four engaging little lions on its feet.

* Oxford: Lincoln College

Oxford was in the diocese of Lincoln in the Middle Ages, and the foundation of this college of St Mary and All Saints was due to the bishop, Richard Fleming, who obtained a royal charter in 1427; the foundation charter is dated 1429. It was of modest size, for a warden or rector and seven fellows, with seven deacons. It was intended for the training of clergy, but the chantry motive too was prominent. Three Oxford churches were appropriated to it: St Michael at the North Gate, St Mildred, and All Saints. Of these, St Mildred was demolished and its site included in that of the college. All Saints, standing just to the S, was initially used by the college as its chapel. The establishment of the college also included two chaplains, to serve the cure of souls in All Saints and St Michael's. The college encountered difficulties and was nearly extinguished later in the century, but it was rescued by Bishop Thomas Rotherham (later also the founder of a college in his native town of Rotherham), who is regarded as the second founder here. He obtained letters patent in 1478 confirming the status of the college, and by his new statutes of 1480 the foundation was enlarged to twelve fellows. The original buildings form the present Front Quad, completed with the S side late in the century. Licence was obtained for a chapel in 1441, and a modest structure was formed at an upper level in the N range, but All Saints continued to be used for some of the college's religious functions. Finally in 1629–31, partly through the generosity of Bishop Williams of Lincoln, the college was provided with its own full-sized chapel, forming the S side of Chapel Quad. This, however, was

not the end of the use of All Saints by the college: in 1971 it was made redundant, and was converted at a cost of £420,000 into the college library, opened
in 1975. The architect of the conversion was Robert Potter.

All Saints is now a magnificent structure built in 1706–9 following the
destruction of much of its medieval predecessor by the collapse of its spire.
The architect is said to have been an amateur, Dean Aldrich of Christ Church.
It has a broad, rectangular body of ashlar, five bays in length, with paired
Corinthian pilasters, a dentilled cornice and a balustraded parapet. The main
windows are very large and round arched, and above is a low attic storey with
short segmental-arched windows. The N and S doorways are straight headed
with a segmental pediment, and are covered by shallow but very tall pedimented porches or porticos on paired Corinthian columns. The massive W
tower was added in 1717–20, with the involvement of Nicholas Hawksmoor,
and is a splendid ensemble. It has a lower stage with banded rustication.
Above is a stage having pilaster buttresses with banded rustication and large

Lincoln College, Oxford:
the library (former All Saints
Church), from the south-east

round-arched belfry openings containing intersecting tracery. There is a large cornice, a balustrade, and then a tall circular stage with free-standing Corinthian columns; an openwork parapet surrounds a short octagonal spire.

The interior is equally splendid. It is a great undivided space, three bays wide, faced in ashlar. Its conversion cannot be ignored, however: the principal change is that, except at the W end, the floor is raised, allowing a lower floor level that was partly excavated beneath. This is a fine conversion, and there are elegant stairs up and down from the W end, with excellent woodwork; but some injury has been done to the proportions of the building. The walls have features comparable to those of the exterior; the pilasters show bases at the present floor level, and the windows disappear behind book-cases so that we cannot see how low they come. The glazing is clear throughout. There is a splendid plaster ceiling, divided into panels, with large coving penetrated by the attic windows. The admirable library furnishings of oak reuse much old work, including rich eighteenth-century carving incorporated in the study carrels. Some good mural memorials, five hatchments and a moulded Royal Arms remain on the walls. Survivors from the old church are a recumbent alabaster effigy of 1616, with some colour, and a fine iron-bound round-topped medieval chest. Incorporated in the E part of the lower level is the seventeenth-century Senior Library, an exquisite panelled room brought in its entirety from its previous location in the college.

Lincoln College, Oxford: the chapel, from the north

The chapel of 1629–31 is in almost conventional Perp. style. It is of moderate size, a rectangle four bays in length; the windows are arched and traceried, in three lights except for the large E window of six. There are battlements, and the entrance doorway from the courtyard is three-centred in a square label. Internally it is delightful, and has scarcely been altered since the seventeenth century. Its panelled canted roof has varied ornamental and heraldic devices. Separating the W bay as an antechapel is a fine late-seventeenth-century screen, with Corinthian pilasters and columns, a central broken segmental pediment and pedimented flanking sections containing vertical oval openings. Attractive panelling all round has an enjoyable motif of an enriched rectangular panel with a broken pediment; the section behind the altar is little emphasized. The stalls have marquetry and figures standing on their ends; these are of 1686, but the back stalls are early seventeenth century and have misericords. The communion rails too are late seventeenth century. Particularly evocative of its time, and characteristically pre-Laudian, is the pulpit: it is portable, and spends much of its time in front of, and obscuring, the altar. It is of chamfered square form, and has the same decorative motif as the panelling. All the windows have their original glass of 1629–30, finest in the E window but all forming a splendid and most enjoyable set. The chapel is in perfect condition following major repairs about 1995; small as it is, it is an exceptionally attractive building.

* Oxford: Magdalen College

William Waynflete was associated with academic colleges throughout his career; in 1443 he became Provost of Eton. In 1448, soon after he became Bishop of Winchester, he obtained licence to establish a college in Oxford, to be known as Magdalen Hall. For this, he obtained properties on the S side of the High Street. In 1456, however, Waynflete became Chancellor of England, which gave him access to resources that enabled him to re-establish the college on a more generous, indeed lavish scale. He now acquired the thirteenth-century hospital of St John the Baptist, which was dissolved, and its site became that of the new college of St Mary Magdalen. A charter of incorporation was granted in 1457. There was then a delay, and building work did not begin until 1467, and then only on the precinct wall. But when construction of the main buildings started in 1474 it was to a purpose, and the chapel and hall seem to have been complete and the buildings occupied in 1480. The founder gave statutes in this year, by which the college had a president, forty fellows, thirty other scholars, four chaplains, eight clerks and sixteen choristers. Also attached to the college was a school, with a master and usher. Waynflete died in 1486; the buildings were completed about 1509. At the Valor of 1535, the annual income of Magdalen was more than twice that of any other Oxford college except for the former Cardinal College. The choir is still essentially as it was founded in 1480, and has a fine reputation; its sixteen boy choristers are educated at Magdalen College School.

Magdalen College, Oxford: the cloisters, with the north side of the chapel

The name of the college is pronounced 'maudlin'. The buildings are splendid, and are laid out on a spacious scale. The centre is a large quadrangle with cloister walks and buildings all round; the E half of the S side is the hall, the W half the chapel. S of these is a narrow irregular court, the S range of which incorporates what was the late-thirteenth-century chapel of the hospital, converted to rooms in 1665–6. In this range stands the famous tower, which is thus separate from the college chapel. It was built in 1492–1509; it is 144 ft (43.9 m) high, in four main stages, with polygonal buttresses, long twin three-light belfry openings and elaborate openwork battlements with large corner and intermediate pinnacles. It is well known for the traditional singing from its summit by the choir at dawn on May morning.

The chapel is of 'T' plan and, as at All Souls, is a reduced version of that at New College. Its body is of five bays, with the antechapel two bays in length. It is of regular ashlar, with buttresses of large projection, pinnacles and battlements with beneath them a frieze of beasts, fleurons, busts and other devices. The windows are of three lights, long and transomed. A battlemented projection contains the rich W doorway, four-centred in a square label, with the arch of its outer order formed by flying ribs. At the NW is a block known as the Muniment Tower, containing a lobby with a fine tierceron vault, from which a doorway opens to the chapel.

Tall two-bay arcades on pillars of four shafts and four hollows open to the transepts. Covering the whole chapel is a tierceron vault of plaster, looking like

stone: this was introduced by James Wyatt in 1790. Further extensive alterations were made by Cottingham in 1829–34. Cottingham designed the
attractive stone veranda screen, with vaulting inside, which carries the organ
and separates the chapel from the antechapel. Also mostly due to him is the
treatment of the sanctuary: the walls have close stone panelling, and above this
the E wall has three tiers of canopied niches with images. On the N side, the
panelling is open to a fan-vaulted chantry chapel, built for the founder. Much
of this is now a replica, replacing original work moved in 1830 to Theale in
Berkshire, where a new church had been built by the sister of the president, Dr.
Routh. The tomb with recumbent effigy of the founder's father, who died about
1450, was placed in the chantry chapel at this time. Also of about 1830 are the
stalls, but thirty-two original stalls remain in the antechapel, all but two with
misericords. There are some good mural memorials, together with many late-
medieval brasses, mostly in the antechapel. A painted casket or shrine, with
twisted columns, is perhaps early-eighteenth-century French work. The brass

Magdalen College, Oxford:
the outdoor pulpit

eagle lectern is of 1633. The glass in the main chapel is Victorian, but in the antechapel is all seventeenth-century work in grisaille, appearing as shades between black and brown. The W window has seventeenth-century tracery, and its glass, based on Michelangelo's 'Last Judgement', was restored to its place in 1997. Outside, in the corner S of the W front, is an outdoor pulpit, corbelled out, with a canopy. It too is late Perp.

* Oxford: Merton College

The founder of this college was from an early age associated with the Augustinian Priory of Merton in Surrey; he was perhaps educated there, and later acted as its legal clerk. This may have led to his being noticed by the king, Henry III, and his career advanced until in 1261 he was made Chancellor of England. He became known as Walter of Merton. He first obtained licence in 1262 to vest in Merton Priory his manors of Malden and Farleigh in Surrey,

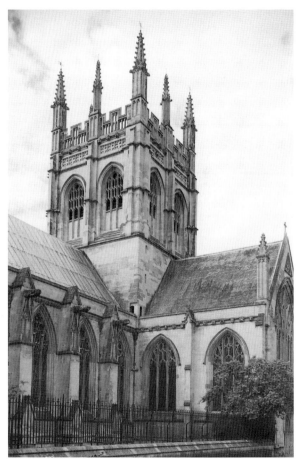

Merton College, Oxford: the
chapel, from the north-east

for the support of clerks studying at a university. In 1263–4, he established eight of his nephews in Oxford to study at the university, and made provision for others. In September 1264, he issued a document that is regarded as the first statutes of his foundation, providing for the maintenance of twenty scholars at Oxford or another university. In this period, he had set up an organization in his manor house of Malden in Surrey (*see* Appendix IV), with a warden and several priests, which appears to have been the administrative centre of his scheme. But Walter's ideas now focused on founding an establishment at Oxford, and from 1266 he made purchases to acquire a site. One of these carried the advowson of the Church of St John the Baptist, which was to serve the foundation. In 1270, he issued new statutes, though these still involved the warden being in Malden. Having ceased to be Chancellor in 1264, Walter was again appointed to the position in 1272 by Edward I, and this seems to have enabled him to devote further resources to his college. He issued his third and final statutes in 1274, by which time the warden was in Oxford and Malden was no longer involved. The number of fellows was not specified, but a bull of Pope Nicholas III in 1280 refers to forty fellows. There seem also to have been about twenty-five students living in the town.

Although both Balliol and University Colleges may claim some 'firsts', Merton was the first fully formed academic college at either university, and in its scale and scope it far exceeded all others until the foundation a century later of New College. It acted as a model for others to follow. Buildings were soon begun; some thirteenth-century work still remains, including part of the hall. In 1292, the Church of St John the Baptist was appropriated: in this, this first academic college was like most non-academic foundations of the time. In about 1290, a replacement church was begun, on a very large scale; the chancel was completed in 1297. The old church, which stood just S of the new, was demolished a few years later, though some fragments were perhaps incorporated in Mob Quad, which covered its site. The crossing of the new church was built about 1330–5; there was work on the S transept about 1367, and then the transepts were completed in the early fifteenth century. Finally the tower over the crossing was finished in 1448–51. Blocked arches show that a nave and aisles were intended, but they were never built, so Merton ended up with the 'T' plan that had already been adopted at New College. It is an outstanding building, one of the great college chapels. Restoration took place mainly in 1849–51, under Butterfield. It continued to be parochial until 1891.

The chancel is aisleless, in seven bays; it has large side windows of three lights, with fine early Dec. tracery in four different designs, and a huge E window of seven lights, with much enrichment in its tracery. There are large panelled buttresses, gargoyles and a straight parapet. Internally, the windows have two orders of attached shafts and their hood-moulds are linked. A rich composition of doorway, triple sedilia and large double piscina is apparently entirely of 1851. At the SE is a large early-fourteenth-century sacristy.

The splendid Dec. crossing arches have six orders of sunk quadrants, and the arches to the intended nave aisles are similar. Otherwise the transepts are

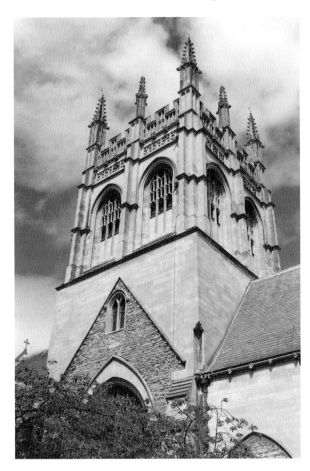

Merton College, Oxford:
the west end of the chapel,
showing indications of the
intended nave and aisles

Perp., though not identical. In the S transept, a very large double piscina with shelf and central shaft is set under a crocketed gable between moulded buttresses rising from the floor. It is clearly reset: did it come from the chancel? The tower is very broad and stately, one of the characteristic landmarks of Oxford; it has slender set-back buttresses, twin three-light openings on each side, and openwork battlements with eight pinnacles.

The roofs are of the restoration. There are several large medieval brasses, also some fine mural memorials. An extraordinary and beautiful font of green marble, a rectangular pedestal carrying a very large oval bowl, was a gift in 1815 from the Tsar. The massive screen, with its central section standing forward on fluted Corinthian columns, was reassembled in 1960 from surviving parts of the original, which was of 1673 and by Wren; it had been ejected in 1851. The especially fine twin-sided brass lectern is of 1504. Almost all the glass of the chancel is original, though considerably restored; most windows include the name of their donor, Henry de Mamesfeld, fellow from 1288 to 1296. A little more old glass is in the transepts.

* Oxford: New College

This famous institution, founded by William of Wykeham, Bishop of Winchester, represented an important step forward for the academic college, both in its scale and in its comprehensive and careful planning. It was also a remarkable innovation in that the founder conceived it alongside his other college of St Mary at Winchester, to provide a staged education of boys for the priesthood. As at Winchester, he began early, planning the acquisition of land from 1368, and by 1376 there were sixty scholars associated with the proposed college. Its foundation is usually dated to the licence granted by Richard II in 1379. Building began in 1380, and was sufficiently advanced for the members to take possession in 1386. The cloisters, the last major part completed, were consecrated in 1400. Its formal name was St Mary College of Winchester in Oxford, but the present name was used almost from the first. Alongside the academic aspect, the life had much of the character of a chantry college. It was for a warden and seventy scholars or fellows, and to serve the chapel there were ten chaplains, three clerks and sixteen choristers; the canonical hours were to be maintained, together with seven masses daily. Its choir, still with sixteen choristers, continues to this day.

The buildings reflect the splendid scale of the foundation. They are laid out around a very large quadrangle, the N side of which is formed by the chapel, with continuing E from it the hall. The N boundary of the precinct is the

New College, Oxford: the west front of the chapel, seen from the cloister

medieval town wall, the maintenance of which was an obligation placed on the college when the land was acquired; it is still well preserved. W of the quadrangle is a large, rectangular cloister, free standing as at Winchester; it has three-light traceried openings and a timber wagon roof. Its N side is attached to the town wall, one of the bastions of which was replaced by a tall bell-tower, which thus stands well separated from the chapel. The approach to the college from either New College Lane or Queen's Lane is most engaging, with several right-angle bends leading to the lofty entrance gate-tower.

New College, Oxford: the antechapel, looking north

The chapel is in the 'T' plan, and was the first to be so planned. It has an aisleless body of five bays, at the W end of which is an antechapel with transepts which can alternatively be read as a very short aisled nave of two bays. The scale is that of a very great church. Externally it is of fine ashlar, with deep buttresses, a straight parapet and large panelled pinnacles. The W range of the quadrangle attaches to the S transept, but the SE corner of the transept projects into the court. A doorway beside it opens to a vaulted passage which leads to the entrance doorway. The body of the chapel has regular very large arched windows of four lights, traceried and transomed. The transepts are roofed in the E–W direction. Their E sides have very large six-light windows, while the main W window is of seven lights.

The interior is very impressive, but it has suffered much restoration. Wyatt in 1789–94 carried out a major remodelling which included a plaster vault and a plaster reredos. In 1877–81, Sir Gilbert Scott returned the chapel to more responsible forms of Gothic. His are the hammerbeam roof and the great reredos covering the windowless E wall, with four principal tiers of statuary, though the reredos must represent approximately the original form. The transepts have exceptionally tall two-bay arcades, their arches resting on pillars of four shafts and four large hollows, with a further slim shaft in the middle of each hollow. The large balcony screen is of the restoration, though it incorporates the original doors; it carries an impressive organ of 1969. Much of the woodwork of the stalls is Victorian, but the back row of seats is ancient, with their original sixty-two carved misericords, which are particularly good. The triple stepped sedilia with large piscina and credence retain a little original work. The N side has a comparable arrangement, and here a long narrow recess contains the gilt crozier of William of Wykeham. There are many fifteenth- and sixteenth-century brasses in the floor of the antechapel. Also here are some fine mural memorials and a large statue of Lazarus by Jacob Epstein, acquired in 1951. The glass throughout the main chapel is of the eighteenth century. In the antechapel all the windows have fine original late-fourteenth-century glass, except that the great W window has glass of 1795 designed by Sir Joshua Reynolds, its qualities long a matter of controversy.

* Oxford: Oriel College

The first founder of this college was Adam de Brome, who among other positions was rector of the university Church of St Mary. He obtained royal licence in 1324, but in 1326 the college was refounded by Edward II, who is regarded as co-founder. It was due to the king that the Church of St Mary was appropriated. The college was called the House of Blessed Mary the Virgin, but the name Oriel College soon came into use, derived from a property acquired as part of the site in 1329. It was also sometimes in its earlier years known as King's Hall or King's College, after its royal founder. It was initially for a provost and ten fellows, but benefactions of the fifteenth and early sixteenth centuries increased the number of fellows to eighteen.

The Church of St Mary served the college as its chapel in its first years, and continued in use for some of its religious life until the Reformation, even after a chapel was built in the college about 1373. A second chapel in the college apparently replaced the first in the fifteenth century. However, the entire college was rebuilt in 1620–42, the present chapel being of 1637–42. It is quite small, though it adopts the Oxford 'T' plan. Its body has three bays, with

Oriel College, Oxford: the chapel, looking east from the gallery

three-light arched windows containing typical seventeenth-century tracery. A heavily moulded three-centred arch divides it from the antechapel, which has a N–S roof. Externally, as internally, the building is quite simple; it is faced in ashlar and the N and S sides are battlemented. The W wall faces the court; above the entrance is an oriel window, of which the principal purpose is to balance that of the hall in presenting a symmetrical façade to the court. This oriel opens to a room which was originally unconnected with the chapel but formed part of a set of rooms occupied by J.H. Newman when he was a fellow; he is said to have used it as an oratory. In 1884 this room was connected to the chapel; it has been restored and the window was in 2001 given striking new stained glass.

Much of the woodwork is of the seventeenth century. The beautiful panelling has arches in simulated perspective, and the stalls have large ball finials. There are richly carved communion rails. The eagle lectern is dated 1654. In 1884, the screen was moved further W, so that instead of an antechapel there is now only a lobby, with a gallery above. The shallow S end of the antechapel became a vestry, the N end a ladies' pew. Oriel College was the home of the Oxford Movement, and its fellows included Keble and Wilberforce as well as Newman. It is interesting that despite this there were no major alterations to the chapel.

The Church of St Mary is the university church; as such, it served and still serves as the place for major events in the university's life. An especially remarkable aspect is its many very moving historical associations. Here in Queen Mary's reign the trials of Cranmer, Latimer and Ridley were conducted, leading to their being burnt at the stake for their beliefs. In 1641, the Virgin and Child on the porch was used as a charge against Archbishop Laud at his trial. In the eighteenth century John Wesley preached many notable sermons here. Newman was vicar from 1828 until 1843, before his departure to become a Roman Catholic convert and a cardinal.

St Mary's is a splendid and very large mainly Perp. church. Two especially memorable parts, however, are not of this period. The tower, attached to the N side, was begun in the late thirteenth century. Its lower part is sober, with angle buttresses and very long three-light belfry openings of intersecting tracery. But above this is a riot of Dec. richness, added in about 1310–20, encrusted with ball-flower. There are an openwork parapet, many image niches containing statues, and two tiers of finials and pinnacles; from this exuberant display there emerges the splendidly tall spire, with tall transomed

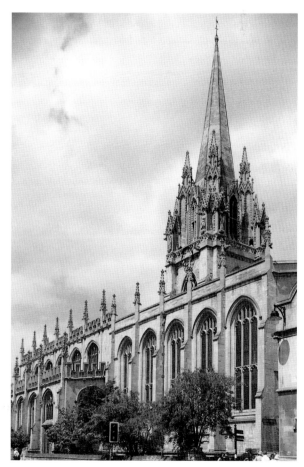

Oxford: St Mary, from the south-east

spire-lights at its base. Some of what is seen is the result of an extensive but good restoration in 1894–6. The other most remarkable part of the church is the latest: the tall, shallow S porch of 1637, designed by Nicholas Stone. This has bold classical features including a broad round arch with pendant, a broken pediment, volutes and, most strikingly, a pair of very large spiral columns. Yet it is also Gothic, with battlements, pinnacles and a fan vault. The original statue of the Virgin and Child remains in its large shell niche.

The roofs are low pitched throughout. The aisled nave of six bays dates from the end of the fifteenth century, with pinnacles and richly panelled battlements. The windows are mostly of four lights, but the W window is of seven. The arcades have pillars of a sophisticated Perp. section carrying finely moulded two-centred arches. Between the clerestory windows are tall canopied image niches. The lofty aisleless chancel of five bays was under construction in 1463. Its windows are of three lights, tall and transomed, with an E window of seven; externally it has deep buttresses, a straight parapet and pinnacles. The excellent triple sedilia have four-centred arches, cusped and sub-cusped. There is an attractive late-seventeenth-century timber reredos with fluted Corinthian pilasters, but above this appear seven canopied image niches of the original reredos. They have relatively recent statuary.

An outer N aisle extends two bays W of the tower: this is the Adam de Brome Chapel, built about 1328 probably for the use of the college. It has a low Dec. arcade of two continuous hollow chamfers, but its windows are now

Oxford: St Mary, looking east from the gallery

Perp., matching those of the nave. In it is the tomb-chest of Adam de Brome, though only the top is original, with just the indent of his brass. E of the tower runs another attachment separated by a space from the chancel. This is partly Dec., in two storeys, the lower one vaulted. It was the Congregation House, the first building of the university, with the university library occupying the upper storey. Its lower room now serves as a coffee house. In the upper room in 1942 was held the meeting that led to the foundation of the Oxford Committee for Famine Relief (Oxfam).

A refitting of the church in 1828 provided an attractive stone choir screen in Perp. style. This now carries the splendid large organ of 1987, in a case of eighteenth-century style. The pulpit, pews and W gallery are also good work of 1828. There are many excellent mural memorials. The Adam de Brome Chapel has eighteenth-century panelling and fittings as the court of the chancellor of the university. In the chancel are original mid-fifteenth-century panelling and traceried stall-fronts with poppy-head ends; there are no misericords. The rich communion rails are of 1673.

* Oxford: The Queen's College

The proposal for the foundation of this college was due to Robert of Eglesfield, a chaplain to Queen Philippa, wife of Edward III, whom he involved and named as founder and patroness. Its charter and statutes both date from early in 1341. The queen helped with the endowments, and the foundation was intended to be on a very large scale, for a provost and twelve fellows, together with up to thirteen chaplains and as many as seventy-two poor boys, from whom choristers would be chosen. In the event, the resources were far from sufficient for this establishment, and the number of fellows was not reached until the end of the sixteenth century. However, the endowments gradually grew, and from the mid-fifteenth century the college began to prosper. Membership was intended to be open to all, but with a preference for those originating in the counties of Cumberland and Westmorland.

Buildings were constructed mostly in the late fourteenth century. The chapel was built in 1373–82; it was three bays long, to which an antechapel of two bays was added about 1516, bringing it to the standard Oxford 'T' plan. It is well known from old illustrations. However, starting in the late seventeenth century, new buildings were added and then the entire medieval college was demolished and replaced. The new chapel was built in 1714–21, and to Front Quad the hall and chapel present a symmetrical façade, the W half being the hall, the E half the chapel. Their splendid style owes much to Wren and Hawksmoor, though the actual architect is uncertain. The exterior is of fine ashlar, with Tuscan plasters above which are a frieze, cornice and intermittent balustrading. The windows are large and round arched. The centrepiece of the façade has four giant Tuscan columns carrying a pediment containing rich sculpture; above is an impressive cupola of stone, octagonal but with paired Ionic columns

Queen's College, Oxford: Front Quad, showing the south side of the chapel

standing outside the diagonal faces. From here, a stately, stone-vaulted passage passes through the range, with an enriched doorway opening to the chapel.

The interior of the chapel is aristocratic in both its scale and its quality. Its elaboration is baroque. It is seven bays long, to which is added a semicircular apse; the two E bays and the apse are not seen from the court. Internally, a large shell niche replaces one window in each side. There are Corinthian pilasters, a richly decorated cornice and a ceiling with a large cove. Elaborate plasterwork, arranged in large panels, is applied to the ceiling; above the sanctuary is a large painting of the Ascension by James Thornhill, of 1716. The splendid great screen has Corinthian columns, with a central round arch and scrolly pediments with urns. This is original, as are most of the other fittings. The stalls and the panelling behind them have a fine dignity. The two great brass chandeliers are of 1721, but the brass eagle lectern pre-dates the building, being of 1662. The communion rails are of wrought iron. Rather startling in these classical surroundings are two late medieval brasses mounted on the wall of the apse. Most of the glass is old: some is contemporary with the building, but some is seventeenth century, and four windows are of 1518.

Oxford: St George

St George in the Castle was the first college to be founded in Oxford, but it was not an academic college. In 1071, William the Conqueror entrusted the building of a castle in Oxford to his compatriot Robert d'Oilly. In 1074, d'Oilly, with Roger d'Ivri, founded a college in the Church of St George within the castle; a parish was attached, and it is possible that the church existed before the castle. The college had prebendaries, but it is not known how many. Being in a royal castle, it had royal privileges, and vestiges of these seem to have persisted throughout the Middle Ages; but the original college ceased when it was in 1149 given to the recently founded Augustinian Abbey of Osney, which stood close by. Under Osney, some sort of collegiate establishment seems to have been maintained in St George's; in the early fourteenth century Osney claimed to provide two canons and thirteen ministers for its services. In the late fifteenth century, it was refounded in a modified form, with five chaplains under a canon of the abbey as head. The statutes of this period survive; some scholars were also attached, of whom there were six in 1523. However, it was not an independent establishment, and it ended in 1539 when the abbey was dissolved.

The remains of the Church of St George in their state at the time of writing are perhaps the most extraordinary of all collegiate survivals. The castle was sufficiently intact to be used by both sides in the Civil War, but it was slighted in 1651. However, the site continued to be used as a prison, which was rebuilt at the end of the eighteenth century and much remodelled in 1848–56. It continued as such until it was closed in the 1990s, and at present remains as it was when the last prisoner left; however, conversion to a hotel and shops is

Oxford: St. George. The crypt

planned. Just two ancient structures survive, both associated with the church, both early Norman, and both in their different ways very puzzling.

The first is approached via steps down beside a long stone prison block. It is a crypt which was apparently originally beneath the chancel of the church. It is low, dank, windowless and without lighting, but it is a most evocative place. It is three bays wide and four long. Very short cylindrical pillars carry big capitals, four of which have crude but bold incised leaf designs. The walls have pilaster responds, and the whole is covered by groin vaulting. On the E side is rough masonry, curved to present a convex face to the crypt. This crypt is the earliest Norman work in Oxford, convincingly of the time of the foundation. Bafflingly, however, it is reported to have been rebuilt and even moved in 1794 and to have been again altered or rebuilt in 1848.

The other is a massive and tall tower, originally set in the curtain wall and clearly intended for military use. Immediately below its W face is the river. This face is almost windowless; the E side has two apparently late square-headed

Oxford: St. George. The tower, from the south-east

openings. It is an impressive but strangely crude structure, showing a marked but irregular batter and several uneven offsets. Its parapet is straight and has in each side two cross-loops and the remains of blocked round-arched openings. At the SE corner is a very large diagonal projection containing the staircase. The tower is in a semi-ruinous condition, but still has a roof and timber floors. It is known as St George's Tower, and remarkably it served also as the W tower of the church. It stands directly W of the crypt and in line with it, though set a little askew; its E side opens in a low but massive round arch, unmoulded, with plain imposts. This now gives on to a murky and sordid chamber forming the end of the prison block, but it must originally have opened to the nave. The date of the tower is not agreed, but its crudeness and the absence of architectural ornament surely favour its being early. Both tower and crypt are important buildings; it is hoped that they will soon be more fully understood following archaeological investigations.

Oxford: University College

The date of the act which led to the foundation of this college was the earliest for any academic college in Oxford, but it was not the first to become a college. William of Durham was a notable scholar and churchman, once Archdeacon of Caux; at his death in 1249 he left 310 marks (£206 13s 4d) to the university for the purchase of property, the income from which was to be employed to maintain ten or more Masters of Arts, who were to be studying divinity. From this bequest, the university bought properties in 1253 and subsequent years. But in 1280, it reassessed the use it had made of the bequest and found it wanting, in particular that 160 marks had not been used in accordance with the donor's wishes. It then laid down what may be accounted the foundation charter of the college, which was initially to maintain four Masters of Arts. Statutes were issued in 1292; they included provision for the saying of soul-masses for benefactors. The establishment became known as University Hall; only later was the title 'college' used. The university issued new statutes in 1311, and after 1330, probably after receiving a major benefaction, it purchased four adjoining properties on what became the permanent site of the college. In its early years, the college used the Church of St Mary (*see* Oriel College); by the 1330s it seems to have had some form of chapel, but in the closing years of the century, a permanent chapel was built. From the mid-fifteenth century, further construction produced a complete quadrangle, with hall and gate-tower. By 1535, it had a master and twelve fellows. Beginning in 1635, the college was completely rebuilt, a new court to a single consistent plan being completed with the consecration of the chapel in 1666. A recent historical connection of the college is with former United States president Bill Clinton, who was once a Rhodes scholar here.

University College, Oxford: the north side of the chapel, from Front Quad

The S side of what is now Front Quad is symmetrical, with its W half occupied by the hall and its E half by the chapel. Work on these had begun in 1639, and the shell of the chapel was roofed by 1641; but a long pause then ensued. Both hall and chapel are battlemented and have arched windows of three lights with typical seventeenth-century tracery. Outside, Perp. panelling continues below the windows. In the centre, containing the two entrances, is a feature taken up higher, with oriel windows and a gable: but its present form dates from 1802. The E end of the chapel has original paired panelled pinnacles, but the large five-light window with elaborate tracery is Victorian.

The interior has more Victorian work, by Sir Gilbert Scott in 1862. It includes the roof and the excessively large and elaborate corbels supporting it. Further work of his in the sanctuary has been concealed by curtains. The building is six bays in length. Separating the W section as an antechapel is a splendid oak screen of the late seventeenth century, with Corinthian pilasters and columns, a segmental pediment and vase finials. There is excellent seventeenth-century panelling with a boldly projecting cornice; the tall straight-topped reredos has Corinthian pilasters. Of the same period are the stalls, with big ball finials. The two brass chandeliers are of the eighteenth century, as is the brass eagle lectern. There are some good memorials in the antechapel. Most of the windows are filled with excellent glass made for them in 1640–1 by Abraham van Linge, which was stored for about twenty years before being installed.

Rutland

The smallest county appropriately has just one small but charming collegiate church. There was also an attempted foundation at Tolethorpe, but this seems to have been unsuccessful (*see* Appendix IV).

* Manton

Sir William Wade was Member of Parliament for Rutland from 1342 to 1352. In 1351, he founded in the Church of St Mary at Manton a chantry college for three chaplains, one to be master. In addition to the canonical hours, there were to be three masses daily. The endowments were increased in 1360, 1364 and 1383, and the rector, John Wade, brother of the founder, in 1383 purchased the advowson from the Crown and gave it with the rectory to the college. By 1491, however, there were only a master and one chaplain, and this seems to have remained the number thereafter. The college was dissolved in 1548, at which time its annual value was £26 18s 8d.

The church is on a small scale, but is complex, unspoilt and most engaging. Its earliest features date from about 1190–1200. It is towerless, but the W front is an impressive EE structure, faced in ashlar: the lean-to aisles each have a small lancet, and the centre has three flat buttresses, the central one pierced by a narrow lancet, the side ones rising to circular chimney-like pinnacles.

Manton, from the south-east

Above is a tall and massive stone belfry with twin triple-chamfered openings for the bells; this is original work, though the top has been altered. The nave has a clerestory of modest square-headed Perp. openings, and most of the aisle windows too are Perp. The roofs are mostly low-pitched. There is a small sanctus turret on the E gable of the nave. The little S porch rather surprisingly has a room above, rising well above the aisle. There are relatively large transepts, the N one quite ambitious, with large traceried three-light windows; these transepts were probably added for the college, though remodelled in the fifteenth century. The chancel is of brown stone, contrasting with the rest, and has a date tablet of 1796; it is in classical style, with simple round-arched windows having plain impost and key stones.

The interior is delightful. The arcades are of four bays, round arched but otherwise entirely EE in style, with slender cylindrical pillars. On the N side, the W bay has a double respond rather than a pillar, suggesting that a previous, shorter nave was first given a N aisle and then extended a bay W, following which the S aisle was added to the whole. There is a blocked round-arched N doorway. Similar to the arcades but pointed is the chancel arch. Image brackets flank the E window of the S transept, and a good coffin-lid with foliated cross is here. The W wall of the N transept oddly projects halfway across the aisle; it is panelled, and has a panelled stone lintel crossing to the wall above the arcade. In the W wall of the transept there is a large recess with a panelled four-centred arch, whose purpose is puzzling. Also in the transept is a particularly good piscina. The chancel is internally simple; its roof is Victorian.

The fine circular font has good blank arcading round its bowl, and rests on five octagonal shafts; it is late Norman. There are simple eighteenth-century altar rails. An attractive pillar alms box is dated 1637, and a chest is of similar period. On the wall above the chancel arch is a large George III Royal Arms, repainted in 1975. In the N chapel, a small brass reads (in Latin), 'Here lies William Wade, founder of this chantry, on whose soul may God have mercy.'

Shropshire

There are more collegiate churches in Shropshire than in almost any other county. They are varied, and include good examples of all types, but particularly striking is the number of small churches of portioners in the county; this seems to be a regional characteristic. Three are included here; others appear in Appendix IV. The colleges of canons include two in the town of Shrewsbury, of which St Mary is an outstandingly splendid and important church. Shropshire's largest church is Ludlow, which was closely associated with a college of fraternity priests. There are especially attractive and interesting chantry colleges at Battlefield and Tong.

* Battlefield

This fine church, in its peaceful and evocative setting, owes its existence to a stirring event in English history: here in 1403 was fought the Battle of Shrewsbury, when a large rebel army under Henry Percy, known as Hotspur, in alliance with others, met and was defeated by the forces of King Henry IV. Hotspur was among those killed, and about 1,600 bodies were buried in a mass grave. Henry IV is cited as founder of the college, and he provided the endowments, but the initiative came from Roger Ive, Rector of Albright Hussey, in which parish the site lay. Licence was granted in 1406, initially for a perpetual chantry of two chaplains. The church was built from 1406 to 1409. During its building, more ambitious plans were developed by Richard

Battlefield, from the south-west

Hussey (lord of the manor), Ive and the king, and in 1410 a new foundation charter was granted for it as a chantry college of a master and six chaplains.

The principal purpose of the college was intercession for those killed in the battle; the church is thought to have been built close to the site of the mass burial. The college appropriated the church of Albright Hussey, and Roger Ive became the first master, holding the position until he resigned in 1447. In practice the number of chaplains was established as five, in addition to the master. Limited functions both as a school and as an almshouse seem to have been included. Some accommodation must have been provided early on, but under

Roger Phelips, master from 1454 to 1478, a new set of six chambers was built for the chaplains. The tower was added to the church about the end of the century. At the Valor of 1535, the annual income of the college was given as £56; it was dissolved in 1548. By this time it had replaced Albright Hussey as the parish church, and so continued in use. It was neglected in the eighteenth century, and the nave roof finally collapsed; the nave remained roofless and was walled off from the chancel, the roof of which was propped up by Doric columns. An extensive but very good restoration was carried out in 1860–2, by S Pountney Smith. There is no village, and the church became redundant in 1982; it is now in the care of the Churches Conservation Trust.

The Church of St Mary Magdalene is a noble and regular structure, 94 ft (28.7 m) long, of fine ashlared limestone. It is aisleless and has no structural division between the nave and the chancel. Entry is through the W tower, which is large, with shallow diagonal buttresses, a band of ornament below the battlements and eight crocketed pinnacles; its good proportions are a little spoilt by the bulky rectangular stair projection at its SE corner. The nave has four bays and the chancel five. In the chancel the windows are taller than in the nave, and the fine parapets (entirely of the restoration) are of openwork and have pinnacles. The E gable has a large original statue of Henry IV in armour. A surprising feature of this closely dated building is that three of the chancel windows differ from their fellows and have pure reticulated tracery; since they must have been built at the same time as the rest, even though their style was then out of date by sixty years,

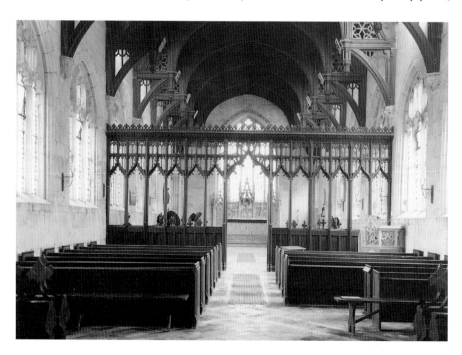

Battlefield, looking east

there is a lesson here for modern antiquaries! Traces on the S side of the chancel indicate that the collegiate buildings were attached here. A vestry is attached by a passage at the NE corner, of about 1862 but well matching the rest.

There are original triple cinquefoiled sedilia and a modest ogee piscina. The excellent Victorian roofs are of hammerbeam form, lower pitched over the chancel, and resting on original head corbels. All the fittings are good Victorian work, with a timber screen, pews, stalls and a stone pulpit. There are two large hatchments and a series of painted coats of arms of knights who fought in the battle. A large and appropriate canopied tomb-chest against the N wall of the sanctuary is of the early nineteenth century. In the vestry are some old glass of French origin, and a display concerning the battle. Mounted in the chancel is a fine and rare survival, an oak carving of the pietà, Our Lady of Pity, probably of the early fifteenth century.

* Bridgnorth

The foundation of this college was due to Roger de Montgomery, 1st Earl of Shrewsbury, who established it in 1083–6 at Quatford (*see* Appendix IV), where he also began a castle and planned a new town. A picturesque story is told about how his foundation was due to a storm at sea involving his second wife, Adeliza. In 1098, Robert de Bellesme became the 3rd earl, and moved from Quatford to the strongly defensible site 2 miles away at Bridgnorth, where he began a new castle. On the accession in 1100 of Henry I, he sided with the new king's rebellious brother Robert; the rebellion failed, and all the earl's possessions were forfeit to the Crown, including the patronage of the college. The college was now established in the chapel of the castle of Bridgnorth, dedicated (like Quatford) to St Mary Magdalene. Being in royal patronage, Bridgnorth became a royal free chapel; it was among the many royal free chapels in the diocese of Coventry and Lichfield, and was one of those of which the freedoms were acknowledged by the bishop in 1281. It had a dean and five canons, and was also served by five vicars; most of the deans and canons through its history were absentees in royal service. Following a petition of the townspeople in 1330, it also became a parish church. Its annual value was estimated as £81 in 1535, but as over £100 in 1546 and 1548. It was dissolved in the latter year, but its parochial function continued. By this time the castle was in decay, but it and the town were put into a state of defence in the Civil War, and suffered a siege in 1646. The church survived this too, and since the redundancy in 1978 of the Church of St Leonard, it has been the town's only parish church.

The medieval church is well known from a good picture and plan made in about 1792: it comprised a long chancel, a nave of three bays with a N aisle and a W tower. It was on a moderate scale, and the sixteenth-century antiquary Leland described it as 'a rude thynge'. It was demolished in 1792 and replaced by a new church which was consecrated in 1796, the architect being the famous engineer Thomas Telford, who has given his name to the county's new town. It is approximately on the site of the medieval church, but whereas

Bridgnorth: the east
(ritual north) side

the latter was conventionally oriented E–W, the new building has its axis N–S, allowing its entrance façade to appear at the end of a vista down East Castle Street. The houses of the town have covered part of the site of the castle, but the ruin of the Norman keep is still to be seen close to the church, and the site is spectacular. Telford's church is a fine and bulky building of good ashlar, with Tuscan pilasters, a large cornice and a straight parapet, in a style considered to show French influence. Its main body is externally in three large bays, with a single tier of large, very tall round-arched windows, separated by paired pilasters. Its entrance façade to the N is impressively dignified, with four attached Tuscan columns carrying a pediment; in the centre the wall surface is rusticated, and here is the round-arched doorway. Above rises the tall tower: on a rusticated square base, the belfry stage has attached columns carrying a bold cornice, above which is a stage chamfered almost to octagonal plan, with round-arched niches, surmounted by a copper dome.

Entry is through the base of the tower, which is internally circular. The main space is strikingly broad, and is divided into a nave and aisles by tall Ionic columns, six each side, carrying a straight entablature. There is a cornice but the flat ceilings are plain. A shallow gallery runs across the entrance wall; side galleries were removed in 1889. A large, round arch opens to a short chancel, which is flanked by lofty chambers used for the organ and vestry. Originally the chancel ended straight; a semicircular apse was added in 1876 by the architect Sir Arthur Blomfield, a good match to the rest. There is a baldachino over the altar. The eighteenth-century fittings have, alas, been almost entirely obliterated. However, clear glass has recently replaced Victorian tinted glass, and the whole interior has beautiful restrained decoration.

* Burford

This is another of the county's portionary churches, almost certainly originally a pre-Conquest minster; it had two priests at the time of Domesday. By 1291 it was divided into three portions. The rectories belonging to each portion

Burford, from the west

stood close to the church, though particular responsibilities seem to have been allocated to the rectors for chapels in outlying parts of the large parish. The revenues were here divided among the clergy in a way that did not give equal portions. The total annual value in the sixteenth century is given as £26. No change took place at the Reformation, and the particular interest of Burford is that technically it retains its portionary status today. In 1849, three parishes were formed out of the original, in which the rector of the first portion was to serve Nash and Boraston, that of the second portion to serve Whitton, while that of the third portion served the mother church. New rectories were built close to their churches for the rectors of the first and second portions. Further changes took place starting in the 1950s, and in 1974 all the benefices became part of a team ministry based on nearby Tenbury Wells (Worcestershire). However, the portionary arrangements were preserved, and today Burford still has three separate benefices: in the relevant church directories there are separate entries for Burford I, Burford II and Burford III. They all, however, have the same incumbent, so their separate existence is largely nominal.

The Church of St Mary comprises a W tower, nave and chancel, but it is quite substantial and indeed is strikingly long. Flat buttresses on the chancel indicate its Norman origin. Some windows in the nave, though renewed, are Dec., which is the period of the modest N and S doorways; the latter has its ancient doors. Most of the effect of the church, however, is due to its extensive Victorian work, largely of attractive Arts and Crafts character by Sir Aston Webb from 1889. The nave and chancel have battlements, in the latter with fancy enrichment, and there are pinnacled buttresses. Externally the most striking of Sir Aston's work is the very broad tower, in two big stages, of which just the ashlar masonry of the lower stage is ancient. Its style is an enriched Perp., with angle buttresses, pairs of two-light belfry openings, much panelling, openwork battlements and large, square corner pinnacles themselves battlemented and pinnacled.

The tall tower arch, of continuous mouldings, is Perp. Beside the S doorway is a stoup recess. The charming trefoiled piscina set diagonally on a corner of the Victorian sedilia is medieval, probably Dec. This is a dark interior, its walls stripped of plaster; much of its distinction is due to the very rich Victorian contributions. Particularly beautiful is Sir Aston's chancel roof, a panelled timber barrel vault with very large angels. He also designed the very striking gilt chandeliers and sanctuary lamps. All timber furnishings are of excellent quality, including a rich chancel screen.

There are also important ancient contents. A very long chest is probably late medieval. The octagonal font is good Perp. work, with a panelled stem and large fleurons on the bowl. There are many memorials, the most important being in the chancel to members of the Cornwall family. In the centre is a plain tomb-chest of the early sixteenth century, with a recumbent oaken effigy of a knight, restored and heavily repainted in 1938. Similarly restored is a perhaps thirteenth-century arched recess, with tomb and painted inscription. On the N side is a fine ogee tomb-recess enriched with ball-flower, again coloured, containing the recumbent effigy of a lady. There is a large brass of about 1370. The finest thing here, however, is the great memorial to Richard Cornwall and his parents, dated 1588 and untouched by restoration. It is a standing wall memorial of oak, 11 ft (3.4 m) high, with pediment and fluted Ionic pilasters, externally painted with texts and representations of the apostles. It opens as a triptych, the side panels having heraldry and the centre a painting of the three commemorated; the base also opens, and shows Richard Cornwall in his shroud. In its design, this memorial may be unique.

* Holdgate

The church was mentioned in Domesday Book, with one priest. At that time, the manor was held by a Norman called Helgot, from whom the place takes its name. He built a castle here, and he and his son Herbert generously endowed the church; its construction was probably due to them, a consecration being recorded between 1115 and 1119. It also appears to have been at this time that it was made portionary, although this status was not documented until 1189: it

Holdgate, from the south-west

had three portions, one each for a priest, deacon and sub-deacon. In 1205, the portioners were described as canons, and it seems probable that their function was indeed collegiate. In the fifteenth and sixteenth centuries, and again in the eighteenth and nineteenth centuries, many rectors (holders of the priest portion) were absentees. The portions continued after the Reformation, but the sub-deaconry ceased in the early seventeenth century. The rectory and the deaconry were united in 1888.

The church has a hilltop setting within the earthworks of one of the two baileys of the castle, of which the mound is immediately E of the churchyard; part of a tower of the castle remains, incorporated in what is now a farmhouse. It is a small but lovely church, consisting simply of a chancel, nave and W tower, dedicated to the Holy Trinity. The tower is of engaging proportions, very broad but quite short, in two stages without buttresses; it has battlements, small corner pinnacles and very modest openings, those of the belfry all differing. Its base is EE and the upper stage is Perp. The nave, however, is Norman. Within the nineteenth-century S porch, the doorway is a splendid piece in three orders, with two orders of shafts; it has good capitals and its arch is enriched with a great variety of motifs, including pellet, beakhead and orthogonal chevron. Also Norman is the W window, which now opens into the tower; there is no tower arch. There is a Dec. tomb-recess in the S side, and two windows are of similar period. The chancel arch is of the 1894–5 restoration, as are the roofs; the chancel is stripped of plaster. There are several authentic lancets in the chancel, including two in the E wall, and also a large three-light, square-headed Perp. window. On the S exterior of the chancel is a sheila-na-gig corbel, probably of Norman date.

The unusual pews are quite tall, with plain probably late-medieval ends, but they have doors, thinner and clearly fitted later; these have mouldings of Jacobean type, but an inscription of 1707 on a desk attached to one pew may date this work. In the SE corner of the nave is the family pew of the Cressets, formerly on the N side; it has a large double seat with rich Jacobean decoration. The church formerly had stalls, of which just one carved misericord survives; it is not kept in the church. The plain polygonal pulpit is late eighteenth century, as are the communion rails. A decayed Royal Arms painted on boards is of 1757. The finest item is the Norman font: its circular bowl has a variety of boldly carved motifs, and a cable moulding runs round the top. Its stem has zigzag in relief, and the base has grotesque heads at the corners. This charming church is in only fair condition, and some of the fittings are decayed; but the parishioners are working to improve matters.

* Ludlow

Although this glorious church was never appropriated to the college of fraternity priests that used it, it owes much of what it is to this association. The Palmers' Guild, founded in the mid-thirteenth century and incorporated in 1339, was an exceptional institution. Dedicated to SS Mary and John the Evangelist, it was not only of dominating importance within the town, but had

Ludlow, from the north-west

members all over Wales and southern England. By 1284 it supported three chaplains, and this number had become eight to ten by the later fifteenth century. The chaplains were formed into a college, and occupied a building erected in 1393–4; this was extended about 1446, and in addition to its fraternity priests, it housed a similar number of chantry priests serving in the church, who were also administered by the Palmers' Guild. The guild moreover provided the church with boy choristers, singing men and an organist. Its charter was renewed during the reign of Henry VIII, and although the guild was visited by the chantry commissioners under the Act of 1545, negotiations went on for some years and it was not surrendered until 1551. Most of its endowments were transferred to the corporation, and continued provision was secured for the grammar school and almshouses which it had supported.

Splendidly situated on its hilltop, the Church of St Laurence is one of the greatest of all parish churches. Its external length is over 200 ft (60 m); it is splendid in its architecture and equally fine in its contents. Internally, the height is especially impressive, but the building is also wide. Though it is

Ludlow, looking east

predominantly a Perp. fabric of the fifteenth century, significant Dec. parts are also evident, and just a little is even earlier. Dominant in distant views of Ludlow, the tower is of especially elegant and sophisticated design. It has polygonal buttresses and its openings are of distinctive depressed four-centred form, with Y-tracery; it is not ornate, but it has a rich battlemented parapet with corner and intermediate pinnacles. Inside, its many-shafted Perp. pillars and richly moulded arches are splendidly lofty, and its lower stage forms a lantern, crowned with a lovely timber vault.

All the Perp. work is faced in ashlar inside and out; the roofs are low pitched and the parapets are straight, with pinnacles. Entry is by a remarkable two-storeyed Dec. S porch, hexagonal in plan, externally uneloquent but internally splendid, with a fine vault and a rich EE doorway to the church. The nave has six bays of uniform Perp. arcades, with two-centred arches on tall pillars of four shafts and four waves, only the shafts having capitals; above are clerestory windows of form similar to the tower openings. Most of the windows in the aisles, however, are Dec., and the W window of the N aisle has lavish ball-flower. Also mainly Dec. are the long transepts, but their walls were obviously raised in Perp. times; great half-arches cross to the tower pillars. Tall chapels flank the chancel, of three bays in their mostly late Perp. windows but opening by just one huge arch to the chancel. Above these arches, the chancel has a clerestory; the remaining three splendid bays of the chancel are of the glasshouse type, their great side windows of five lights having two transoms. The E window has nine lights, with three transoms. Panelling continues below the windows, and there are quadruple sedilia. Outside on the N is an original sacristy.

The roofs throughout are ancient, and are very fine; the main roofs are panelled, with bosses, and that in the chancel has angels. The N chapel is that of St John the Evangelist, which was used especially by the Palmers' Guild; it is notable for the survival above its altar of a fine ceilure of about 1500. Especially notable in the chancel are the stalls, original except for the canopies, with twenty-eight fine and entertaining carved misericords; the timber for them was purchased in 1447. The excellent rood screen is of veranda type, with rich coving and cornice. There are further fine medieval screens at the chapel entrances and across the transepts. Other ancient woodwork includes a long medieval chest. Quite extensive and notable medieval stained glass survives. There are many good memorials, including some impressive post-medieval tomb-chests with recumbent effigies. Above the N transept screen is the organ, dated 1764, in a very fine case. Most of the nave furnishings are good quality nineteenth-century work.

College Street runs past the W side of the churchyard. In it, the college buildings still survive in part, though much rebuilt in the eighteenth century and later; they are built round a quadrangle, and were in 1874 converted into the cottage hospital.

Newport

This college shared the functions of a chantry foundation and one of fraternity priests. In 1432, Thomas Draper obtained licence to establish a chantry for two priests, to celebrate in the Chapel of St Mary which he was causing to be built in the parish Church of St Nicholas. One priest was serving by 1435, but although papal indulgences were obtained in an attempt to increase the endowment, it seems the resources were insufficient. Thomas then joined with the town's Guild of St Mary, and in 1442 they obtained licence to establish in the church a college of a master and four chaplains. Two of the chaplains were to serve Thomas's original chantry. The advowson of the church was purchased for the college, and in 1452 the first master was appointed; the masters had responsibility for the cure of souls. The statutes specified the stipend of the master as 10 marks (£6 13s 4d) per annum, of the other chaplains as 7 marks (£4 13s 4d), and of the college servant as 13s 4d. Dissolution took place in 1547, at which time one of the chaplains serving Draper's chantry was also teaching grammar in a school.

The church, though large and generally of late-medieval aspect, was all either rebuilt or heavily restored in Victorian times, when major eighteenth-century alterations were removed. Externally the nave and aisles are of smooth ashlar and have low-pitched roofs and battlements. The S aisle is of 1883–5, the N of 1890–1 and the S porch is dated 1904. However the clerestory, of two windows per bay under depressed arches, may be genuine Perp. work. The chancel appears totally Victorian, with a S chapel and on the N an organ-chamber and vestry. The best feature is the W tower, tall and bulky, in four

Newport, from the south-east

stages with battlements, angle buttresses and a SW stair turret. It is genuine Dec. work, though externally mostly refaced.

Internally, the nave is broad and lofty. Its five-bay arcades on octagonal pillars are entirely of the 1880s. However its fine roof, with moulded timbers and many bosses, is authentic late-medieval work. Two arched tomb-recesses in the N aisle are ancient but have been moved from elsewhere. Also old is the tower arch, of three continuous chamfers. Perhaps old, though scraped, is the S chapel arcade, of two short bays. The chancel has elaborate Victorian features, including a hammerbeam roof with coloured angels. An early-sixteenth-century tomb-chest carries recumbent alabaster effigies of man and wife. The plain octagonal font bears the date 1660. An unexpected distinction of the church is its extensive collection of benefaction boards; particularly good is the group in the tower, all large and carrying dates in the eighteenth century.

* Pontesbury

Though not mentioned in Domesday Book, this was probably a pre-Conquest minster. By the thirteenth century it was a church of three portioners. Unusually, only a part of the tithe was common and divided between the portioners, other parts being allocated individually, with the result that the portions were not equal; the income of the third portion was about half that of the others, suggesting that it was originally intended for a deacon. One of the portioners, usually but apparently not always the rector of the first portion, was often styled dean. All three portioners seem to have been usually resident. The combined income of the portions in 1535 was given as nearly £43. The portionary arrangement continued unchanged after the Reformation; a system was operated whereby the rector of the first portion was responsible for services for twenty-six weeks of the year, and the others for thirteen weeks each. In 1840, the bishop assigned responsibility for areas of the parish to each of the portioners, and partly as a result of this there was much friction between the portioners in subsequent years. In 1909, the first and second portions were merged, but two portions still exist today, though both are held by one rector. A residence belonged to each portion: that of the first portion, just E of the church, is known as the Deanery and is still occupied by the rector today, but unfortunately its fine eighteenth-century structure was replaced in 1965; the second, later known as the Manor House, was also demolished in the late twentieth century, while the third, known as the Old Rectory, still exists.

The Church of St George is large and quite impressive, but only the chancel is medieval. This is of about 1300, of irregular red sandstone. It has two-light side windows containing Y-tracery and a fine five-light E window with tracery mostly but not entirely of intersecting pattern. Its plain roof is old, and there are a good trefoiled piscina recess and a large aumbry with shouldered lintel, containing moulded doors dated 1652. The rest of the church is dignified and broad, in a good EE style; it dates from 1829, by the

Pontesbury: the chancel, from the south

architect John Turner, and is an attractive example of the Gothic revival architecture of its time. It is an aisled nave with five-bay arcades on tall quatrefoil pillars, a clerestory of single lancets, paired lancets in the aisles, a S porch and straight parapets. The arcades seem to incorporate material from their medieval predecessors. Set in the SW corner is the tower, bulky and tall, with angle buttresses, a straight parapet and large lancet belfry openings. The medieval nave too was aisled, but its tower, which was Norman and is quite well known from old illustrations, stood on the N side; its collapse in 1825 brought down much of the nave and precipitated the rebuilding.

Plaster was stripped from the whole interior in 1897. The fittings of 1829 have all been replaced. The W end has a gallery containing the organ, beneath which is a screen which incorporates seventeenth- and eighteenth-century panelling. Much more seventeenth-century work is incorporated in the pews and in panelling round the walls; especially fine is the very rich panelling of the chancel. The font is good Norman work, with a cylindrical stem carrying a circular bowl, the underside of which is given large scallops. A series of carved timber coats of arms hangs in the chancel, and the many mural memorials from the sixteenth century and later include some fine pieces.

* Shrewsbury: St Chad

This was of pre-Conquest origin, and may well have been the earliest church of the town, perhaps originating in the seventh century. It also had an important college in late Anglo-Saxon times, possibly with sixteen canons; however, the entry in Domesday Survey is ambiguous, and it may be that the college had then ceased to exist. It was refounded or reconstituted early in the twelfth century perhaps by Bishop Roger de Clinton, with a dean and ten canons; it remained in the patronage of the bishops of Coventry and Lichfield throughout the Middle Ages. Two clergy referred to as sacristans, vicars or curates were responsible for parochial services. Vicars choral are first mentioned in 1326; there seem to have been eight, but there were only four in 1548, the year in which the college was dissolved. Despite its large number of canons, it does not seem to have been a thriving institution; the annual income as recorded in 1535, 1546 and 1548 varies, but all assessments were less than £50, and the value of a typical prebend was only in the region of £1.

The church was substantial: cruciform with a central tower, and reported as 168 ft (51.2 m) in length. Its central tower collapsed in 1788, bringing down the N nave arcade and much else. A replacement church was built on a new site; the ruins of the old were cleared away with the exception of the S chancel chapel, which remains preserved in a spacious churchyard. It is a broad rectangle with two three-light traceried windows in both the S and E sides, its large scale reflecting that of the former church. A Trans. Norman date is shown by the broad depressed round arches in the N and W sides, both blocked, and by the former crossing pier which forms the NW corner. The stair originally of the S transept forms a large projection at the SW corner. A short stretch of wall

Shrewsbury: Old St Chad, from the south-west

Shrewsbury: St Chad, looking across the nave

projecting at the NE contains a blocked lancet window of the chancel and below it triple Perp. sedilia, with miniature vaulting enriched with fleurons. Good doors dated 1663 occupy the reset Perp. entrance doorway. The unused interior is evocative, with most of its contents pre-dating 1788. There is a Dec. tomb-recess. The very large circular Norman font bowl remains, with a decorative pattern of lozenges. Other contents include some good memorials and seventeen hatchments. W of the church stood some timber-framed college buildings, of which a small part survives.

The replacement church was built in 1790–2 to a classical design by George Steuart. It is very large and stately, and on a splendid site. It was highly controversial at the time, and in plan it is unique. Its body is circular, externally with a rusticated lower stage containing rectangular windows, above which are tall round-arched windows, paired Ionic pilasters, a cornice and a parapet with intermittent balustrading. Internally a great gallery goes round most of the circle, resting on Ionic columns, with thin fluted Corinthian columns rising to support the flat ceiling, which has beautiful restrained plasterwork and a large central Glory. The columns are actually of cast iron. A short sanctuary is formed within the circle, oriented to the NW, with an arch on lavish paired Corinthian columns and a very large enriched Venetian window.

The entrance front has a pedimented portico of four Tuscan columns. Behind this is the massive, rusticated square base of the tower, surmounted by a very large octagonal stage with four tall round-arched belfry openings; above this is a lofty cylinder surrounded by eight free-standing Corinthian columns, carrying a dome. The entrance hall under the tower is circular; to each side is a vestry, externally tall and dignified, with a pedimented E wall. That to the right was in 1914 extended by a windowless apse and made into a chapel. Connecting the entrance hall to the church is another large and very distinctive compartment, in plan a circle slightly extended laterally, with the gallery stairs curving elegantly up each side.

Much of the fine woodwork of the interior is original, but the pews have been cut down. There are many mural memorials and, as at old St Chad's, a remarkable collection of hatchments, twenty-one in all. In the window behind the altar, and in several others, is dramatic pictorial glass of the 1840s. The striking pulpit of brass and copper dates from 1882.

* Shrewsbury: St Mary

St Mary's is the largest, and was long the most important, parish church in Shrewsbury. It was of early origin, and had secular priests attached to it from an early stage; it had royal freedoms, which may have been due to King Edgar (ruled 959–75). In the thirteenth century it had a dean and nine prebendaries. Interestingly, the prebends were named after saints, and since their feast days were spread fairly uniformly through the year it is suggested that this is a relic of an early organization in which the canons were responsible in rotation through the year for the services in the church. It was a royal free chapel throughout its life;

Shrewsbury: St Mary, from the south-west

with others in the diocese of Coventry and Lichfield, its exemption from ordinary jurisdiction was acknowledged in 1281 by Bishop Meuland. From the early thirteenth century most canons were normally absent, though it seems that usually one remained in residence. In addition, it had several vicars choral and at least one parochial chaplain, though little is known about these. By the sixteenth century, two of its prebends seem to have lapsed. Though an important college, it was not wealthy; in 1548, the year of its dissolution, its annual income was given as £38. Its peculiar status survived the Reformation, and it was not until 1846 that it came under the jurisdiction of the bishop.

When in the 1980s there was a reorganization of the parishes in the town, St Mary's was startlingly chosen for redundancy; it is now the most important church vested in the Churches Conservation Trust. It is of impressive size and splendour, with an external length of over 200 ft (60 m) and a spire reaching 222 ft (67.7 m). It contains work of all medieval periods in a complicated and occasionally baffling growth; work showing some characteristics of the transition between Norman and EE is prominent. During Victorian restoration, foundations of the preceding Anglo-Saxon church were discovered beneath the present nave.

The massive W tower is Norman in its three lowest stages, with flat angle buttresses and simple round-arched openings; the W doorway and the low slightly pointed arch to the nave are of several unmoulded orders. The fourth stage is Perp., its yellow ashlar contrasting with the red of the stages below; it has paired two-light belfry openings and openwork battlements with big corner pinnacles. The commanding, slender spire has three tiers of lucarnes. In the nave, the large and lofty four-bay arcades are round arched but in all other respects are very fine EE work, with pillars of many shafts, stiff-leaf capitals and finely moulded arches. Above there is much blank wall and then a Perp. clerestory of paired windows. The great chancel arch conforms with the arcades, but is pointed; two large, apparently EE two-light openings in the wall above it are a late-Victorian insertion. The nave has a very fine late-medieval roof, low pitched, with splendid large bosses and richly moulded

Shrewsbury: St Mary,
looking east

timbers divided into small quatrefoiled panels. It looks very authentic, but it is an admirable restoration after most of it was brought down in 1894 by the collapse of the top of the spire.

The aisles have three-light Perp. windows. The N porch is Victorian, but the S porch is notable very late Norman work, with capitals almost of stiff-leaf type and a depressed round arch with splendidly rich decoration including openwork chevron. The doorway to the church is similar, and the porch has a vault; the room above is a Dec. addition. There is thought to have once been a central tower; the transepts are E of the chancel arch, and are a complex mixture of Norman and EE work. They have tall lancet windows including spectacular N and S triplets, internally and externally shafted, with stiff-leaf capitals. Each had a barrel-vaulted E chapel, that on the S now reduced to a recess. The S transept has another rich late-Norman doorway.

The large and lofty chancel is partly EE; traces suggest that it was once vaulted, but it now has a Perp. clerestory similar to that of the nave. On its N side is a single-bay Dec. chapel, with fine features including a spherical triangle window. E of this, the chancel has a great triplet of very acutely pointed lancets, internally very rich and repeated in an inner plane, with a wall passage. On the S side, a single Norman sedile remains, with chevron; its companions have been destroyed, and the present sedilia further E are Victorian, as is the great E window. There is a very broad and lofty Dec. S chapel, divided into four bays, with finely traceried three-light S windows and triple ogee-cinquefoiled sedilia.

Splendid and fascinating as its architecture is, it is the glass that is regarded as the church's finest possession. Outstanding is the Jesse Tree of about 1340 in the E window, which was probably originally in the town's Greyfriars Church. Almost all the other glass was brought here between 1829 and 1851 under the then vicar, William Rowland: there is very extensive early-sixteenth-century glass from Altenberg in Germany, glass of about 1479 from Trier, also in Germany, glass of about 1535 from Liège in Belgium and much more. Despite this, the church is not dark. It has many mural memorials and some large monuments, including a fine tomb-chest of about 1315 with a recumbent effigy. The octagonal Perp. font rests on an octagonal stem which is unusual in being hollow, with openwork panelling.

* Tong

In 1409, Sir Fulke de Pembrugge (Pembridge) died. In 1410 his widow Isabel, with two others, obtained licence from the Crown to purchase from Shrewsbury Abbey the advowson of the Church of St Bartholomew at Tong, and to establish in it a chantry college of a warden, four chaplains and two clerks. The first warden was instituted in March 1411, and statutes were drawn up in the same month. The principal purpose of the college was intercession for the souls of Sir Fulke and Isabel's two previous husbands, Sir Thomas Peytevin and Sir John Ludlow. An almshouse was also to be

Tong, from the south-west

supported for thirteen poor people, of whom seven were to be so infirm as to be helpless. In 1415, the endowments of the dissolved alien priory of Lapley (Staffordshire) were added, and revised statutes were devised in 1423. About 1510, a further chantry was established in the church by Sir Henry Vernon, the priest of which was also to live in the college. The annual income of the college in 1546 was given as £56; it was dissolved in that year, though the almshouse continued, supported by the lords of the manor.

The church was almost entirely rebuilt for the college, and is exceptionally interesting and evocative. It is not particularly large, but it is of spectacular and individual character, and its medieval contents are outstanding. All parts have battlements and it bristles with pinnacles. The main roofs are low pitched, but the aisles are lean-to, and the nave has no clerestory. There is a central tower, and the church seems cruciform; but the transepts are simply a continuation of the aisles. The tower is very distinctive: above a short square stage, it turns octagonal, with pinnacles on the transition; this stage has battlements and pinnacles, and carries a short stone spire with one set of lucarnes, each of which carries yet another pinnacle. There is a S porch and a three-bay aisleless chancel, coeval with which is a substantial sacristy on the N side. An additional chapel, again battlemented and pinnacled, is attached to the S side of the S transept.

The windows in the aisleless chancel are tall, in three lights, and the transomed E window has five lights. There are triple sedilia and a large piscina recess. In the nave, the arcades are of three bays, with octagonal pillars and arches of two moulded orders; the S arcade in part differs, and seems to include some thirteenth-century work. A stair is incorporated in the NW crossing pillar. The roofs throughout are original, with moulded timbers and some large bosses. The floors, incongruously of red Victorian tiles, slope steadily up to the E.

In place of the transept S wall, there is a splendid arrangement with many lavish image niches; in this, a very richly panelled depressed arch and an ogee doorway open to the Vernon (or Golden) Chapel, a superb little building added in 1510 for Sir Henry Vernon's chantry. It retains its stone altar and several painted consecration crosses, and has a fan vault of two bays, with pendants; one of its vault springers curiously and clumsily hangs in space in front of the arch. In the arch is a tomb-chest with splendidly preserved recumbent effigies of Sir John and his wife, in alabaster. On the W wall of the chapel is the very distinctive memorial to Sir Arthur Vernon, who died in 1517: it is in the form of a bust holding a book, set on a panelled corbel with a canopy above. The central part of the church is crowded to an extraordinary degree with further late medieval memorials; one is a tomb-chest with recumbent effigies of Lady Isabel de Pembrugge, the founder of the college, and Sir Fulke. Most others are to Vernons, who succeeded Sir Fulke as lords of the manor. In the S transept is the great Elizabethan two-decker Stanley monument, with effigies: this was originally in the sanctuary. A brass of 1510 commemorates a priest of the college.

Tong, looking east

The octagonal font is set against a nave pillar. Some fifteenth-century glass remains in the W window. The attractive pulpit was given in 1629. Seating in the nave is medieval pews, with traceried straight ends; well-preserved parclose screens of 'L' plan separate as chapels the E part of the aisles with the transepts. The chancel screen remains in position, and the chancel has its set of sixteen stalls, with traceried fronts, poppy-head ends carved as figures and tall crested back panelling. Some of the misericords have foliage, but two have a green man, and that on the master's stall has the beautiful form known as a lily crucifix.

The collegiate building stood S of the church; it was demolished in the early nineteenth century. To the W of the church, one ruined wall remains of the almshouse, which was rebuilt on a new site in the late eighteenth century.

Somerset

Somerset had two medieval colleges, neither of them major, of which only one has its church today. The county's outstanding collegiate possession is at Wells, which has the finest remaining example of a college of vicars choral (*see* Appendix I).

* North Cadbury

This college owed its origin to Lady Elizabeth, the widow of Sir William Botreaux, who had died in 1391. She caused the parish Church of St Michael to be rebuilt, and in 1417 obtained licence to convert it into a chantry college for a rector and six chaplains, with four clerks. The licence was renewed in 1423 by her grandson, another Sir William, but it is doubtful whether the foundation was ever completed, and it almost certainly never achieved its intended size. At its dissolution in 1548, it was 'commonly callyd a college and hathe ben tyme out of mynde'; there were a rector and two chaplains, and the annual income is given as £28.

The church built for the college is uniform, stately and splendid, of typical Somerset type. It is of fine regular masonry, and has low-pitched roofs with straight parapets throughout, running from nave to chancel without external distinction. Only the W tower is earlier than the rest, though still Perp.; it is tall, in three stages, but has little enrichment and its diagonal buttresses are rather clumsy in effect. Its battlements and the blunt spirelet top of its stair turret are modifications of 1905. The nave has five bays, with arcades of finely moulded two-centred arches on pillars of four shafts and four waves. Both the clerestory and the aisle windows have three lights. There are virtually identical N and S porches: two-storeyed, with a panelled front and a crocketed ogee hood-mould over the arch rising to an image niche, flanked by little two-light windows. Each has a stair turret carrying a blunt spirelet (the model for that on the tower), and internally has a tierceron vault.

North Cadbury, from the north

The tall chancel arch unusually has two pairs of identical capitals: the lower pair supported the rood beam. A rood access doorway is on the N side. The chancel is aisleless, three bays long, with large three-light windows set high, below which the walls are blank for the canopies above the former stalls. An original sacristy is attached below window level on the N side. There are attractive triple sedilia, but they seem to be all restoration, as perhaps are the gorgeously coloured large canopied image niches which flank the E window.

The roofs throughout are original and are excellent: especially fine is the nave roof, with cambered tie-beams, tracery and large foliage bosses. It rests on very large shield-bearing angels. The chancel furnishings are indifferent, but mounted on a wall are three misericords from the stalls, which were removed in 1850. Most of the pews are medieval, with poppy-head ends having tracery with entertainingly varied motifs; one has the date 1538. Under the tower are three tomb-chests, two of which are Jacobean. The third was formerly in the chancel, and has the recumbent effigies of a knight and his lady, almost certainly the original Sir William Botreaux with Lady Elizabeth, the founder of the college. It is of fine quality; its sides have carvings, including a fairly intact Virgin and Child, and also retain some painted heraldry. Close by is the Perp. font: its octagonal bowl has a different design on each face, and rests on a square stem with four attached shafts. The whole interior is very light, with predominantly clear glass; a little medieval glass remains, mostly in the W window.

North Cadbury, looking east

Close beside the church stands the splendid mainly Elizabethan mansion of North Cadbury Court: church and mansion are set high, and make a beautiful sight from the valley to the south.

Stoke-sub-Hamdon

This chantry college was established in 1304 by Sir John Beauchamp, who obtained royal licence in 1303 and papal confirmation in 1309. It had a provost or warden and four chaplains, and served in the private Chapel of St Nicholas, which was a free-standing building in the courtyard of the family's manor house. The manor house and chapel had been built in the later thirteenth century; after 1333 the manor house was fortified, and was sometimes referred to as a castle. The domestic buildings provided for the college stood in the village, about ¼ mile from the chapel. In its life, the college was almost monastic, the chaplains being required to take vows of obedience, chastity, and lifelong residence, and to have no property. Five masses were to be said daily. Rules specified the habits to be worn, including that for moving between the collegiate buildings and the Chapel of St Nicholas. The parish Church of St Mary, 1 mile away at East Stoke, was appropriated to the college, and served by a vicar.

For perhaps half a century, the college seems to have fulfilled the intentions of its founder, but from then on its story was one of steady decline. By 1361, the male line of the Beauchamps here ended, and in the early fifteenth century the manor house passed to the Crown, and was allowed to fall into ruin. Already in 1375 there were disputes about the payment of the vicar in the parish church, and the vicarage was abolished, the church being served either by a chaplain or by a curate found by the provost. By 1444, the college had only three chaplains, and the collegiate building seems to have been ruinous; the bishop suspended the provost for mismanagement and ordered repairs. By the 1540s, there was only an absentee provost, employing one curate for the parish church and one for the chantry, in which mass was now said just three times a week. The college was dissolved in 1548; the parishioners petitioned for the Chapel of St Nicholas to be retained as a chapel of ease, but to no effect, and together with the manor house it has completely disappeared. As described by Leland shortly before its end, it seems to have been substantial, with a series of monuments, mostly with recumbent effigies commemorating the Beauchamps.

The domestic buildings, however, survived in secular use. In the early twentieth century they became known as the Priory, and are now owned by the National Trust and in part open to the public. They were much altered in the fifteenth century, and again later. The main building, which was restored in 1967, includes a substantial hall and a small chapel.

Staffordshire

Staffordshire has an impressive series of six collegiate churches. They have a unique uniformity in that all were colleges of canons (or in one case portioners), all were of early or fairly early origin and, most remarkably, all were royal free chapels. Tamworth was a late addition as a royal free chapel, but the others, together with Derby All Saints, Bridgnorth and Shrewsbury St Mary, seem to have been intentionally formed at an early stage into a group in royal patronage. Some events in their histories are shared. With only one exception, the collegiate churches of Staffordshire are splendid and important medieval buildings. The county also has an attractive if modest college of vicars at Lichfield.

* Gnosall

The first syllable of the place-name is pronounced 'know'. This Church of St Lawrence may have been a pre-Conquest minster; certainly by the early twelfth century it had a small community of priests and the status of royal free chapel. With other Staffordshire colleges, its royal patronage was given away in the twelfth century by King Stephen to the Bishop of Coventry. It continued as a church of four portioners (often called prebendaries), in the patronage of the bishop, who was occasionally referred to as the nominal dean. Some aspects of its royal free status remained, and under Edward I an attempt was made to regain its patronage for the Crown, but without success. The prebendaries became non-resident early on, and the church was served by four vicars;

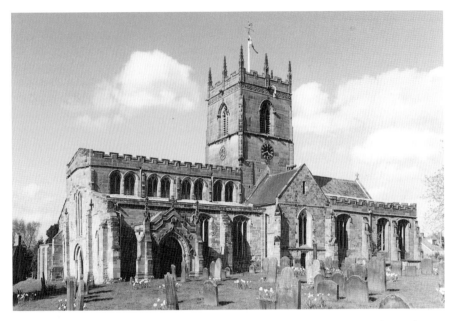

Gnosall, from the south-west

Gnosall: the south transept from the crossing

a house may have been provided for them in the early thirteenth century, and certainly a new one was built shortly before the dissolution. The annual value in 1535 was just over £47; dissolution was in 1546.

This is a splendid church, a magnificent sight both externally and internally, although it is only of larger-medium size. Its setting in the village too is beautiful. It is cruciform, and the crossing and transepts are basically Norman. The crossing arches are massive and impressive: the W arch is richest, with shafts and rich if rather shallow decoration, including chevron; a shallow roll goes round the soffit of the arch. The capitals are much damaged but show decorative patterns. Notable Norman work also appears in the S transept: its W side has good blank arcading (now cut through by an EE arch to the aisle), and above this is a triforium-like gallery, giving access from the transept stair turret to the tower, with two fine twin openings.

The rest of the church is later. Externally a fine display is made by the Perp. crossing tower, which has shallow diagonal buttresses, battlements with a band of panelling below and corner and intermediate pinnacles. The nave has three-bay EE arcades with double-chamfered arches on tall octagonal pillars; with these go the modest lancet triplet in the W wall and the W and S doorways, the latter with stiff-leaf capitals. There is an externally battlemented Perp. clerestory of paired two-light windows, arranged (unlike the arcades) in four bays. The aisles have three-light probably Perp. windows under shallow segmental arches; they are taller on the S side. There is a quite elaborate Victorian S porch. Attached by a passage on the N side is a recent parish room, called Chapter House.

The chancel is also three bays long. Its N wall has windows similar to those of the nave. The five-light E window is Dec., with enterprising tracery. Along the S side of the chancel is a battlemented late-Perp. chapel, as wide as the transept, with a relatively plain arcade. It is suggested that its structure originated in the thirteenth century and was separated from the church, forming the vicars' residence. Both transepts were partly remodelled in the Perp. period, and the N transept was given a shallow E chapel. Odd raking buttresses were applied in the early nineteenth century to this transept. The furnishings are excellent, but mostly of the nineteenth or twentieth century. In the S transept is a tomb-chest with the damaged late-medieval alabaster effigy of a knight; also here are an effigy of a child and a battered medieval chest.

* Penkridge

Penkridge church is of pre-Conquest origin; there is some evidence to suggest that it was founded by King Eadred (reigned 946–55). Nine clerks are recorded in Domesday Book, though not the nature of their community. In 1136, with others, the church was given by King Stephen to the bishop, Roger de Clinton, perhaps in gratitude for gaining the pope's recognition of his status

Penkridge, from the south

as king. By the 1180s it had returned to the Crown, and was established as of royal free status, with a dean and probably seven prebendaries. In the early thirteenth century, the advowson of the deanery was granted to the Archbishop of Dublin, and this soon led to the deanery itself being permanently united with the archbishopric of Dublin. Penkridge still, however, retained royal free status, and, like Stafford and other neighbouring colleges, was involved in disputes between kings and bishops over this in the late thirteenth century. In the 1280 dispute, Archbishop Pecham of Canterbury excommunicated the clergy of Penkridge, but not the dean, the Archbishop of Dublin. Penkridge was among those acknowledged in 1281 by Bishop Meuland in its privileges as royal free chapel. Its annual value in the sixteenth century is given as £106; at this time in addition to its dean and prebendaries it had six vicars, two chantry priests and others. It was dissolved in 1548. It continued to be a peculiar of the archbishops of Dublin until the nineteenth-century reforms.

The church is large, dignified and beautiful. It is of good red-brown sandstone ashlar, with a W tower and a nave and chancel both of four bays, aisled and clerestoried. The roofs are low pitched, and it is uniformly battlemented, with small pinnacles. It dates from the thirteenth to the sixteenth centuries, but is regular and consistent in its effect; this is assisted by a late Perp. remodelling, in which many of the windows surprisingly employ the Y-tracery form; some may be as late as Elizabethan.

The tall tower is in three stages, finely proportioned, with shallow diagonal buttresses; most of its features are Perp., with large three-light belfry openings, a frieze of shield-enclosing quatrefoils and battlements with eight pinnacles. The lofty nave has tall cylindrical pillars, moulded capitals and arches of two orders, the inner chamfered, the outer with a filleted roll: these are EE. Above is a Perp. clerestory of tall paired two-light, square-headed windows. The roof of moulded timbers is a good replacement of 1881. In its E part, the S aisle becomes broader and forms a chapel. The two narrower W bays of this aisle were in 1999 formed into a large lobby, with a glazed screen to the church and a gallery room high above. This room communicates with a room over the S porch, which has a Perp. fireplace and is now used as a chapel 'set aside for the visitor or pilgrim'.

The tall chancel arch has Dec. features, but it was raised by 8 ft (2.4 m) in 1881. Although the height of the chancel is less than that of the nave and its aisles are narrow, it is lofty and noble in its effect. Its arcades resemble those

Penkridge, looking east

of the nave. The five-light E window is Dec., with beautiful flowing tracery. In the chancel arch is a very rich and impressive wrought-iron screen, of surprising provenance: it is Dutch work of 1778, and was brought from Cape Town in the 1880s. Smaller gates, excellently matching its style, were made for the aisles. Most furnishings are nineteenth century, but in the sanctuary there remain some late medieval stalls, with misericords. There is a Perp. parclose screen. Three large memorials are all to Littletons: two are tomb-chests of Elizabethan date, with multiple recumbent effigies. The third is early seventeenth century and is in two tiers, both of which carry the recumbent effigies of a knight and his lady; on their fronts are kneeling effigies of their children, all named. There are also two late-medieval incised slabs. The octagonal font is of 1668, with ornamental motifs characteristic of the date; it is inscribed 'restored 1864', probably also the date of the engaging wrought-iron bracket hinged from the wall, from which its cover is suspended.

* Stafford

The first mention of a collegiate church here is in Domesday Book, when it is described as having the king's thirteen prebendary canons; this was probably a pre-Conquest royal foundation. Stafford is associated with St Bertelin, an eighth-century hermit, and immediately SW of the present church there stood, as a separate but related building, an Anglo-Saxon church or chapel of St

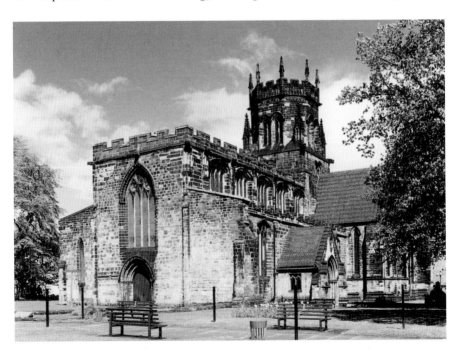

Stafford: St Mary, from the south-west

Bertelin. This was demolished in 1801, but its footings were excavated in 1954 and may still be seen. Whether the canons of 1086 served in St Bertelin's or in a predecessor of the present Church of St Mary is unknown. Stafford (with Gnosall, Penkridge and Wolverhampton) was given by King Stephen in 1136 to the Bishop of Coventry, but it returned to the Crown under Henry II. The church was much involved in the controversies of the thirteenth century concerning royal free chapels; the story of the events, including the physical assault on the church in 1258, has already been told in Chapter 2.

Stafford remained a royal free chapel throughout the rest of the medieval period, though in 1446 Henry VI gave the advowson to Humphrey Stafford, Duke of Buckingham. It returned to full royal control in 1521, on the execution of the then duke. It had a dean and twelve canons throughout, but whereas the deanery and three of the prebends were of substantial value, the remaining prebends were always small. The canons who held the latter seem not to have provided vicars; there were four vicars choral, four clerk vicars and a chantry chaplain, who also taught in a school. The annual value is given as £73; the college was dissolved in 1548. The college house stood on the S side of the churchyard; it was demolished in 1736–8. A curious piece of much later history here was the attempt in 1929 by the rector, Lionel Lambert, to revive its royal free status, so that the bishop would have no automatic right of entry. After lengthy legal proceedings, the case failed.

The church is large and stately, and is well set in a large open churchyard in the centre of the town. It is cruciform, with a central tower, and is aisled throughout; both the nave and the chancel have five bays. It is in excellent condition, but this is in part due to George Gilbert Scott, who here undertook his first major restoration, beginning in 1842. He was most destructive in the chancel and S transept, in both of which a Perp. clerestory was removed and a high-pitched roof put on. He was also responsible for all three E windows and for most of the windows of the S chapel and S transept, which either are lancet groups or have geometrical tracery.

The nave arcades are noble work of about 1200: the pillars are of quatrefoil plan with a square fillet between the foils, carrying volute capitals, cruciform imposts and acutely pointed arches of two finely moulded orders. The renewal of details here has been extensive, but seems to be good. Above are a lofty Perp. clerestory of four-light windows, and the original low-pitched roof of finely moulded timbers; externally it is battlemented. Similar good late-medieval roofs cover the aisles; the N aisle windows are Perp., the S are Dec. Also original are the four-light geometrical W window and the fine EE W doorway. Only the S porch is by Scott. The fine crossing goes with the nave arcades, with arches of three orders; above the W arch is good EE arcading with double shafts; two of the six arches are open, but curiously they are not symmetrical. Externally the tower is Perp. and is very distinctive. Above a short square stage it turns octagonal, with twin two-light openings in the cardinal directions, and crowned by panelled battlements with pinnacles; it formerly carried a spire, the fall of which in 1594 caused much damage to the chancel and probably the S transept.

Stafford: St Mary, looking east

The chancel arcades are late thirteenth century; they have filleted quatre-foil pillars and deeply moulded arches, and the E pillar is a double respond, presumably indicating an extension. Both chancel chapels are broader than the nave aisles; the N one retains its low-pitched roof. The N transept is different from the rest of the church, and has never been restored: except for its Perp. clerestory and battlements, it is a Dec. showpiece. Its very broad N window is in seven lights, with lavish tracery; also fine are the E and W windows, and the interior has Dec. panelling, with crocketed gables and ogee details. It has a spectacular N doorway, externally in four shafted orders, with rich leaf capitals and lines of ball-flowers and fleurons in the hollows of its arch.

The many mural memorials include one to Izaak Walton, author of *The Compleat Angler*, who was baptized here. In the N transept are two larger memorials, one a tomb-chest of 1562 with two recumbent alabaster effigies. The large font is exceptional: it is Norman, but of most unusual type, with a curving bowl of quatrefoil form, resting on lions and other beasts. Its design must reflect influence from Italy or the East. It carries a quite long, curiously enigmatic inscription in Latin.

* Tamworth

This place was important in early times; Offa, King of Mercia in the late eighth century, had a palace here. St Edith or Editha, to whom the church is dedicated, is believed to have been a grand-daughter of Alfred the Great and to have married the Danish king Sihtric at Tamworth in 926; she may have established a religious community here. The early collegiate history of the church is not known, but by the mid-thirteenth century it had a dean and five or six canons, in the patronage of the Marmion family, who were lords of Tamworth. When the last Marmion lord died, Edward I claimed it as a royal free chapel, alleging that it had been under royal patronage in the time of Henry II. This resulted in prolonged litigation, but by about the mid-fourteenth century its royal free status was established. Its prebends were frequently held by absentees, and in 1319 six chaplains or vicars are recorded. In 1442 the dean, John Bate, provided additional statutes, mainly to improve the lot of the vicars, giving them security of tenure and increasing their stipend from £5 to £6 a year. A house was also allocated for their use. The annual value of the college in the sixteenth century is given as £58; it was dissolved in 1548.

Tamworth, from the south-east

The church is extremely large; it has much of interest, and has not been spoilt by the considerable restoration to which it has been subjected. The exterior is all of ashlar. It has a W tower with a most impressively bulky presence; it is Perp., in four stages, with twin two-light belfry openings and buttresses with diagonals in their angles. It is battlemented and has crocketed corner spirelets, bringing the height to about 130 ft (40 m). Internally it has a timber vault resting on stone springers, and opens to the church by a large doorway above which is a great unglazed seven-light Perp. window. Its stair turret in the SW corner has the rare curiosity of being double, with two interleaving stairs which never meet.

At first sight, the church seems to be a fairly uniform aisled nave and chancel, with the chancel longer than the nave. The impression of uniformity

Tamworth, looking east

is due to the low-pitched roofs with straight parapets and a Perp. clerestory throughout, of windows in three or four lights; the nave is slightly higher. Internally there is no structural division between the nave and the chancel. The nave has splendid Dec. arcades of four very large bays, with finely moulded arches on pillars of quatrefoil section with a fillet between the foils. E of these is the most memorable oddity of the church: each side has a tall and fine Norman arch, with rolls, billet and some zigzag. Rough masonry on each side, and even some battered remains of more zigzag and a shaft, show that this was once a crossing; it ceased to be that following a major fire in 1345, which caused the rebuilding of most of the church. The former crossing was incorporated in the chancel, adding to its already great length. Features of the crossing area have been thought to show pre-Conquest traces.

The aisles of the nave are very wide, with very large mostly Dec. windows. There is a vaulted N porch of the EE period, now with a glazed arch and used as a bookshop; it has an upper chamber. A thirteenth-century crypt is below part of the S aisle. The transepts remain, though they do not project beyond the aisles; only the one on the N has a N–S roof. They, too, have good Dec. features; a two-bay arcade divides the S transept from the S aisle.

The chancel has no arcades. On its S side is a short chapel containing the organ, and then nineteenth-century sacristies; the chancel wall here shows Norman features including nook-shafted flat buttresses, and there is a large Norman window, now internal. The impressive but unusual E window has a thick central mullion and apparently Dec. tracery, but it may be nineteenth century. On the N side is the broad and fine St George's Chapel, mainly Dec. but with a seven-light Perp. E window; canopied image niches flank this window, and there is a tomb-recess on the N side. Remarkably, this chapel communicates with the chancel by three very rich tomb-recesses which have arches opening each side, cinquefoiled and sub-cusped; three unglazed Dec. windows are above.

The roofs are mainly of good medieval work. The slender wrought-iron chancel screen is probably eighteenth-century work. There is a series of medieval tomb-chests with recumbent effigies in the tomb-recesses N of the chancel and elsewhere, though most of the effigies are mutilated. One is to Baldwin de Witney, dean during the rebuilding following the fire. There are some notable later memorials too, especially, in the tower, a very large and magnificent baroque standing wall memorial of about 1680, with two half-kneeling figures. Some of the nineteenth-century glass is fine.

Tettenhall (*now West Midlands*)

The Church of St Michael and All Angels was reported in 1401 to have been founded by King Edgar (ruled 959–75). Whether or not this was so, it appears in Domesday Book. Only in the thirteenth century do we hear of it as a royal free chapel, possessing a dean and five prebendaries, but these probably existed in Norman times if not earlier. In the late thirteenth century, as at other Staffordshire royal free chapels, there were disputes concerning its status; it was among those whose freedoms were in 1281 acknowledged by the bishop. A later period of confusion arose from 1338 when, the manor having been granted to Lord Ferrers, the Ferrers family claimed patronage of the college; but from 1374 it was firmly back in royal hands. There seem to have been four vicars, and eventually also two chantry priests; a house for the vicars existed in the sixteenth century. Dissolution took place in 1548, and the property was purchased in 1549 by Walter Wrottesley, who thereby acquired the privileges over the deanery which had formerly belonged to the dean, including the right

Tettenhall, from the south

to hold a secular court with such functions as proving wills and recording marriage bonds. These were retained by the Wrottesley family until the nineteenth-century reforms.

The church was substantial though not especially large. It had a chancel with N and S chapels, an aisled and clerestoried nave with a two-storeyed S porch and a W tower. Much of it was thirteenth century, and the nave arcades were fourteenth; the S aisle was rebuilt and much enlarged in the early nineteenth century, and again rebuilt in 1882–3 to the designs of G.E. Street and his son, A.E. Street. There were late medieval stalls with misericords. Alas, almost all was destroyed by fire on the night of 2 February 1950. Rebuilding took place to the designs of the architect Bernard Miller, and it was reopened in 1955. Of the old church, only the W tower and S porch were retained. The tower is Perp., of ashlar, with shallow diagonal buttresses, two-light arched belfry openings and battlements. Its arch to the nave, of continuous mouldings, is entirely renewed. The fine vaulted porch is of 1882–3.

The rebuilding was to an entirely new plan and design. It is striking, but not everyone will like this architecture; it is of medieval inspiration but some features, especially the principal windows, are far from medieval in character. All is ashlar-faced inside and out. It has a very broad nave, with three-bay arcades of large pointed arches resting on very short cylindrical pillars carrying large stylized leaf capitals; there is a further small bay at each end. Above is a modest clerestory of two-light windows, and much is made of the oak roof, the trusses of which come low. The broad aisles have lean-to roofs, but are dominated by cross-gables containing very large triangular-headed traceried windows. There is a short structural chancel, liturgically the Lady Chapel and at first separated from the nave by a wall, in front of which was the high altar; after later controversies, the wall was removed. The Lady Chapel has cinquefoiled circular windows; it is flanked by vestries and an organ-chamber. Furnishings throughout are of oak. The large circular Norman font survives: ejected from the church in Victorian times, it is now in the modern daughter church at Pendleford.

* **Wolverhampton** (*now West Midlands*)

This was certainly of pre-Conquest origin, and perhaps of royal foundation. There seems to be sufficient evidence to accept the story of the church of Hantun or Hampton being founded or more probably refounded in 994 by the lady Wulfrun, whose name was then combined with the existing name to give its present form. At this period the church was dedicated to St Mary, but it had

Wolverhampton, from the south

been changed to St Peter by the mid-twelfth century. As with the other collegiate churches of Staffordshire, it was a royal chapel, and in this case we know much of its rather convoluted history during the Norman period. It was given by the Conqueror to his chaplain, Sampson, who later became Bishop of Worcester, to which it became attached. It was then obtained by Roger, Bishop of Salisbury, apparently illicitly. After Roger's death, King Stephen gave it, with three other Staffordshire colleges, to the Bishop of Coventry, Roger de Clinton, but by the reign of Henry II it was back under full royal control. It retained royal privileges throughout these changes. Another surprising episode followed: Peter of Blois became dean at the end of the twelfth century, and there survives a letter he wrote to Pope Innocent III, in which he describes in lurid terms the corruption and iniquities of the canons of the time. He resigned, and with the agreement of the king, the pope and the archbishop, Wolverhampton was to become a Cistercian monastery; the first monks actually arrived. But the archbishop died in 1205, and the scheme was abandoned. Wolverhampton remained a college of a dean and six canons, with a seventh canon added in 1294. It shared in the thirteenth-century disputes which affected the royal free chapels of Staffordshire, and was one of those which the bishop in 1281 acknowledged as exempt from his jurisdiction. Many of the deans and canons through its history were in royal service, and few were resident. In 1385 there were five vicars, and in 1531 there were seven, with two chantry chaplains.

William Dudley, dean from about 1457 to 1476, was also Dean of Windsor, and in 1480, by letters patent of Edward IV, the two deaneries were combined. Although in 1548 the dean argued that the terms of the 1547 Act which permitted Windsor to continue should apply also to Wolverhampton, the college was dissolved in that year. However, one of the first acts of Queen Mary was to reinstate it, on the grounds that its dissolution had been invalid because of its connection with Windsor. This was eventually confirmed in a charter of Elizabeth I, so the college continued, except for the period of the Commonwealth. It also remained a royal peculiar, and shared its dean throughout with Windsor. It was finally dissolved in 1848, following the death of the last dean, and the peculiar was abolished.

St Peter's has a notable setting, on the highest point of the hill on which the town stands; it is a fine and important church, especially striking both inside and out for its loftiness. There has been much renewal, especially externally. It is cruciform, and the earliest work is the crossing, its relatively small triple-chamfered arches of about 1300 much restricting views through the church. Also partly of this period is the S transept, with a tall five-light E window and a good trefoiled piscina recess. All other medieval work is Perp., of the second half of the fifteenth century or later. The nave has five bays, with richly moulded two-centred arches on tall octagonal pillars. Above these, the clerestory is surprisingly divided into six bays, with pairs of very tall square-headed transomed two-light windows. This clerestory continues in the S transept. The lofty aisles have large windows, mostly of Victorian work, and

Wolverhampton: the pulpit

the W front is all Victorian. Unusually, the aisles have a kind of clerestory, of continuous timber-framed windows, concealed behind the battlements. The large S porch is vaulted; its upper storey is entirely Victorian.

The tall crossing tower is in three stages, all panelled, with twin two-light openings in the top stage, and battlements with corner pinnacles. The very large E and N windows of the N transept are extraordinary: their arches are only slightly pointed, and they are divided by just a single massive, moulded mullion. Can this be the authentic Perp. form? Running up each side of the one to the E are Perp. panelling and a series of large image niches. This transept has the only remaining medieval roof, with bosses and moulded timbers. The long chancel, with its polygonal apse, is of 1862–5, by the architect Ewan Christian, replacing a predecessor of 1682–4, itself built because the medieval chancel was said to be in ruins. This chancel is a fine work of its period, with tall windows of Dec. tracery. Its striking roof has hammerbeams and in the apse is formed into a two-stage timber rib vault, with beautiful colouring.

The nave is dominated by the organ, cantilevered out from its E wall. It also has a W gallery of 1610, with a baluster front. The fine octagonal font has a stem with figures in trefoiled niches and a bowl with differing motifs on its faces: it appears to be Perp., but is inscribed '1660'. There are medieval screens to the S transept. Divided between the chancel and transepts are twelve stalls with misericords; surprisingly, these are not original to the church but were brought from Lilleshall Abbey in 1546. Fine memorials include two Elizabethan tomb-chests with recumbent effigies. A splendid bronze statue with two reclining cherubs is set on a tall pedestal: this is part of a great memorial of 1634 to Admiral Sir Richard Leveson by Le Sueur, which was removed for melting down during the Commonwealth, just these pieces being saved by Lady Leveson. An outstanding possession is the Perp. pulpit, of stone, with panelling and vine trails; it is quite large and rests on a slim shafted column. Curling round the pillar to which it is attached is its original staircase, with a stone handrail, at the bottom of which sits a most engaging lion. Outside, near the S porch, stands a remarkable pre-Conquest column or cross, perhaps of the ninth century: it is tall and circular, with much intricate ornament.

Suffolk

Suffolk has an interesting and varied series of colleges, including several unusual or even curious examples. Most were of chantry type, and several have especially fine churches.

* Bury St Edmunds: College of Jesus

Jankyn, or John, Smyth, a wealthy merchant, was the leading citizen and an important benefactor to Bury St Edmunds. In the great parish Church of St Mary, he established a chantry for himself and his family, and was responsible in the 1460s and 1470s for the construction of the chapels flanking the chancel and probably of the sanctuary; the N chapel was known as the Jesus Aisle. In 1480 he founded the College of Jesus, the first master being appointed in December. Jankyn Smith died in June 1481, and his foundation was confirmed by letters patent of Edward IV later that year. It was intended for a warden and six chaplains, who were attached to chantries in the Church of St Mary. However, although served by the college, the church was not appropriated and so not truly collegiate. The college stood about 400 yd from the church. It later also accommodated some others, including at least one chantry chaplain of the Church of St James, the parochial vicars of both churches, and four poor men. Dissolution took place in 1548; nothing remains of the buildings, though the site is known.

Both churches stand within the beautiful precinct of the former great abbey, to which they were appropriated; that of St James was in 1914 raised to cathedral status. St Mary's is an outstandingly noble and splendid building, largely but not entirely of uniform fifteenth-century Perp. work, over 200 ft (60 m) in length. Its condition and quality are wonderful; restorations have been light, and it remains very authentic. The nave is of ten bays, with very tall arcades of two-centred arches on slim pillars of four shafts and four hollows, longer on their N–S axis; their mouldings are continuous but for a diminutive capital on the E and W shafts. The arcades are reflected in blank arcading on the aisle walls, framing the large three-light windows, which are four-centred with tracery and a transom. The clerestory has two windows per bay, of two lights under four-centred arches. Externally the whole is battlemented, the gables are stepped, and much of it is ashlar faced. The W front is impressive, with its three very large windows. Polygonal stair turrets flank the E gable of the nave, carrying quite tall crocketed spirelets.

Bury St Edmunds: St Mary, from the south-west

The supreme feature of the nave is its hammerbeam roof, the hammerbeams carrying very large angels with outstretched wings; intermediate trusses are arch-braced. It has every enrichment: the wall-posts are carved as figures, there are angels on the wall-plates, and the spandrels have tracery. All the other roofs of the church are original and fine too. There is a remarkable, very lavish N porch, built about 1445, with many image niches, stone panelling, a richly crocketed gable and pinnacles surmounted by beasts. Inside, it has a flat stone ceiling with ribs as if it were a vault, and a great openwork pendant in the centre. Also on the N side near the W end is the tower; this too is Perp. but

Bury St Edmunds: St Mary, looking east

earlier, built of flint and pebble. It is very broad, with angle buttresses and battlements; it has three stages but is relatively low. It stands halfway into the aisle, no doubt a reminder of the narrower aisles of an earlier nave.

The chancel has no clerestory; its arcades are similar to those of the nave, but a little lower. Its four-bay flanking chapels are of similar design and height to the nave aisles. An arch opens to the sanctuary, which extends one bay further.

Most furnishings are good-quality nineteenth-century work, but there are some fine medieval pieces. In the E bay of both chancel arcades is an early-sixteenth-century tomb-chest with two recumbent effigies and a helm carried by a beam above. A brass with two kneeling figures probably represents Jankyn Smith and his wife Ann. The E bay of the S nave aisle is the Chantry of John Baret, containing his impressive tomb-chest with lengthy inscriptions and a cadaver effigy. Its roof has remarkable intricate painted decoration. There are partly ancient stalls with poppy-head ends, but they have no misericords. Some old work remains in the parclose screens. The octagonal font rests on a stem with four lions and four humans; the carvings on its bowl were, however, removed in 1783.

A charity in the town founded by Jankyn Smyth still functions. One of his many other bequests was for an annual service in commemoration of his death; although chantries ceased in 1548, this service is still held, in 1982 reaching its five-hundredth anniversary. It is said to be the oldest endowed service in England.

* Denston

The foundation of this chantry college was due to the will of John Denston, owner of the manor house; his executors, Sir John Howard and John Broughton, in 1475 obtained royal licence for its establishment. Its clear annual value in 1535 and 1548 was only £22. It was suppressed in the latter year, when it had a warden and just two priests, probably the original number. So this was a small and one might suppose minor college, yet for it the Church of St Nicholas was rebuilt very splendidly; it is a uniform and exceptionally fine late Perp. structure. Only the W tower is earlier, though also Perp.; it is rather smaller and less ambitious than the rest, of roughly rendered rubble, in two stages, with diagonal buttresses, long two-light, square-headed belfry openings and plain battlements much patched in brick. The church has tall battlemented aisles throughout its seven bays of length, with tall three-light arched windows which have tracery and an embattled transom. Also of three lights are the clerestory windows; there are battlements above. The E window has five lights. There is a fine S porch with a straight parapet and little embattled angle pinnacles, large side windows and a stoup recess in an external projection with an embattled hood. Inside, it has a fan vault, and the four-centred doorway contains its original traceried doors.

This is a lofty church. The arcades have very tall pillars, longer on their N–S axis, with to E and W a circular shaft carrying a little capital, a large hollow in the diagonals and a polygonal shaft N and S. Battlemented corbels support the low-pitched roofs, which are of good moulded timbers; they have the striking

Denston, from the south

feature of large panels in front of the wall-plates, along which leap large carved beasts. A very impressive aspect of this church is the exceptional uniformity and completeness of its medieval fittings, well matching the perfection and nobility of the structure. The woodwork is in good repair, polished and stained (much of this was done in 1842), so that nothing is battered or decayed. The church is divided E–W only by the battlemented rood beam, set very high, a rare survival. Below, the base of the screen remains in position. A turret on the N side housing the rood stair curiously is one bay E of the screen, and must have given access to the rood loft by a bridge. Also largely original are the parclose screens and the tower screen. The stalls have traceried fronts and ends with poppy-heads and beasts; four of them, facing E, have carved misericords. Most of the pews are medieval; they too have poppy-head ends carrying a beast, with another beast on the arm-rest. In the S aisle, however, there are some eighteenth-century box pews, plain, of deal. Also plain, indeed humble, is the octagonal pulpit, which is Elizabethan or Jacobean. There are charming early-eighteenth-century communion rails with twisted balusters, groups of four balusters forming the posts. Medieval glass fills the E window, though much of it is jumbled. The large octagonal font on its thick panelled stem is a Seven Sacraments example (an East Anglian speciality), the panels on its bowl representing the seven sacraments and the crucifixion; it is remarkably perfect, except that the heads have been knocked off its figures.

The S chapel has a surprising pair of tall probably late-eighteenth-century wooden gates in front of its altar. Mounted in this chapel is a helm together

Denston, looking east

with a sword, spear and other armour. Set beneath the arcade here is a large tomb-chest commemorating a death of 1822. In the corresponding position on the N side is a remarkable late-medieval altar-tomb, its sides open in large arches to show inside the effigies of the two deceased in their shrouds which, however, are partly open to reveal them. These are probably John Denston and his wife Katharine; brasses formerly on the top have been lost. In the centre of the chancel floor and in the nave are early-sixteenth-century brasses. There are two hatchments and a Royal Arms of Queen Anne. This wonderful church is in immaculate condition following extensive repairs in the 1980s. A house just to the W is said to incorporate remains of the domestic accommodation of the college.

Glemsford

This Church of St Mary had a small college of a dean and canons, established apparently in the reign of Edward the Confessor. The college continued in existence for 200 years, but little is known, and the last references to it are from the mid-thirteenth century. The church is Dec. and Perp., so no features visible today go back to its collegiate period. It is quite large and stands high, an impressive sight as viewed from the valley below; the exterior is quite attractive, but there is considerable Victorian work. It comprises a W tower, a nave with clerestory and broad aisles under low-pitched roofs, N and S porches, and a chancel flanked by chapels of two bays with the sanctuary

Glemsford, from the south

projecting further. The tower is of three stages, with diagonal buttresses and battlements; it was refaced in 1868. Its belfry openings have reticulated tracery in three lights. Also Dec. in style but probably Victorian are the clerestory windows of the nave. The S side of the church, facing towards the village, makes a fine show of uniform Perp. work. It has a plinth of shield-enclosing quatrefoils, a battlemented parapet with pinnacles, and a splendid display of panelling in flint flushwork covering its surfaces. Its long three-light transomed windows are without tracery in the aisle, but in the chapel are taller and traceried. The S porch has two-light side windows and its front has three empty canopied image niches. The N side of the church is simpler, having mostly rendered surfaces and lacking pinnacles.

The interior is disappointingly bland. The surfaces are uniformly whitewashed, and most windows have Victorian tinted glass. The nave arcades are Dec., in three large bays, with double-chamfered arches on octagonal pillars, their details differing slightly on the two sides. Finer than these are the tall two-bay Perp. arcades of the chancel, having two-centred arches of complex mouldings on pillars of four shafts and four hollows, with capitals only to the shafts. The blocked rood stair can be seen. Old roofs with moulded timbers remain over the N aisle, N chapel (which is occupied by the organ and vestry) and S porch. The S door is medieval, with fine tracery. There is a good octagonal Jacobean pulpit. The octagonal font has square panels outlined by fleurons and carved with different motifs; its panelled octagonal stem has damaged angels on alternate faces. In the tower are two enjoyable benefaction boards of 1833. A large iron-bound medieval chest has an arched top, and is made of poplar.

* Ipswich: Cardinal College

Thomas Wolsey was born in Ipswich about 1474. He entered the Church and advanced rapidly; he was noticed by the king, and in 1515 was made Chancellor of England. He also rose to become Archbishop of York and a cardinal. About 1523 he determined on an ambitious project for a pair of academic colleges after the manner of Eton and King's College, Cambridge, both called Cardinal College, one to be at Oxford (*see* page 276), the other at Ipswich. Much of their endowment came from the dissolution of a number of mostly small monasteries. In Ipswich, the Augustinian priory of SS Peter and Paul was dissolved and its site became that of the Cardinal College of St Mary. There were to be a dean, a sub-dean, twelve priest fellows, a schoolmaster, eight choristers, eight clerks and fifty poor scholars; a dozen poor men were also to be maintained. Papal sanction was obtained in 1527, royal licence was granted in 1528, and the foundation stone of the new buildings (now preserved at Oxford) was laid on 15 June of that year. Staff were appointed in September, including as schoolmaster William Goldwin, previously Master of Eton. By January 1529, both the educational and liturgical functions were operating, and a report to Wolsey from Goldwin in that month stated that the school house was already too small for the number of boys being educated. Building work was going on day and night in July 1529. But late in that year, Wolsey fell from power, having failed to procure from the pope the king's divorce from Catherine of Aragon. In his disgrace, all of Wolsey's property was forfeit; his college at Ipswich was dissolved in November 1530, and demolition quickly followed.

The parish Church of St Peter became the chapel of the new college; it is said to have served previously also as the church of the priory, though this is not certain. It returned to parochial use after the college ended. Some changes were made for its collegiate function, though since there was also work here in the fifteenth century it is hard to identify these with certainty. It appears as a fine, large-scale town church: it has a chancel with flanking chapels and a nave with aisles and clerestory, S porch and W tower. The tower is tall and majestic, of knapped flint, in three stages, with diagonal buttresses and

Ipswich: St Peter, from the south-west

stepped battlements enriched with flushwork. It dates from about 1450, but was largely rebuilt, authentically, in 1881–2. Its fine W doorway has fleurons, crowns and other motifs in the hollows of its mouldings, and is flanked by very large canopied image niches containing miniature fan vaults: these features may be of Wolsey's time.

The nave has uniform late-thirteenth-century arcades of four large bays, stately in effect, with arches of two hollow chamfers on pillars of quatrefoil plan having a keeled fillet between the shafts. On the S side there is a Perp. clerestory, but the N side has sexfoiled circular openings probably contemporary with the arcade. The S aisle wall has a straight parapet and restored Perp. windows. On the N, however, the aisle wall is externally rough and patched, irregularly buttressed, with a curious arched buttress or chunk of wall at the NW; it has Dec. windows. Internally this aisle has a blocked rood doorway and a fine but mutilated thirteenth-century piscina, with shafts and richly moulded arch. The S porch has traceried side windows, a finely moulded round arch with Tudor roses in the spandrels of its square label and an image niche over; this is probably due to Wolsey. The chancel has two-bay arcades. The N chapel was added in 1878, and the very large chancel E window and much else are alterations of that time. A now unrecognizable carving on an E buttress is said to have been the arms of Henry VIII, showing that Wolsey made alterations here too.

The church stands close to the docks, and has been redundant since the 1960s; it is in the care of the Ipswich Historic Churches Trust, by whom it is leased out for an alternative use. Just a few furnishings and memorials remain. Its outstanding possession is the large Norman table font of Tournai marble, strikingly carved with a series of lions. It is set on a limestone pedestal perhaps of Wolsey's time, with octagonal corner shafts and mutilated figures between. The E wall of the churchyard is of Tudor brick, and at its S end it connects to a gateway also of brick. Though not large, the gateway has flanking octagonal turrets and carries a coat of arms; other than the church, it is the only surviving structure from the college.

Mettingham

This is a most curious example of a college. What one finds at the site are the substantial remains of a fourteenth-century castle, built by Sir John de Norwich, who was granted licence to crenellate in 1342. Sir John was a soldier, and had given good service to the Crown against the Scots and the French. His grandson was another Sir John, on whose death in 1373 the castle descended to a cousin, Catherine de Brewse, who was a nun at Dartford in Kent. When she died in 1380 it was passed to trustees with the intention that it be given to the college of Raveningham (*see* p.238), fairly close by in Norfolk, which had been founded by the earlier Sir John de Norwich. Before this could happen, the castle was sacked in 1381 during the Peasants' Revolt; but the transfer of ownership was completed in 1382. It was then proposed to move the college to Mettingham, but there were difficulties with the nunnery of Bungay, to which the parish church of Mettingham was appropriated; it was not until 1394, after the college had a period at Norton Subcourse (*see* p.234), that it indeed transferred to Mettingham.

This was a large college of chantry type, for a master and twelve fellows, dedicated to the Blessed Virgin. The numbers fell in the sixteenth century, but there were still a master and nine fellows in 1534. Its annual value was the large sum of £202, and there were fourteen boys being boarded and educated. It was dissolved in 1542.

The puzzling aspect here is the absence of evidence for buildings appropriate to a college. The present remains are principally the main front of the castle, with its impressive tall gatehouse. Behind this are farm buildings, a house of 1880, and some further ruins of medieval structures, apparently military. Within the castle there formerly stood a mansion, of which there is a description from 1562, at which time it was in some decay. The date of this mansion is unclear, but it was probably used by the college, as evidenced by the arms of the last master being recorded as appearing inside. Most perplexing is the question of the collegiate chapel, which for a college of this size should have been substantial. The parish church could not have been used: it is a mile away and moreover is small. Yet nothing is known of the ruins or foundations of a chapel, nor is there any mention of one in the surviving documentary evidence. Presumably it was demolished shortly after the dissolution, and only excavation could tell us more.

Stoke by Clare

This important college has an interesting but confusing history; and confusion continues about what may be seen today. Its origins were in a pre-Conquest college in nearby Clare (*see* Appendix III), which in 1090 became an alien Benedictine priory, and in 1124 was removed to Stoke by Clare. There was damage by fire about 1392–5. Its alien connection was severed in 1395, but in 1415, at about the time of the suppression of alien monasteries, its patron, Edmund Mortimer, Earl of March, began its conversion to a college. He obtained a charter in 1419, and the statutes are dated 1423. The college was for a dean, six canons, eight vicars (why not seven?), four clerks and five choristers; the canons held prebends, this being a rare late example of their employment. It was a major college: in 1535 it had the very large annual value of £324. It was dissolved in 1548, and the last master, Matthew Parker, went on to become Archbishop of Canterbury under Queen Elizabeth.

After the dissolution of the college, its buildings were converted into a mansion, which was mostly rebuilt in the eighteenth century and is now a school, Stoke College. This incorporates some medieval walls, thought to be Norman, though what they represent is disputed. The greatest uncertainty, though, is whether the college used its own church, either the former priory church repaired after the fire or a replacement, or whether it used the parish church, which stood only 200 yd away, and still exists today. The college was dedicated to St John the Baptist; the parish church, previously dedicated to St Augustine, was rededicated to St John the Baptist in Victorian times, reflecting the belief of the time that it was the church of the college. It is a fairly large church, and was extensively rebuilt in the late-Perp. period. However, it is not especially fine, and though it has some old fittings there are none that suggest a collegiate connection. The arguments are complicated but, on balance, it seems better to believe that the collegiate church no longer exists.

* Sudbury: St Gregory

This is the mother-church of the town; it was important before the Conquest, and was possibly collegiate at that time. If so, however, it later ceased to be and was simply parochial until it was made collegiate in 1375 by two brothers born here, John of Chertsey and Simon of Sudbury. The founders had in 1374 obtained the advowson of the church from Nun Eaton Priory, and the church was appropriated to the college. It was of chantry type, for a warden and eight chaplains. Simon of Sudbury was at this time Bishop of London, and was made Archbishop of Canterbury later in 1375; he crowned Richard II in 1377. In the Peasants' Revolt of 1381 he took refuge in the Tower of London, but was caught by the mob and beheaded. In the sixteenth century, the number of chaplains in the college was low, but not through lack of funds: the annual value in 1535 was £122. When surrendered in 1544, it had only the warden and two chaplains.

Sudbury: St Gregory, from the south-east

Sudbury: St Gregory, looking east

This remains the most important of the three old churches in this attractive town. It stands in a spacious churchyard, at the W end of which is a stone archway in a piece of brick walling, which was the entrance to the otherwise vanished college buildings. It is a large and stately church, all in Perp. style: it was probably largely rebuilt for the college, but there were alterations 100 years later. It is mostly of flint and rubble, battlemented throughout, with low-pitched roofs; it is mainly but not entirely uniform. The fine W tower is in four stages, with diagonal buttresses, battlements and a straight-topped polygonal stair turret near the SE corner. It is stately though not lavish; on the S side is an external canopied tomb-chest, with a panelled front: this is worn, and its former brasses have gone.

The nave has aisles and a clerestory, both with three-light windows under four-centred arches. On the S side is a large attachment of which the W half is the porch, while the E half forms a chapel opening from the church; internally the W wall of the porch has a range of panelling incorporating two tall windows. The entrance doors are original, with excellent tracery; the W doors in the tower are similar. The lofty four-bay arcades are fourteenth century; they differ in details but have pillars with large semicircular shafts E and W and half-octagonal shafts N and S, while their arches have sunk-quadrant mouldings. The chancel, the axis of which deviates to the S, is long and lofty, in four bays, aisleless except that it is overlapped on the N side by a chapel of one bay. E of this is a late-medieval sacristy of brick. The windows in the chancel are large and set high; the side ones are of three or four lights, and externally continue below their bases as recessed blank panelling. Internally, the details here are not rich; a plain arched recess serves for sedilia. Two windows on the S side reflect the exterior in continuing below as recessed blank panelling, rather attractively containing nineteenth-century paintings.

The roofs are ancient, mostly with good moulded timbers. A surprisingly rich doorway opens to the tower stair, and contains its ancient door. The fine octagonal font with a panelled stem is Perp. A particular treasure is its exceptionally fine fifteenth-century cover: very tall, like an openwork spire, richly pinnacled and traceried, suspended from the roof. There is a beautiful medieval oak chest, with three locks. A magnificent brass-bound chest is dated 1785. The medieval stalls survive, with nineteen carved misericords. A few panels remain from the former screen, one having an interesting painting. There are a few good mural memorials, as well as many matrices of former brasses. Two large eighteenth-century tomb-chests occupy much of the chapel beside the porch. In the sacristy is preserved a gruesome relic: the head of the murdered archbishop.

* Wingfield

This is an especially attractive example of a chantry college, notable for the beauty and interest of the church and its contents; it is also memorable for the survival alongside the churchyard of its collegiate buildings. The village is well known for the moated Wingfield Castle, begun about 1384; the college was earlier, dating from 1362. Its foundation was undertaken by Lady Eleanor Wingfield and Thomas Wingfield, widow and brother of Sir John Wingfield, whose wishes they were carrying out as executors. The church was appropriated. The initial establishment was a provost or master and three priests, later increased apparently to a provost and nine priests, with three choristers; three poor boys were also supported. Whether or not these numbers were achieved, in 1532 there were only a master and four priests, and they said they were two short. The college was dissolved in 1542.

The Church of St Andrew is large and splendid. It seems to have been extensively rebuilt in connection with the foundation of the college, though further building took place about 1415, including the addition of the splendid S chapel in which is buried Michael de la Pole, 2nd Earl of Suffolk, son of the builder of the castle. The church is not all uniform, and indeed possesses a rather bafflingly random mixture of parts in Dec. and Perp. styles. It comprises a W tower, nave and long chancel, with lean-to aisles; the walls are of flint with some brick, and the roofs are fairly low pitched. The nave and chancel are of almost the same height; both have a clerestory of three-light Perp. windows, in the chancel set so closely as to be almost continuous. In the N aisle, the windows are Perp., large, of three lights with panel tracery, but the S aisle has two-light windows with Dec. tracery. Also Dec. is the tall S porch, with two-light side windows, an enriched canopied image niche and a straight parapet with quatrefoil panelling; inside are a large arched stoup recess and a richly moulded Dec. doorway. The S chapel of the chancel has three-light Perp. windows with panel tracery, but its E window is again of Dec. character. The very large five-light chancel E window is Perp. In place of a N chapel there is a narrower attachment. The tower is large but not tall, in three stages, with diagonal buttresses and plain battlements; its W window is Perp.

The nave has uniform five-bay arcades of double-chamfered arches on tall octagonal pillars. Both aisles have in their outer wall a rather curious rood-stair arrangement. The long chancel is especially splendid. Its N side is open only by a four-centred arch in the first bay, but on the S side there is one partic-ularly broad arch followed by two further arches; all these arches carry very remarkable decoration, the hollows of their mouldings being set with fleurons

Wingfield, from the south-east

and with shields appearing to hang on stone strings. The two E arches on the S side also have the badges of the three great families here: wings for the Wingfields, leopards' heads for the de la Poles, and the Stafford knot. Above the arches is a crested cornice. The E arch contains the large tomb-chest of Michael de la Pole and his wife Katharine, carrying their excellent recumbent effigies, which are of oak; against its N side are the triple sedilia, which in this position are without canopies. Set diagonally in each E corner of the S chapel is a muti-lated image niche. In the N side of the chancel, a very rich doorway with crocketed ogee hood opens to the attachment, which was presumably at least partly a sacristy; it is mostly but not entirely divided by a floor and has original timber screens. Its upper level opens to the chancel by two squints. W of the

Wingfield: the sanctuary

doorway, a very large enriched arched recess with crocketed ogee hood and flanking pinnacles contains a tomb-chest with the effigy of Sir John Wingfield, originator of the college. E of the doorway is a Perp. recess with a very depressed arch and again much lavish detailing, occupied by the third major memorial here: the tomb-chest of John de la Pole, Duke of Suffolk, who died in 1491, with his wife Elizabeth, sister of Edward IV. Their effigies are of alabaster. Above is a helm of timber, rather startlingly carrying a Saracen's head as crest.

Everything in this church is beautifully preserved. Much old work survives in the roofs; that of the nave is arch-braced and has shield-bearing angels along its sides. The base remains of the rood screen, a good deal restored, with traceried panels. Also partly original are the parclose screens, which have coving. The fifteen stalls are entirely medieval, with misericords. There is a large medieval chest. The excellent octagonal font has panels containing lions alternating with shield-bearing angels, while four lions are against the stem. There is a little ancient glass. An amusing relic is a hudd, a portable shelter for the parson to use at the graveside, probably eighteenth century: this one is open in its lower part.

Fifty yd to the S is College Farm, now Wingfield Arts. This is a charming building presenting to the road an eighteenth-century front, but behind this it retains much of the timber-framed structure of the original college buildings.

Surrey

Surrey had just two colleges, both of chantry type; of these, Lingfield is a fine example. There was also an interesting collegiate story at Malden (*see* Appendix IV).

Kingston upon Thames

This small non-parochial chantry college dedicated to St Mary Magdalen had its origins in about 1304, when Edward Lovekyn, a citizen of London but native of Kingston, with his brother Richard, built a chapel, and in 1309 endowed it and established in it one chantry priest. This may have been an augmentation of an existing small hospital, though if so, that function seems later to have been given up. In 1351–5, Edward's heir John Lovekyn, a fish-monger who was altogether four times Lord Mayor of London, rebuilt the chapel and obtained royal licence to convert the foundation into a college of a warden or custos, one other chaplain and a clerk. He died in 1368, and in 1371 William Walworth, who had been his apprentice, added endowments to support a further chaplain. Lovekyn and Walworth were also involved with Walworth's College in London. The annual income in 1535 was almost £35; the last warden, Charles Carew, seems to have been attainted and executed in 1540. He was not replaced, but at least one chaplain continued until 1547.

Kingston upon Thames: Lovekyn Chapel, from the south-west

The college was then surrendered to the Crown, and in 1561 under Queen Elizabeth it was granted to the governors of the new grammar school, and the chapel became the schoolroom. It was restored in 1886, and in the early twentieth century was used as the school gymnasium. Following a very recent restoration, this attractive survival is now used by the school mainly for music.

The building is known as the Lovekyn Chapel. It is undivided and quite small (the internal length is 38 ft/11.6 m), but it is uniform, relatively lofty and of good quality. It is in three bays, with straight parapets; the E end is flanked by battlemented octagonal turrets. There has been much external renewal. The E and W windows are of three lights, with tracery transitional between Dec. and Perp. The large two-light side windows have Perp. tracery; the W bay, containing the doorways, is windowless. In all three bays, the side walls are internally framed in a large blank arch of continuous mouldings. Between the two W bays, each side has a large shallow rectangular recess, and immediately above it another which has a multi-cusped depressed arch; the purpose of these features is obscure. There is a damaged piscina recess, ogee-cinquefoiled, with shelf; a hexagonal image bracket rests on a large head corbel of a king. The ceiled roof shows its rough crown-post trusses. Part of the N side is masked by a two-storeyed domestic attachment, mostly nineteenth century but with a W wall of perhaps Elizabethan red brick.

* Lingfield

The Cobham family of Starborough Castle near Lingfield was a branch of the family from the place of that name in Kent, where they were also involved in college foundation (*see* p.190). At Lingfield, licence for the foundation of the college was granted in 1431 to Reginald, Lord Cobham, with three others; Lord Cobham was the principal founder. The advowson of the Church of St Peter was obtained for the college from Hyde Abbey, Winchester, by which it had long been held, and the church was appropriated. This was a chantry college, for a provost or master, six chaplains and four clerks, and it also supported thirteen poor persons. In 1535, the annual value was given as £75. The college was surrendered to the king by the provost, with five others, in 1544.

The church, now dedicated to both St Peter and St Paul, is large and fine. It is usually considered that, apart from the tower, it was constructed on the foundation of the college, but a recent suggestion is that the E part dates from the 1360s, which is the date of the first of the major Cobham memorials here. However, it seems uniform in style throughout. The nave and chancel are of the same height, respectively four and three bays in length, and have a N aisle of full length and identical width. The walls are of ashlared sandstone, with regular buttresses; the side windows have three lights without tracery, under pointed-segmental arches. A boldly projecting polygonal turret on the N side contains the rood stair. Beneath the chancel is a low crypt. A S aisle similar to but narrower than its partner extends along two bays of the chancel, with a medieval sacristy E of it. This aisle continues W, but then comes the tower,

Lingfield, from the south-east

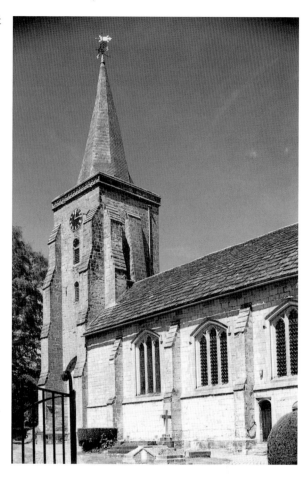

which is fourteenth-century and is plain in its features. It has big angle buttresses and in addition large raking buttresses on the E and W sides, presumably later reinforcements. Above are a straight parapet of quatrefoil mouldings and a fairly short chamfered spire of shingled oak. The nave continues a bay further W from the tower.

The arcades have finely moulded arches on slender pillars of four shafts and four hollows. The one to the N nave aisle has a larger bay spacing than in the chancel, and its arches are four centred. The arcade to the short S aisle of the nave has two small bays. The large E buttresses of the tower come down inside the church, but are largely concealed by the organ. A slender chancel arch and arches across the aisles rest on pillars no larger than the others. The roofs are original, boarded, of depressed wagon form. Their covering throughout is of Horsham stone slabs.

The contents are especially fine. The back row of the stalls is mostly original and has eleven misericords, with very good carving; five further stalls on

Lingfield: the chancel, looking north-west

the N side are missing. Both sides have parclose screens, of which much is original. In the centre of the chancel is the excellent tomb-chest with recumbent effigies of Reginald, 3rd Lord Cobham, founder of the college, and his wife Anne. Several other major memorials to Cobhams are in the N chapel, including that to the 1st Lord Cobham, founder of the family here, who died in 1361. One tomb-chest carries a large brass, and there are further fine brasses in the floor, forming a notable series. The good octagonal Perp. font has a medieval crocketed ogee cover, suspended from the roof. A large parish room was formed in the W end in 1999, with a glazed screen. The college buildings stood just W of the church; they are now represented by a beautiful early-eighteenth-century building known as The College.

Sussex

This county had five collegiate churches, all important and interesting. Of these, Arundel and Steyning are major buildings on a very large scale, while Bosham is of remarkable interest both historically and architecturally. In addition, the county possessed a college of vicars at Chichester, much of which survives.

* **Arundel** (*West Sussex*)

A probably pre-Conquest collegiate church here (*see* Appendix III) was in the mid-twelfth century replaced by a small alien Benedictine priory, a cell of the Abbey of Séez in Normandy. In the mid-fourteenth century, Richard, Earl of Arundel, established a chantry of three priests in the Chapel of St George in the castle, and in 1354 obtained licence to increase it to a college. For some reason nothing more was done until his death in 1376, when he left by his will of the previous year 1,000 marks for the foundation of the college, to have six chaplains. Meanwhile, however, partly as a result of the state of war with France, the monks had withdrawn, and after Richard's death the new earl began negotiations to establish the college in the priory church instead. This led in 1380 to the dissolution of the priory and its conversion into a collegiate church. The new foundation was large, consisting of a master and twelve chaplains with two deacons, two sub-deacons and four choristers; it was dedicated to the Holy Trinity, but the church retained its dedication to St Nicholas.

Arundel, from the south-west

In a single campaign between 1380 and 1400 the church was completely rebuilt, and new buildings were also constructed for the college; nothing remains from the monastic era. The annual value of the college in the sixteenth century was given as £168; it was surrendered in 1544.

The church is a major building, cruciform with a central tower, and very fine. The roofs are low pitched throughout; though over 220 ft (60 m) long externally, the church is too low to compete with the spectacular Victorian accents of the nearby castle and Roman Catholic cathedral. It is of flint, in a Perp. style that still has some memories of Dec. The nave is of five bays, with three-light arched windows in the aisles and a clerestory of quatrefoiled circles. There is a substantial medieval W porch, but the S porch is Victorian. The arcades have large arches of two hollow-chamfered orders with a deep hollow between, resting on pillars of four shafts and four hollows. Stone benches are set below the aisle windows. The clerestory continues in the transepts, which project only slightly beyond the aisles. Within the NE crossing pillar is the tower stair, with large doorways for entry and rood access, retaining their ancient doors. The tower has two external stages, both with openings having depressed segmental arches; it has a straight parapet and a pyramidal roof.

The chancel is wider than the nave; it is long and noble, in four bays. It has large traceried S windows of four lights and an E window of seven. On the N side, a broad, lower Lady Chapel is attached to its three W bays. This is apparently an afterthought. Its arcade has details similar to those of the nave, but

Arundel, looking east from the gallery

instead of pillars has short pieces of wall; the two W bays at the lower level are continuous wall, as backing for the stalls. Above are clerestory windows of four lights. E of the Lady Chapel is a medieval sacristy. The chancel has a beautiful timber vault, now of 1886 but incorporating many bosses and other fragments from the original.

From the beginning, the chancel was used only by the college, and was separated from the rest by a great iron grille, which is still in place. After the dissolution, the chancel became the property of the earls of Arundel, who paid 1,000 marks for it, the grant being dated just twelve days after the surrender. They used it principally as a mortuary chapel; it is now known as the Fitzalan Chapel. Since the family has remained Roman Catholic, this has led to the unusual (but not unique) situation of a church building which is partly Anglican and partly Roman Catholic. Relations were bad in the Victorian era and led to the building of a wall completely dividing the two; but in 1969 the wall was fully removed and was replaced by glass with doors, which on rare occasions have been opened to allow joint events or services. Normally, however, the Fitzalan Chapel remains effectively a separate building which may only be approached from the castle grounds.

Some late-fourteenth-century wall-paintings survive in the nave, with several much-repainted consecration crosses. There is a striking seventeenth-century Royal Arms in an architectural frame. The octagonal font is contemporary with the church. Also probably of this date is the remarkable pulpit; it is of stone, set against the SW tower pillar and standing forward as three sides of a polygon, covered by a frilly canopy with an elaborate vault.

The most important contents, however, are in the Fitzalan Chapel, and form an outstanding collection. On the S side is the exceptionally fine chantry chapel of the 9th Earl of Arundel, who died in 1487: it is in three large bays, with columns supporting a tall canopy, and with further twisted columns standing outside; its surfaces are covered in busy decoration. Within it is a strange arrangement of one tomb-chest upon another, from which the two outstandingly fine effigies were in 1982 removed to a more visible position; unusually, they retain much original colour. Opposite is a comparable structure commemorating the 10th, 11th and 12th earls, erected in 1596, a time when it could no longer functionally be a chantry chapel; it is in a remarkable mixture of medieval and Renaissance styles. The many further memorials include several more medieval tombs with effigies, one of which has the tomb below open to show a cadaver effigy. There are some late medieval brasses. The 14th Duke of Norfolk and his wife have their tombs in a low Victorian addition on the S side. Both the Fitzalan and Lady Chapels have stalls with misericords, all much restored. Attached to the S side of the Fitzalan Chapel there still stands the large quadrangle of the domestic buildings of the college, extensively restored and now used as homes for the elderly.

* **Bosham** (*West Sussex*)

The Church of the Holy Trinity at Bosham (pronounced 'bozzam') is a specially evocative place, its fascinating history matched by its architecture and its exquisite setting, separated from the shore by the National Trust's Quay Meadow. Its site may have been occupied by a Roman building. As told by Bede, when St Wilfred came in 681 to preach to the South Saxons, he found a small community already here, led by one Dicul, a monk or priest from Ireland. By the time of Edward the Confessor, the religious community, now of secular canons, was so important that its annual value was over £300. Edward gave it to his chaplain Osbern, a Norman who after the Conquest became Bishop of Exeter. It already had royal freedoms; after Osbern's death it reverted to the king, and in 1120 Henry I granted it to Bishop Warelwast of Exeter, who in 1121 reconstituted it as a college of a dean and six canons holding prebends. The nominal dean was the Bishop of Exeter; one of the canons, the sacrist, was the acting head. All the canons were required to provide a

Bosham, from the south-east

vicar, one of whom was the parochial vicar. After the Bishop of Exeter supported Thomas à Becket, Henry II in 1164 bestowed the college instead upon the Bishop of Lisieux; but in 1177 it returned to Exeter. It continued as a royal free chapel, and there were disputes concerning its peculiar status between the bishops of Exeter and of Chichester, only 4 miles away. From the record of visitations by the bishops of Exeter, its life does not seem to have been of a high standard; there were reports of neglect of the church building, of the absence of vicars, of vicars frequenting taverns, of a vicar living with a widow, and even of the attempted murder of the sacrist by a vicar. The college had an annual value of £47 in 1535; it was dissolved in 1548.

It was from Bosham that the then Earl Harold sailed in 1064 to Normandy for his ill-fated meeting with Duke William; the church appears on the Bayeux tapestry. This representation is conventional rather than representational, but much of the church that saw Harold sail still exists today. It is of the early eleventh century. The W tower, bulky and tall, is excellent Anglo-Saxon work, roughly rendered, with quoins mainly of long-and-short work; string-courses, now partly broken away, divide it into four stages. The openings are mostly plain and round-headed, with a few Perp. insertions. The W side has an original belfry opening, a twin with a mid-wall shaft. Above is an attractive broach-spire of shingled timber. Also characteristic is the unmoulded small round tower arch, with long-and-short responds; above are a triangular-headed doorway and, higher up, a round-arched opening, set off-centre. Architecturally the finest Anglo-Saxon feature is the chancel arch, lofty and sophisticated, with elegant roll mouldings and rather strange moulded capitals carrying large square abaci. The bases are rather improbably said to be Roman. Beneath the floor close by lies a stone coffin containing the remains of a child, said to be the daughter of King Cnut (Canute); a memorial to her was set in the floor in 1906.

Most of the rest is thirteenth and fourteenth century, and is fairly large. It is internally light and very beautiful, though Victorian restoration has replaced the roofs, removed internal plaster and renewed many window details. The axis of the chancel droops noticeably to the S, and its W part retains Anglo-Saxon walling; this is followed by Norman walling from an extension, its extent indicated by a plain arched piscina, and then a further extension of the early thirteenth century which has left it long and mostly EE. It has an internal string-course round the E part, a trefoiled double piscina, tall lancet pairs with moulded rere-arches and shafts of Purbeck marble, and an especially splendid E window of five lancets with free-standing shafts. Also EE is a two-storeyed sacristy on the N side. A small but fine cinquefoiled recess contains a fourteenth-century tomb-chest with a damaged recumbent effigy of a lady.

The nave has large four-bay EE arcades on cylindrical pillars, the two sides slightly different. A clerestory of circular windows on the N side is probably also EE. Both aisles were widened in Dec. times; there is a post-Reformation S porch partly of brick, covering a Dec. entrance doorway with its ancient

Bosham, looking east

doors. A fine Dec. tomb-recess has large heads on the cusps of its cinquefoiled arch. The floor of the E part of the S aisle is raised above a beautiful crypt, rib-vaulted in two bays, formerly a charnel-house.

The font is late Norman, having an octagonal Purbeck marble bowl with blank arches on its sides, resting on a cylinder and four shafts. There is an ancient chest, said to be thirteenth century. A few fragments of buildings belonging to the college are incorporated in old houses N of the church.

* Hastings (*East Sussex*)

Following the Battle of Hastings, the Conqueror ordered the construction of a stone castle on the cliff above the town. By 1069 it had been granted to Robert, Count of Eu, and it was he who established a college of ten canons in its Chapel of St Mary. It was apparently not until the late twelfth century that one of the canons was identified as dean. In the thirteenth century, by the division of one of the prebends into three, the number of canons was increased by two. All the canons were expected to provide vicars. Both a choir school and a grammar school were supported, each the responsibility of one of the canons. In 1244, the castle reverted to the Crown, and under Edward I the claim was made that the college was a royal free chapel, exempt from the jurisdiction of the bishop. This resulted in a lengthy dispute, but was upheld. In the early fourteenth century, some parts of the castle fell into the sea, and in 1339 Hastings was plundered by the French, with extensive damage to the chapel and the canons' houses. Repairs were undertaken, and the college continued; at a visitation by royal commissioners in 1345, four of the vicars were ejected for keeping mistresses, and refusing to give them up. From this period, the castle was no longer garrisoned, and the college had sole occupation of the site. The town declined in importance, and in 1447 the college was given to Sir Thomas Hoo, and its royal exemptions ceased. By the sixteenth century, the castle was in ruins, and the college seem to have been in decay; the number of canons had fallen to seven, and their provision of vicars seems to have ceased. Its annual value was given as £61, and it was dissolved in 1546. Although in the late fourteenth century it had acquired parochial responsibilities (replacing a parish Church of St Andrew), the church was abandoned and fell into ruin.

In 1824, the owner of the site, Thomas Pelham, Earl of Chichester, arranged for the clearance and excavation of the castle ruins; some fallen sections were re-erected, and it was laid out as a public attraction. The church is a major part of what remains: it had a nave, a S aisle (apparently with a solid wall rather than an arcade to the nave, so interpreted as a cloister), a central tower with a chapel on its S side, and a short chancel considerably angled towards the S. Continuing W from the nave was a narthex, with twin W towers. Much of what remains is early Norman, with masonry of irregular stone and a little herring-bone. The windowless N wall of the nave served also as the curtain wall; it survives substantially, and the NW tower stands fairly high, with a Norman window and half of another. Otherwise the W part is represented

Hastings: the nave, looking east

only by wall bases. The W side of the central tower forms the tallest piece of the ruins, having been re-erected in 1824, and its arch is the most impressive piece of architecture: pointed, its inner order resting on corbels, with worn but good-quality early-thirteenth-century mouldings. It is flanked by small doorways with lintels, the N one opening to a spiral stairway. A recess for sedilia remains in the chancel. The chapel S of the tower has a large early Norman arched altar recess, in each side of which is a small rectangular aumbry.

At the same time as the ruins were cleared, the earl had laid out below the cliff a crescent of houses, Pelham Crescent, with as its central feature a new church of St Mary-in-the-Castle, designed by Joseph Kay and built in 1825–8. For these the cliff had to be quarried away, removing more of the castle site, so that on a map the two churches appear very close together. The new building was technically a proprietary chapel, but was in effect the successor to the medieval church. However, in 1970 it was declared redundant, and there followed a sad story of deterioration and vandalism. This was finally reversed between 1987 and 1998, with restoration costing several million pounds partly funded by National Lottery grants, leading to its becoming a centre for the performing arts, a use for which it seems ideal. It is a remarkable building in classical style, facing the sea with a bold pedimented portico of plain Ionic columns. The centre behind this is recessed, with three large round-arched windows; to each side are projections containing lobbies and gallery stairs. Above and behind the portico is a screen wall.

Hastings: St Mary-in-the-Castle Arts Centre, looking across the auditorium

The extraordinary and very large interior is in plan two-thirds of a circle; the altar was against the straight wall behind the portico, facing S. At each side of this wall is an opening to a box or private pew. Round the rest runs a great gallery, resting on radial walls; from it rise blue Corinthian columns which carry the tremendous moulded ceiling, with light coming from a large and beautiful lantern. The few windows at the back of the gallery look straight on to the rock face. All is beautifully decorated in white and pale yellow, and the original box pews in the gallery have been excellently restored. Few fittings remain in the auditorium, though many minor memorial tablets are under the gallery. Unusually for an Anglican church, there is an immersion font, constructed in 1930.

South Malling (*East Sussex*)

This place is just outside Lewes; the name is pronounced 'mauling'. The College of St Michael the Archangel was of very early origin, a foundation by King Caedwalla before 686 being suggested on evidence from Leland. From the ninth century, it was a property of the archbishops of Canterbury. It was probably originally monastic, but secular canons are recorded at Domesday. The college was refounded in about 1150 by Archbishop Theobald, for a dean and three canons, with a sacrist and a penitencer (the latter an unusual office), together with four vicars. Though lying physically within the diocese of Chichester, the college and the churches attached to it formed a peculiar of Canterbury. The canons had houses, and in 1515, under Archbishop Warham, a house was built for the vicars. The annual value in 1535 was given as £45; the college was dissolved in 1545. Following this, the church fell into decay, and despite being parochial was allowed to be demolished. A new church of St Michael was eventually built in 1628–32.

There is some uncertainty about the site of the college. At Old Malling Farm, half a mile NW of the present church, there are some medieval remains, including some ruined walling in which old illustrations show an apparently Norman archway, since lost. This is often regarded as the remains of the college. However, there is a probably more persuasive case that the present church occupies the site of its medieval collegiate predecessor. It contains a few medieval features, though probably reset; there is some evidence of the foundations of a larger building around it; and nearby is the large house known as the Deanery, now mostly seventeenth century. It may be that Old Malling was the site of the college in pre-Conquest times, but it seems likely that it was later occupied by the house of the archbishops, who sometimes stayed here.

The existing church is small and simple: it is a broad single cell of flint with a S porch and W tower. Its original rectangular mullioned windows were replaced throughout by lancets or cusped lancets in 1873; the outline of the former E window is visible externally, but oddly has small stiff-leaf capitals at each side, presumably reset. The interior has little of interest; it is uniformly painted cream, with fittings of about 1990. The very small octagonal font is probably early seventeenth century. A stone of 1873 reproduces an inscription of 1628, when the 8-year-old John Evelyn, later well known as a diarist, laid a foundation stone. Pre-Victorian character is retained by the porch and tower. The porch has a moulded round arch with keystone and imposts, set in a square label, above which is the date 1628. The plain doorway, which contains its original door, is also round-arched. The attractive tower is low and unbuttressed, with a pyramidal roof and a few elementary rectangular openings. Its W window is a broad cusped-ogee single light, clearly Dec. This is probably also the period of the arch to the nave, which is round, double-chamfered, on half-octagonal responds. None of this is sufficient, however, to give any hint of the character of the medieval church.

* Steyning (*West Sussex*)

This church was of early origin and importance, and King Ethelwulf of Wessex, father of Alfred the Great, was buried here in 858. It was no doubt a minster, and may have had secular canons throughout. It was under royal patronage, and before the Conquest was granted to the Abbey of Fécamp in Normandy. It was certainly collegiate in the twelfth century, with apparently a provost and three canons holding prebends. Despite the association with Fécamp, it retained the privileges of a royal free chapel. In about 1260 the college ceased, probably as a result of a decision by Fécamp, and the church became simply parochial, served by a vicar, since the rectory was appropriated to the abbey. At about this time, the present dedication to St Andrew replaced that to the local St Cuthman. The church reverted to the king during the French wars, and in 1461 it was given to Syon Abbey. It was cruciform with central tower, but after Syon had been dissolved the eastern parts fell into disrepair. In 1578 the chancel chapels were demolished, and by early in the seventeenth century the chancel and tower too had been removed, and a W tower constructed instead.

Following these demolitions, all that remains of the medieval church is four bays of aisled Norman nave: but these are glorious, on a very large scale and of very high quality. The earliest work is the W side of the former crossing, with a splendid tall arch carrying chevron ornament. Both of the arches from the aisles to the former transepts are fine, too, though dissimilar: that on the N is of three unmoulded orders, but that on the S has two orders of rolls and capitals of complex and sophisticated design. The nave itself is late Norman; it has massive, tall cylindrical pillars with circular capitals and imposts, and round arches of three orders. Above are round-arched clerestory windows, each set in a shafted recess which is prolonged down to a string-course above the arcade. The windows have linked hood-moulds, and on the N side they have two orders of shafts; between the bays is a vertical moulding. Externally the N clerestory is plain, but on the S side the windows have two orders of shafts and linked billet hood-moulds; both sides

Steyning, from the south-west

have a corbel-table with grotesques. It is the arcades that are outstanding: their capitals have variations on the theme of scallops, while their arches are heavily loaded with ornament, including much chevron, all in great variety and originality. No two are identical, and even the soffits of some arches are ornamented. Their hood-moulds are charmingly decorated with rosettes. The aisles retain only one original window, the rest being Perp., large and simple, in two lights. One nook-shafted flat buttress is applied to the S aisle. The tall S doorway is Norman, restrained in its ornament, with continuous roll-mouldings of which the outer has a kind of chevron imposed upon it. It contains its ancient door.

The tower is big and plain, of a chequer of flint and stone, with large diagonal buttresses and a straight parapet; though not short it only just reaches the ridge of the nave roof. As is evident inside, it replaces at least one further bay of nave. There is a large, plain S porch of knapped flint, probably fifteenth century and formerly two-storeyed; it was altered in 1766. Probably in the seventeenth century a short new chancel was constructed, with flanking chapels: the walls of the latter remain, with a few simple mullioned windows, but there is now an assertive Victorian lancet E wall. Between the chancel and chapels, each side has two tall, narrow, completely unmoulded round arches; of what date can these be?

The large, square Norman font of marble has a raised zigzag on its faces; it rests on a cylinder and four shafts, which are good replacements. A large

Steyning, looking west

Royal Arms of Queen Anne is set in an enriched frame. An excellent refurnishing scheme of 1981–5 provided modern chancel fittings and beautiful early-sixteenth-century panelling from elsewhere as a reredos. It also fitted the organ into the tower, largely concealing the late Victorian tower arch. In the porch are two early ornamented coffin-lids; one is suggested as being that of King Ethelwulf.

Warwickshire

This county has a fine series of six collegiate churches, of varying types. Warwick must be unchallenged as the finest, but Stratford-on-Avon too is among the major examples. Much of interest and beauty may also be found among the others, of which Astley, once of great size, is now an evocative and fascinating fragment.

* Astley

In 1338, Sir Thomas Astley of Astley Castle founded a chantry for four chaplains in the parish Church of St Mary, of which the Astley family had long been patrons. He increased this to seven chaplains in 1340, and in 1343 made it into a chantry college, at which time he undertook the complete rebuilding of the church, which was appropriated to the college. The constitution which Sir Thomas gave to this chantry college was unusual: it had a dean and two prebendaries, with three vicars, three chaplains and a clerk. At the Valor of 1535, its annual value was £40; it was dissolved in 1545. The church constructed for Sir Thomas was on a magnificent scale, cruciform, with a central tower which carried a notably tall spire known as the 'lanthorn of Arden'. Further chapels were added in late medieval times. After the dissolution, the roofs of the church were stripped of lead and it became ruinous; the tower fell about 1600. It was rescued for the parish by Richard Chamberlaine in 1607–8: he demolished most of the ruins but repaired the chancel, which he made into the nave and provided with a new chancel and W tower.

Today, Astley is a tiny village with a still striking castle, which has, alas, since the mid-twentieth century become a ruin, and close to it the church, which is of remarkable and engaging character. The nave (formerly the chancel) is on a tremendous scale, in three large and very lofty bays. It is mostly rendered, and has deep buttresses and tall three-light Dec. windows with curvilinear tracery, which both inside and out have ogee hood-moulds with finials. Above the present low chancel arch, the upper half of the former great E window appears, blocked but still showing its Perp. tracery in seven lights. Flanking it inside are two large image niches. Outside, it has an ogee hood-mould, above which is a Dec. rose window. On the N side is a rich crocketed ogee doorway, blocked, which once opened to an attached structure. The S side has a plain

Astley, from the north-east

Astley, looking east

Perp. doorway, covered by a small and simple timber-framed porch probably of 1607–8. The flat panelled timber ceiling of the nave is partly ancient.

The tower and chancel are both in Perp. style, but are surprisingly different in character. The tower is of red ashlar, and though not tall is of a bulk to match the nave. It has diagonal buttresses and battlements with small corner and intermediate pinnacles; some heraldry and panels of fleuron decoration appear. By contrast, the delightful chancel is of cream ashlar, sophisticated and elegant but very small beside the rest. It appears externally as in two bays, with buttresses, a straight openwork parapet and again some heraldry. All three windows in the E bay have three lights and are four-centred, while the windows in the W bay are of Y-tracery form, and are blocked. Inside, it has a very charming depressed barrel vault of plaster divided into three bays by transverse arches, with ribs, cusping and much pretty enrichment.

Most notable among the contents are the stalls, now at the E end of the nave: there are nine each side, with carved misericords. They have shafts carrying a battlemented canopy on cinquefoiled arches, and the back panels have vivid paintings of apostles and prophets, original though much repainted in the seventeenth century. Concealed behind them on the S side there are known to remain the piscina and triple sedilia, hacked back to make way for them. The oak pulpit of chamfered square form is late seventeenth century, and has at the back a recess for a seat, with a finely carved back. Of similar date is the reading desk. Other timber furnishings are mainly nineteenth century, and include in the chancel eight more canopied stalls of a design related to that of their medieval companions. The three-sided communion rails of wrought-iron date from about 1700. Many seventeenth-century painted texts adorn the nave walls. A little medieval glass remains. The octagonal font is mutilated Perp. work. A brass of about 1400 is mounted murally, and collected together within an iron railing at the W end are three surviving recumbent effigies of the fifteenth and early sixteenth centuries.

* Coventry: St John the Baptist (*now West Midlands*)

Known also as the College of Bablake, this college owed its existence to the Guild of St John the Baptist, founded in 1342. In 1344, the Dowager Queen Isabella (widow of Edward II) gave land known as Babbelak or Bablake as the site for a chapel for the guild, on condition that two priests sang masses for the royal family. This chapel, thought to be represented by the present chancel, was consecrated in 1350. The guild flourished, and in 1357 further endowments were provided for the chapel and its staff was increased to six priests. More land was given, and the building was successively enlarged. In 1362 an anchorite was established in a cell probably N of the N chancel aisle. At some point, the priests were formed into a college. In 1392, the Guild of St John the Baptist was amalgamated with those of Holy Trinity and St Mary, and the number of priests was now nine, one of whom was warden. The

Coventry: St John the Baptist, from the south

priests eventually reached twelve, and there were also singing men; a school was attached, for which one of the priests was responsible. The annual value in 1535 was £45, and in 1536 there were only a master and eight priests. Dissolution took place in 1548, and the buildings were granted to the mayor and corporation. The chapel had never been parochial, but surprisingly it was retained in a limited ecclesiastical use; in 1608 it was repaired, and a series of lectures and sermons was established in it. In 1648 it housed Scottish prisoners after the battle of Preston; in 1658 it was in use by a small body of Congregationalists. By the early eighteenth century it was approaching ruin, but, with the growth of the city, it was made a parish church by Act of Parliament, its parish being taken from that of St Michael. It remains so today, High in usage, with an active congregation.

The church probably reached its present extent by the end of the fourteenth century, but most of what is now seen seems to be the result of fifteenth-century rebuilding. It is a fine and very distinctive building, compact in plan but remarkable for the loftiness of its proportions. It is cruciform, with aisles and a central tower; the transepts do not project on plan, and indeed the tower and transepts seem to have been inserted after the church had reached its present size. The nave is of three bays, the chancel of two. There are some surprising irregularities, with the chancel deviating sharply to the N, and the N transept strikingly out of square. The roofs are low pitched, mostly with straight parapets; nineteenth-century restorations by Sir Gilbert Scott have resulted in much external refacing. The tower is tall, in two stages, with a straight parapet on three sides but battlements on the N; there is a polygonal stair turret at the NE, but the other corners have battlemented circular bartizans, giving the tower an engagingly unusual appearance. The bartizans seem to date only from the nineteenth century.

The windows in the aisles are arched and traceried, of three or four lights. Those of the S nave aisle, continuing into the transept, have pretty tracery, probably of the late fourteenth century. The very large transomed W window is in six lights, flanked externally by image niches. In the chancel the arcades have two-centred arches on tall pillars of eight shafts and eight hollows, with small capitals only to the shafts. The chancel clerestory has very distinctive tall and narrow windows in pairs, with two pairs per bay; they are transomed and almost square headed. Panelling continues below them to the arcade arches. The crossing arches, though tall, are less so than the rest; they have fine mouldings and carry a vault. The transepts have fenestration in two storeys, with clerestory windows E and W similar to those in the chancel, though broader. In the nave, the lozenge-shaped pillars have sixteen shafts, each shaft having a little capital. Its N clerestory is of three-light arched windows with reticulated tracery, almost certainly reused from elsewhere. Some stone panelling appears internally, also some interesting large carved corbels. An unusual Royal Arms of metal, cut out and partly moulded, is of 1812. Otherwise the contents are entirely of the twentieth or late nineteenth century.

Coventry: St John the Baptist,
looking east

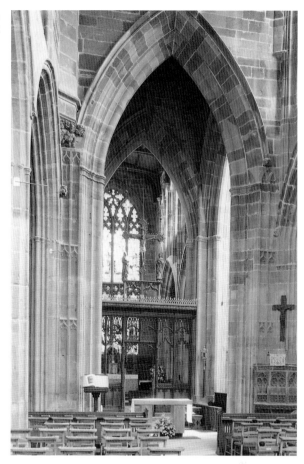

The collegiate buildings stood to the N. They were mostly timber framed, and eventually formed a complete quadrangle, the N range being Bablake or Bond's Hospital, an almshouse founded in 1506. This still exists and serves its original purpose. The E range was in 1560 remodelled to form a boys' hospital, later Bablake School: the school has moved elsewhere, but the building remains and is most attractive. The S range, which separated the quadrangle from the church, has gone, and the W range is now of the nineteenth century.

* Knowle (*now West Midlands*)

Knowle was formerly in the parish of Hampton in Arden. In 1396, Walter Cook, a native of the place and canon of Lincoln, obtained a faculty to rebuild the Chapel of Knowle, and to dedicate it to SS John Baptist, Laurence and Anne. He gave endowments sufficient to support a priest, and obtained licences enabling its use by the inhabitants for most purposes, including burials and baptisms. In 1402, Walter and his father Adam were granted letters patent to establish a small perpetual chantry in the church. This involved negotiations with Westminster Abbey, which owned the manor: Walter paid 300 marks (£200) and allocated to the abbey the patronage of the chantry, the abbey in return agreeing to provide 10 marks a year for the support of a chantry chaplain. Walter Cook's career advanced such that in time he held in plurality at least four other lucrative positions. In 1413, with six others, he founded a fraternity, the Guild of St Anne of Knowle, attached to the church. Then in 1416, with Lady Elizabeth, widow of John, Lord Clinton, he obtained letters patent to establish in the church a college for ten priests, one to be warden. This was a foundation of unusual character in that its members were to include both chantry priests, presumably an augmentation of the earlier chantry, and the priests of the fraternity. It is doubtful whether the planned numbers were ever reached; in 1535, there were three chantry and three fraternity priests, and the annual value was £51. The college was dissolved in 1547, but the commissioners decided that the chapel should remain for the benefit of the inhabitants. It became a parish church only in 1850.

The church is quite large, and is almost entirely Perp. It is largely of ashlar, red in parts and cream in others; this variety illustrates the complexity of its building history, in which the description of the *Victoria County History* distinguishes seven phases. Most of it seems nevertheless to be due to Walter Cook. The roofs are low pitched throughout; on the S side all have battlements and pinnacles, whereas on the N these are absent. There is a W tower of three

Knowle, from the east

stages, with diagonal buttresses and battlements, which contains the entrance. The aisles have three-light arched windows with tracery, and there is a clerestory, also of three-light windows. Four bays from the W, the roof steps down slightly, without a chancel arch; a clerestory continues for two more bays. The first of these bays has on the S side a chapel continuing the line of the aisle, and on the N a transept-like chapel; the next bay is aisleless (though the N side now has an organ chamber and vestry). That this was originally the full extent of the chancel is indicated by the remains exposed on the S side of a piscina and triple sedilia. However, there follow two further aisleless bays, with long windows of three and four lights, and an E window of five; this extension was probably associated with the establishment of the college. Internally ashlar faced, it makes a fine effect. The E bay is canted in, and externally shows low on each side a broad blocked four-centred arch: the E wall once abutted on to another building, and these arches opened to a passage under the sanctuary, probably to maintain the processional route round the church. The consequent high internal floor level explains the impossibly lofty positioning of the piscina and triple sedilia, which have ogee arches and other details similar to their predecessors further W.

Both arcades have octagonal pillars, moulded capitals and double-chamfered arches; they are not identical, and it is suggested that the N arcade is reused thirteenth-century work. The chapel bay on the N side is completely different, with a rather crude four-centred arch. Some old work remains in the

Knowle, looking east

roofs, with moulded timbers. The octagonal font is Perp., with a quatrefoil on each face. Most furnishings are nineteenth century, but the back row of stalls on each side is medieval, with altogether eleven misericords, mostly carved. Also medieval is the screen, though it is much repaired: it has intricate small tracery in single-light divisions, and elaborate ribbed coving with pendant arches below the front beam. In 1860 it was moved one bay E of its medieval position, adding another confusing factor to the layout of the church. The N chapel is finely fitted out as a Great War memorial, with a stone screen in Perp. style. There are two ancient dug-out chests. A fine hourglass of 1674 on the pulpit has, alas, been stolen. Immediately W of the church stands the splendid timber-framed Guild House, of Walter Cook's 1413 foundation.

Maxstoke

This is a fascinating place, but as a collegiate church Maxstoke is a marginal and puzzling case. The great person here was Sir William de Clinton, later Earl of Huntingdon and the builder of the splendid castle, licensed in 1346. In 1330 he purchased the advowson of the parish church, and in 1331 obtained licence to found in it a college of a warden and five chantry priests. The rector, John Lynie, was made the first warden; in 1332 Sir William augmented the endowments, and it seems that priests were appointed and the college began to function. In 1336, however, he decided instead to establish an Augustinian priory, for a prior and

Maxstoke, looking east from the gallery

twelve canons. Its foundation charter was dated 1337, and the endowments of the college were transferred to it; it was consecrated in 1342.

The remains of the priory, now a farm, are an evocative sight. Most of the impressive precinct wall remains, with the large gatehouse; inside can still be seen (despite a recent partial collapse) a tall surviving fragment of the central tower of the otherwise vanished church. Immediately outside the NE corner of the precinct is the parish Church of St Michael. This is of a single Dec. build, clearly of Sir William's time; it is a single cell, very unusual for a parish church, and is not large. Was it built for the college, perhaps as the chancel of an intended larger church? Or can it be explained by the alternative suggestion that it was the *capella ante portas* (chapel outside the gate) of the priory? It is of good ashlar, three bays long; its E window is of four lights, with good flowing tracery, while the other windows are of two lights, also traceried. There is a trefoiled single light low-side window. The blocked N doorway has two continuous chamfers. Entry is by a probably early-nineteenth-century W doorway, which may be contemporary with the very small W tower which has been added inside the W end, of brick but ashlar faced above roof level.

The interior is given considerable charm by its surviving eighteenth-century work. There is a plaster ceiling with plain rectangular panels, a very large cove, and a quite sophisticated dentilled cornice. Of similar sophistication is the panelled front of the W gallery, which rests on Tuscan pilasters and columns of stone. The sanctuary has good dignified panelling with fluted pilasters, and simpler panelling continues all round the church. Fine inlay enriches the oak pulpit, which is a chamfered square in plan. Though cut down, the pews are of eighteenth-century origin. The font in use is Victorian, but there is also an eighteenth-century baluster font. A small Royal Arms is of Queen Anne, and on the walls are five hatchments. There is a fine large medieval chest, and in the floor are some medieval tiles from the priory site. A little medieval glass remains.

* Stratford-on-Avon

The Church of the Holy Trinity was important before the Conquest, but its collegiate story begins only in 1331. John de Stratforde, Bishop of Winchester, who had earlier been rector here and was to become Chancellor of England and Archbishop of Canterbury, founded a chantry college for five priests to serve in the Chapel of St Thomas of Canterbury in the church. In 1337, the founder purchased the advowson of the church for the college, and from 1340 the college had a warden and five priests, the warden being also the rector. About 1353, a substantial collegiate building of stone, with a common hall, was begun W of the church by the founder's nephew, Ralph de Stratforde, Bishop of London. In 1415 the privileges of the college were confirmed by Henry V, and the church was now legally appropriated; from this time the heads of the college were styled dean. In 1515 an endowment was given for four choristers. The annual value is given in 1535 as £124; dissolution took place in 1547. The college house was finally demolished about the end of the eighteenth century.

Stratford-on-Avon, from the north

Stratford-on-Avon, looking east

Exquisitely situated close to the river, the church is a very large and impressive building, cruciform with a central tower, with an external length of approximately 200 ft (60 m). It has some splendidly rich Perp. work of the late fifteenth century, built under two successive deans, but EE and Dec. contributions remain. The nave is of six bays; the arcades of double-chamfered arches on octagonal pillars are Dec., and with them go the aisles, with Dec. windows, not all uniform but mostly of three lights. This work was at least partly due to John de Stratforde, the Chapel of St Thomas of Canterbury being in the S aisle. Above the arcades is now a splendid Perp. clerestory, almost continuous with its two tall three-light windows in each bay, and panelling below comes right down into the arcade spandrels. The clerestory is externally of ashlar and battlemented. Also Perp. is the great W window, of nine lights. The timber roof, which is divided into panels, is fine. There is a splendid Perp. N porch of two storeys, with battlements, pinnacles, a quatrefoil plinth and image niches; inside, its walls have excellent blank arcading, and it has a vault. The richly panelled doors to the church are fine original work, as are the porch doors and the W doors.

The E limb, including the transepts, deviates noticeably to the N. The transepts are basically EE: they have large five-light Dec. windows in their end walls, but retain lancets elsewhere. Also Dec. are the relatively low crossing arches, with good rich mouldings including sunk chamfers; the crossing has a lierne vault. Externally, however, the tower shows a lower part of about 1200, with flat buttresses and large openings of two pointed arches under a round containing arch. Above this is a Dec. stage with large traceried circular openings. This has battlements and corner pinnacles, within which rises the tall stone spire, which is of 1763. The long and noble five-bay battlemented chancel is of the Perp. glasshouse type. It has lavish panelling inside and out, and tall arched windows of four lights, transomed and traceried; the E window has seven lights, under a four-centred arch. There are lavishly enriched doorways to N and S; the former once opened to a large attachment in two or three storeys, demolished about the beginning of the nineteenth century. The triple sedilia are splendidly rich, with large nodding-ogee canopies carrying finials; below the seats there are richly carved busts of angels. The piscina has similar features.

The church contains many fine things. In the chancel there are the twenty-six fifteenth-century stalls, their fronts and poppy-head ends largely original; they have a particularly entertaining set of carved misericords. Two more misericords are mounted murally. The chancel screen is partly ancient, traceried in single-light divisions; more completely authentic is the fine and tall medieval screen which now separates the N transept as the choir vestry. The font in use is a copy of the mutilated Perp. one preserved in the chancel. The striking pulpit of dark green marble is of 1900. There are some important large monuments and very many mural memorials, the greatest concentration being in the chancel. Among the latter is the memorial that makes this a major tourist shrine, to William Shakespeare, died 1616, with his bust; his tomb is in the floor below. It is interesting that he was able to be buried here because he was lay rector, a position he had acquired by purchase.

* Warwick: St Mary

St Mary at Warwick is a church of especial magnificence, one of the most important of the collegiate churches. Warwick's first college was not attached to this church: a pre-Conquest foundation was attached to the Church of All Saints (*see* Appendix IV), which later became enclosed within the castle. The first Norman Earl of Warwick, Henry de Newburgh, planned to make St Mary's collegiate. After his death, his son Roger founded the college in 1123, and soon afterwards the canons of All Saints transferred to it; the new college had a dean and five canons. It was unusual for its date in showing a strong chantry motive: the canons were to pray for the families of the founder and of the king; but in its constitution it was a college of canons. The earls of Warwick were the patrons throughout its life. In the thirteenth century, there were six chaplains or vicars, and the dean and canons had become absentees, a situation the bishops of Worcester tried to correct, perhaps successfully. In 1468, Richard Neville, Earl of Warwick ('Warwick the Kingmaker') and his wife Anne added endowments to provide for four more priests and two clerks. In 1535, the annual value is given as the large sum of £334, and there were a dean, five prebendaries, ten priests or vicars, a parish curate and six choristers. The college was dissolved in 1544, and was granted to the corporation of Warwick.

The external length of the church is 228 ft (69.5 m), and the tower is 174 ft (53 m) high, a notable landmark. Only the medieval chancel and the structures flanking it survived the great Warwick fire of 1694. Below the chancel is an impressive Norman crypt, with thick piers, scalloped capitals and a rib vault. The E bay is a late-fourteenth-century extension, as is the entire chancel above. This is a splendid Perp. structure in four bays, with richly panelled surfaces inside and out and flying buttresses on the N side. The large four-light side windows are set high, and the E window is of six lights. Expecially glorious is the vault, of tierceron type; it is depressed, but remarkably its major ribs are duplicated by flying ribs springing from a lower point. The fine sedilia are quadruple; a fifth compartment contains the piscina. Most of the chancel fittings are relatively recent, but in the centre is the splendid tomb-chest with the recumbent effigies of Thomas Beauchamp, Earl of Warwick, and his wife, Katherine; Thomas, who died in 1369, was responsible for the rebuilding of the chancel.

There is a complex of medieval attachments on the N side, mainly sacristies in two storeys. The lower level has a tierceron vault, and is divided into two parts by an original stone screen. Projecting N is the chapter-house, with a half-octagonal end; it has recessed seats set beneath septfoiled canopies. Its roof is of timber. It is now almost filled by an enormous early seventeenth-century canopied memorial.

Alongside the chancel to the S is the Chapel of Our Lady, usually known as the Beauchamp Chapel, which was built in 1443–64 and consecrated in 1475. Because of its lavish architecture, its exceptional contents and its remarkable state of preservation, this is the greatest fame of Warwick. Externally, it has very rich panelling, numerous image niches and very deep buttresses, of which

Warwick: St Mary, from the south

Warwick: St Mary, looking east

the tops have a distinctive openwork form implying flying buttresses. The internal panelling is equally rich. It has six-light windows, and a seven-light one to the E; the last has two especially thick mullions which, with the reveals, are internally covered in canopied image niches, complete with their original images, all unmutilated and outstandingly fine. The strikingly original vault is of modified lierne form. Much colour was restored in the 1970s, particularly on the statuary and the roof bosses, to fine effect. Also notable is the extensive remaining original glass, especially in the E window. The startlingly white Gothic reredos, containing a large relief of the Annunciation, is eighteenth-century work in plaster. The entrance to the chapel, from the W, is formed by an internal porch, in convincing Perp. Style; remarkably, this dates from 1704.

In the centre of the chapel is the Purbeck marble tomb-chest of Richard Beauchamp, founder of the chapel. This is a supremely fine and well-preserved piece, with a recumbent effigy of gilt latten. It is covered by a hooped metal framework or hearse. Also fine are the weepers around the tomb, including a

Warwick: St Mary.
The Beauchamp Chapel,
looking east

memorable representation of Richard Neville, the Kingmaker. Several other very fine memorials in the chapel are of the sixteenth or seventeenth centuries. There are medieval stalls with back panelling, but they are relatively plain and lack misericords. Between the Beauchamp Chapel and the chancel is a space occupied by several small chambers, the finest being the tiny Dean's Chapel, with exquisite detailing including a miniature fan vault with pendants. There are more medieval fittings here.

The rest of the church dates from 1698–1704, and was designed by Sir William Wilson. Its style is a curious yet committed mixture of Gothic and classical, and must be accounted a success. It has a W tower and an aisled nave of four bays with transepts, all on a very large scale (it is in fact slightly larger than its medieval predecessor). The tower stands outside the W front, its base open by three heavy pointed arches. It has Gothic blank arcading but many large niches almost of classical type. The tall parapet has crocketed corner and intermediate pinnacles, but incorporates many round-arched openings. Buttresses of medieval type are a feature of the body of the church, but there are also balustrades, urn finials and pediments to the transept ends. It is a hall church, the aisles being of full height, and has a Gothic rib vault of plaster, with bosses of cartouche form. The huge windows have pointed arches and are in three lights, with heavy tracery of a type resembling that of seventeenth-century Oxford chapels. The pillars are of four shafts and four hollows, with classical foliage capitals; the W pair is massive, the tower having been begun here, but removed after showing cracks. There are many mural memorials and the eighteenth-century font of marble, but most furnishings in this part of the church are recent.

Westmorland (*now part of Cumbria*)

The small county of Westmorland never had any collegiate foundations.

Wiltshire

The three medieval colleges of Wiltshire were all founded by bishops; substantial churches remain at two. Had it not become a house of Bonshommes, Edington would be another, and the finest (*see* Appendix III).

* Heytesbury

The church of Heytesbury was given to Salisbury Cathedral in about 1115 by Henry I, to form part of a prebend. The value of this prebend was soon increased by other gifts of property, and it seems that within a few years there were already canons at Heytesbury. Its establishment as a collegiate church was formalized in a charter by Bishop Jocelyn of Salisbury in about 1160; the college was of a dean and four prebendaries, two each of priests and deacons,

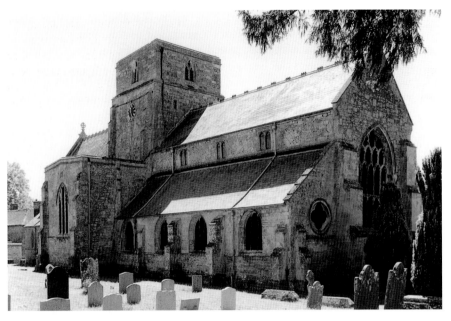

Heytesbury, from the north-west

Heytesbury: screen to the north transept

the dean being the canon of Salisbury who held the Heytesbury prebend there. In the thirteenth century, the holder of the deanery of Heytesbury became and remained the Dean of Salisbury; the college and its property became a peculiar of his, the other prebends being in his gift. The dean was clearly normally non-resident. There were four vicars, and later also at least one chantry chaplain. In 1535, the annual value was given as £91, including the income of the dean. This college was one of the few that survived the Reformation unscathed, with the Dean of Salisbury continuing to be Dean of Heytesbury, and regularly appointing clergy, normally of course non-resident, to all four prebends. This situation was ended by the Cathedrals Act of 1840, which dissolved the college and abolished the prebends, subject to the life interest of the existing holders.

The church, dedicated to SS Peter and Paul, is large and noble in character; it is cruciform, with a central tower and lean-to aisles to both nave and chancel. Post-Reformation mutilations included the removal of the chancel aisles; these were reinstated in the 1865–7 restoration by Butterfield, but are of a stone ill-matched to the old work. Most of the structure is EE, but some parts show considerable restoration. The roofs are Victorian except for the depressed plastered wagon roof over the nave. The chancel has strikingly lofty and dignified arcades of three bays (reopened in the restoration): the arches are triple-chamfered, and the E pillars and responds are of complex composite form with free-standing marble shafts. There is a clerestory of lancets above. Internally the E wall has a remarkable lofty tripartite arcade on Purbeck marble shafts, standing free of the wall; the central arch frames a single enormous lancet. Also EE is the crossing, with large triple-chamfered arches on responds with clustered shafts, of which the main ones are keeled. Externally the tower has a short, considerably recessed Dec. upper stage, with two-light reticulated openings and a straight parapet. The S transept has a very fine EE arch to the E, but its long three-light S window is probably seventeenth century. The N transept, which is lower than the rest, was the Hungerford Chantry, remodelled in the late Perp. period; it has springers for a vault (apparently a fan vault), and a small panelled four-centred archway to the E. The four-bay nave is impressive, with tall, fairly thick octagonal pillars, again carrying triple-chamfered arches. Above there is a small Perp. clerestory, and the large aisle windows (which are mostly authentic) are of a curious, probably Perp., design, without tracery and set at the mid-point of the wall. A large quatrefoiled opening over the chancel arch is probably Victorian. The S porch and S doorway are certainly Victorian. The W wall has a fine transomed five-light Perp. window, and circular windows to the aisles, apparently medieval but given Victorian cusping.

The furnishings are mostly Victorian (the medieval stalls were destroyed in the restoration); the chancel has some inoffensive Victorian decoration of coloured tiles. There are many mural memorials, and beautifully mounted on a plinth of 1959 are the effigies from a destroyed memorial of 1623. The outstanding feature is the stone screen to the N transept. This is late-Perp. work, tall, its openings divided into three lights, with two transoms; it has a rich doorway with a much-crocketed ogee hood, and is crowned by splendid fan-vaulted coving.

Salisbury: De Vaux College

De Vaux College (the name rhymes with 'low'), or Domus de Valle Scholarium (House of the Valley Scholars), which was dedicated to St Nicholas, was an interesting and apparently unique institution among the medieval colleges. It was probably founded in 1262 by Bishop Giles de Bridport, for a warden, two chaplains and twenty scholars; the warden was to be a member of the cathedral chapter. It stood close to the Hospital of St Nicholas (which still exists today), and may have been associated with it. In 1280, Bishop Roger de Wickhampton attached three more chaplains, though it is not clear that they were to celebrate in the chapel of the college. The college certainly had a chantry function, but the most interesting aspect is its scholars: Bishop Bridport's charter describes them as poor, needy, honourable and teachable, and specifies that they should study theology and the liberal arts. This has been claimed as the earliest academic

De Vaux College, Salisbury, from the south. Engraving by R. Benson, 1826

college in England. It seems that in the thirteenth century Salisbury was an important centre of learning, and this may have been reinforced by the time when, in 1238, Oxford was placed under an interdict, and some masters and scholars moved from there to Salisbury and other places. It appears that Bishop Bridport's foundation might have developed along the lines of the colleges of Oxford and Cambridge had it not become clear by the early fourteenth century that Salisbury was not to become a university city.

The college has been much discussed, but knowledge of its function in its later years is limited. However, it certainly maintained an academic element, and seems to have had a connection with Oxford University;

usually some of the scholars (or fellows) were in residence, while others were apparently away studying. In 1346 there were at least eleven graduate scholars, and the numbers seem to have been maintained through most of the next two centuries. A chapter resolution of 1526 ordered all scholars to leave Salisbury and move to Oxford or elsewhere, but the significance of this is not clear, and there were still nine fellows at the time of its dissolution in 1542. The annual value in 1535 was £94. The site was immediately S of the cathedral close, and significant buildings survived into the early nineteenth century. Now all that can be said is that there are a few medieval remains incorporated in two mainly eighteenth-century houses – most obviously the flint-built N wall of De Vaux House, which has a late-medieval chimney breast inside.

Salisbury: St Edmund

The dedication is to St Edmund of Abingdon, a former treasurer of Salisbury Cathedral, who was canonized in 1247. This was a newly created parish; the college was founded in 1269 by Bishop Walter de la Wyle, the church having been begun a little earlier. The college was intended for a provost and twelve priests; although not organized as a college of canons, it appears that it did not have a chantry purpose. In 1339 Bishop Wyville complained that there had never been more than seven priests; new endowments were then added and by 1362 it had attained its planned numbers. The church seems to have been entirely rebuilt in the first years of the fifteenth century, but the college then encountered more financial problems and in 1431 there were only three priests. When visited in 1478 by Bishop Beauchamp, there seem to have been none. The bishop took remedial action and appointed six priests. In 1535 the college had the substantial annual income of £102. Dissolution took place around 1543, when a layman was made provost.

What the visitor finds now is a large, apparently all-Perp. church, but in two ways it is not what it seems. It consists of a W tower, a nave with aisles of full height under pitched roofs and a chancel with flanking chapels. The nave and aisles appear as uniform Perp. work; however the E limb seems mainly of Victorian masonry, though it is in a reasonably matching style, and both chapels have authentic five-light Perp. E windows, each flanked internally by four mutilated image niches. There is a Perp. piscina in the S chapel. The explanation is surprising: the present nave was originally the spacious collegiate chancel of a very large cruciform church, the central tower of which fell in 1653, causing severe damage. The nave and transepts were then demolished, the former chancel being made the body of the church, with a new tower completed in 1655. A small chancel was added at the E end in 1766, and then in 1865–7 this was replaced by the present chancel and chapels, two bays long, with the sanctuary extending a further bay. The architect was Sir Gilbert Scott. Most features of the former E walls of the aisles were re-erected in their new positions.

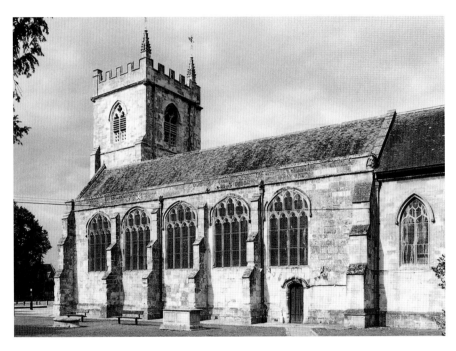

Salisbury: St Edmund, from the south

Set in its beautiful large churchyard, the church makes a fine sight. Externally all is of ashlar, with regular buttresses; the medieval parts have straight parapets and large, uniform four-light N and S windows with panel tracery. There are good reused Perp. entrance doorways in the W sides of the tower and S aisle. The tower is large but not tall, in three stages, with slightly set-back buttresses, battlements and corner pinnacles (one is missing). It could very nearly pass as genuine Perp. work, but above the W doorway is a large pedimented cartouche containing an inscription referring to the collapse and reconstruction. The seventeenth-century W walls of the aisles too are a good match to the medieval work, and their five-light windows are reused pieces. Internally, the present nave is very broad and has five-bay arcades of two-centred arches with double hollow chamfers, resting on tall, slim pillars of four shafts and four hollows. Some ancient work remains in the roofs. A substantial two-storeyed block attached to the N side of the church was built as a mausoleum and vestries; it is partly of 1766 but mostly early nineteenth century.

The second surprise for the unwary visitor comes on entry; the church became redundant in 1973 and is now the Salisbury Arts Centre. The interior is divided by partitions and curtains into bar, restaurant, art gallery, auditorium and offices. The art is mainly 'pop'; many surfaces are painted black, and some backstage areas are untidy. This may jar upon the church lover: but the building is in use, filled with life and maintained, so we should probably be grateful. All the ecclesiastical fittings have been removed, but some memorial tablets remain.

The college buildings stood just E of the church. After the dissolution they became a large house, mostly rebuilt in the Elizabethan period, then finely remodelled in the eighteenth century. In 1927 this was bought by the corporation and became the Council House, as it remains today.

Worcestershire

This county possessed just one college.

* Elmley Castle

Some confusion has clouded modern understanding of this college. Shortly after the Norman Conquest, a castle was begun by Robert d'Abitot, high on the hill above the village. It included a chapel, which at some stage was served by five clerks, perhaps formed into a college. The castle had fallen into decay by the beginning of the fourteenth century, and whether clerks still then served in its chapel is unknown. However, by this time its lord was Guy de Beauchamp, Earl of Warwick, and in 1308 he founded a chantry college intended for eight chaplains, with four clerks. Instead of being in the castle, this was in the village and was attached to its Church of St Mary, the advowson of which was granted to the college; the church was appropriated in the

Elmley Castle: St Mary, from the north

following year. In 1311 the planned size was reduced to seven chaplains and two clerks; one of the chaplains was warden. In 1463, Richard Neville, the then earl, augmented the endowments sufficiently to provide an eighth chaplain. The annual value in 1536 was £56; the college was dissolved in 1545.

The church is of medium size only, externally attractive but in its internal appearance much spoilt by the removal of plaster in 1878. Some herring-bone masonry in the chancel implies an eleventh-century date, but its windows are Dec. and Perp., with a nineteenth-century chancel arch and E wall. The nave has aisles under low-pitched roofs, a N transept and a N porch. The N side, facing the village, has battlements, and its windows are mostly square-headed late-Perp. work; the blocked E window of the transept has five lights. The S aisle has varied Dec. and Perp. windows. This aisle may have been added for the college; the chancel seems to have been extended E about the same time. The attractive W tower is unbuttressed, in three stages, with battlements; most of its details are Perp., but the two lower stages are clearly EE, with a lancet N window and blocked former belfry openings.

The arcades are of four bays, with octagonal pillars and double-chamfered arches, perhaps fourteenth century; irregularities include two square pieces of masonry instead of pillars on the S side. In the transept are the blocked openings to the former rood stair. The roofs are replacements, but there are attractive old stone floors. The seating is delightful, almost all of late medieval pews, with plain straight ends, well preserved and little repaired. Just one group is later, with simple perhaps Jacobean ends. A vestry area has partly eighteenth-century screenwork. Also ancient are the doors to the porch and the church. The font is remarkable: its octagonal bowl is late-Perp., but its square base with a cylindrical stem is surrounded by four large and boldly carved dragons, thought to be twelfth- or early thirteenth-century work. Two outstandingly fine memorials dominate the transept. The seventeenth-century Savage memorial is a tomb-chest with three recumbent alabaster effigies and four kneeling sons at their feet. The huge canopied standing wall memorial of about 1700 to the Earl of Coventry was to have been erected at Croome d'Abitot, but was exiled to Elmley by a family quarrel. It is lavish in its details, with a semi-reclining effigy and four allegorical figures. Also here is a medieval coffin-lid with enriched cross.

A substantial part of the collegiate building remains, now forming three houses, one known as The Old College, close to the churchyard gate. Of the castle, little more remains than earthworks; nothing is known of the chapel.

Yorkshire: East Riding and the City of York

The fine series of collegiate churches in this riding includes in Beverley and Howden two of the most magnificent in existence. Also of much interest are Hemingbrough and Lowthorpe. At York, St William's College (*see* Appendix II) is the finest example of a college for chantry priests serving in a cathedral.

* Beverley

Beverley Minster, or the parish Church of St John the Evangelist, is arguably the finest building described in these pages. Of the three great collegiate churches that were effectively subsidiary cathedrals in the large diocese of York, it is the only one which was not elevated to cathedral status in the nineteenth century. However, it possesses in full measure the splendour, richness and generosity of scale that belong to cathedrals, and indeed it ranks with the greatest of them. Its early origins are unclear, but it may be that a monastery was established about 700 by Bishop John of York, who in 1037 was canonized as St John of Beverley. His tomb here was an object of pilgrimage through the Middle Ages. It is suggested that it was refounded in about 934 by King Athelstan for secular canons. Certainly before the Conquest it had seven canons. This remained its basis throughout the Middle Ages, though one further canon was eventually added; it had no dean, the Archbishop of York being regarded as the head. Its constitution was unique. The canons did not have true prebends, their emoluments coming mainly from a common fund; their positions were known by the names of altars in the church, of St Andrew, St James, St Martin, St Mary, St Michael, St Peter and St Stephen. The canon of St Martin also had responsibility for the Chapel of St Mary in the town (which itself became a very large and important church). There were also a provost, who was not necessarily a canon, and a precentor, chancellor and treasurer who, uniquely, were not canons. In addition, it had nine vicars, ten or more clerks, eight choristers and later about fifteen chantry priests. The college ran a grammar school, under the control of the provost, and a song school, under the control of the precentor. Beverley figured as a cathedral in one of Henry VIII's schemes for new sees. However, this did not happen, and the college was suppressed in 1548.

The minster is cruciform with double transepts; the main transepts have two aisles, whereas the E transepts have just an E aisle. Its external length is 365 ft (111.3 m); the nave has eleven bays, the main transepts project three bays beyond the aisles, and the chancel has four bays to the E crossing, beyond which are two further bays, the E one aisleless. It is a wonderfully homogeneous building, despite the fact that it was begun at the E end in about 1225 and only finished with the W front in the fifteenth century. It is all of beautiful cream-coloured limestone, excellently preserved and mostly very authentic. Major repairs and restoration were carried out in the unusual period of 1716–31, including considerable new work in a style sympathetic to its surroundings: the architect was Nicholas Hawksmoor. Famously, the N transept front, which had threatened to collapse, was pushed back to the vertical by means of an immense timber frame. The most obvious work of this time is the low central tower, which has windows with ogee hood-moulds of gothick character; until 1824 it carried an ogee dome or cupola of timber.

Beverley Minster, from the
south-west

Beverley Minster: looking south
across the transepts

The chancel and transepts are uniform EE work. Mouldings are deep, dog-tooth is employed, there are both stiff-leaf and moulded capitals, and much Purbeck marble appears, mainly for shafts and imposts. The pillars are of four major and four lesser shafts, the latter keeled. The triforium has no passage, but is remarkable for having two planes of arcading, of four arches per bay, the front ones trefoiled, the rear set lower and simply arched. Each bay of clerestory has a single large lancet, set internally and externally in blank arcading. The vaults are quadripartite throughout. Trefoiled blank arcading runs round the aisles. An especially lovely feature is the great double staircase set into the wall of the N chancel aisle, of the utmost EE sophistication; it led to an octagonal chapter-house, which was demolished in 1550. The end walls of the transepts have two tiers of great lancet triplets, just the upper group being graduated in size. There is an impressive portal below. Some Perp. windows have been inserted in the chancel aisles, and the E wall has a great Perp. window of nine lights, its tracery internally doubled up to the level of the transom. A further Perp. addition is a single-bay chapel at the NE corner.

The nave is Dec., but remarkably it continues without alteration the main features of the previous system. However, large windows of excellent flowing tracery are employed, of three lights in the clerestory and four in the aisles, and there are lush foliage capitals. Purbeck marble is largely abandoned after the first bay. A surprising aspect is the continuation of dog-tooth ornament. The blank arcading in the N aisle is of a rich ogee-trefoiled design. There is a lavish two-storeyed N porch; this is Perp. work, as are several aisle windows here. The W front, with its wonderful pair of tall towers, is perhaps the supreme feature of the whole exterior, showing Perp. work at its finest. However, almost all of its extensive statuary is nineteenth century.

The contents of the minster include some outstanding treasures. Finest of all is the great Percy tomb, in the arch between the sanctuary and the NE transept. This is a crowning achievement of the Dec. style, in almost perfect condition, its lavish and lofty canopy having nodding-ogee arches and retaining much outstanding figure sculpture. Behind the altar is a further fine Dec. screen, of veranda type, in this case significantly restored; and on the S side are superb quadruple Dec. sedilia of timber. Several other rich timber screens are Perp. work. There are splendid early-sixteenth-century stalls with canopies and sixty-eight carved misericords. The screen between the nave and the chancel, which carries the organ, is Victorian. A remarkable relic is the frith stool, a pre-Conquest stone chair or throne. One fine Norman piece remains: the very large circular font, of black marble, with elegant fluting or scallops, resting on a large square base. Suspended above it, its superb cover is of 1713. There are some other fine eighteenth-century fittings too. A little medieval glass remains, mainly in the E window.

The exterior is especially well seen across the rough meadow which still survives immediately to the SW. There are no remains of the collegiate buildings or of the canons' houses. To the W was the Bedern, originally the common residence of the canons but later occupied mainly by the vicars choral.

* Hemingbrough (*now North Yorkshire*)

This important church, dedicated to St Mary, was in the patronage of the prior and monks of Durham Cathedral. It was a valuable rectory, and a strenuous attempt was made by Durham in the mid-fourteenth century to appropriate it, permission being obtained in 1356 from the king and the Archbishop of York; but papal sanction was not forthcoming. Instead, in 1426, licences were obtained from the king and Archbishop Kempe of York for it to be made collegiate, with a provost, three prebendaries, six vicars and six clerks. The Prior of Durham is said to have spent £171 on this project. It was a chantry college, and its prebends were bursal; the members were to pray for Henry VI and his progenitors and descendents. Four of the vicars had a parochial role. The income of the college in 1535 is given as £78; it was dissolved in 1545.

The church is large, interesting and very attractive. It is of good limestone, cruciform, with a crossing tower; its building history is complicated and it is far from uniform, but much of the exterior makes a bold Perp. display. It is the

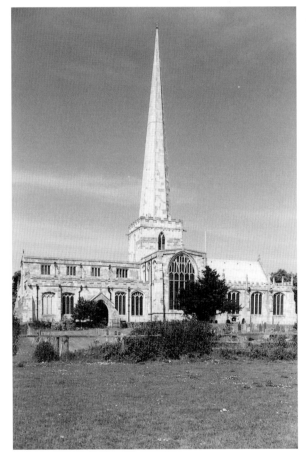

Hemingbrough, from the south

Hemingbrough: the chancel, looking west

spire, however, which is memorably unique: above a modest tower, which rises 63 ft (19.2 m) to its battlements, the plain stone spire soars to a height of 189 ft (57.6 m). These proportions are comically unusual, but it is both impressive and aesthetically successful. The spire is a fifteenth-century addition to a Dec. tower and crossing; there is no ringing chamber, so the ringers have to stand in the centre of the church.

The earliest features inside are the two E bays of the nave arcades, of about 1190: they have round arches with a chamfer and a roll, on cylindrical pillars with octagonal imposts. There is a double respond, then the two W bays, which are a little later and have acutely pointed arches of two chamfered orders. Above is a late Perp. clerestory of square-headed windows. The W window has five lights, with panel tracery. Both aisles are battlemented and the S one has pinnacles too, with both Dec. and Perp. windows. The N aisle was rebuilt wider in late Perp. times. There is a broad S porch which covers a fine EE doorway with a continuous filleted roll-moulding; above is a Dec. image niche of nodding-ogee form. Also EE is the acutely pointed W doorway.

The N transept surprisingly has a W aisle, very narrow, with an arcade of two dissimilar bays. The fenestration in this transept is Perp., the E and W sides having a clerestory of three-light windows; however, the E wall has an EE arch and the blocked remains of two lancet windows. The S transept has similar Perp. features. It has no aisle, and its W side has two very long late-thirteenth-century cusped lancets; another, now internal, is on the E side.

There are five impressive image corbels here. The five-light E window of the chancel is early Dec. On the N side of the chancel is a Perp. chantry chapel of a single bay, E of which is a two-storeyed medieval sacristy. Along the S side of the chancel is a fine late-Perp. chapel, externally of ashlar, with battlements and pinnacles. It has an excellent arcade of four bays, with four-centred arches on pillars of four filleted shafts and four hollows.

Other than over the chancel, the roofs are low pitched and mainly ancient; several are fine. Both sides of the chancel have original parclose screens. The stalls are mostly authentic, but only one old seat remains, with its misericord: its carving suggests this is EE, which if true is exceptionally early for a misericord. The nineteenth-century pews have a fine set of medieval ends, straight-topped, mostly with tracery designs. It is startling to learn that the hexagonal pulpit of apparently Jacobean type dates from 1717. Fragments remain from a former Elizabethan chancel screen, with a pedimented top but tracery of medieval type. The font has a circular Norman bowl, with ambitious but rather irregular blank arcading. On the walls are some worthy memorials. There is a late medieval cadaver effigy, the shroud opened back to shocking effect. In the N transept is an unusual Perp. stone table or pedestal, with tracery designs. Also in this transept is a curiosity: the top 8 ft of the spire, set up here when they were replaced in 1989.

* Howden

From 1080, the patronage of this church belonged to the Prior and Convent of Durham. In 1267, Prior Hugh de Darlington and Archbishop Walter Giffard of York, acting in concord, elevated it to collegiate status, with five prebendaries and five vicars. There was no dean or master, but the canon who held the prebend called Howden had some precedence. The patronage belonged to Durham, but members were instituted by the Archbishop of York. In 1279, a sixth prebend was added, with a further vicar, and in 1319 Archbishop Melton established a vicar who had the cure of souls. There were also three chantry priests, later increased to five. In 1535 the value was given as only £61; dissolution seems to have taken place in 1548. The church was not damaged, but in the years that followed the lay impropriators who acquired the property of the college did nothing to maintain the chancel, despite a lawsuit in 1600. As a result, in 1609 the chancel was separated from the rest of the church and abandoned. It finally collapsed in a thunderstorm in September 1696, and the roof of the chapter-house followed in 1750.

The Church of SS Peter and Paul was entirely rebuilt probably in the years following 1267, and is exceptionally large, majestic and rich. It is cruciform with a crossing tower, and is externally over 250 ft (76 m) in length. The transepts and crossing came first, together with a chancel that may have been begun just before 1267. The aisled nave followed, and was completed with the W front in about 1306–11. Finally in the early fourteenth century a spectacular new aisled chancel, vaulted throughout, replaced the one of the thirteenth century. Though it is in ruins, the chancel remains an impressive sight. Both the nave and the chancel are six bays in length.

Dominating the exterior is the splendidly large and lofty central tower, externally Perp., with two tall stages above the level of the pitched roofs. Both stages have on each side two three-light openings, the upper ones four-centred and transomed, the lower ones exceptionally long, with two transoms. The transepts are lower than the nave and the chancel; they both have an E aisle, of which that on the S was extended E in Perp. times, and remains in use; the N one is roofless. There is a large, pinnacled two-storeyed S porch, internally vaulted in two bays. Extending W from it is a large attachment constructed about 1500; this was the grammar school, and has no internal communication with the church. The W front is impressively rich, with blank arcading and four crocketed stone spirelets on hexagonal openwork turrets.

The nave has large and tall arcades, with finely moulded arches on pillars of filleted quatrefoil plan. They carry a clerestory of two two-light windows

Howden: the tower seen through the ruined east window

Howden, looking east

per bay, with a wall passage. The aisle windows have three lights, with good tracery. Many capitals have foliage. The large crossing arches are of four hollow-chamfered orders. Both transepts have an E arcade of three bays (in the N transept blocked); in the bays that opened to the chancel aisles a very rich four-centred Perp. doorway has been inserted. Distortion here shows the subsidence of the tower. In the E tower arch, the former pulpitum now closes the church; it is a Perp. veranda screen, with lavish enrichment including four canopied image niches which still contain their images. The vaulted central passageway now forms a little chapel.

Even richer is the chancel. Its E wall remains complete in its main elements; its buttresses and the space above its enormous window have a profusion of image niches. The arcades have fallen, but the responds show that they had quatrefoil pillars, and the clerestory windows were of three lights. The wall of the N aisle is fairly ruinous, but one of its three-light windows retains its tracery; the buttresses continue as ragged pinnacles high above the walls, and no doubt carried flying buttresses. On the S side the wall stands to full height, and attached here is the splendid octagonal chapter-house: this is early Perp., and has large three-light windows under ogee hood-moulds. For its protection it was reroofed in 1984, though it remains ruinous and is not internally accessible.

The interesting contents include a surprising amount of medieval statuary, mostly brought in the late eighteenth century from the ruined chancel, and rather decayed. Against the SE tower pillar is a stone structure which may be a tomb-chest or a shrine base, on which stands a medieval statue of St John of

Howden. There are many memorials, some large, including medieval recumbent effigies and a brass of a knight. The large octagonal font is striking Dec. work, each side of the bowl having a rich cinquefoiled-ogee blank arch on slim shafts which curve up from the corners of the stem. Several medieval chests remain, in varying states of decrepitude; an enormous lozenge-shaped Royal Arms dates from 1718.

* Lowthorpe

Licence was granted by the Crown on 26 January 1333 to Sir John de Heslerton, patron of the Church of St Martin, to elevate it to collegiate status, with a rector (also known as master or warden), six chantry priests and three deacons or sub-deacons. Its foundation was completed later that year. The first two chantries were known as those of the Trinity and of St Mary. The third was the chantry of the archbishop, with his predecessors and successors, and King Edward II. The fourth was the chantry of the chapter, for the deans and canons of York Minster, living and dead, their successors, and William de Ros the second. The fifth was the chantry of the founder, with his wife and their parents, their children, their heirs, living and dead, and John de Hothum, Bishop of Ely. The sixth was the chantry of the patron. In 1364, Sir Thomas de Heslerton added a seventh chantry priest, who was to pray for Sir Thomas and his wife Alice while they lived, and for their souls after their deaths. The college continued in this form until its dissolution in 1548.

Lowthorpe, from the south-east

The church today is a remarkable and evocative building, partly in ruins. It appears to have been entirely rebuilt as a uniform Dec. structure on the establishment of the college, though post-medieval changes have left some puzzles. It is of good ashlar, aisleless, with a W tower; its length was reduced soon after the dissolution, with a new E wall and apparently a new wall dividing the nave from the chancel. Later, the chancel became ruinous, and was abandoned. Finally, in 1859 the remaining nave was patched up and altered: its walls were lowered and their upper parts rebuilt, they were given mostly two-light Y-tracery windows, and a S porch was added. However, the S doorway with its continuous mouldings is Dec. Internally the nave is humble, with a poor boarded hammerbeam roof and basic furnishings including pews of deal. Its E wall is apparently Elizabethan, with a pointed arch of unusual character, its capitals having a band of leaves and flowers. This now opens to a little polygonal sanctuary, windowless, externally of brick, said to have been provided in 1777. The tower is very modest in scale and character, and its date is uncertain: it has W buttresses and a square-headed, perhaps Elizabethan, W window. Its stonework rises no higher than the nave roof, above which is an elementary belfry stage of brick, probably of about 1777, with simple battlements, obelisk corner pinnacles and arched belfry openings with wooden Y-tracery.

Though of the same width as the nave, the roofless chancel is of much greater presence and splendour. Its walls have the remains of battlements and contain large three-light windows with fine reticulated tracery, all now blocked with brickwork. Its E wall has a blocked four-light window with mullions and a transom, square headed below a pointed arch. The E buttresses demonstrate the demolition of the former E end, each showing the jamb of another large window, and that on the S having what is probably part of the sedilia. Surprisingly set in the E wall is a small ogee-trefoiled piscina recess. High in the S wall is a puzzling trefoiled recess with iron bars.

The chancel has many decayed ledgers and several indents of former brasses, one being the top of a large, low tomb-chest. One of two brasses from this was in the nave until it was stolen in 1999. Also in the nave is a remarkable large, rather worn slab with recumbent effigies of a husband and wife, their bodies covered by a sort of tree with foliage at the foot; dotted between the branches are thirteen heads, presumably representing children. It is probably Dec., and may well commemorate members of the de Heslerton family.

Sutton-on-Hull

This Church of St James the Great, serving a village now immersed in the outer spread of Kingston upon Hull, was originally a chapelry to Wawne, but by 1291 had become in most respects a rectory. In 1346, the lord of the manor, Sir John de Sutton, obtained licence to appropriate the church and to found in it a chantry college consisting of a master and five chaplains. The college was established in the following year, with as master Thomas de Sampson, the founder's uncle, who was previously rector. In 1380, new statutes were given, and two clerks were ádded to the foundation. Dissolution took place in 1547. The church was apparently rebuilt in 1347–9, on becoming collegiate; but curiously it is of two distinct builds, both Dec., the chancel being of stone whereas the aisled nave is of red brick, an early use of that material. Whilst three-light square-headed windows are used throughout, their design differs between the nave and the chancel, yet with nothing to indicate which is earlier. It is suggested that the founder was responsible for the rebuilding of the nave, while the master rebuilt the chancel.

This is not a large church, but the chancel is relatively long; it is externally an attractive building, but less so inside, where the Victorians' hand has been

Sutton-on-Hull, from the south-east

heavy. Most of the N side of the chancel is covered by vestries and the organ-chamber; two original windows remain here, now internal. The nave has narrow aisles with low-pitched roofs. On the S side there are battlements and a brick doorway of two continuous chamfers; on the N the battlements were removed in 1889. At the W end, after a straight joint, there is a further bay of the aisles, Perp., also of brick, and with a straight parapet. This bay goes with and embraces the tower, which has one string-course below the belfry stage, a renewed five-light W window and stone battlements with small corner and intermediate pinnacles.

This brick nave originally had heavy four-bay arcades of brick, with massive piers, but in 1866–7 slender arcades of stone were substituted, pleasant but of no interest. The panelled surfaces of the thick tower piers are also Victorian, though the three tower arches remain original, with two large hollow chamfers; with these go the arches crossing the aisles. The roofs are renewed, the chancel arch is new, and so are the double sedilia. In the chancel, until 1870 central but now at one side, is the large Perp. tomb-chest with a fine recumbent effigy of Sir John de Sutton, who died in 1357. In the N arch of the tower is an excellent oak screen, with bold ogee arches and delicate Perp. tracery. On a nineteenth-century base, the circular font bowl must be of about 1200: it is plain but for a band of nailhead round the rim.

York: St Mary and the Holy Angels

This college was often in later medieval times referred to as St Sepulchre, for reasons which are unclear but were perhaps associated with its use as a churchyard chapel. It was founded in about 1179 by Archbishop Roger of Pont-l'Evêque, for a sacrist and twelve canons; the canons were to be four priests, receiving an annual stipend of 10 marks (£6 13s 4d), four deacons whose stipend was £5, and four sub-deacons receiving 6 marks (£4). The college was in the patronage of the archbishops, and had a chantry function; its constitution seems to anticipate those later chantry colleges that had bursal prebends. In 1258, Archbishop Sewal de Bovill added several further clergy. There seem at times to have been problems in relations with the clergy of the minster; some of the college prebends could be held in plurality with minster canonries. Its annual value was given in 1546 as £165; it was dissolved in 1548. The chapel was physically separate from the minster, but stood immediately N of the W end of its nave, where there remains a blocked doorway thought to have led to it. Little is known about it, although excavations before 1847 are supposed to have exposed parts of its foundations.

Yorkshire: North Riding

Unlike the other Ridings, the North Riding had no major college; the college of Middleham however has an interesting history.

Middleham (*now North Yorkshire*)

In 1461, the nine-year-old Richard, Duke of Gloucester, came to live in Middleham Castle, in the household of the Earl of Warwick (the 'Kingmaker'). Richard's eldest brother had just become king as Edward IV. In February 1477, Edward granted licence to Richard to make collegiate the parish Church of SS Mary and Alkelda at Middleham, with a dean, six chaplains, four clerks, six choristers and a 'clerk sacristan' responsible for the cure of souls. This was one of several collegiate foundations begun by Richard, none of which was fully completed. It was established in January 1478; the rector, William Beverley, became the first dean, and chaplains were appointed. In 1481, the Archbishop of York confirmed the foundation, and that it was a royal free chapel exempt from his jurisdiction. In July 1482 its statutes were confirmed by a papal bull. Successive further endowments were added. This was a chantry college, with the purpose of offering prayers and masses for the House of York. In 1483 Richard succeeded to the throne as Richard III, but he was killed in 1485 at Bosworth Field, and Henry Tudor became king as Henry VII. Most of the endowments were confiscated; the college continued in little more than name, with only the dean and the clerk sacristan. As such, it survived the Reformation, as did its royal privileges. Curiously, in the early nineteenth century the then dean, Dr. Wood, attempted to revive it, and appointed six canons, one of whom was Charles Kingsley. But in 1845, the college and the peculiar were finally dissolved, subject to the life interests of the dean and canons.

The church is attractive, but in size and ambition it is no more than a village church; more spectacular is the great ruined castle, not far away. Probably

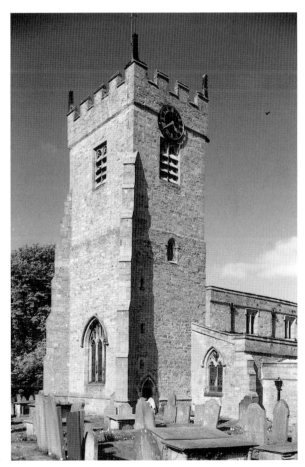

Middleham, from the
south-west

rebuilding or enlargement of the church would have followed had the college continued. Externally it is mainly Perp., with square-headed windows, but some Dec. features appear, notably the four-light E window and the windows of the S chapel. The walls are of irregular stone and the roofs are low pitched, with straight parapets. The W tower is in two stages, with diagonal buttresses, battlements and small corner pinnacles; its belfry openings are square headed.

More quiet Dec. work appears inside, especially the four-bay arcades, with octagonal pillars and double-chamfered arches. The Perp. clerestory windows are set over the arcade spandrels. Further Dec. pieces are the chancel arch, with continuous mouldings, the round arch from the chancel to the S chapel, and the mutilated S doorway, above which is a good carved panel of the crucifixion. The N side of the chancel is Victorian, with an organ-chamber, a vestry and a clerestory of quatrefoils. Victorian stencilling covers the chancel walls.

The furnishings are of excellent quality, but include little that is ancient. The plain octagonal font is Perp.; it has an elaborate and richly coloured canopy of the spire type, suspended from the roof, which is partly original and was reassembled in 1898. Mounted murally is a very fine memorial to an abbot of nearby Jervaulx Abbey, who died in 1533. A parish room in the W end is of 1997, and the pews and panelling of the nave are late-twentieth-century work. The chancel fittings date from the early twentieth century; the stalls, of which there are ten, have most unusual and attractive tall canopies resting on slender shafts. They are successors to the collegiate stalls; the six for the canons each had a dedication to a saint.

This church is of particular interest to the societies, English and American, dedicated to the memory of Richard III.

Yorkshire: West Riding

The dominating collegiate church of this riding is that of Ripon, now the cathedral. That of Rotherham also is a splendid building.

Acaster Selby (*now North Yorkshire*)

This College of St Andrew was founded about 1470 by Robert Stillington, at that time Bishop of Bath and Wells and Chancellor of England. It was a chantry college for a provost and three priest fellows, who were to celebrate for the souls of King Edward IV, the queen, their son Prince Edward, the founder and all Christian souls. Robert Stillington was subsequently involved in the Lambert Simnel rebellion, and died in 1491 as a prisoner in Windsor Castle. Despite this, his college continued; it had an annual value of £28 in 1535 and was dissolved about 1548. Attached to it was a school, and at the dissolution the commissioners recommended that this should continue; a former chaplain, William Gegoltson, was still schoolmaster in 1571. A new school was later built in the village, but closed in the twentieth century. However, Robert Stillington's charity has survived to our own times, and distributes dictionaries and other educational materials to children of the village.

The college was non-parochial; however, the parish church of Stillingfleet being on the other side of the River Ouse, without a bridge, the college chapel functioned also as a chapel of ease for the local inhabitants. This did not prevent its destruction after 1548, and nothing but the moated site remains NE of the village. It shows evidence of former buildings of brick, and it can be said that the chapel was cruciform. The people of Acaster Selby continued to travel to church in Stillingfleet, and in a tragedy on Boxing Day 1833, eleven were drowned. Eventually in 1850 a chapel of ease was built, an unremarkable small building dedicated to St John, charmingly approached through a field. It contains a good Perp. font, of unknown provenance.

Pontefract: St Clement (*now West Yorkshire*)

Following the Norman Conquest, Ilbert de Lacy was granted huge estates in Yorkshire which became known as the Honour of Pontefract and were controlled from the great castle he caused to be built. In the inner bailey of the castle, there was built in about 1085 a Chapel of St Clement, containing a college of a dean and three prebendaries. The castle and estates remained with the de Lacys, and in 1351 became part of the Duchy of Lancaster. When in 1399 Henry Bolingbroke became the first Lancastrian king as Henry IV, his predecessor Richard II was imprisoned in the castle until his death, perhaps murder, the following year. One of the prebends had been held as early as 1291 by the prior of the Cluniac priory of Pontefract, and at the time of the dissolution of the priory, the prior was also dean of the college. The college was valued in 1535 at £49; it was dissolved in 1548.

The chapel was moved or rebuilt more than once. The Norman chapel seems to have been demolished at some time in the Middle Ages, a new chapel being built further N within the bailey. This was rebuilt in 1499–1505, and was presumably the building that appears, pinnacled and battlemented, in a drawing of about 1560. However, this in its turn was replaced soon afterwards by another building constructed against the curtain wall, SE of the site of the Norman chapel. Traces of this Elizabethan chapel may still be seen. Nothing is visible of the late-medieval chapel, and its site has not been excavated. However, the remains of the earliest chapel were excavated in 1881–2 and again in 1982–6, and enough survives to be of interest. It comprised a nave, chancel, and apsidal sanctuary, the last a later Norman addition; the walls stand 2 or 3 ft high, of good ashlar. Two demi-columns on bases in the apse probably carried a vault. The responds of the arch to the apse have a demi-column and on the W side two orders of shafts. Externally the apse has shallow buttresses with nook-shafts. The chancel, wider than the apse, is unbuttressed; it has the base of a priest's door, and the footings of the chancel arch are visible, but without details. The nave was wider again, but except for its beginning it remains covered up.

* **Ripon** (*now North Yorkshire*)

About 655 a monastery was begun under King Alchfrith of Northumbria, who a few years later brought Wilfred here as its second abbot. Under Wilfred, from about 672, a great church of stone was built, as we are told, 'in the Roman manner'; Wilfred was a protagonist of Roman as opposed to Celtic ways in the church. For a period from about 678, he was banished and Eadhed was made bishop, Ripon becoming a cathedral. This ceased when Wilfred returned in 686 as Bishop of York, after which he again spent much time at Ripon. Wilfred died in 709, and less is known about the history of Ripon in the following years; it was apparently destroyed by the Danes in the late ninth century, and again by Eadred in about 948. However, it was re-established, and in 995, when the body of St Cuthbert was removed from Chester-le-Street, it came first to Ripon before continuing to its final resting place in Durham.

At some stage the church became collegiate; seven prebends are supposed to have been established by Archbishop Ealdred after 1061, and this remained the number throughout the Middle Ages. There was no dean. In Norman times, St Wilfred was added to St Peter in the dedication; the major rebuilding which is the basis of the church we see today began in about 1175. Six vicars choral were instituted in 1303, and they were formed into a college in 1414 (*see* Appendix I). In 1439, in addition to the canons and vicars there were six deacons, six thuribulers and six choristers. Among the canons, the precentor had precedence, and was to be permanently resident. A school was in existence in the fourteenth century. In 1535, the annual value of the college was given as £334; it was dissolved in 1547. Remarkably, however, it was re-established in 1604 by James I, and some of its former revenues were returned to it; it now had a dean and five prebendaries, a sub-dean being added soon after, and there were two vicars choral, six lay clerks and six choristers. The college was again suppressed during the Commonwealth, but was restored with the return of Charles II. Then in 1836 its chapter was again altered when Ripon became a cathedral, the first of the new sees of the nineteenth and twentieth centuries.

By the standards of the greater cathedrals, Ripon is relatively small; its internal length is given as 280 ft (85.3 m). It is nevertheless a magnificent building, well worthy of its cathedral rank. Its structure has work of several periods, with some surprising irregularities, but it has much that is of exquisite beauty and much that is lovable. Restoration has been significant, but has mostly done little harm. It is set in a beautiful large churchyard, but has no close. It is cruciform and has three towers, which until the mid-seventeenth century all carried timber spires. The W front is one of its finest features, a pure and sophisticated EE piece, with carefully judged use of shafting, arcading and dog-tooth ornament; its effect is restrained rather than lavish. It has two tiers of five great lancets, and three portals below; the flanking towers have buttresses of moderate projection rising without offset to the full height.

Ripon Cathedral, from the north-west

This front originally terminated an aisleless EE nave, of which internally just the extreme E and W ends remain. The rest has been replaced by a beautiful quiet aisled structure of the early sixteenth century, in five bays, externally battlemented, with large five-light arched and traceried clerestory windows and three-light aisle windows. Internally, the arcades have great dignity, with beautiful richly moulded arches. The aisles are vaulted in stone, but the main space has a richly ribbed vault of timber; both are nineteenth century, probably completing the original intentions.

The transepts and parts of the E limb are of the late twelfth century: their Trans. Norman design shows elegant and slender mouldings of EE type, but with many round arches. The transepts have an elevation of three stages, and have E aisles; the E side of the S transept has been rebuilt in Perp. style, and the low-pitched, panelled main roofs here are Perp. The battlemented central tower is low; it and the crossing arches are in a most extraordinary condition, apparently the result of a partial collapse followed by an unfinished scheme for total rebuilding. The N and W sides are Trans. Norman, whereas the S and E are Perp.; the earlier tower arches are broad and round, whereas the other two now have narrower but taller pointed arches, resting on massive piers of many orders. This leads to an unfortunate lop-sided appearance as viewed from the nave, as only the SW pier has been replaced by the new form. The collapse probably also brought down much of the S side of the chancel and the E side of the S transept.

Ripon Cathedral, looking east

The chancel has six bays. The first three bays on the N are of beautiful Trans. Norman work, comparable to that of the transepts; the arcade has pointed arches, and there are a triforium and clerestory with sophisticated detailing incorporating both round and pointed arches. Opposite them are three bays of Perp. work, with fine panelling of the wall surfaces; the glazed triforium has round arches, no doubt to be in keeping with the rest. The three E bays on both sides are a fine uniform early Dec. structure, with windows of geometrical tracery; the triforium is again round arched, the clerestory windows have two planes of tracery and it culminates in a magnificent E window of seven lights. As in the nave, the aisles have stone vaults and the main space has a nineteenth-century timber vault.

Along the S side of the chancel is a building in two storeys. Its upper stage is Dec. and is now the library. The lower stage is mainly Norman, with an apsidal E termination; it was divided in medieval times, the vaulted W part becoming the chapter-house. This, however, is not the earliest work to be seen at Ripon: for remarkably there still remains the crypt of Wilfred's church, dating from about 672. It was probably below his high altar, and is now below the crossing. It is reached by descending through narrow stairs and passages, which are later. Small, plain arched doorways open to two chambers, with tunnel vaults and various small arched recesses in their walls, all coated in hard plaster. This is one of the most moving places that may be visited in all England.

Among the many fine fittings is an impressive late-Perp. choir screen of stone, carrying the organ; its statuary, however, is not medieval. The splendid stalls have very rich canopies and retain their thirty-four excellently carved misericords: they are of about 1490. Other worthy contents include the Perp. font of black marble, with concave-octagonal base, stem and bowl. There are many fine memorials, some of medieval date. A few striking modern fittings have been introduced.

* Rotherham (*now South Yorkshire*)

In 1480, Thomas Rotherham caused to be built the Jesus Chapel of the parish Church of All Saints, to contain a chantry. Originally known as Thomas Scott, he was a native of the town; amongst other notable positions he was at this time Bishop of Lincoln, and later in the year became Archbishop of York. Also in 1480, he obtained licence to found the College of Jesus, which was established in 1483; it was for a provost, two fellows, later increased by his will to

Rotherham, from the north-west

Rotherham, looking west

three, and six choristers. A particular direction was given that the provost should preach widely in the neighbourhood. The three fellows were to teach in schools respectively of song, grammar, and writing and arithmetic, and the college was also to provide accommodation for other chantry chaplains of the town. Already belonging to Rufford Abbey, the church was not appropriated; however, the college was to celebrate in its chancel on Sundays and festivals, and at other specified times in the Jesus Chapel. The remaining services could be either in the Jesus Chapel or in the chapel in the college buildings, which stood a short distance E of the church. These were of brick, laid out round a quadrangle, and included a building to house the three schools. They have long disappeared and the site is now occupied by Woolworths. In 1548 the college had an annual value given as almost £123; it was dissolved in that year.

This is a very impressive and very large cruciform church, with a commanding central spire 180 ft (54.9 m) in height. It has a fine position in the centre of the town, with the land dropping steeply to an open square to the N. Externally it is all Perp. work of high quality, and only the E limb shows obvious departures from uniformity. It is faced in ashlar, rather black in colour; external renewal is considerable, most noticeably on the S side of the nave. It has low-pitched roofs with battlements and pinnacles throughout, and the buttresses are panelled. The nave is of four bays, with aisle windows of four lights, traceried and transomed, and a clerestory of two three-light windows per bay. The W window has seven lights. There is a large S porch, much renewed. Both transepts are of full height, with end windows of six lights. The chancel too has a clerestory, added in 1508–12, with rather curious uncusped tracery. It is flanked by differing two-bay chapels stopping short of the E end: that on the S side is the Jesus Chapel. A medieval sacristy, also with battlements and pinnacles, is E of the N chapel. The tower is splendid, each side having two arched openings of four lights; the battlements have corner and intermediate pinnacles, and the crocketed spire is distinguished by the very effective large pinnacles rising from the base of its diagonal faces.

The interior is as fine as the exterior. It too is all faced in ashlar. The nave arcades are large and tall, with complex pillars longer on their N–S axes carrying castellated capitals with a broad band of foliage and finely moulded two-centred arches. Shafts rise to the splendid roof, which is original and impressively panelled, and carries very large foliage bosses; it is surprisingly but attractively painted blue, with the bosses gold. Fine too are the crossing arches; above them on three sides are a pair of two-light windows, now all internal, and it has a beautiful vault of a type intermediate between tierceron and fan. In the chancel there is earlier work; the arcades, with slim octagonal pillars, the triple ogee-cinquefoiled sedilia and a small piscina of similar form are all probably Dec. Three varied image niches are disposed around the E window.

There are eighteen stalls, with excellent original traceried fronts and poppy-head ends, though only two misericords remain. There are also some medieval pews here, with traceried ends: they are entirely original and very charming. An original parclose screen with coving divides the S transept from the Jesus Chapel. The very fine octagonal pulpit, dating from 1605, is rich in design, with Ionic columns standing out at the angles. The splendid large tester is later. In the N chapel are a plain medieval chest and a late-Perp. canopied tomb-chest, its back plate carrying an amusingly naïve brass with the date 1561. There are good nineteenth-century oak pews, some of which have been rather startlingly bleached to accord with the stalls and screenwork provided with the 1994 nave altar.

Wales

Wales had few collegiate churches, and none that compare architecturally with the more important English examples. Many Welsh churches are of early origin, and peculiar to the early Church in Wales was the *clas*, a kind of religious community with both clerical and lay members. It seems that it was because of this that Wales in the Middle Ages had very many portionary churches: these, however, are a specialist subject, and are not addressed in this book (though the possibly portionary Holyhead nevertheless demands inclusion). Of the four colleges below, two were founded by Thomas Bek, Bishop of St Davids and elder brother of that other notable founder of colleges, Bishop Anthony Bek of Durham. In addition, Wales has two particularly interesting establishments that do not meet the criteria for this gazetteer, at Ruthin (*see* Appendix III) and Brecon (*see* Appendix VIII).

Abergwili (*Carmarthenshire*)

This college was founded by Bishop Thomas Bek, initially in 1283, in the church of Llangadog (*see* Appendix IV). Probably in 1287, however, he changed the plan, and college was established instead at Abergwili. It was large, with a precentor and twenty-one canons holding prebends, of whom seven were priests, seven deacons and seven sub-deacons; most canons were expected to have vicars, who were to be of the same order, and there were also several clerks and choristers. In 1334, its constitution was adjusted by Bishop Gower, giving the positions of chancellor and treasurer to two of the prebendaries, who with the precentor were required to be resident. This was an important college, and its canons were frequently English absentees.

In 1540, at the request of Bishop Rawlings, the college was dissolved by Henry VIII in order to transfer its endowments and its function to the buildings of the former Dominican friary at Brecon (*see* Appendix VIII) where, remarkably, it still exists in modified form. Abergwili, however, remained important, for the collegiate buildings were given over to a new use as a palace for the bishop, more conveniently and centrally located in his diocese than St Davids. The palace was soon rebuilt. It was here that Richard Davies, who was bishop from 1561 to 1581, with William Salesbury translated the Book of Common Prayer and much of the Bible into Welsh. There was a severe fire in 1903, after which it was again largely rebuilt, and it remained the home of the

Abergwili, from the south

bishops until 1974. It then became Carmarthen Museum, although the bishops still live in a smaller house close by.

It is probable that the college used the parish Church of St David, though it has been suggested that it had a separate building. A description of the church as it existed in the early nineteenth century indicates that it was not a major building; it was towerless, consisting of a chancel, nave and broad S aisle with a four-bay arcade of pointed arches on massive octagonal columns, together with a S porch and a S transept. Nothing, however, remains of this church, as it was replaced in 1842–3 by a new building immediately N of its site, typical of its time and quite large; the architect was C. Nelson. Its main part is a broad space six bays long, undivided E–W, with regular buttresses and lancet windows; the W wall has a graduated triplet of lancets, and the E wall an equal triplet with a foiled circle above. A relatively narrow N aisle runs along the central four bays; it has a N porch, and the bay W of the aisle is occupied by the tower which is quite small, in two stages, the upper with triplets of very narrow lancet openings. It carries a stone broach spire. The arcade is plain, with two continuous slight chamfers. It continues blank in the bays to E and W, and the same motif is applied to the other walls. Arcading and much black marble shafting enrich the E wall. Several good mural memorials pre-date the church. Set in the floor is a damaged coffin-lid with a foliated cross. The church is attractively decorated in white and pale blue. To its E is the wall of the former bishop's grounds, with the palace just beyond.

* Holyhead (*Anglesey*)

The foundation of this Church of St Cybi is attributed to that saint in the sixth century. It is situated in the small but impressive rectangular Roman fort standing immediately above the harbour, the walls of which remain largely intact. The establishment of a college was apparently due to two local magnates of the twelfth century. It had a dean and three prebendaries, who may really have held portions. There were certainly further clergy, since in 1553 there were twelve in receipt of pensions. The annual value of the college had earlier been given as £24, and it was dissolved in about 1547. Its canons were frequently English, and following Edward I's conquest of Wales it may have had royal freedoms. Its churchyard fills the fort, and contains a second small church, Eglwys y Bedd, which from 1748 was used as a school.

The church is mostly a quite ambitious Perp. rebuilding attributed to about 1480–1520, comprising the transepts, aisled nave and S porch. They have low-pitched roofs, battlements and pinnacles; below the battlements of the S transept are a quatrefoil frieze and a series of bold and interesting carvings. Against the W side of this transept is a very large polygonal stair turret, on which the frieze continues. The windows in the transepts are quite small, whereas in the aisles they are large, in three lights with tracery, under four-centred arches. The richest part of the building is the S porch: each side has another large three-light window, unglazed, and there is a fan vault (rebuilt

Holyhead, from the south

Holyhead, looking east

in Sir Gilbert Scott's restoration of 1877–9). Large canopied image niches are set diagonally in the corners flanking the doorway, above which are a small image of the Trinity and much busy, rather undisciplined stone panelling. Inside, the arcades are of three bays, and there is a crossing; the arches are all four-centred and richly moulded. The N arcade has octagonal pillars; the S arcade, which is much taller, has pillars of four shafts and four hollows. Each side has a low clerestory.

The three-light E window is medieval, as is a small low-side window, but otherwise the chancel has lancets dating largely or wholly from the restoration. On the S side is a chapel of two bays in enriched Perp. style, added in 1896–7. This is the Stanley Chapel, and contains behind an iron screen a marble tomb-chest with a recumbent effigy by Hamo Thornycroft, attended at head and foot by spectacular life-size angels. The church has a W tower which, unlike the rest, is of primitive character; it is thought to date from the early seventeenth century. Its irregular walls include one offset, and it has plain rectangular belfry openings, battlements and a short pyramidal roof. It is longer on its N–S axis, and its W side partly incorporates the Roman wall.

Internally the church is dark, with extensive Victorian glass, and is rather cluttered with dark Victorian furnishings. The plain octagonal font is rustically inscribed 1662.

* Llanddewi-Brefi *(Cardiganshire, now Ceredigion)*

A strong tradition connects this site with St David and a synod in the sixth century. Its early associations are confirmed by a number of inscribed or carved stones thought to date from the seventh to the tenth centuries, which are preserved under the tower. In 1287 the bishop, Thomas Bek, reorganized it into a college for a precentor and twelve canons, probably four of each order. As in the other Welsh colleges, its prebends were often held by English pluralists; at one time William of Wykeham was a prebendary. Its annual value was given in 1535 as £38 6s. Dissolution came in or soon after 1547.

The Church of St David is stately and on quite a large scale, built of the local rubble stone. It was cruciform, but following neglect both transepts became ruinous or collapsed around 1800. Their arches are blocked, each having a small window or an opening above a door containing wooden intersecting tracery. The crossing tower, 70 ft (21.3 m) high, is large and impressive. All four arches are tall, pointed and unmoulded. It has a pointed barrel vault, its axis E–W, with rough openings to allow access for bells and bell-ropes. The arches are perhaps thirteenth century, and the upper part of the tower fifteenth; its openings are small and it has a battlemented parapet above a shallow corbel course, with a pyramidal roof and a square battlemented turret.

Both the nave and the chancel also became ruinous in the early nineteenth century; the nave, which had a S aisle, was entirely demolished in 1832, and a new nave constructed. This was again largely rebuilt in 1874, to the designs of

Llanddewi-Brefi, from the south-west

R.J. Withers. It is broad, stately and simple, with large lancet windows; entry is by a W porch. The chancel, which deviates noticeably to the N, was also rebuilt after 1832, though not totally; it too was remodelled by Withers, in this case in 1886. It has lancet windows similar to those of the nave; its N side is windowless. Many of the furnishings are good late-twentieth-century work. In the SW corner, a pedestal carries a life-size statue of St David, dated 1960.

* St Davids: St Mary's College (*Pembrokeshire*)

It was about 1365 that the College of St Mary was founded by Bishop Adam Houghton, with John of Gaunt and his wife Blanche, for a master, seven priest fellows and two choristers. It stands immediately N of the cathedral, with its chapel parallel to the cathedral nave. From about 1487, this college served also as the college of the vicars choral of the cathedral, whose buildings stood just to the E (*see* Appendix I). It thus acquired a unique double function, and had a master, seven priests, between fifteen and twenty-seven vicars choral and eight choristers. It was dissolved in 1549.

Both the chapel and the college buildings fell into ruin after the dissolution. Some fragments of the buildings remain, standing N of the chapel, partly as ruins and partly as barrel-vaulted undercrofts incorporated in the early-nineteenth-century house known as Cloister Hall and its outbuildings. The chapel remained as a largely complete shell; it was reroofed in 1966 and is now St

Mary's Hall, used for refreshments and exhibitions. It is on a large scale, a very lofty aisleless building of four bays, standing over a quite high barrel-vaulted undercroft. On the N side, the wall of the chapel is set back from that of the undercroft, and has large regular buttresses. At the W end, there is a lower attachment containing broad stairs rising to the chapel entrance; it has the springers of former vaulting. Its S part rises as a quite tall but relatively thin tower, straight topped, with narrow cusped single-light belfry openings; a surprising, very deep buttress projects from its SW corner. A cloister was built between the college and the cathedral, the S wall of the chapel showing the springers and four-centred arch shapes of the former cloister vault.

The restoration did not seek to conceal the chapel's former ruinous condition. Modern plain mullions with two transoms divide the tall arched windows into four lights, but outside these there remain a few fragments of the original Perp. tracery. The large E window is in five lights. A moulded string-course runs round the interior, above which the walls are of rough unplastered slate rubble, softened by long curtains. The low-pitched roof is plain, painted yellow and

St Davids: St Mary's Hall,
from the south-west

cream. There are no side windows in the E bay; on the S side this bay formerly connected with a building above the E cloister walk. The W wall is largely blank; the stonework of the entrance doorway and flanking openings is entirely of the restoration. At the time of writing, an appeal is in progress with the objective of recreating the cloister and its buildings.

APPENDIX I
Colleges of Vicars Choral

Colleges of vicars choral were established at almost all of the English medieval cathedrals that had a secular organization, though at only one of the Welsh cathedrals. This is an important category of college, but a college of vicars did not possess a collegiate church, since its members served in the cathedral. Most of these colleges survived the Reformation with little immediate change. Vicars choral also existed at many colleges of canons, and were sometimes provided with a separate common residence; uniquely at Ripon, this was incorporated, and so also appears below.

Chichester (Sussex, now West Sussex). The vicars choral of Chichester formed a flourishing community in the late fourteenth century. A major scheme for their accommodation was undertaken about 1397–1403, when a hall was constructed, its E part standing over a fine late-twelfth-century vaulted undercroft. On its S side was built a long rectangular courtyard containing houses for twenty-eight vicars, originally with timber cloister walks all round. In the S side of the courtyard was a gatehouse. To the W of the hall was a thirteenth-century Chapel of St Faith, which was probably used by the vicars. The whole was connected to the cathedral by a covered walkway, which became the E walk of the cathedral cloisters. Not until 1465 was the college incorporated.

Many of the buildings remain, forming a fine and engaging group. The vicars' hall is in good condition and is used regularly. It is large and has a number of interesting features, especially a rectangular projection on the S side forming a pulpit, and the lavatory or washing place, which is like an enormous rectangular bracket piscina in front of an ogee recess. At the E end of the hall is the vicars' parlour. The undercroft is now used as a restaurant. The houses along the W side of what is known as Vicars' Close still form an attractive range, showing some Perp. features although their appearance is now mainly seventeenth and eighteenth century. Originally each house had just one room up and one down. The gatehouse and most of the S range have disappeared; the E range remains but is walled off from the rest and turned round so that it now forms the backs of shops in South Street. Also remaining in part is the Chapel of St Faith, converted to a house, with the roofless E part as its garden. Amusingly, a corner of the Perp. cloister passes through the lower part of its W end, with a timber partition separating it from the chapel interior.

Exeter (Devon). The vicars here were formed into a community in the fourteenth century, for which buildings were constructed under Bishop Brantingham in 1387–8, with houses along both sides of a street known as Calendarhay. The buildings included a hall and both an inner and an outer gatehouse; no chapel is known but it was perhaps in the upper level of the inner gatehouse. There were twenty-four vicars, and the college was incorporated in 1401. The number of vicars was reduced after the Reformation, and from 1613 the college had just a custos and three vicars; there were also then eight lay vicars, who were not members of the college. It was dissolved in 1933. Some of the former vicars' houses survived until the 1850s and 1860s; the inner gatehouse was pulled down in 1872. The hall remained in good condition, with excellent early-sixteenth-century panelling, until it was largely destroyed in the bombing of 1942.

A public path running SW from the cathedral follows the line of Calendarhay. At its end remains the ruin of the hall, with tall two-light transomed windows in one side wall. An Anglo-Saxon doorway from the Church of St George, which once stood close by, was in 1954 curiously set up inside the ruin.

Hereford. The cathedral had thirty-three canons including the dean, but there were twenty-seven vicars, of whom one was custos. They were incorporated in 1396 by charter of Richard II. Their first buildings were probably constructed about this time; the hall survives, a good deal altered, now at the back of a fine eighteenth-century house (29 Castle Street). The vicars apparently found this situation too far from their work, and in 1472 Bishop Stanbury gave them a new site just SE of the cathedral; the new buildings were constructed in 1473–5. There were no changes in the 1540s, but in 1583 the college was reduced to twelve vicars. With numbers later further curtailed, it survived as a corporation until 1937.

Apart from some modernization, the buildings of 1473–5 remain complete, and are an exceptionally fine and delightful survival. They form a square quadrangle of uniform two-storeyed stone ranges. A cloister walk runs all round, with pairs of broad two-light openings under very depressed arches. The upper storey comes forward over the walks, and has simple single-light windows; the internal walls dividing the houses of the vicars from each other and from the cloister walks are timber framed. Many of the windows in the outside of the quadrangle are now eighteenth century. In the centre

Hereford: quadrangle of Vicars' College, looking north-west

of the E side is the chapel, projecting a little further E; it now seems to be mainly seventeenth century. Attached to the S side is the large vicars' hall, which was entirely rebuilt in the eighteenth century and has regular sash windows.

The entrance is at the NW corner of the quadrangle, through a fine two-storeyed porch added early in the sixteenth century. This has a fan vault and an original traceried door; the passage from it to the cloister curiously turns through a right-angle bend. Also rather awkwardly attached to the porch and apparently a later addition is a covered walk connecting the college to the SE transept of the cathedral. It has cloister-like openings in its E side, and is enjoyable especially for the excellent and varied carving applied to its roof timbers. The buildings remain in cathedral use, though no vicars choral now live here. The chapel is used as the cathedral Sunday school.

Lichfield (Staffordshire). This cathedral had thirty-one canons, which also was the number of vicars. Housing was first assigned for the vicars in about 1240, and in 1315 under Bishop Langton a site was allocated to them NW of the cathedral; this may previously have been occupied by two prebendal houses. The buildings were mainly timber framed, constructed around two courtyards, with the hall occupying part of the range between the two. The hall was rebuilt on a larger scale in about 1390, and a chapel was built or rebuilt in about 1474 on the S side of the S courtyard. The hall was again rebuilt in 1756, but by 1800 it had been subdivided, probably marking the end of corporate life here; the chapel has gone. However both courtyards remain and their buildings are mostly used as residential accommodation; one or two are still occupied by vicars choral. The whole forms a delightful enclave within the close. The N or upper courtyard is known as Vicars' Close. Its N side is a charming and largely unspoilt timber-framed range, and the E and part of

Lichfield: north side of Vicars' Close

the S sides are also of timber; the rest is now of eighteenth-century brick. Several timber-framed sections remain too in the lower courtyard, but this has mostly been turned to present a façade to the exterior, the parts facing the court now forming a pleasant jumble.

Lincoln. There seem to have been vicars here from the late twelfth century. Buildings for them were begun by Bishop Sutton (1280–99), and they were incorporated in 1440. The number of vicars seems to have been variable but always smaller than the number of canons; in 1535 there were twenty-five. The Vicars' Court still exists, a large irregular quadrangle on the steep hillside S of the cathedral. At least part of all four ranges remains, stone built, in two storeys, much altered but still showing some original features; that on the S side is the most complete, and originally comprised lodgings for six vicars, three on the ground floor and three on the upper level. Part of the W range stands as a ruin. Both the hall and the chapel have disappeared. The gatehouse remains, in the N side, and has a panelled tunnel vault.

Lincoln: east side and gatehouse of Vicars' Court

London: Minor Canons' College. The constitution of St Paul's Cathedral was unique. It had thirty prebendaries, and there were also thirty vicars choral, who were all in minor orders, there being no priest-vicars. In addition, there were twelve further priests known as minor canons, who shared with the vicars choral responsibility for the music of the cathedral. The vicars choral had a common hall standing W of the cathedral, but they were never formed into a college. In 1353, a hall and houses were bequeathed for the common life of the minor canons. This was confirmed by the dean, the bishop, and in 1373 by a papal bull; in 1394 it became a college by charter of incorporation from Richard II, known as Minor Canons' or Pettie Canons' College. One of the minor canons was warden or custos. As a corporate body, this college still exists today. It is a unique survival, untouched by the Reformation and not extinguished by the nineteenth- and twentieth-century reforms, the only subsidiary college associated with a cathedral to retain its corporate identity. It was reduced by the Act of 1840 to six, and in the twentieth century to just three minor canons: they still take part in the services, as well as having individual roles in the life of the cathedral. Two of the minor canons are entitled to the designation 'cardinal', though understandably they do not normally use it today!

The medieval college building, probably mostly late fourteenth century, stood close to the N side of the cathedral. Following the Great Fire of 1666, houses were built for the minor canons round a court in the SW corner of St Paul's Churchyard; this was known as St Paul's College. It was destroyed in the early nineteenth century, and today the three minor canons together with the residentiary canons occupy the partly seventeenth-century houses of Amen Court, W of the cathedral.

Ripon (Yorkshire, WR, now North Yorkshire). The collegiate church of Ripon (*see* p. 412) was not unusual in that its vicars had their own residence; its six vicars were instituted in 1303 by Archbishop Thomas de Corbridge, and from 1304 had a building known as the Bedern, standing to the W of the church in the street now known as Bedern Bank. But Ripon was unique in that, by charter of Henry VI in 1414, its vicars were incorporated in their own right. They were to elect one of their number as proctor. A new Bedern was constructed for the incorporated college, on a site just N of the minster, said to have been built round a quadrangle, with a hall and chapel. Unsurprisingly, this college did not survive the dissolution of the collegiate church to which it was attached. The building on its site is now known as the Old Deanery, and is of the seventeenth century and later, having been built for the dean when in 1604 a college was re-established at Ripon.

St Davids (Pembrokeshire, Wales). A common residence for the vicars choral existed here from 1287 and was due to Bishop Thomas Bek, who also appears as a founder of colleges elsewhere in his diocese. At least initially, only some of the vicars were accommodated here. It stood N and NE of the cathedral, on what is now a hillside of rough scrub and trees. This site is immediately E of where, in about 1365, the College of St Mary was founded (*see* p. 422). The college of vicars was perhaps not incorporated, and in about 1487 it was merged with the College of St Mary. Although much may be seen of the latter, nothing remains of the vicars' buildings.

Salisbury (Wiltshire). Salisbury has the finest of all cathedral closes, but in it the college of vicars is no more than a minor element. This cathedral had fifty-two canons, and by 1222 all, whether resident or not, were required to have a vicar. The norm here was for them to live in the house of the canon to which they were attached. Other vicars, especially those of non-resident canons, lived in houses in various places in the close: in later years these were often houses belonging to chantries in the cathedral, many of the vicars adding to their income by also serving as chantry priests. Salisbury was the last of the English cathedrals to form its vicars choral into a community: a building was provided for them in 1409 at the NE corner of the close, and was known as the Vicars' Hall; it had previously been a large canon's house. The college of vicars choral was incorporated immediately, by charter of Henry IV. Not all vicars were expected to live in it, though after 1442 all those who did not live in the house of their canon were required to do so. The Vicars' Hall was a large, rambling building of many ages, partly timber framed, built round a small courtyard and with a substantial hall. The college continued beyond the Reformation, but by 1620 the vicars ceased to use the Vicars' Hall as a residence; it was leased out, and later divided into two. It still stands today, numbered 12 and 13, one of the many interesting ancient houses of the close: it is a good deal altered and lacks the hall, which was demolished in 1814.

Wells (Somerset). Wells possesses the finest, best-preserved and most beautiful of all colleges of vicars. There were vicars choral at Wells from the mid-twelfth century; their number was equal to the number of canons, and by the mid-fourteenth century there were fifty, still either living with their canons or lodging outside. In 1348, under Bishop Ralph of Shrewsbury, they were formed into a college and incorporated, and from then until the 1360s buildings were constructed for them. These remain largely complete today and form a street, known as the Vicars' Close, running N from the cathedral, with a terrace of twenty-one stone houses down each side; this accommodated forty-two vicars, so presumably a few still lived elsewhere. Each house has one principal room downstairs and one upstairs, with at the front a prominent chimney-breast carrying a tall chimney. Interestingly, about 1410–20 they were given front gardens, each with a wall and a little battlemented gateway. There are many seventeenth- and eighteenth-century windows, and some houses have been combined so that they now form twenty-eight units, but they retain much of their original aspect.

Wells: Vicars' Close, looking north

Closing the street to the N is the delightful chapel. This was provided immediately but was rebuilt or much remodelled about 1470–5 by the executors of Bishop Bekynton, when it was given an upper floor forming the vicars' library. Across the S end of the street is the entrance gateway, the passage of which has a tierceron vault; above it is the fine Vicars' Hall, where the vicars took their meals. This still has some Dec. windows, and it incorporates a readers' pulpit and two charming oriel windows. It was much altered in about 1457, when at its W end it was given a tower and a broad staircase up from ground level.

From this end was constructed a bridge known as the Chain Gate, connecting with the head of the chapter-house staircase. This bridge is a delightful feature; it gave the vicars their own private entrance to the cathedral. Despite the perfection of its structural survival, like the other vicars' colleges its existence as an institution was ended in the 1930s.

York. There were thirty-six canons here, each with a vicar choral. A common dwelling for the vicars was established as early as 1248; it came to consist of dwellings for thirty-six vicars arranged round a courtyard, with a hall built probably in the early fourteenth century, and a small chapel which was consecrated in 1349. It was known as the Bedern; the name (used also at Ripon and elsewhere) may mean 'house of prayer', but this is not certain. It was incorporated under Henry V in 1421. The site is 150 yd SE of the minster, on the opposite side of Goodramgate, from which it was entered by a gatehouse; the street was crossed by a gallery which allowed the vicars to reach the minster without mingling with the crowd. As with the other colleges of vicars, it lost most of its financial independence in the Victorian reforms, but lingered on until it was finally dissolved in 1936.

The Bedern is still entered through a timber archway from Goodramgate. In 1850 it

York: Bedern Hall

became a street; the residences of the vicars had disappeared, and in the nineteenth century it was known for its crowded and degraded housing. Much of it is now occupied by modern houses. The chapel still remains, a small rectangle, but its walls were in 1961 reduced to about half their original height, perhaps because of the lean they had acquired; it was given a utilitarian roof, and is used as a store. By the early twentieth century, the hall was part of a confectionery works. More fortunate than the chapel, it was restored in 1979–80, and is now in excellent condition and very attractive, owned by the city and used for functions. Its walls are extensively patched in brick and its large arched windows have mostly lost their tracery, but it still has its original scissor-braced roof.

APPENDIX II

Chantry Colleges Without a Collegiate Church

Cathedrals, like other important churches, had many chantry priests in the late Middle Ages, for whom in a number of cases a college was established. As with the colleges of vicars, they were colleges without a collegiate church. Also listed below are two colleges of chantry priests who served in monastic churches. Several of the colleges listed here, though of interest and known as colleges, were not incorporated.

Campsey Ash (Suffolk). This chantry college was founded in about 1347 for a warden and four chaplains, to celebrate in the Chapel of the Annunciation in the priory church of Augustinian canonesses, which had been established about 1195. The college was founded at the instance of Maud, Countess of Ulster, mainly to pray for the souls of her first and second husbands, William de Burges, Earl of Ulster, and Ralph de Ufford. This lady in 1347 entered the convent as a nun. In 1354, however, apparently mainly because the priests had to live outside the priory precincts in the village some distance away, the college moved to Bruisyard (*see* Appendix III). It existed there for no more than twelve years, and by 1390, the college of five chaplains was again established at Campsey Ash, where buildings were now constructed for it within the precinct, though completely separate from those of the priory. It continued until the dissolution of the priory in 1536. Nothing survives of the priory church, but significant parts of the timber-framed buildings belonging to the college are incorporated in the present house, known as Chantry Farm.

Exeter (Devon): College of Annuellars. This was the college for the chantry chaplains of the cathedral, of which there were at least eighteen; the name comes from the *missae annuellariae*, annual masses or obits, which would be among the duties of these priests. This was a very late foundation, of 1528–9; it was never incorporated, though this was probably intended but was prevented by its dissolution in 1548. A recent study has told us much about it: its principal part was laid out round a rectangular courtyard which was almost closed at its N end by St Martin's Church. It had eighteen houses for the chaplains. A significant part is incorporated in No. 5 the Close, with most of three chaplains' houses and the fine hall (now divided by a floor), which has its stone fireplace and arch-braced roof with bosses. It is now used as a restaurant. Ruins further NE, formerly thought to be part of the college, in fact belonged to a large canonry.

King's Lynn (Norfolk): Thoresby's College. This was founded about 1500 by a wealthy merchant and three times mayor, Thomas Thoresby, principally for the accommodation of thirteen fraternity priests of the Trinity Guild. These priests celebrated mainly in the great monastic and parochial Church of St Margaret, but also in the town's chapels of St James and St Nicholas. Thomas Thoresby was associated with the rebuilding of the S chapel in the Church of St Margaret, and established there a chantry of two priests together with a charnel priest who had already been there. These too were housed in his college. The quadrangle of buildings erected for the college in 1508–11 remains, though it has been much rebuilt, especially in the early eighteenth century.

Lincoln: Cantilupe College. Sir Nicholas and Lady Joan Cantilupe founded this college about 1360, for a warden and seven chaplains who were to celebrate at the altar of St Nicholas in the cathedral. Close to the chancel of the cathedral, on the S side, they established a house for the communal living of the chaplains. The college did not long continue as the founders intended: by 1437 its revenues had declined, perhaps through mismanagement, such that it had only a warden and one chaplain. It is unlikely that the numbers ever recovered, but it survived to be dissolved in 1547. The chantry house still stands, appearing as two linked buildings, of ashlar and showing a few medieval features.

London: Holmes College. In the late fourteenth century, Adam of Bury, one-time Lord Mayor of London, with Roger Holmes, a canon of St Paul's Cathedral, built a Chapel of the Holy Ghost inside the cathedral, near its N doorway. By Adam's will, a chantry of three priests was to be established in it. Roger Holmes was an executor, and in 1386 the dean and chapter assigned a site SW of the cathedral for a residence for these chaplains, who were increased to seven by Roger Holmes's will. It was called a college, though it was not incorporated. It had declined to four chaplains by the end of the fifteenth century, and was dissolved in 1548.

London: Lancaster College. Following the accession to the throne in 1399 of the House of Lancaster in the person of Henry IV, a chapel was built in the chancel of St Paul's Cathedral for the tomb of his father, John of Gaunt, Duke of Lancaster, who had died in the same year, and his wife Blanche. In 1403, a chantry was established here, and a building was provided S of the cathedral as a common dwelling for its chaplains. It became known as Lancaster College and had ordinances, but was never incorporated; it had just two chaplains, with some others of unclear status. Dissolution took place in 1548.

London: St Peter's College. St Paul's Cathedral had a very large number of perpetual chantries. In about 1318, land was acquired just W of the cathedral, and buildings constructed for the use of the chantry priests. In 1391, Bishop Braybrook ordered that chantry priests should take their meals in its common hall. It had statutes, and accommodated more than thirty priests. Though known as a college, it was not incorporated, ownership remaining with the dean and chapter. It was sometimes known as 'presteshous'. With the other colleges attached to the cathedral, it was dissolved in 1548, and the buildings given over to other uses.

Wells (Somerset): New College. We first hear of a common house being allocated for the chantry priests of the cathedral in 1334; in about 1384, a building in the market place was purchased for them by Bishop Harewell. A purpose-built college was provided in about 1399 through the initiative of Bishop Ralph Erghum. It was built on a site that had been occupied since 1235 by the cathedral school, and was known as the New College of St Anne and St Catherine, or sometimes as Mountery. It was for fourteen chantry priests, and later at least seventeen. Dissolution took place about 1547. It stood on North Liberty, just N of the Vicars' Close, and after the Reformation was used as a private house. It was demolished in 1755, when the large house called The Cedars was built on the site. This remained a private house until the twentieth century and then, completing the circle, became the main building of the Wells Cathedral School.

York: St William's College. Licence for this college was first granted in 1455 by Edward IV, and a new licence was given in 1461 by Henry VI to George Neville, Bishop of Exeter, and his brother Richard, Earl of Warwick. George Neville became Archbishop of York in 1464. The college occupied the sites of two former prebendal houses, close to the E end of the minster, and was constructed about 1465–7. It was for twenty-three chantry priests of the minster, who were to be known as fellows and to elect one of their number as provost. The dedication was to the city's own saint, who as William FitzHerbert had been archbishop on two occasions in the twelfth century; he was great-grandson of William the Conqueror. The college was dissolved in 1548. The building was then in lay hands for 350 years, but it was purchased in 1902 and returned to ecclesiastical use as a meeting place for the Convocation of the Province of York; it was restored by Temple Moore in 1906–11.

St William's College, York: the courtyard

This is a particularly fine and beautiful survival, set around a rectangular courtyard. The walls of the ground floor are of ashlar, while the upper storey is of timber, elegantly jettied. There are many four-centred doorways, and quite a large passage for the entrance. Other parts have later brickwork, and there are seventeenth- and eighteenth-century windows; the whole makes a most attractive ensemble. Among the restorations are some windows with timber tracery. The former hall is now divided. There was a chapel, but this no longer exists.

Richard III, in his short reign (1483–5), began the foundation of a further college at York, to have the spectacular complement of a hundred priests, serving in the minster. Construction of its buildings was begun, but the project came to an end with the king's death at Bosworth Field.

APPENDIX III

Collegiate Churches That Later Became Monastic

Because of their ultimate development, these are to be regarded as monastic churches, even though they had a collegiate stage in their histories. The change from college to monastery (most frequently Augustinian) happened to many establishments in the twelfth century, but a few others followed in later years. Listed here are monastic churches that had previously been collegiate at any time after the Norman Conquest (establishments that became monastic before the Conquest do not appear). There is, however, some element of selection.

Arundel (Sussex, now West Sussex). This was a probably pre-Conquest college, and in the twelfth century it had ten prebends. However, in about 1150 it was appropriated to the abbey of Séez, and became an alien Benedictine priory. Remarkably, in 1380 the Church of St Nicholas again became collegiate (*see* p. 363).

Bedford. The Church of St Paul was of pre-Conquest origin; it had perhaps been monastic, but by the Norman Conquest it was collegiate, with six canons. About 1165, it was converted into an Augustinian priory, which fifteen years later moved to a new site and became Newnham Priory, in what are today the E suburbs of Bedford. This became important, but there are virtually no remains. St Paul's, however, continued as the principal church of the town; it is today a very large mostly Perp. and Victorian building, with a few EE features.

Boxgrove (Sussex, now West Sussex). Domesday Book reports clerks in this Church of St Mary; it was probably a small pre-Conquest college. In the early twelfth century, it was given to the Abbey of Lessay in Normandy, and became an alien Benedictine priory. This grew, and was made denizen in the fourteenth century. Much of the exquisite, very large priory church remains in use, with a little early-twelfth-century work.

Bromfield (Shropshire). This was an important pre-Conquest college with twelve canons; Edward the Confessor gave it a grant of liberties in about 1060, and it was of royal free status. During the early twelfth century the canons were gradually replaced by monks, and a charter of 1155 established it as a Benedictine priory. Part of the Church of St Mary survived the dissolution; it includes a little early Norman work.

Bruisyard (Suffolk). This small chantry college of the Annunciation, for a warden and four chaplains, had a curious history. It was originally founded in 1347, and attached to the church of the nunnery at Campsey Ash (*see* Appendix II), but in 1354 it was re-established on a new site in the parish of Bruisyard, where a chapel and buildings were constructed for it. In 1366, however, it was dissolved and its buildings became an abbey of Franciscan nuns or minoresses, which continued until 1539. A few fragments remain incorporated in Bruisyard Hall, the house on the site.

Chester: St Werburgh. This church originated in the early tenth century and was collegiate, with a warden and twelve canons. In 1086 the canons were apparently living in separate houses. In 1092–3, Hugh Lupus, Earl of Chester, made it into a Benedictine abbey, which was a large and important house. In 1541 it became the cathedral, with a change of dedication (*see* Appendix VIII).

Christchurch (Hampshire, now Dorset). The town was originally known as Twynham. This college was a pre-Conquest foundation, dedicated to the Holy Trinity, and had the large number of twenty-four canons. The present building was begun under Ralph Flambard in about 1094. It was converted to an Augustinian priory in 1150. The magnificent, very large church remains complete, a most exceptional monastic survival; the nave and transepts are basically Norman.

Cirencester (Gloucestershire). Perhaps founded in the ninth century, the church was collegiate at the time of Domesday Book, when its dean was Reinbald or Regenbald, who had been Edward the Confessor's chancellor. From 1117 Henry I converted it to Augustinian canons; by its charter of 1133, the existing secular canons were allowed to hold their prebends for life. The church was rebuilt on a majestic scale, and a new Church of St John Baptist was built a little way to the S for the parish. The Abbey of St Mary became the richest Augustinian house in England, but has almost totally vanished. Excavations have revealed much of its layout, and that of its very large Anglo-Saxon predecessor.

Clare (Suffolk). A college for seven canons was established in the early eleventh century in the Chapel of St John Baptist here. This stood within the castle established after the Conquest, and in 1090 was converted by Gilbert de Clare into a Benedictine priory, dependent on Bec in Normandy. Curiously, this priory was in 1124 moved to Stoke by Clare, probably to allow for enlargements to the castle, and in the early fifteenth century again became collegiate (*see* p. 353). Part of the castle keep of Clare remains on its mound, but nothing else.

Colchester (Essex): St Botolph. This was founded probably in about 1093, as a house of secular canons. However, it seems that from the beginning the canons were interested in joining a religious order. The Augustinian order was proposed and, with a recommendation from Anselm, Archbishop of Canterbury, two canons went to France to learn the rule. On their return, early in the twelfth century, St Botolph's was converted into an Augustinian priory. This was the first Augustinian house in England, and retained a nominal precedence over all others throughout the Middle Ages. The impressive ruin of the Norman nave and W towers remains.

Dorchester (Oxfordshire). Dorchester is a place of exceptional interest. The Church of SS Peter and Paul was founded in 634 as the seat of a bishop, the first being St Birinus. The see was later moved away, but from about 869 it was again a cathedral, with a vast

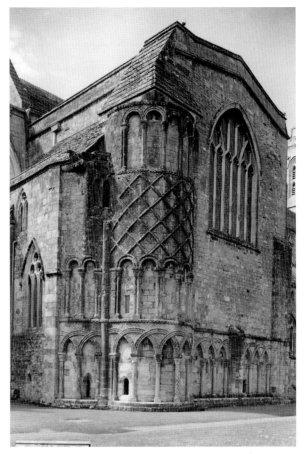

Christchurch Priory:
the partly Norman
north transept

diocese extending to the north. In 1072, the see was moved to Lincoln by the first Norman bishop, Remigius. Dorchester remained collegiate until Augustinian canons were introduced in about 1140 by Bishop Alexander. The large and exceptionally inter-esting abbey church survived the dissolution and remains largely complete; it has a Norman core probably built in the first monastic years.

Dover (Kent). This was a seventh-century foundation, said to be due to Eadbald, King of Kent. It certainly had royal privileges in Norman times and was important, with twenty-two canons. It was dedicated to St Martin. In 1131, Henry I gave it to Canterbury Cathedral, and it was at first made a house of Augustinian canons, and then in 1136 a Benedictine priory. Some of its buildings, especially the exceptionally fine Norman refectory, remain as part of the present-day Dover College, a school.

Edington (Wiltshire). Edington is a church of particular architectural interest and beauty. It was founded in 1351 as a chantry college by William Edington, Bishop of Winchester; his initial proposal was for a master and two chaplains, but by 1353 the number of chap-lains was increased to nine. In 1358, however, probably under the influence of the Black

Edington, looking east

Kirby Bellars, from the south-west

Prince, the founder changed it into a house of Bonshommes. This was an order of regular canons, a variant of the Augustinians, which reached a total of three houses, the others being at Ashridge (*see* Appendix IV) and Ruthin (*see* below). They did not use the term 'abbey' or 'priory', and their heads were styled 'rector'. The master of Edington resigned, and was replaced by a brother from Ashridge, who became rector. The house ended in the dissolution of the monasteries, in 1539. The large and exquisite Church of St Mary, St Katherine and All Saints built for the foundation remains complete. It was consecrated in 1361, and is striking for its style, transitional between Dec. and Perp. It is cruciform with a central tower, a three-bay aisleless chancel and a nave of six bays with aisles and a clerestory. A charming feature is the elaborate seventeenth- and eighteenth-century plaster ceilings, that of the crossing in the form of a fan vault. There are some good contents, including a few stalls with misericords.

Gloucester: St Oswald. This was an important early site, originally monastic, but converted to secular canons after 972. It had royal freedoms, and in Norman times there were six prebends. It was given by Rufus to the Archbishop of York, who in 1152 or 1153 made it into an Augustinian priory. Of this there remain some ruins in a park. These include four Norman arches formerly between the nave and the N aisle, and the remains of an Anglo-Saxon arch which must originally have opened to a porticus.

Hartland (Devon). The college is thought to have been founded before the Conquest by Githa, wife of Earl Godwin. In the 1160s, it was re-established as an Augustinian abbey. This was a major house; just a few medieval fragments remain incorporated in the mansion on the site. However, the abbey was built anew in this location, and the college must have been attached to the predecessor of the present large Perp. parish church of St Nectan.

Hatfield Peverel (Essex). The church was originally founded in the late eleventh century for secular canons, it is said by Ingelrica, wife of Ranulph Peverel. About twenty years later, her son William converted it into a priory of Benedictine monks, a cell of St Albans. It remained small. Part of the church, now dedicated to St Andrew, is still in use; it is mostly fifteenth century.

Hereford: St Guthlac. The College of St Guthlac was of pre-Conquest foundation, and stood within the walls of the castle. In 1143 it was amalgamated with the Benedictine Priory of St Peter (itself previously collegiate: *see* below), and moved to a new site as the Priory of St Guthlac. There are no remains on either the old or the new site.

Hereford: St Peter. This collegiate church was founded before 1084 by Walter de Lacy. In 1101, Walter's son Hugh granted it to Gloucester Abbey, which made it into a Benedictine priory, though it seems the prebends were not extinguished for some years. In 1143, it was combined with the College of St Guthlac (*see* above), and the whole moved to a new site as the Priory of St Guthlac. St Peter's Church remained parochial, and exists today, though it has no work going back to the Norman period. It possesses fifteenth-century stalls with misericords, said to have come from the priory.

Kirby Bellars (Leicestershire). Sir Roger Beler, King's Justice, in 1316 founded in the church a chantry for two chaplains, but by 1319 increased this to a chantry college for the large establishment of a warden and twelve chaplains. Some poignancy attaches to it from the murder of its founder in 1326. The system here employed prebends; it seems that as a result there were difficulties in maintaining an effective community and, in consequence, in 1359 it was converted by the founder's son, another Sir Roger, into an Augustinian priory for a prior and twelve canons, almost the last Augustinian house. This continued until dissolution in 1536, when there were a prior and eight canons.

The Church of St Peter is partly EE and partly Dec. Most impressive is the W tower, carrying a splendidly lofty broach spire with three tiers of lucarnes; this is probably of about 1300. Plaster has been stripped from the interior of the church, to ugly effect. The Dec. N aisle has been demolished, but its four-bay arcade is visible inside. The S arcade is EE, but its very wide aisle is a Dec. enlargement. A pair of tomb-recesses here contains alabaster effigies probably of the later Sir Roger Beler and one of his wives. The chancel is aisleless. The collegiate, later monastic, buildings stood at some distance to the N.

Launceston (Cornwall): St Stephen. This was an early monastery, and by time of the Norman Conquest was a house of secular canons. In about 1127 it was replaced by an Augustinian priory of the same dedication but on a new site. This was important, but there are now only slight remains. The earlier Church of St Stephen on the hill to the N remained parochial, and still shows a little Norman work.

Morville (Shropshire). Morville was an important pre-Conquest college, with eight canons. After the Conquest, most of its endowments were taken for the foundation of Shrewsbury Abbey, and in about 1138 it was made into a very small Benedictine priory, a cell of Shrewsbury. The mainly Norman Church of St Gregory remains in use; some of the structure can be associated with a consecration in 1118.

Oxford: St Frideswide. Apparently founded in the early eighth century, this house was originally for nuns, of whom the first head was Frideswide. In 1002 it was burnt in the Danish troubles. It was rebuilt and at this period, if not earlier, was a college of secular canons. It contained the burial place of the saint. It became a priory of Augustinian canons in about 1122, which was suppressed in 1524 for Wolsey's new Cardinal College (*see* p. 276), later Christ Church (*see* Appendix VIII); the former priory church is now the cathedral.

Plympton (Devon). Founded before 909, Plympton is reported to have had five prebends in early Norman times. In 1121, Bishop Warelwast of Exeter converted it into the Augustinian Priory of SS Peter and Paul; its secular canons are said to have been transferred to Bosham (Sussex: *see* p. 366). The priory became very large and important, but there are only slight remains today.

Ruthin (Denbighshire, Wales). The name is pronounced 'rithin'. This is a very interesting but problematical establishment. The town was founded in the late thirteenth century, and what was at first a Chapel of St Peter was built. In 1310, John de Grey, lord of Ruthin, founded an establishment for seven priests in the Church of St Peter, which was now parochial and was completely rebuilt. This is often regarded as a chantry college, but either then or later it had associations with the Bonshommes, an order of regular canons similar to the Augustinians, whose other houses were at Edington (*see* above) and Ashridge (*see* Appendix IV). Its existence seems to have been chequered, and it apparently ceased some time before 1478, although it was later revived. It may well have been for some of its life a college, and at other times a house

Ruthin, looking east

of Bonshommes, but the latter was presumably its final state, since it was dissolved in 1536 with the lesser monasteries.

Attached to it was a school. Gabriel Goodman, Dean of Westminster from 1561 to 1601, was born in Ruthin. In 1574 he refounded the school, and in 1589–90 he founded Christ's Hospital, an almshouse for twelve poor people; for their endowment, he purchased much of the old college property. The incumbent of the church was made warden of the hospital, and to this day has the title of warden. The church is attractive and on quite a large scale; the building of about 1310 had a chancel, an axial tower and a nave. A S aisle almost as wide as the nave was added later in the century. The chancel was demolished in 1663, probably following damage in the Civil War, and the aisle is now used as both nave and chancel. There has been much renewal. The upper part of the tower was taken down in 1754 and rebuilt in 1858–9, with a tall stone broach spire. The greatest glory of the church is its timber roofs, probably of the early sixteenth century, divided into many carved panels, with bosses. Attached to the N side is part of the original collegiate accommodation, a two-storeyed range running N, its lower level vaulted. Until 1954, this was the residence of the warden. Close by are the grammar school building, of 1700, and the almshouses, rebuilt in 1865. The group forms a charming precinct.

St Germans (Cornwall). The church was perhaps founded very early; from about 936 it was a cathedral. It was united with the cathedral of Crediton in 1042, the see being moved in 1050 to Exeter. Secular canons continued here until the late twelfth century, when Bishop Bartholomew replaced them with Augustinian canons. St Germans is notable for the impressive remaining part of the church, which has a W front with twin towers. Much of it is late-Norman work, built when it became Augustinian.

Southwark (London, but Surrey until 1888). This was a pre-Conquest foundation, possibly early, and apparently of secular priests. In 1106 it became the Augustinian Priory of St Mary Overie (Overie meaning over the water from the city). This was a major house, and its very fine mostly thirteenth-century church survived the dissolution. It suffered badly in the nineteenth century, but in 1905 became Southwark Cathedral.

Taunton (Somerset). A pre-Conquest foundation here, dedicated to SS Peter and Paul, was probably of secular canons; it became an Augustinian priory in about 1120 and grew to be large, but hardly anything remains.

Thetford (Norfolk): St Mary. This was a pre-Conquest religious house, probably collegiate. In about 1071, the bishop, Herfast, transferred the Anglo-Saxon see of East Anglia from North Elmham to this church as part of the Norman policy of moving bishops' seats to important towns. As a cathedral it was served by secular canons. However, in about 1094 the see was moved again, to Norwich. In 1104, the church was re-established as a Cluniac priory, but in 1107 buildings for the priory were begun on a new site, to which the community moved in 1114. The old site seems to have been left unused; what remained became in 1335 part of the endowment of the new Dominican friary. There are no remains.

Upholland (Lancashire). A college for a dean and twelve chaplains was founded by Sir Robert de Holland in 1310, in a Chapel of St Thomas the Martyr. However, it seems that it was difficult to find satisfactory priests who would stay in the place, and in 1317–19, at the instigation of Sir Robert, Bishop Langton refounded it as a Benedictine priory. The magnificent chancel built for the priory remains in use.

Waltham (Essex). This very historic Church of the Holy Cross was of early origin; it was refounded by Earl Harold and dedicated in 1060, with a dean and twelve canons. As king, Harold prayed here before the Battle of Hastings; and here, it is thought, he was brought back for burial. The college was of royal free status. Under Henry II in 1177, however, it became an Augustinian priory, soon promoted to abbey status. A vast new cruciform church was constructed, standing E of the previous nave and crossing, which were retained for parochial use. When dissolved in 1540, this was one of the churches considered for elevation to cathedral rank: but it was not to be, and the great Norman nave which had been built for the college is the only part of the church to remain today.

APPENDIX IV

Other Churches with Collegiate Connections

Appearing here are churches that at some time after the Norman Conquest were collegiate or had collegiate associations, but do not meet the criteria for an entry in the gazetteer. Included are churches that ceased to be collegiate before 1200; establishments that never had more than two clergy; churches of colleges that were licensed but apparently never established; establishments sometimes listed as colleges but more probably to be regarded as hospitals; some churches of portioners (but churches of just two portioners and Welsh churches of portioners are not usually mentioned); and a variety of other marginal cases. This is inevitably a selection.

Alberbury (Shropshire). There was a church on this site before the Conquest, probably a minster; in the early twelfth century it had four portioners. In 1221–6, Fulk Fitzwarin founded an Augustinian priory on a site elsewhere in the parish, which in 1230 became an alien priory of the Grandmontine order. By 1262, the church and its portions had

Alberbury, from the south

been appropriated to the priory. A vicarage was established in 1289, but aspects of its portionary status continued in the provision of another priest and a deacon. In 1441, the church went to All Souls College, Oxford, which continued to appoint a Welsh-speaking curate in addition to the vicar, no doubt to serve the large Welsh element in the parish. The church of St Michael is attractive, despite considerable rebuilding and restoration. Its long chancel is of 1846, but on the foundations of its predecessor. The nave has been much renewed, but has a notable roof. The finest features are the massive N tower, mainly of the late thirteenth century, and the splendid Dec. Loton Chapel on the S side.

Ashridge (Hertfordshire). This was usually called a college, but it was a house of Bonshommes, founded in 1283 by Edmund, Earl of Cornwall. There were only three houses of this order, the others being at Edington and Ruthin (for both, *see* Appendix III); Ashridge was the earliest. The Bonshommes were regular canons, and the life was definitely monastic, very similar to that of Augustinian canons; however, they did not use the name abbey or priory, and their clergy were called brethren. The College of the Precious Blood at Ashridge ended in 1539, in the dissolution of the monasteries. It is now a very large, mainly early-nineteenth-century mansion in Gothic revival style, used as a business school, incorporating just small medieval remnants.

Bakewell (Derbyshire). The Church of All Saints is often referred to as collegiate, but it was a very marginal case. At the time of Domesday Book, it had two priests. In 1154 its patronage became forfeit to the king, and in 1192 it was granted to the dean and chapter of Lichfield (still the patrons today). At this time it was reported to have three prebends; however, these ceased soon afterwards. The church, though much rebuilt, is large and impressive, cruciform with a central tower and spire. An extensive display of pre-Conquest carved stones vividly attests to its early origin.

Bampton (Oxfordshire). An important minster recorded about 955 was given by Edward the Confessor to Leofric, who in 1069 gave it to the see of Exeter, in whose hands it remained. From the thirteenth century it had three portionary vicars, who continued until the nineteenth century. Much of the impressive cruciform church is of the twelfth and thirteenth centuries.

Barnard Castle (Co. Durham). In 1471 the castle came into the hands of Richard, Duke of Gloucester, who in 1483 was to become king as Richard III. In 1478, his brother Edward IV granted him licence to found within the castle, presumably in the Chapel of St Margaret in the outer bailey, a large college of a dean, twelve chaplains, eleven clerks and six choristers. But (unlike his college at Middleham, licensed on the same day) nothing more is heard of this scheme, which probably finally foundered with Richard's demise at Bosworth Field in 1485.

Barton (Isle of Wight). The unusual establishment founded here in 1275 was for an arch-priest, five chaplains and a clerk. Its charter required perpetual celebration for the living and the dead, and it thus seems to have been very like a chantry college; but the chaplains followed the Augustinian rule, and the life was much like that of a small Augustinian priory. It is usually referred to as an oratory. The dedication was to the Holy Trinity. Owing to the decline of its endowments the community ceased in 1439, when it was appropriated to the College of St Mary at Winchester. A few medieval fragments remain in the mostly Victorian house now on the site, known as Barton Manor, close to the grounds of Osborne House.

Berkeley (Gloucestershire). There was here an important pre-Conquest minster or college, but this ceased by the mid-twelfth century. However, the Church of St Mary remained important throughout the Middle Ages, and there were reportedly ten chaplains in 1338, presumably serving chantries. It is a splendid and very large building, with a detached tower; its core is impressive EE work, and it is notable for its extensive wall-paintings.

Blyth (Nottinghamshire). This was a royal free chapel probably of pre-Conquest origin; it was granted by King Stephen to Lincoln Cathedral, and later in the twelfth century became a possession of Rouen Cathedral. It had four prebends. At some time, the college ceased, but Edward I later attempted unsuccessfully to recreate it with its royal freedoms (*see* Tickhill, below). Blyth, however, is a puzzle: the college was unrelated to the Benedictine priory founded here in 1088, so it seems that it must have used another church building; but historical or archaeological evidence of such a site is lacking.

Bramber (Sussex, now West Sussex). After the Conquest, William de Braoze was given the large lordship of Bramber. He had built a castle by 1073, and immediately outside it founded a borough and a church with a dean and canons. But, at least partly because of disputes with the Abbey of Fécamp, owner of nearby Steyning, before 1096 the college was given up and its endowments transferred to the newly founded Benedictine Priory of Sele close by. Much of the original aisleless, cruciform church of Bramber remains; it is dedicated to St Nicholas. This well-documented case may well exemplify other short-lived early collegiate foundations of which record has been lost.

Hackington (Kent). This brief but remarkable story reflects the tensions there could be between a bishop and the community of a monastic cathedral. In 1186–7, Archbishop Baldwin of Canterbury obtained a papal bull and began the foundation of a major new college in this place just outside the city; it was to have forty canons, and be dedicated to SS Stephen and Thomas of Canterbury (the latter, murdered in the cathedral in 1170, had been canonized in 1173). Building began and the first canons moved in. But the prior and monks were bitterly opposed to it, on the grounds of the loss both of the revenue which was diverted to the new college, and of their own power and influence. The prior appealed to the pope. The archbishop was supported by the king, Henry II. A major dispute ensued; the archbishop blockaded the monks in their own monastery. But in July 1189, the king died; his son became Richard I. Both Baldwin and Richard were anxious to proceed with the Third Crusade. Richard visited Canterbury and an agreement was reached whereby the college was abandoned; instead a college was to be established at Lambeth (*see* below). The buildings at Hackington had been demolished by 1191. No relationship has been established between the presumably partly built college and the existing partly Norman parish church; even the location of the college is not certain, though it may have been W of the church where later there stood Place House, the residence from about 1227 to 1540 of the archdeacons of Canterbury.

Halstead (Essex). Licence was first granted in 1341 to Sir Robert Bourchier, Chancellor of England, to found a chantry college of eight chaplains in the parish Church of St Andrew, but nothing happened. In 1412, licence was granted to Richard Clifford, Bishop of London, for a college of a master and four chaplains, to be known as Bourchier's Chantry. However, part of the endowment was never realized, and the actual foundation was on the reduced scale of a master and one chaplain. Much of the interesting but restored church is fourteenth century, with good memorials.

Kirkby Overblow (Yorkshire, WR, now North Yorkshire). This was a chantry college for a provost and four chaplains, founded apparently in 1362 by the executors of Henry, 2nd Lord Percy. However, it had a curious arrangement whereby the chaplains spent most of their time celebrating not at Kirkby Overblow but elsewhere; three in the chapel of Alnwick Castle, the seat of the Percys, and the fourth in a chantry in York Minster. The Church of All Saints is not large. It has a few medieval parts, but its main attraction is its work of 1780–1 in Gothic style.

Lambeth (London, but Surrey until 1888). After the defeat of Archbishop Baldwin of Canterbury in his plan to found a college at Hackington (*see* above), he determined instead on establishing a college at Lambeth. It too was to be dedicated to SS Stephen and Thomas of Canterbury; the site was acquired by exchange of lands with the Bishop of Rochester. It was probably begun in 1190; after the death of Baldwin on crusade in the Holy Land it was continued by his successor Walter. It seems likely that the church was to be on the largest scale, and was seen by the archbishops as a future cathedral for them in the capital, ideally placed just opposite Westminster. However, it proved as much a subject of dispute as its predecessor, with the prior and monks of the cathedral opposing it, but the king (Richard I) taking the archbishop's side. Following the king's death in 1199, the archbishop was finally in 1200 obliged to accept the closure of the college and the demolition of its church. However, in the early thirteenth century Lambeth Palace was begun here, still today the London residence of the archbishops. No remains survive from the college, which probably stood just N of the present grounds. The fine chapel of the palace is of the early thirteenth century.

Lazenby (Yorkshire, NR, now North Yorkshire). In 1290, John de Lithegrenes and his wife Alice began the foundation of a chantry college or hospital dedicated to St Mary, to have a master and five chaplains, celebrating in the Chapel of St John the Baptist. It seems unlikely that their intention was fully carried out, though some establishment came to exist. In 1443 it was transferred to the Abbey of Jervaulx, which until the dissolution provided two chaplains to maintain a chantry at Lazenby. Lazenby (3 miles from Northallerton) is no more than a hamlet; even the site of the former chapel is unknown, though it may have been at what is now known as Grange Farmhouse.

Ledbury (Herefordshire). The Church of St Michael is often described as the county's finest parish church. It was almost certainly a pre-Conquest minster. The place was important, and the bishops of Hereford established a residence here. St Michael's continued with two portioners, together with a vicar who was responsible for the cure of souls. There seem to have been plans for the foundation of a substantial college in the church in about 1330, and again in 1400–1. The earlier of these is linked to the attractive but highly improbable suggestion (still presented in the church guidebook) that the unusual outer N chapel of the church was built as a chapter-house. Neither of

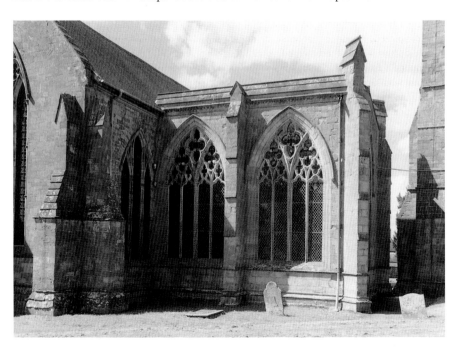

Ledbury: the outer north chapel

these collegiate proposals came to fruition. The portions continued until the nineteenth century.

The church is very large (its external length is 178 ft/54.3 m); its basis is Norman, and work of that period remains at both ends. Much of the rest is Dec. The nave has no clerestory and is flanked by broad, lofty aisles under pitched roofs, which continue without division as chapels flanking the chancel; externally, the S side is impressively long and largely uniform. The outer N chapel has its longer axis N–S and is Dec., of the most spectacular architecture here, with great richly traceried four-light windows thickly encrusted inside and out with ball-flower. In the chapel there is a very fine thirteenth-century effigy of a priest. Another striking feature of the church is its detached tower, standing just to the N, a massive EE structure in four stages; its upper part and its thrillingly tall stone spire date from 1733.

Llangadog (Carmarthenshire, Wales). In this church, in 1283, Bishop Thomas Bek founded the first of his two colleges, for a precentor and twenty-one prebendaries. However, it seems that by 1287 he had decided on its transfer to Abergwili (*see* page 418). It is not clear to what extent the college functioned at Llangadog, but there do seem to have been some canons here, perhaps continuing for a year or two after 1287. The Church of St Cadog, at the time of the college dedicated to SS Maurice and Thomas of Canterbury, is cruciform with W tower, but not large. It remains medieval in its plan, but other than in the tower almost every feature was replaced in the restoration of 1888–9 by D. Jenkins.

London: All Hallows Barking. This church was of early origin; its name derives from Barking Abbey, Essex, to which it was appropriated. Associated with it was a Chapel of St Mary, in which was established in 1442 a Guild of St Mary. In 1465, the guild obtained royal licence to endow two chaplains in the chapel. Richard III is said to have increased this to a college of a dean and six canons, but the foundation was probably not completed, no doubt because of the king's early death at Bosworth Field. At the dissolution in 1548, there were five priests and five conducts, but they were probably not incorporated. The church was largely Perp. and quite large; it survived the Great Fire but was largely destroyed in 1940. Rebuilt in the 1950s, it is of remarkable interest and beauty. The Chapel of St Mary stood parallel to it on its N side, and would have been on the far side of the present road; nothing remains.

London: Jesus Commons. The nature of this establishment is uncertain. There was certainly a building here in which lived a number of priests; it may have been established before 1400. Little is known, and there is no evidence of incorporation. It is mentioned in 1539 and 1543; it subsequently disappeared, though it is suggested that this did not happen until the reign of Queen Elizabeth.

London: Leadenhall. Simon Eyre, a draper, left 3,000 marks (£2,000) at his death in 1459 for the foundation in the Chapel of Leadenhall of a college for a master, five priests, six clerks and two choristers, with masters of grammar, writing and song. Nothing seems to have been done, but in 1466 Edward IV gave licence for the establishment in the chapel of a Fraternity of the Holy Trinity and the Sixty Priests of London. This fraternity was connected with a hospital called the Papey, and cared for sixty aged, sick or blind priests, and the principal purpose of the establishment was as a hospital. The Chapel of Leadenhall survived until 1814: old pictures show an attractive, regular Perp. structure, not large; it was aisleless, in four bays, with a W vestibule.

London: St Katharine by the Tower. Sometimes referred to as a college, this was a hospital, founded in 1147 by Queen Matilda. Strictly, like the Tower itself, it stood in Stepney. It was very large and had a master and three brethren, under the Augustinian rule; its income in 1535 was given as £315. It continued after the Reformation, but was moved in 1825 for the building of St Katharine's Dock, when its buildings were demolished. These included a magnificent and very large chapel, which had been built in the late fourteenth century. As an institution, the hospital still exists, and after being elsewhere has returned to Stepney, where its modern chapel still contains the original stalls with misericords. The great memorial to John Holland, Duke of Exeter, is in St Peter ad Vincula in the Tower (*see* page 223).

London: St Thomas, London Bridge. A London Bridge of stone was first begun in 1176 and completed in 1209. Building was in the charge of Peter de Colechurch, a priest of the nearby St Mary Colechurch. Near its centre was constructed a chapel, dedicated to St Thomas of Canterbury, which was served initially by two priests and four clerks, who were members of the Brothers of the Bridge. It is sometimes referred to as a college, but it was not an independent corporation. Chantries were founded in the chapel, and the number of chaplains increased. In 1538, the Corporation of London decided that it should be served by only two priests and a conduct, and in 1548 it was closed.

Houses had been built on the bridge by the end of the thirteenth century. The chapel was entirely rebuilt in 1384–96; it is quite well known from old illustrations. Its pier was especially large and was elongated on the downstream side, so that the W front of the chapel faced the roadway; it was 60 ft (18.3 m) long, of five bays plus a polygonal apse, with large arched windows. Below it was a vaulted lower chapel. After closure, it was converted to commercial and residential use. The bridge was widened in 1758–62, when the houses were removed; the lower chapel remained until 1832, when the bridge was demolished following its replacement by a new structure to the design of Rennie.

Malden (Surrey, now London). Walter de Merton, twice Chancellor of England, was the founder of Merton College, Oxford (*see* page 288), effectively the first academic college. His first moves towards an educational foundation were in 1262, but it was some time before its nature was settled. He owned the manor of Malden, and many of the properties with which he endowed his foundation were in the vicinity, and included Malden Church. From 1263, the manor house of Malden was used as part of his designs, and had a resident warden and several priests. It has been considered that from 1263 to 1264 Malden contained a number of scholars who then moved on to Oxford, but this is doubtful; it was not intended as a feeder college to that at Oxford in the manner of the much later Winchester and Eton. Certainly by 1264 or soon after, Walter's plans were established as the foundation of a college in Oxford, and the principal purpose of Malden was the administration of its Surrey properties. So, interesting as it is, it was probably never a college in its own right; however, it was part of the foundation, and only in 1274 did the warden and priests move to join the scholars in the college at Oxford.

The manor house still exists, now mainly of the early eighteenth century, standing close to the Church of St John the Baptist which was no doubt used by the establishment. The church was small; only the flint walls of the short chancel are medieval, with Perp. windows of 1609–11, a time at which the rest of the church was rebuilt, a nave and W tower of red brick. These now form a S aisle and chapel to the large new nave and chancel constructed in 1866–7 and 1875.

Melmerby (Cumberland). The foundation here of a chantry college for a master and seven priests was begun in 1342 by Sir Robert Parvyng, chancellor to Edward III. However, probably as a result of Sir Robert's death the following year, it was never completed. The Church of St John the Baptist is now largely Victorian.

Newark (Nottinghamshire). The Church of St Mary Magdalen is one of the greatest parish churches; it is now predominantly Perp., but also has substantial EE work. In late-medieval times it had as many as fifteen chantry chaplains; several of its chantries had been founded about 1350 by survivors of the Black Death. Soon after 1361, one Alice Fleming provided a mansion for the accommodation of the chantry priests; the life lived here and the practices in the church resembled those of a college. However, though sometimes mentioned in collegiate listings, it was not incorporated, nor was it in medieval times referred to as a college.

Norwich: Beck College. This unusual establishment was not really a college. A house of Pied Friars ceased in the fourteenth century; its premises then became a property of the Hospital of Beck (near East Dereham). The hospital used it both as its town house and as a residence for chantry priests of the city, particularly those celebrating in the adjacent Church of St Peter Parmentergate. Although the way of life is said to have been collegiate, it had no revenues of its own and was not incorporated. A fragment of the buildings may survive, and the late Perp. Church of St Peter Parmentergate remains, now used as a counselling centre.

Osmotherley (Yorkshire NR, now North Yorkshire). This Church of St Peter had three portioners, under the patronage of the bishops of Durham. Following disputes between the bishop and the Archbishop of York, in 1322 the revenues were appropriated to York and the church was thereafter served by a vicar. The church is minor, with a pleas-ant late-Perp. W tower, a small but sophisticated perhaps post-Reformation S porch, and a Norman S doorway of two orders. Much else dates from 1892–3.

Pevensey (Sussex, now East Sussex). This was a royal free chapel, founded probably in the early twelfth century in the Church of St Nicholas. In about 1150 it was given by King Stephen to Chichester Cathedral, and any claim to royal freedoms was soon given up. A college probably existed, but it presumably ceased following the gift. Despite its strikingly long chancel, it is unlikely that the existing fine mainly EE church ever served a college.

Pontefract: Holy Trinity and the Blessed Virgin Mary (Yorkshire, WR, now West Yorkshire). Founded in 1485 by Sir Robert Knolles, a citizen of London, and Constance his wife, this was known as Knolles Almshouses, referred to as a *domus collegiata*. It had a master, several chaplains (there were six in 1535) and two clerks, with thirteen debilitated poor and two servants to care for them. The statutes give extensive details of the religious observances that were to be maintained. But, as recorded in the chantry certificates, the 'hole necessitie' of the house was 'the mainte-nance of hospitalitie, Goddes service daily, and the reliof of pore people, and the kepynge of .... xiiij poore folkes iij servants and iij children'. It was allowed to continue as an almshouse and survived into the twentieth century, but not into the twenty-first.

Quatford (Shropshire). This collegiate church for a dean and five prebendaries was founded in 1083–6 by Roger de Montgomery, 1st Earl of Shrewsbury. About the beginning of the twelfth century, the college moved to Bridgnorth (*see* page 307) 2 miles away, where it was established in the chapel of the castle. The Church of St Mary Magdalene at Quatford is no more than a small village church; it has some Norman work, especially a fine chancel arch of tufa, but this seems to be of later date than Quatford's collegiate period.

St Kew (Cornwall). This was apparently an early monastery, which from the tenth century was a house of secular canons. Early in the twelfth century, it became a property of Plympton Priory, and from soon after this time it was served by two regular canons from there. The church is a very fine Perp. building, and possesses some notable stained glass.

St Michael's Mount (Cornwall). This famous island rock off Marazion was the site of an important religious community long before the Conquest. It seems to have been given by Edward the Confessor to the great Abbey of Mont St Michel in Normandy, of which it became a subordinate priory until the dissolution of alien monasteries in 1414. St Michael's Mount was an important place of pilgrimage throughout the Middle Ages. In 1460 it was given to the Bridgettine Syon Abbey (Middlesex), which established in it a staff of an archpriest and two chaplains. These remained until 1538, when it was dissolved just before the abbey. Though this final state perhaps resembled a college, it was not independent; moreover, the priests presumably belonged to the Bridgettine order, which had both nuns and religious men.

The church on the summit of the rock remains complete, comprising a nave, central tower and chancel. Its walls are probably basically Norman, but most details are Perp., at which period also was added a Lady Chapel at the NE corner.

St Teath (Cornwall). The name is pronounced 'teth'; St Tetha is believed to have been a female hermit of Welsh origin. This was a church of portioners, sometimes referred to as prebendaries, in the presentation of the bishops of Exeter; there were apparently three portions, but one seems to have been appropriated before 1259 by Bodmin Priory, which put in a vicar. The church is of typical Cornish type, medium sized, undivided E–W and predominantly Perp. It is low and internally rather dark. In a window recess is a damaged recumbent effigy of a priest, and there is a fine series of memorials on slate.

Shrewsbury (Shropshire): St Alkmund. This establishment is believed to have been founded in the early tenth century by Aethelflaed, daughter of Alfred the Great. At the Domesday Survey, it had a dean and twelve prebendaries. It was dissolved in about 1145, when its possessions were given as endowments to the Augustinian Lilleshall Abbey, which was then being founded; so it can be seen as another case where regular canons replaced secular canons. The church remained parochial; it is large and possesses one of Shrewsbury's two great spires, 184 ft (56.1 m) high, on a Perp. W tower. The rest of the church was rebuilt in 1794–5, in early Gothic revival style.

Shrewsbury: St Juliana. Often referred to as St Julian, this church was closely related to the castle Chapel of St Michael, and had similar royal freedoms. It may have been collegiate in its early days, and it seems to have had three portions in the early thirteenth century; but these apparently soon ceased. It is large and retains its medieval W tower, but the body of the church was rebuilt in classical style in 1749–50, with further modifications in 1846. Long closed as a church, it was until recently used as a craft centre.

Shrewsbury: St Michael. The castle of Shrewsbury was royal; within its inner bailey was a Chapel of St Michael which seems to have served a parish in the northern suburbs of the town. It may have been a pre-Conquest minster, and certainly had royal privileges. However, there is little evidence that it was ever collegiate. In 1409, it was given as an endowment to the new College of Battlefield. Nothing now remains of the chapel. When a new church building was erected in 1830 in the northern suburbs (in the parish of St Mary), it was dedicated to St Michael probably in remembrance of the medieval St Michael's; this church still exists, but is now a Freemasons' hall.

South Molton (Devon). The Church of St Mary Magdalene appears in some lists of collegiate churches. It was probably a pre-Conquest minster, and at Domesday Survey had four *presbyteri*. But there are no later references to multiple clergy, so it probably came to an end in Norman times. The church today is large, with some good Perp. work, but is much spoilt by nineteenth-century alterations and extensions. Its finest feature is the excellent Perp. pulpit, of stone.

Thornbury (Gloucestershire). This impressive, mostly late-fifteenth-century Church of St Mary stands next to the great castle, which was begun in about 1511 by the 3rd

Thornbury, from the south

Duke of Buckingham. The duke obtained licence to establish in the church a large chantry college of a dean, a sub-dean, eight priests and others; some of the rebuilding of the church may have been carried out in preparation for this. However, the duke was executed in 1521, and the college never came into existence.

Tickhill (Yorkshire, WR, now South Yorkshire). In the late thirteenth century, Tickhill Castle became royal, and Edward I attempted to re-establish in its chapel of St Nicholas the defunct royal free chapel formerly 4 miles away at Blyth (*see* above). However, it is doubtful whether a college ever came to exist here, and certainly it was not permanently established. Some remains of the chapel are possibly incorporated in the present house.

Tolethorpe (Rutland). A Hospital of SS Mary and Anne was founded here in 1301 for seven poor men, with a chaplain as warden. In 1359, Sir William de Burton, having rebuilt the chapel, obtained papal licence to increase this to a college for a master and six chaplains. However, there is no evidence that this happened. In 1379, a master and one chaplain are recorded, but a little later only a chantry remained, served by a chaplain from nearby Little Casterton, and in 1410 even that ceased. The site is marked by earthworks just NE of Tolethorpe Hall; it has not been excavated.

Towcester (Northamptonshire). This little chantry college was licensed in 1448, fulfilling a process begun by William Sponne, who was Rector of Towcester and also Archdeacon of Norfolk, and died in 1447. It had only two priests, and the Church of St Lawrence was not appropriated. In the church, which has work from the twelfth century onwards, is the monument to William Sponne, with his effigy above and his cadaver below. Part of the college building still stands, NW of the church.

Wappenham (Northamptonshire). In 1327, a chantry for a warden and five priests was founded in this church of St Mary by Gilbert de Middleton, Archdeacon of Northampton. However, it was not incorporated. The spacious chancel may have been rebuilt in connection with this foundation.

Warkworth (Northumberland). Not the least remarkable feature of the large and splendid ruined castle of Warkworth is the large collegiate church (more correctly chapel) which was probably begun under Henry, 2nd Earl of Northumberland, in about 1420. However, there is no documentary evidence of the college being established, and it is virtually certain that the church was never completed. It remains as well-preserved wall-bases of ashlar, and divides the bailey into two. It has an aisled nave of four bays, and two of the pillar bases stand high enough to show their quatrefoil plan. There are transepts with diagonal buttresses, and the crossing pillars have multiple shafts.

The chancel too must have been aisled, but no pillar bases are visible; the arrangement of the E end is unclear, abutting other domestic buildings of the bailey. The interior of the church is now well-kept turf, the level rising from W to E so that the walls of the E part stand 8 or 9 ft above the bailey; there are substructures here which are well preserved. These are two crypts, one beneath the N transept and a larger one beneath the chancel: both have a tunnel vault of depressed four-centred form, and four-centred window openings. A fairly broad passage with a vault of similar form

Warkworth: remains of collegiate church, viewed from the keep

passes beneath the E part of the chancel, forming the communication between the two parts of the bailey.

Warwick: All Saints. This church was of pre-Conquest origin, possibly early, and after the Conquest stood within the castle. When Roger, Earl of Warwick, founded a major college in the town's church of St Mary (*see* page 386) in about 1123, it absorbed the earlier college, whose canons transferred in 1128. The exact site of All Saints is not known.

Warwick: St James. Founded in 1383, the Guild of St George the Martyr (later combined with a second guild) maintained two chaplains in the Chapel of St James, set above the West Gate. It was dissolved in 1546, but the charming chapel and quadrangle of timber-framed buildings became Lord Leycester's Hospital in 1571, which still exists today.

Winchester: Holy Trinity. This was a chantry or small college for a warden and one chaplain, founded in 1317 by a prominent merchant, Roger de Inkepenne. Its chapel stood on the N side of the cemetery of the Nunnaminster, above a charnel-house. It was dissolved in 1548, and has vanished even more completely than the nunnery; its exact site is not known.

Wroxeter (Shropshire). This small village is visited mainly for the very interesting remains of the Roman city. The church was an Anglo-Saxon minster, and had four priests in 1086. It was given in 1155 to the recently founded Augustinian Abbey of

Haughmond, but it still had three portioners in the late thirteenth century. These seem to have been abolished in 1347, when the abbey instituted a vicarage. The church was declared redundant in 1980, and following a major programme of restoration and archaeological investigation was vested in the Redundant Churches Fund (now the Churches Conservation Trust). It has a very complicated and interesting structural history, starting with Anglo-Saxon work in the N side, using stone taken from the Roman ruins. Other parts are Norman. The tower is Perp., and curiously incorporates many artefacts said to have come from Haughmond Abbey after its dissolution in 1539. The churchyard gates hang from elegant Roman pillars, brought from the ruins in 1868; also probably Roman in origin is the gargantuan circular font.

APPENDIX V

Collegiate Churches in Castles

These appear in the gazetteer unless otherwise indicated.

Arundel (Sussex). Proposals of 1354 and 1375 were for a college in the chapel of the castle; but the college as actually established in 1380 was in the parish church close by.

Barnard Castle (Co. Durham). This was a late-fifteenth-century proposal that came to nothing (*see* Appendix IV).

Bridgnorth (Shropshire)

Clare (Suffolk). *See* Appendix III.

Elmley Castle (Worcestershire). A doubtful case.

Exeter (Devon)

Fotheringhay (Northamptonshire). The initial foundation here was attached to the chapel of the castle, but the college established in about 1411–15 was instead in the parish church.

Hastings (Sussex)

Hereford: St Guthlac. *See* Appendix III.

Holdgate (Shropshire)

Holyhead (Anglesey, Wales)

Leicester: Newarke College. The college occupied the Newarke, or New Work, a walled, semi-fortified area adjoining the castle.

Leicester: St Mary de Castro

London: St Peter ad Vincula

Mettingham (Suffolk). A special case: a pre-existing castle in 1394 'became' a college.

Oxford: St George in the Castle

Pontefract (Yorkshire, WR): St Clement

St Michael's Mount (Cornwall). A special case, not a true college: *see* Appendix IV.

Shrewsbury (Shropshire): St Michael. *See* Appendix IV.

Stoke-sub-Hamdon (Somerset). The castle was really a fortified manor house.

Tickhill (Yorkshire, WR). Probably never came into being: *see* Appendix IV.

Wallingford (Berkshire)
Warkworth (Northumberland). *See* Appendix IV.
Warwick: All Saints. *See* Appendix IV.
Windsor (Berkshire): St Edward
Windsor: St George

APPENDIX VI

Royal Free Chapels

The royal free chapels fall into two groups. The majority were founded or obtained royal free status before about 1150. After a pause, some further royal free chapels were established from the mid-thirteenth century onwards; the latter are indicated by an asterisk. All are included in the gazetteer unless otherwise noted.

Blyth (Nottinghamshire). *See* Appendix IV.
Bosham (Sussex)
Bridgnorth (Shropshire)
Derby: All Saints
* **Fotheringhay (Northamptonshire)**
Gnosall (Staffordshire)
* **Hastings (Sussex)**
London: St Martin le Grand
* **London: St Peter ad Vincula**
* **Middleham (Yorkshire, NR)**
Oxford: St George
Penkridge (Staffordshire)
Pevensey (Sussex). *See* Appendix IV.
* **St Buryan (Cornwall)**
Shrewsbury (Shropshire): St Juliana. *See* Appendix IV.
Shrewsbury: St Mary
Shrewsbury: St Michael. *See* Appendix IV.
Stafford
Steyning (Sussex)
* **Tamworth (Staffordshire)**
Tettenhall (Staffordshire)
* **Tickhill (Yorkshire, WR).** *See* Appendix IV.
Wallingford (Berkshire)
* **Westminster (London): St Stephen**
Wimborne Minster (Dorset)
* **Windsor (Berkshire): St Edward**
* **Windsor: St George**
Wolverhampton (Staffordshire)

In addition, the following royal free chapels of the early period became monasteries in the twelfth century. As such they continued to enjoy some special privileges. All appear in Appendix III.

Bromfield (Shropshire)
Dover (Kent)
Gloucester: St Oswald
Waltham (Essex)

APPENDIX VII

Establishments That Survived the Dissolution

In the process of dissolution, a very few colleges were exempted. Some other small colleges of canons or churches of portioners simply seem to have been missed. Other colleges were dissolved, but later refounded. Some of these survivors, but again not all, were finally dissolved in the nineteenth century, mainly by the 1840 Act. Not included here are cathedrals, colleges of vicars choral, academic colleges or churches of only two portioners. Except where otherwise noted they appear in the gazetteer. Those still today existing as institutions in some form are indicated by an asterisk.

Bampton (Oxfordshire). Portioners. *See* Appendix IV.
* **Brecon (Wales)**. A unique case: *see* Appendix VIII.
Bromyard (Herefordshire). Portioners.
* **Burford (Shropshire)**. Portioners.
Chulmleigh (Devon). Perhaps portioners.
* **Cobham (Kent)**. Dissolved, but refounded in 1598 as an almshouse, the New College of Cobham.
Heytesbury (Wiltshire)
London: Whittington's College. Dissolved, refounded under Queen Mary, but again dissolved under Elizabeth.
* **Manchester**. Dissolved, but refounded under Queen Mary. Was not again dissolved, but was in 1847 reorganized as the cathedral.
Middleham (Yorkshire, NR)
* **Pontesbury (Shropshire)**. Portioners.
* **Ripon (Yorkshire, WR)**. Dissolved, but refounded under James I.
* **St Endellion (Cornwall)**
Southwell (Nottinghamshire). Dissolved, but refounded under Queen Mary.
Tiverton (Devon). Portioners.
* **Windsor (Berkshire): St George**
Wolverhampton (Staffordshire). Dissolved, but refounded under Queen Mary.

APPENDIX VIII

Colleges Created Under Henry VIII from 1540

The period of the dissolution of the monasteries (1536–40) was followed by some constructive foundation of establishments to be served by secular priests, mostly based on dissolved monasteries. Six were new cathedrals. Of the other new colleges, some were academic, some were of canons. Several of these foundations were short lived, but others have continued to the present day.

Brecon (Breconshire, now Powys, Wales). In 1540–1, on the initiative of Bishop Barlow of St Davids, the College of Abergwili (*see* page 418) was transferred to the more important location of Brecon, where it was installed in the buildings of the thirteenth-century Dominican friary, which had been dissolved in 1538. As such it became Christ College, with a charter of Henry VIII dated January 1541. The constitution and endowments of Abergwili were transferred largely unchanged, so it had twenty-two prebendaries; it also provided a school, with a master, an usher and twenty scholars. It was visited by the chantry commissioners in 1548 but, exceptionally, was allowed to continue. The bishops of St Davids continued to take an interest in it, and there were regular visitations. However, its constitution was not ideal for its educational function,

Christ College, Brecon: the chapel, from the north-east

and the prebendaries did not always give adequate support. Its existence was chequered, and at times the number of pupils fell as low as seven; in 1845 it closed for two years. Finally, in 1853 it was refounded by Act of Parliament; the prebends were abolished, and it became a normal public school. It has since flourished; it was given extensive Victorian buildings, and there are further additions of the twentieth century. Thus Bishop Bek's foundation of 1283, originally at Llangadog, uniquely continues after two moves as an important institution in the twenty-first century.

Remaining from the friary are the chapel and two halls. The chapel is a remarkable survival, dating from about 1250. The chancel is intact, but the nave fell into ruin after the Civil War, though its tidied-up walls remain, with some features; it was given a N aisle in the fourteenth century. Now forming the antechapel is what was the cross-passage of the friars' church; at its N end, a fourteenth-century chapel is now the vestry. The chancel, though restored, is a large and noble building of very fine EE design. Its N side has a continuous range of close-set lancets, with shafts, moulded capitals and finely moulded rere-arches. On the S side, only the four lancets towards the E end match their partners, the rest of the wall being windowless; buildings were attached to this part. The E window is a Dec. alteration. There is a superb group of double piscina and quadruple sedilia, all with trefoiled arches resting on shafts. The fittings are mostly Victorian, but in the antechapel are six battered stalls with misericords; they have startlingly crude carvings. Religious life remains important in the school, and the chapel is used every day.

Bristol. This Augustinian abbey, dedicated to St Augustine and founded in about 1140, was dissolved in December 1539. It became a cathedral in 1542, with a dean and seven canons. It remains a cathedral today, though there was an intermission from 1836 to 1897.

Burton upon Trent (Staffordshire). The Benedictine Abbey of SS Mary and Modwen was dissolved in 1539; but it was one of two dissolved abbeys chosen to become colleges of secular canons. As such, it was re-established in 1541 for a dean and four prebendaries, with six choristers, five singing men and others. However, this situation only lasted four years, and it was dissolved in 1545. Part of the very large church remained in parochial use, but was replaced in 1719–26 by a new building on roughly the same site. Medieval fragments including parts of the infirmary survive, incorporated in later buildings.

Cambridge: Magdalene College. This was a refounding of 1542 by Thomas, Lord Audley, who had been Lord Chancellor since 1533, and had played a prominent and not always attractive part in some of the later events of the king's reign. It used the site and buildings of Buckingham College, a monastic college founded in 1428. Though much remodelled, the original fifteenth-century quadrangle remains in use, including the hall and chapel.

Cambridge: Trinity College. Founded in 1546 by Henry VIII, probably under the influence of his final queen, Catherine Parr, this immediately became the largest college in Cambridge, a rival to Christ Church at Oxford. It was formed out of King's Hall (*see* page 93) and Michaelhouse (*see* page 95), with some other smaller establishments and new endowments partly from dissolved monasteries. The king died a month after its foundation, and perhaps as a result there was no grand architectural scheme; but the college has the largest court in either university as a result of the work of Dr. Thomas Neville, master at the end of the sixteenth century.

Chester: St Werburgh. The Benedictine Abbey of St Werburgh (*see* Appendix III) was chosen in 1541 for promotion to cathedral rank, in preference to the collegiate church and former cathedral of St John Baptist in the same town (*see* page 112). Its dedication was changed to Christ and St Mary, and it supported a dean and six canons.

Gloucester. The great Benedictine abbey of St Peter had been founded in the seventh century. When surrendered in January 1540, it briefly became a collegiate church pending its establishment in 1541 as a cathedral, with a new dedication to the Holy Trinity. It was given a dean and seven canons.

Oxford: Christ Church. Established in November 1546 by Henry VIII, this was the final form of what had been Wolsey's Cardinal College (*see* page 276), with its former priory Church of St Frideswide serving both as college chapel and as a cathedral to replace Osney (*see* below). This amalgamation of the cathedral with the college enabled a substantial part of their endowments to be regained by the Crown.

Oxford: Osney. This great Augustinian abbey, founded in 1129, stood on the W side of Oxford; its church was well over 300 ft (90 m) long, and had a central and a very tall W tower. Much of the structure was thirteenth century. Dissolved in 1539, it became a cathedral in 1542, with a dean and seven canons. But after less than four years, it was replaced by the former St Frideswide's priory Church, incorporated in the newly reconstituted college of Christ Church (*see* above). Osney was rapidly unroofed; most of what still stood was demolished to build fortifications during the Civil War, and nothing remains.

Peterborough. The Benedictine Abbey of St Peter was founded in the seventh century. It was dissolved in November 1539, and in September 1541 was raised to cathedral status, with a dean and six canons.

Thornton (Lincolnshire). The Augustinian Abbey of St Mary was dissolved in 1539, and became a college in January 1542; it had a dean and four prebendaries, with choirboys, singing men and others. However, its new life was short, as it was dissolved at the beginning of the reign of Edward VI. Substantial remains survive, now in the care of English Heritage, most notably the enormous fortified late-medieval gatehouse, built largely of brick. There are also ruins of the S transept of the great church and of the magnificent octagonal chapter-house, both of the late thirteenth century.

Westminster: St Peter. The church of this great Benedictine abbey has been the scene of every coronation of an English monarch since that of William I on Christmas Day 1066. As an abbey, it was suppressed in January 1540. However, because of its unique position in national life, it could not be destroyed. Initially, in December 1540, it became a cathedral, with a dean and twelve canons; but it retained cathedral status only until 1550. The canons continued for a time, but in 1556 Queen Mary re-established it as a Benedictine monastery, with an abbot and fourteen monks. It remained thus at the coronation of Queen Elizabeth; but in July 1559 it was again dissolved, and in 1560 finally refounded as a college for a dean and twelve prebendaries. As such it

has remained, one of the two great collegiate churches still existing and fully functioning. Today it has a dean, a sub-dean and just three other canons; it is still a royal
peculiar. The title 'abbey' remains only by tradition.

By any measure, this is one of the very greatest churches of England; and its associations and contents are unique. It maintains a choir school for thirty-eight boy
choristers, the only school in the country entirely dedicated to choristers. Also in the
precinct is Westminster School, which traces its origins back probably to the twelfth
century; it was refounded in 1540 by Henry VIII, and again in 1560 by Queen
Elizabeth.

Glossary

Acolyte: a clerk in minor orders, next below a sub-deacon, who attends the priests and deacons and performs such duties as lighting and bearing candles

Advowson: the right of presenting an individual to a benefice when vacant

Aisle: a subsidiary space alongside the nave, chancel or transept of a church, separated from it by pillars

Altar: a flat-topped table or stone block, consecrated for the celebration of the eucharist

Altar rails: low rails separating the sanctuary from the rest of the church; synonymous with communion rails

Altar-tomb: a tomb-chest with a flat top, resembling an altar

Angle buttresses: a pair of buttresses at a corner of a building, at right angles to each other

Anglo-Saxon: of architecture, that which was prevalent up to approximately 1066

Appropriate: to transfer to the ownership of a religious house or other ecclesiastical owner

Apse: a semicircular or semi-polygonal termination (usually to the east) of a part of a church

Arcade: a series of arches supported by pillars

Ashlar: masonry of stones wrought to a rectangular shape, with smooth faces

Aumbry: a small cupboard, usually recessed into a wall in the sanctuary of a church, used to store the sacred vessels

Ball-flower: a small ornament resembling a ball within a three-petalled flower, characteristic of the Dec. period, usually applied in a series.

Barrel vault (also 'tunnel vault'): the simplest type of stone vault, like a continuous semicircular arch

Batter: an intentional inward inclination of the face of a wall

Belfry: a chamber for bells, usually the top stage of a tower

Benefaction board: a board with painted or inscribed text recording benefactions

Benefice: an endowed ecclesiastical position, with or without cure of souls, yielding an income to its holder

Billet: an ornament characteristic of Norman architecture, comprising regularly spaced small raised rectangular or half-cylindrical blocks

Bishop: a member of the holy orders higher than priest, consecrated for the spiritual government and direction of a territory known as a diocese

Blank arcading (also 'blind arcading'): an arcade applied as ornament to the surface of a wall

Boss: an ornamental projection at the intersection of the ribs of a vault

Box pew: a pew with high wooden sides and a door

Buttress: a masonry feature projecting from a wall, giving it extra strength

Canon: a priest, also sometimes a deacon or sub-deacon, living a life according to the canons (rules) of the church (the canonical life). From the eleventh century, some

461

adopted a rule attributed to St Augustine by which they renounced property; these were canons regular or regular canons, and were effectively monks. Those who did not adopt this rule were canons secular or secular canons

Canonical hours: the services prescribed for eight times of prayer each day, namely matins, lauds, prime, terce, sext, nones, vespers and compline (of these, lauds was abandoned by the Roman Catholic Church in the mid-twentieth century)

Cantarist: another name for a chantry priest

Capital: the crowning feature, often ornamented, of a pillar or shaft

Capitular: pertaining to a chapter

Cartouche: a tablet of approximately oval shape with an ornate frame often carved to resemble a scroll of paper

Cartulary: *see* chartulary

Cathedral (or 'cathedral church'): the principal church of a diocese, containing the bishop's throne

Ceilure: a specially panelled and embellished part of a timber roof above a rood or altar

Chamfer: a long, narrow surface formed by cutting away a right-angled edge at 45 degrees; *see also* hollow chamfer

Chancel: the eastern limb of a church, in which the principal altar is situated

Chancel arch: an arch at the western entrance to the chancel

Chantry: an endowment providing for the daily celebration at an altar of masses for the souls of persons specified, usually but not exclusively after their deaths

Chantry chapel: a chapel, often attached to or screened off inside a church, for the celebration of chantry masses

Chantry priest: a priest who performs chantry masses

Chapel: (a) a place of worship which is not the church of a parish; (b) a subordinate compartment of a church, containing its own altar

Chapel of ease: a chapel for the convenience of worshippers who live at some distance from the parish church

Chaplain: a priest attached to a chapel; often in the Middle Ages synonymous with chantry priest

Chapter: the canons of a collegiate church or cathedral, or sometimes the chaplains of a chantry college, considered as a body, or a meeting of these; also applied to the members of a monastic or other religious house, or of a knightly order

Chapter-house: a room for the meetings of the chapter; in an important religious house it could be architecturally splendid

Charter: a document, usually from the sovereign, by which an institution is incorporated and its purpose and rights specified

Chartulary (also 'cartulary'): the collection of charters, title-deeds etc., belonging to a religious house; also the place in which they are kept

Chevron: a zigzag ornament carved boldly in three dimensions; always associated with Norman work, appearing about 1120. When the plane of the zigzag is at right-angles to the wall, it is here referred to as 'orthogonal chevron', sometimes called 'frontal chevrons'. This is a later variant

Choir (also 'quire'): (a) the body of singers performing a service; (b) the part of the church in which the services are sung. May be, but is not necessarily, co-extensive with the chancel

Choir stall: *see* stall

Cinquefoil: a shape comprising five foils; normally refers to these as applied to an arch, typically in window tracery, having five foils divided by four cusps

Clerestory: a series of windows at an upper level, usually above an arcade

Clerk: a man ordained to one of the orders of the church; either one of the minor orders or one of the holy orders. In the Church of England since the Reformation it is synonymous with 'clerk in holy orders'. The word 'cleric' is usually preferred today. *See* orders

Collate: to appoint to a benefice

Column: a cylindrical pillar or pier, especially in classical architecture

Communion rails: the rail enclosing the sanctuary, at which the sacrament of the eucharist is administered; synonymous with altar rails

Conduct: a hired chaplain, engaged to perform services in a church or chapel in which he is not a member of the foundation

Continuous (of mouldings in an arch or doorway): mouldings that continue without capitals from the responds on to the arch

Corbel: a block projecting from a wall, to support a beam or other load

Cornice: a horizontal moulded projection at the top of a building, or internally below a ceiling; often the top member of a classical entablature

Crocket: a decorative feature in the form of a bud or leafy knob, usually one of a regular series

Cross-gable: a section of roof above an aisle, set at right angles to the axis of the aisle

Crossing: the space at the intersection of the nave, chancel and transepts of a cruciform church

Crown-post: a vertical post standing on the centre of a tie-beam of a timber roof, supporting a collar purlin

Curate: a priest, also called a vicar, who is entrusted with the cure of souls in a parish, usually because the church has been appropriated, so there is no rector to perform the task (the usage as an assistant to a parish priest is post-Reformation)

Cure of souls: the spiritual and pastoral care of the people of a parish

Cusp: a projecting point between two small arcs or foils; typically found in window tracery

Deacon: a clerk in holy orders, of rank immediately below a priest, with the function in mass of assisting the priest

Dean: a name for the head of the canons of a cathedral or collegiate church

Deanery: (a) the residence of a dean; (b) the territory over which a dean has jurisdiction

Dec.: Decorated, a term for the style of architecture used approximately from 1280 to 1360

Demi: half

Demi-column: a half-column, usually attached to a wall or pier

Dentil: one of a series of small square blocks applied as an ornament below a cornice

Diagonal buttress: a buttress projecting diagonally from the corner of a building

Dignitary: a person holding high ecclesiastical rank, a person invested with a dignity; in a college of canons, applied usually to the four senior canons

Dignity: a high ecclesiastical office

Diocese: the territory under the jurisdiction of a bishop

Divine office: the canonical hours

Dog-tooth: a favourite ornamental motif of the EE period, comprising a series of small cut-away pyramids

Domesday Book: the record of the great survey made in 1086 of the lands of England

Double respond: two responds back to back, with an intervening thickness of masonry; this typically represents the surviving fragment of a former wall, and indicates the extension of a previously shorter building

Easter Sepulchre: a recess normally in the north side of the sanctuary, often with a tomb, symbolic of the garden tomb from which Christ rose, and used accordingly in the services for Easter

EE: Early English, a term used for the style of architecture of approximately the period from 1190 to 1280

Episcopal: of or relating to a bishop or bishops

Epistoler: a clerk, usually a sub-deacon, who reads the epistle in the mass

Eucharist: *see* mass

Excommunicate: to exclude a person from all sacraments and benefits of the church

Fan vault: rich late-Perp. form of vault, comprising large concave cones decorated with panelling, of fan-like appearance

Fillet: a narrow raised flat band projecting from a shaft or roll moulding

Filleted: having a fillet

Fleuron: a stylized flower-like architectural ornament, often square. Usually of the Perp. period

Flushwork: the use of cut flint and dressed stone to form a design in a flat wall surface

Flying buttress: buttress supporting a wall at a high level by means of a half-arch, often spanning an aisle

Foil: a small arc between cusps; typically found in window tracery

Foliated: with foils or leaves, as a form of ornamentation

Frankalmoigne: 'free alms', a form of tenure by which religious bodies held lands with religious obligations, such as of prayer for the donor

Fraternity: a body of people, usually both men and women, organized to give religious benefits to its members, including a funeral and prayers or masses for their souls after their deaths

Free chapel: *see* royal free chapel

Gospeller: a clerk who reads the gospel in the mass

Gothick: sometimes used for a style of architecture occurring between about 1740 and 1820, in which the forms of medieval Gothic architecture were imitated, usually with little attempt at authenticity; internal detail is often of plaster

Great tithe: *see* rectorial tithe

Green man: a human head with foliage issuing from its mouth; a popular motif, probably of pagan origin

Habit: the dress or attire of members of a religious order

Hammerbeam: one of a pair of horizontal brackets projecting from the wall at the base of a roof structure, carrying a vertical post

Hatchment: a lozenge-shaped tablet of wood and canvas painted with the armorial bearings of a deceased person

Hebdomadary: a member of the holy orders who takes a weekly turn in the performance of the services in a church

Herring-bone: masonry in which thin stones are laid with successive courses sloping one way and then the other, characteristic of early Norman work

High (or 'High Church'): a church fitted and decorated according to the principles of the Anglo-Catholic arm of the Church of England

Hollow chamfer: chamfer which has a concave instead of a plane surface

Holy orders: *see* orders

Hood-mould: a projecting moulding above a window, doorway or arch; where external, it helps to throw off rain-water

Hospital: a charitable institution for housing and caring for a number of aged, infirm or destitute people

Impost: a horizontal moulded slab at the springing of an arch; where there is a capital, it is the top member of this

Impropriate: to appropriate, but especially, from the Reformation, to transfer ecclesiastical property into lay ownership

Impropriator (usually 'lay impropriator'): a layman who has possession of a benefice and its revenues

Incorporate: to form into a corporation, with a legal identity separate from that of its members

Install: literally, to place in a stall, hence, to invest with an ecclesiastical office

Institute: formally to install or establish in a benefice; sometimes applies only to the spiritual part of a benefice, and is then followed by induction, which applies to its temporalities

Interdict: the exclusion of a person or of all persons in a place from the benefits of the church; or a prohibition on the clergy of a place from performing divine service

Keel: a moulding with an obtuse point, resembling that of a ship

Keeled: having a keel

Lancet, or lancet window: a long, narrow window with an acutely pointed arch; characteristic of the EE period

Lay clerk: since the Reformation, another term for a vicar choral, where he is not a priest

Lay impropriator: *see* impropriator

Lay rector: the same as a lay impropriator

Lay vicar: the same as a lay clerk

Letters patent: a legal term for an open document issued usually by the sovereign, authorizing an agreement or action, such as the foundation of a college; normally on parchment, with the Great Seal attached at the bottom

Lierne vault: a type of vault that includes subsidiary decorative ribs not linked to a springing point

Low-side window: a window set lower than the others and usually originally containing a shutter, near the west end of the chancel; probably used for ringing the sacring bell during mass so that those outside could hear it

Lucarne: a window-like opening in a spire

Mark: two-thirds of a pound, or 13s 4d

Mass: the celebration of the eucharist, in which Christ's Last Supper is commemorated by the consecration of bread and wine

Mensa: altar table, but particularly a medieval one of stone

Minor canon: one of the clergy of a collegiate church or cathedral who is not a member of the chapter; sometimes an alternative name for a vicar choral

Minor orders: *see* orders

Minster: a term which originated in ecclesiastical Latin *monasterium*, a monastery. It came in Anglo-Saxon times to be used also for any important church, often the mother-church which served a region before the full establishment of the parochial system

Misericord: a seat in a stall that is hinged and has a bracket or projection on its underside which, when the seat is in the raised position, can give some support to the standing occupant of the stall; the bracket often carries lively carving

Moiety: half

Mortmain: the condition of land or other property held inalienably by an ecclesiastical or other corporation; many measures, beginning with an Act of Edward I in 1279, attempted to restrict it

Mullion: a vertical bar dividing a window into lights

Multifoiled: with many (i.e. more than five) foils; usually refers to these as applied to an arch

Nailhead: ornament popular in the EE period, comprising a series of small pyramids

Narthex: a room forming the main entrance at the west end of a church

Nave: the main body of the western part of a church, for the accommodation of a lay congregation

Nodding-ogee: a feature with an ogee arch, which also projects forward in a double curve from the plane of the wall

Nook-shaft: a shaft set in an angle or recess, formed for example in a wall or buttress, or in the jamb of a window or doorway

Norman: (a) a person originating in Normandy; (b) the style of architecture prevalent in England from approximately 1066 to 1190

Obit: a mass for the soul of a deceased person celebrated annually, usually on the anniversary of the person's death

Ogee: an arch that curves first one way then the other, coming to an acute point; especially characteristic of Dec. architecture

Order: (a) one of a series of successively recessed arches together forming an enriched, splayed opening; (b) in classical architecture, one of the different formalized designs of column with base and capital: for example, the Ionic, Corinthian and Tuscan orders

Orders: the eight orders, starting from the lowest, are ostiarius (door-keeper), reader, exorcist, acolyte, sub-deacon, deacon, priest and bishop. The highest three, or from the thirteenth century the highest four, are the holy orders; the others are the minor orders. Members may be referred to as 'clerk in minor orders' or 'clerk in holy orders'. In the Church of England since the Reformation, only deacon, priest and bishop have been recognized

Ordinance: the same as statute

Ordinary: the ecclesiastical dignitary who has jurisdiction by right of his position; specifically the archbishop in a province, or the bishop in a diocese

Parclose: a screen that separates a chapel from the rest of the church

Parish: a subdivision of a diocese, having its own church and its own priest with responsibility for the cure of souls, to whom originally its tithes were paid

Patron: a person or body possessing the right of presenting a suitably qualified person to a vacant ecclesiastical position; the holder of the advowson

Patronage: that which is held by a patron; the advowson

Peculiar: a chapel, church, parish or territory that is exempt from the jurisdiction of the bishop in whose diocese it lies; its jurisdiction may instead be with another bishop, with the holder of some other ecclesiastical position or with the sovereign. In the last case, it is a royal peculiar

Pediment: in classical architecture, a formalized gable of low pitch, above an end of a building or often set over a smaller feature such as a window or doorway

Penny (abbreviation 'd'): one-twelfth of a shilling. At decimalization in 1972, it was replaced by the new penny, worth 2.4 times the value of the old

Perp.: Perpendicular, a term used for the style of architecture prevalent from about 1360 to very approximately 1540

Pier: a pillar, usually round or rectangular in section, thick in proportion to its height

Pilaster strip (also 'lesene'): a flat, narrow ornamental band of masonry, without base or capital, projecting from a wall surface; characteristic of Anglo-Saxon architecture

Pillar: a detached vertical structure, of any shape in section, slender in proportion to its height, used as the support for a part of a building

Pinnacle: a tall stone finial, often crowning a buttress or rising from a parapet

Piscina: a small basin with a drain, for the disposal of the water used in the washing of the hands and of the sacred vessels at the mass; it is always associated with an altar (and often indicates the site of an altar now vanished), and is often set in a recess in the wall on its S side

Pluralist: a clerk (usually priest) holding more than one benefice at the same time

Portico: in classical architecture, a formalized porch with columns at regular intervals, usually pedimented

Portioner (also 'portionist'): one of several clergy attached to a church, each receiving a portion of its revenues

Prebend: the property, normally a landed estate and often including a church, assigned to a canon of a collegiate church or cathedral, and providing its revenues to him for his maintenance; also occasionally used for 'prebendary'

Prebendal: of or pertaining to a prebend or prebendary

Prebendary: the holder of a prebend; some prebendaries still exist today, but since an Act of 1840, they only hold the title, and there is no endowment

Predial tithe: a tithe derived from the produce of the land

Present: to nominate or recommend an individual for institution to a vacant benefice

Priest: a member of the holy orders of the level below bishop, with authority to administer the sacraments

Pulpitum: in a large church, a stone screen separating the choir from the nave

Quadrant: a moulding comprising a curve through 90 degrees

Quatrefoil: a shape comprising four foils; normally applies to an opening or the plan of a pillar, having four foils and four cusps

Quire: the same as choir

Quoins: the dressed stones forming the angles of a building

Raking buttress: a buttress the projection of which diminishes uniformly with increasing height. Often a post-Reformation reinforcement

Rector: the holder of the tithes of a parish, who has the responsibility for the cure of souls; where the parish church has been appropriated to a religious house or other person or body, the latter receives the tithes and usually discharges the responsibility for the cure of souls by the appointment of a vicar

Rectorial tithe: in an appropriated parish, the tithe pertaining to the rector, also called great tithe, as opposed to the vicarial or small tithe

Regular: subject to monastic rules (especially applied to a canon)

Rere-arch: an arch in the inner face of a wall spanning the opening of a window or doorway

Reredos: a painted or sculptured screen or feature behind an altar

Respond: a half-pillar attached to a wall, supporting an arch

Reticulated: of tracery, a net-like design characteristic of the Dec. period, formed of multiple repetitions of the same foiled unit with ogee curves at top and bottom

Return stalls: *see* stall

Reveal: an internal side surface, often splayed, of an opening for a doorway or window

Rood: a crucifix, often flanked by the Virgin Mary and St John the Evangelist, set above the entry to a chancel

Royal free chapel: a collegiate church, founded by a sovereign or later coming under the control of the sovereign, and in consequence not subject to normal ecclesiastical jurisdiction

Sacrist: (a) a clerk in holy orders who has charge of the vestments, vessels and other valuables of a church; (b) a title for the head of a college

Sacristy: a chamber attached to a church in which are kept the vestments, vessels and other valuables

Sanctuary: the area surrounding the principal altar in a church; usually separated from the rest of the chancel by the altar rails

Scallop: a decorative pattern of the Norman period, in the form of a series of truncated partial cones, used especially on capitals

Secular: (a) not bound by monastic rules (as applied to canons, clergy, priests or cathedrals); (b) of or pertaining to worldly as opposed to religious matters

Sedile (plural sedilia): a seat on the south side of the sanctuary of a church, frequently of stone and part of the architecture, for the use of the clergy officiating at mass. Often there are three, for the use of a priest, a deacon and a sub-deacon

See: (a) a diocese; (b) the place in a diocese where the cathedral is situated

Segmental: of an arch, one in which the curve represents only a small segment of a circle, because at its base it immediately begins at an angle

Shaft: a slender column, normally for ornamental purposes, especially a small column used in the jambs of a door or window or clustered round a pillar

Sheila-na-gig: a grotesque representation of a female figure with exaggerated sexual characteristics; probably a fertility symbol

Shilling (abbreviation 's'): one-twentieth of a pound; at decimalization in 1972, it became five new pence

Sinecure: a benefice without cure of souls (medieval Latin *beneficium sine cura*)

Small tithe: *see* vicarial tithe

Spandrel: the wall surface above and around the curve of an arch, often limited by surrounding straight mouldings

Spirelet: a small spire, usually set on a base smaller than a tower

Springers: the lowest few stones of an arch or vault

Squint: an aperture cut through a wall, usually to allow a view of an altar

Stall: a seat in the choir of a church for the clergy or choir; normally arranged in rows facing north and south; the return stalls are those at the west end of the choir, facing east

Statute: normally plural, the written rules for the life of a college or other institution

Stiff-leaf: type of stylized ornamental foliage characteristic of the EE period, with stiff stems and bold lobed leaves

String-course: a projecting moulded band running horizontally along a wall surface

Sub-deacon: a clerk of the order below deacon, whose function in the mass is the preparation of the sacred vessels and the reading of the epistle; from about the thirteenth century, regarded as a member of the holy orders

Sunk quadrant: a quadrant recessed below the level at each side, characteristic of the Dec. period

Tenth: a tithe

Tester: a canopy, especially one over a pulpit

Thuribuler: an acolyte who carries the thurible, the vessel in which incense is burnt

Tie-beam: in a timber roof, a horizontal member connecting the base of the roof on each side

Tierceron vault: type of vault that has additional decorative ribs originating at a springing point

Tithe: a tenth part of the production of a property (usually land), in kind or as a payment, allocated for the support of a church, religious house or other ecclesiastical beneficiary

Transept: a transverse arm of a cruciform church

Trans. Norman: Transitional Norman, architecture showing features of both the Norman and the EE styles, which occurs between about 1160 and 1200

Transom: a horizontal member dividing the openings of a window

Trefoil: a shape comprising three foils. May be applied to an arch, typically in window tracery, in which case there will be three foils divided by two cusps; alternatively, an opening of trefoil form has three foils and three cusps

Triforium: an arcaded wall passage above the arcade and below the clerestory of a large church

Tudor: a term sometimes used for the late period of the Perp. style, from about the accession of Henry VII in 1485

Tunnel vault: *see* barrel vault

Veranda type: of a screen, one that is deep and carries a gallery

Vestment: any of several types of attire worn in services by priests and other clergy

Vestry: a room or area in which are kept vestments, sacred vessels etc., and in which the clergy and others robe for services

Vicar: (a) a priest responsible for the cure of souls in a parish in the place of the rector, the rectory having been appropriated. Also known as a curate; (b) a vicar choral; (c) a title for the head of a college

Vicar choral: a deputy to a canon of a cathedral or collegiate church, whose function is principally singing in the choir for the services of the church. Musical skill is required. In medieval times a vicar choral was most often a clerk in minor orders, but some were required to be priests

Vicarial tithe: in an appropriated parish, a tithe pertaining to the vicar; also 'small tithe'

Volute: a feature in the form of a spiral scroll, especially in a capital

Wave: a moulding formed by a convex curve between two concave curves

Zigzag: a Norman form of decoration incised in a flat surface; simpler than chevron.

Select Bibliography

Barrett, Philip *Barchester: English Cathedral Life in the 19th Century* (SPCK, 1993)

Barron, Caroline M. *The Medieval Guildhall of London* (Corporation of London, 1974)

Blair, John 'Secular Minster Churches in Domesday Book' in Peter Sawyer (ed.), *Domesday Book: a Reassessment* (Edward Arnold, 1985)

Butler, Lionel and Given-Wilson, Chris *Medieval Monasteries of Great Britain* (Michael Joseph, 1979)

Clark-Maxwell, W.G. and Hamilton Thompson, A. 'The College of St Mary Magdalene, Bridgnorth, with Some Account of its Deans and Prebendaries' (*Archaeological Journal* lxxxiv, 1927)

Cook, G.H. *English Collegiate Churches of the Middle Ages* (Phoenix House, 1959).

Cranage, D.H.S. *An Architectural Account of the Churches of Shropshire* (Hobson, 1901–12)

Davis, R.H.C. 'The College of St Martin-le-Grand and the Anarchy, 1135–54' (*London Topographical Record*, vol 23, 1972)

Denton, J.H. *English Royal Free Chapels 1100–1300: A Constitutional Study* (Manchester University Press, 1970)

Dodds, Madeleine Hope *A History of Northumberland*, vol. XII (A. Reid; Simpkin, Marshall, 1926)

Duffy, Eamonn *The Stripping of the Altars* (Yale University Press, 1992)

Edwards, K. *The English Secular Cathedrals in the Middle Ages*, 2nd edn (Manchester University Press, 1967)

Elton, Geoffrey *The English* (Blackwell, 1992)

Guy, John *Tudor England* (Oxford University Press, 1988)

Hamilton Thompson, A. 'Notes on Colleges of Secular Canons in England' (*Archaeological Journal*, volume LXXIV, 1917, 139–199). The classic paper for pre-chantry colleges.

Hamilton Thompson, A. *The History of the Hospital and the New College of the Annunciation of St Mary in the Newarke, Leicester* (E. Backus: Leicester, 1937, for the Leicester Archaeological Society)

Hamilton Thompson, A. 'English Colleges of Chantry Priests' (*Transactions of the Ecclesiological Society*, 1943, 92–108). Does for chantry colleges what his 1917 paper did for colleges of canons.

Hamilton Thompson, A. 'The Chapel of St Mary and the Holy Angels, Otherwise Known as St Sepulchre's Chapel, at York' (*Yorkshire Archaeological Journal*, vol 36, 1944–5)

Harrison, Frederick *Life in a Medieval College: The Story of the Vicars-choral of York Minster* (John Murray, 1952). Written with warmth and affection by one of the last members of the vicars' college of York, it gives a fascinating insight into this type of college.

Harvey, John 'The Buildings of Winchester College' in Roger Custance (ed.) *Winchester College Sixth-centenary Essays* (Oxford University Press, 1982)

Henderson, Charles 'Parochial History of Cornwall' in *Cornish Church Guide* (Oscar Blackford, Truro, 1928)

Henderson, Charles 'The Deanery of Buryan' in Charles Henderson, *Essays in Cornish History* (Oxford University Press, 1935)

Hobbs, Mary (ed.) *Chichester Cathedral: An Historical Survey* (Phillimore, 1994)

Jones, Anthea *A Thousand Years of the English Parish* (Windrush Press, 2000)

Keene, Derek *Survey of Medieval Winchester* (Clarendon Press, Oxford, 1985)

Knowles, David and Hadcock, R. Neville *Medieval Religious Houses: England and Wales*, 2nd edn (Longman 1971). This very important work is the only comprehensive modern inventory of medieval religious houses, including colleges.

Little, Bryan *The Colleges of Cambridge* (Adams and Dart, 1973)

Loades, D.M. 'The Collegiate Churches of County Durham at the Time of the Dissolution' (in *Studies in Church History* vol IV, 1967)

Macleod, Roderick 'The Topography of St Paul's Precinct, 1200-1500' (*London Topographical Record*, vol 26, 1990)

McMaster, Ida 'Cropmark of a Medieval Church at Stoke by Clare, Suffolk' (*Colchester Archaeological Group Annual Bulletin*, 31, 1988)

Map of Monastic Britain, 3rd edn (Ordnance Survey, 1978). This covers the whole of England, Wales and Scotland in two sheets, and includes medieval colleges. For England and Wales, it is largely based on Knowles and Hadcock, 1971.

Martin, David and Martin, Barbara 'A Re-interpretation of Hastings Castle, Hastings, East Sussex' (Archaeology South-East, Institute of Archaeology, University College London, 1999)

Martin, Edward 'Mettingham Castle: An Interpretation of a Survey of 1562' (*Proceedings of the Suffolk Institute of Archaeology and History*, vol. XXXVII, 1990)

Morris, Colin *The Papal Monarchy. The Western Church from 1050 to 1250* (Oxford History of the Christian Church, 1989)

Orme, Nicholas 'The Guild of Kalendars, Bristol' (*Transactions of the Bristol and Gloucestershire Archaeological Society*, vol. XCVI, 1978)

Orme, Nicholas (ed.) *Unity and Variety. A History of the Church in Devon and Cornwall* (University of Exeter Press, 1991)

Parker, R.W. 'ArchaeoHistorical Assessment of No. 5 The Close, Exeter' (*Exeter Archaeology Report* 97.30, 1997)

Parkin, E.W. 'The Old Chantry House, Bredgar' (*Archaeologia Cantiana*, vol. XCI, 1976)

Platt, Colin *The Parish Churches of Medieval England* (Secker and Warburg, 1981)

Scarisbrick, J.J. *The Reformation and the English People* (Basil Blackwell, 1984)

Scarisbrick, J.J. 'Henry VIII and the Dissolution of the Secular Colleges' in Claire Cross, David Loades and J.J. Scarisbrick (eds.) *Law and Government under the Tudors* (Cambridge University Press, 1988)

Schofield, John (ed.) with Cath Maloney *Archaeology in the City of London 1907–91. A Guide to Records of Excavations by the Museum of London* (Museum of London, 1998)

Stark, Edwin *Saint Endellion. Essays on the Church, its Patron Saint, and her*

Collegiate Foundation (Dyllansow Truran, 1983)

Tatton-Brown, Tim *Lambeth Palace. A History of the Archbishops of Canterbury and Their Houses* (SPCK, 2000)

Tatton-Brown, Tim 'The Deanery, Windsor Castle' (*The Antiquaries Journal*, vol. 78, 1998)

Tyack, Geoffrey *Oxford: An Architectural Guide* (OUP, 1998)

Yallop, H.J. 'Slapton College' (*Transactions of the Devonshire Association*, 1959)

The Buildings of England series, founded and largely written by the late Sir Nikolaus Pevsner (Penguin Books, 1951–74). For any discussion of an architectural subject in England this great work has made itself indispensable. Publication of new editions, updated and extended by others, is continuing. The companion series *The Buildings of Wales*, written entirely by others, is not yet complete.

The Victoria County History of England (VCH). This vast project to cover the history of England in detail has now been in progress for over a hundred years, but remains incomplete. The general volumes, which are available for most counties, contain a section on religious houses, which includes colleges. Descriptions of buildings are in the topographical volumes, where they exist. The *VCH* is frequently the finest readily available source of information. A proviso is that information in volumes dating from the early decades of the twentieth century may have been superseded by more recent scholarship.

The reports of the Royal Commission on the Historical Monuments of England (RCHME). The Inventories published by the RCHME from 1912 onwards provide superbly comprehensive architectural descriptions of the buildings in the areas they cover, with plans, photographs and archaeological assessment. In addition, there are reports on particular subjects, which may also have collegiate content. However, coverage remains very far from complete.

The listed buildings database of the National Monuments Record (now part of English Heritage). Almost all collegiate churches and surviving collegiate buildings of England may be found described in varying levels of detail in this great database.

Listed building information for Wales from CADW, Welsh Historic Monuments. Most churches have been given an admirably authoritative treatment in their Welsh Churches Project.

Medieval sources are not discussed here. The classic post-Reformation source for colleges, as for all religious houses, is Roger Dodsworth and Sir William Dugdale *Monasticon Anglicanum*; the latest edition is of 1817–30, in six volumes bound as eight. Also valuable is Thomas Tanner *Notitia Monastica*, in the edition of 1787.

Most collegiate churches offer a guidebook dealing with their history and architecture. Some are excellent, and I regret that I cannot list them here. However, caution should be exercised: some are less well informed, and startlingly inaccurate information may occasionally be found!

Index

Collegiate churches that are included in the gazetteer appear in bold type. Page numbers in italic type refer to illustrations; page numbers in bold type refer to principal entries.